ELEMENTS OF SYSTEMS ANALYSIS

for Business Data Processing

SECOND EDITION

ELEMENTS OF SYSTEMS ANALYSIS for Business Data Processing

Marvin Gore

John Stubbe

Mt. San Antonio College

wcb

Wm. C. Brown Company Publishers
Dubuque, Iowa

Contents

Preface

During the four years since the publication of the first edition of *Elements of Systems Analysis for Business Data Processing*, the impact of computer-related technologies on business has continued at an explosive rate. Terms such as "structured design," "data base administrator," "microcomputer," and "distributed data processing" have become part of the working vocabulary of data processing professionals. Job opportunities in all phases of business data processing have continued to expand, and computer systems have become available to businesses in bewildering arrays of shapes and sizes. Developing the information system most appropriate to the solution of a business problem is becoming an increasingly complex process.

Fortunately, systems analysis is receiving increasing recognition as the profession that is responsible for the orderly solution of information system problems, including the effective use of computers. Career opportunities for individuals skilled in the techniques and methodology of systems analysis are great, both within the data processing center and in applications areas throughout the corporation.

Elements of Systems Analysis for Business Data Processing is designed to train students in basic systems analysis skills. The "top-down" approach to systems analysis, which corresponds to the life-cycle phases of a computer-based business system, was introduced in the first edition of this text and is extended in this edition. The integration of systems analysis activities, management reviews, and documentation continues to be the focal point of the text. However, the text has been updated to include newer systems analysis and design tools and techniques that are finding widespread acceptance and use. For example, structured design techniques, such as HIPO charts, structured walk-throughs, and top-down computer program development and testing, have been included at appropriate points in the Study, Design, and Development Phases of the life-cycle of a system. Although revised to improve readability and teachability, the step-by-step method for identifying alternative problem solutions, evaluating them, and selecting the most feasible one remains a key element of the text. This technique called a *feasibility analysis,* is the most important tool of the systems analyst.

Elements of Systems Analysis for Business Data Processing is written in terms the business student can understand. The book is structured so that it can be used in both introductory and advanced systems analysis courses. It can be used in community colleges and also is suitable for the curriculum of a four-year university. The first two units introduce background concepts and acquaint the student with the basic systems analysis tools and techniques. The four units that follow enlarge on these tools and techniques and teach the student to apply them to each of the four life-cycle phases: study, design, development, and operation.

Unit One, Emergence of the Systems Analyst, provides the background concepts most important to the systems analyst's profession. Among these are the life-cycle concept and the concept of a business as an information system.

Unit Two, Tools and Techniques of Systems Analysis, introduces skills that are the working tools of systems analysis. These include coding, forms design, charting, and written and verbal communications. These skills are introduced at this point instead of at the time they are first encountered in the life-cycle process for two reasons: (1) to reinforce learning by allowing the student the opportunity to apply material with which he or she already has become familiar; and (2) to prevent digressions that might interfere with the ability of the student to perceive the dynamics and continuity of the life-cycle process.

Unit Three, The Study Phase, introduces the first of the four life-cycle phases. This unit prepares the student to perform activities essential to identifying a computer-based business system. problem. These include performing an initial investigation, defining system performance, conducting a feasibility analysis, and preparing a Study Phase report. Important features of this unit are the introduction of a continuing case study in the text and an example Exhibit of a complete Study Phase report.

Unit Four, The Design Phase, teaches the student how to perform basic computer-based system design tasks. These include general system design, input design, output design, and file design. The continuing case study illustrates important design techniques and leads to an example Exhibit of a completed Design Phase report.

Unit Five, the Development Phase, acquaints the student with activities that must be undertaken to develop an actual system from a completed design. Two principal topics are preparing for implementation and computer program development. Again, the case study is used to provide illustrative examples, including a Development Phase report.

Unit Six, The Operation Phase, makes the student aware of the operating environment of computer-based business systems. Changeover, routine operation, performance evaluation, and management of change are described. The life-cycle process is reviewed within the context of the management of change, and the importance of management control and of documentation is reemphasized.

Important features of this edition are:

1. A statement of chapter goals and student learning objectives at the beginning of each chapter.

2. Key terms and questions for discussion at the end of each chapter.

3. Careful adherence to the life-cycle "roadmap." The performance of systems analysis activities, cumulative documentation, and critical management reviews are integrated throughout the four phases of the life cycle.

4. Inclusion of a detailed, continuous case study, which provides examples enabling the reader to follow the life-cycle "roadmap" for his or her own future applications. Particularly important are the examples of performance definition; feasibility analysis; and the Study, Design, and Development Phase reports.

5. A reinforcement learning process. Skills are introduced early in the text and then repeated and applied in greater detail in later chapters.

6. The availability of an integrated learning package for the use of those instructors who may wish to teach a course oriented toward measurable student performance. The learning package consists of the text; a student workbook; and an instructional supplement. The workbook contains assignments keyed to a case study that parallels that in the text. The instructional supplement contains unit and chapter goals; and in addition, for each chapter it contains:

   a. Student performance objectives.
   b. Key points, indexed to page and figure number (transparency masters are provided for all important figures).
   c. Answers to "For Discussion" end-of-chapter questions.
   d. Chapter quizzes and answers.
   e. Student workbook problem grading sheets and solutions.

7. Usefulness as a continuing reference. The text can be used not only for an introductory systems analysis course (or courses), but also as a guide for student projects of the type that are the "capstone" of many data processing curricula.

8. Appropriateness to the needs of data processing majors as well as other business students. Programmers are not merely "coders." To develop effective programs, they must understand the general system design and the specific design parameters with which they interface. Systems analysis has been, and will continue to be, the professional growth path most often open to programmers. To be able to take advantage of sudden opportunities and of company policies oriented toward promotion from within, programmers must prepare themselves by both experience and education.

No matter how completely a problem is defined to a programmer, there are always decisions to be made based on an analysis of alternatives and their consequences. Systems analysis provides the methodology and tools for making such decisions. Also, significant system decisions are, all too frequently, left to programmers by default. Programmers should know how to meet their commitments under such circumstances.

9. Usefulness in educating another group of individuals—the largest group of all—the users of computer-based business systems. A *user* may be defined as an individual who, in performing his or her job, must provide input data to, or

use output information produced by, a computer-based business system. In a broader sense, a user is any individual who is affected to a significant degree by a computer-based business system. We only have to go to the nearest bank, supermarket, or department store to encounter computer-based systems with which users interact on a daily basis.

Throughout this book, we have used the grammatical convention "he" (him, his) to refer to male and female systems analysts, managers, users, etc.

We wish to express our appreciation to our students and to the many users of the text for their feedback and suggestions which have been invaluable to us throughout the preparation of this revised edition. We also wish to thank the following reviewers for their comments and critical reviews of the new edition: John Friedrich, San Antonio College (San Antonio, Texas); Delphine Klein, McComb County Community College (Warren, Michigan); John (Jack) Sharp, St. Louis Community College at Florissant Valley (St. Louis, Missouri); Allen Singleton, Essex Community College (Newark, New Jersey); H. D. Weiner, American University (Washington, D.C.). We also wish to thank Charles Harless, graphics technician at Mt. San Antonio College, for the photographs that appear in this edition. Once again, special thanks go to our wives, Iris and Connie, for their patience and encouragement.

January, 1979

Marvin Gore
John Stubbe

UNIT ONE

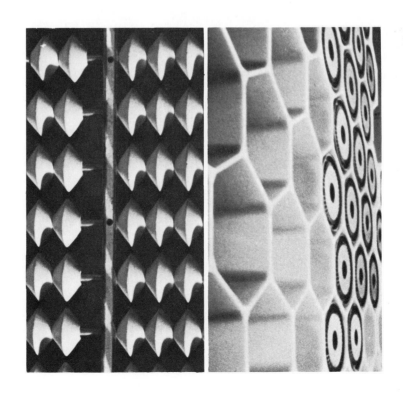

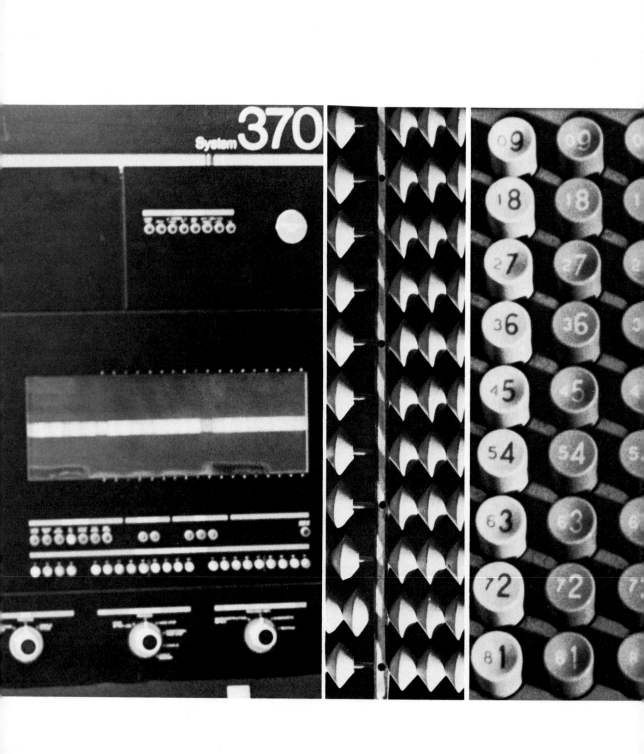

EMERGENCE
OF THE
SYSTEMS
ANALYST

The First Seven Thousand Years

1

Computers have increased rapidly both in number and in capability since they were first used for business data processing in the early 1950s. The goal of this chapter is to review this growth, identifying the systems analyst as the person who is responsible for creating usable computer solutions to business problems. You will learn the principal characteristics of the four computer eras: the Early Era, the Growing Era, the Refining Era, and the Maturing Era; the reasons why difficulties were encountered in using computers successfully to solve business problems during the first three eras; and why the fourth era, the Maturing Era, can be called "the era of the systems analyst."

FROM FINGERS TO COMPUTERS

Business computations have been performed for more than seven thousand years. As long ago as 5000 B.C., primitive man kept track of his possessions, such as horses, cows, and ears of corn, by "finger counting." The early traders and record keepers found that they could extend their digital counting ability by devising simple computational aids, such as hollowed-out parallel grooves in the ground. A pebble placed in the first groove represented a unit of measure. When this groove had been filled with ten pebbles, these were removed, and a single pebble was deposited in the adjacent groove. Thus, a counting process based on powers of ten came into existence, and decimal arithmetic became possible. By 500 B.C., portable calculators (the word is derived from the Latin word *calculus*, meaning "pebble") had been devised by constructing frames containing beads strung in parallel rows. This type of device, still in use today, is called an abacus. Each row of beads in the abacus represents a power of ten. A proficient abacus operator can add two five-digit numbers in approximately five seconds. This is a calculating speed equivalent to that obtained by operators of mechanical desk calculators. Actually, mechanical calculators retain the principle of the abacus. The strings of

4

beads are represented by gears, and the gear teeth are equivalent to individual beads. Only as recently as the mid-twentieth century has modern technology produced electronic calculators and digital computers which far outstrip the abacus in performing business calculations.

Growth and trends in data processing

Since the mid-1950s the growth in the number of computer system installations and in the application of these machines to all aspects of business has been explosive. Computer systems have become available in wide ranges of cost, performance, and size. Computer system sizes commonly are described as *micro, mini, midi,* or *maxi.* To classify machines exactly is difficult, however, because of overlapping capabilities and costs. We will refer to two broad classifications of computers. These are shown on a logarithmic (power of ten) scale in FIGURE 1-1, *Small and large computer systems.* When we refer to "small" computer systems, we will mean micro or mini machines. When we refer to "large" systems, we will mean midi or maxi computers.

FIGURE 1-2, *Growth trends in computer systems,* is a graph that shows the dramatic increase in the number of both large and small computer systems in the United States. The number of large systems is estimated to increase from fewer

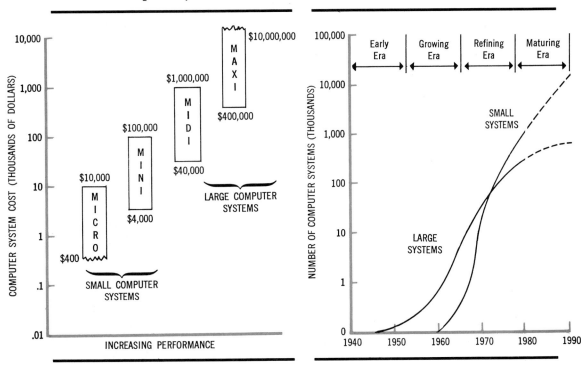

FIGURE 1-1. Small and large computer stystems

FIGURE 1-2. Growth trends in computer stystems

than ten in 1950 to more than 500,000 by 1990. The number of small systems is expected to far exceed even the number of large systems. Progress in miniaturizing computer system components is continuously improving the performance of large and small systems while reducing their cost and size. An important consequence of this progress is the ability to distribute computing power wherever it is needed. Today, distributed data processing systems can serve as small, powerful local computers that can "stand alone" or be connected by a communications link to a large, remote central-site computer. The principal areas of computer applications are military, industrial, process control, scientific, and business. In the 1980s, at least 95 percent of large computer installations will be performing some type of business processing, as will a large percentage of small systems.

Figure 1-2 also shows four time divisions, or eras, which we call the Early Era, the Growing Era, the Refining Era, and the Maturing Era. (Time periods corresponding roughly to these eras often are referred to as "computer generations.") These eras mark significant intervals in the development of computers. They provide a useful time frame for introducing the development of a methodology to improve the general quality of business applictions of computers. We call this methodology "systems analysis." It is the subject of this book, and we shall define it more precisely as we continue.

The Early Era: Machine performance

One method of distinguishing the four computer eras is to identify each with the component that best represents the state of the art in machine design and performance. Thus, as shown in Figure 1-3, *Progress in miniaturization of computer components*, we have progressed from vacuum tubes to transistors to integrated circuits. A single integrated circuit chip of the size pictured is equivalent to several hundred vacuum tubes or transistors. Improvements in reliability and performance through further miniaturization and integration of components will continue in the future.

As an illustration of progress in computer design technology, consider the increase that has occurred in computational speed since people began dropping pebbles into grooves in the ground. Figure 1-4, *The first seven thousand years*, indicates the reduction in time required to add two five-digit numbers. One millisecond is one one-thousandth of a second; one microsecond is one one-millionth of a second; and one nanosecond is one one-billionth of a second. The meaning of these speeds is emphasized by the graph in Figure 1-5, *Seven thousand years growth in speed of addition*. Even more significant is the recent rate of increase in capability. For 4,500 years we crept along, computationally speaking, at a snail's pace. We then increased our computational speed by a factor of twelve and remained pegged at that level for another 2,450 years. Then suddenly, within a mere 25-year time span, our computational speed increased by a factor of more than one billion. Computers, of course, perform more complex arithmetic than the addition of two five-digit numbers. They also store and access large quantities of data and execute logical decisions. In all these respects, too, the growth in technical capability has been similar to the increase in speed indicated in Figure 1-5.

FIGURE 1-3. Progress in miniaturization of computer components

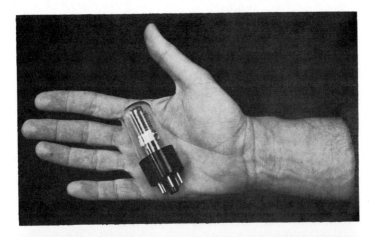

VACUUM TUBE
(Early Era)

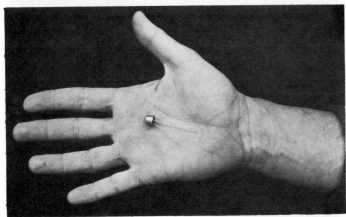

TRANSISTOR
(Growing Era)

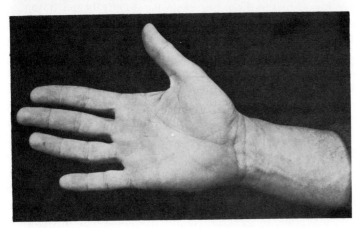

INTEGRATED CIRCUIT CHIP
(Refining Era)

FIGURE 1-4. The first seven thousand years

Equipment	Year	Time to Add Two Five-digit Numbers
STONES	5000 B.C.	60 SECONDS
ABACUS	500 B.C.	5 SECONDS
DESK CALCULATOR	1900	5 SECONDS
DIGITAL COMPUTER	1950	1 MILLISECOND
DIGITAL COMPUTER	1963	1 MICROSECOND
DIGITAL COMPUTER	1975	1 NANOSECOND

Throughout most of the Early Era, emphasis was on improving the internal design of computers. Because of this, we can refer to the Early Era as the era of the computer designer.

The Growing Era: Human-machine interaction

Toward the end of the Early Era and throughout the Growing Era, emphasis shifted to include not only the design of computers, but also improvements in the ways in which humans could communicate with machines.

The internal design of electronic digital computers is oriented around the use of "on-off," or binary, devices. Machine instructions and data are coded in a number system containing only 1's and 0's. The programmers of Early Era computers had to work close to the binary machine design level. Hence, the programs they wrote were said to be coded in "machine language."

Symbolic languages that permit the programmer to write a program using symbols more meaningful than machine language were developed and came into widespread use during the Growing Era. For example, FORTRAN (FORmula TRANslation) is a high level symbolic language used extensively for mathematical computation. FORTRAN may be used for commercial applications; however, a more suitable language, COBOL (COmmon Business Oriented Language), was developed for commercial data processing. Statements such as MULTIPLY HOURS BY RATE GIVING GROSSPAY can be written in COBOL. Clearly, this type of statement is meaningful and easy to remember. Other languages were developed to meet special needs. Examples are APT (Automatically Programmed Tools) for the numerical control of machine tools and RPG (Report Program Generator) for describing a data file and specifying its input and output format.

The high level symbolic programming languages improved human-machine performance in a number of significant ways:

1. The programmer could write fewer instructions. A translator program, called a compiler, was available to generate many machine-level instructions from one symbolic instruction.

FIGURE 1-5. Seven thousand years growth in speed of addition

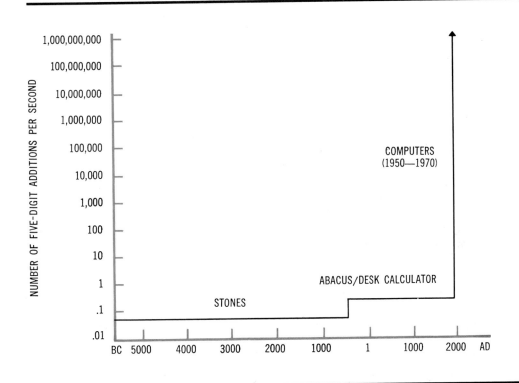

2. Programs could be written in the vocabulary of the user and of the application. Such programs tended to be self-documenting.

3. Symbolic languages were easy to learn and to use. Programmers could be trained more quickly, and assignments could be completed sooner.

4. Symbolic languages could be learned by nonprogrammers. They served as a bridge for improved communication between programmers, problem analysts, and users of the computer program.

5. Symbolic languages were reasonably independent of the machine. As a result, programs tended to remain useful even when equipment was changed.

In addition to symbolic, problem-oriented, programming languages and their translator programs, other aids to the programmer have been developed by computer manufacturers. These include (1) special purpose programs to aid the programmer in debugging and testing his programs; (2) programs to relieve the programmer of the burden of providing the computer with detailed instructions for repetitive input and output operations; and (3) programs to make accessible to him a variety of devices. Collectively, all of these programming aids are called an operating system. Because the Growing Era was a period of extensive improvement in human-machine interaction, we can call this era the era of the computer programmer. However, the need still existed for a better understanding of the computer applications environment, so that the effectiveness of computers as business problem-solving tools could be improved.

The Refining Era: Human-machine-problem interaction

The Refining Era began with the dominance of large, central-site computers and developed into a "computer revolution within the computer revolution." This internal revolution was based on progress in miniaturizing computer components, and it led to the proliferation of small computers and the widespread distribution of computer power. Throughout this era, an enormous effort was required to develop symbolic languages and operating systems. In the 1960s, computer users were plagued with problems encountered in eliminating the "bugs" from one operating system while an even more sophisticated operating system was being developed. Also, while machine technology was changing and operating systems were being developed, attempts were made to apply computers to a broad spectrum of problems, including complex business applications. The success of such endeavors was limited, creating a need for an effective approach to the management of the interaction between humans, machines, and problems, and setting the stage for the emergence of the new profession of systems analysis.

The Maturing Era: Systems analysis

Improvements in computer technology will continue throughout the Maturing Era. Some very large "supercomputers" will be constructed, and complete computers that are "smaller than a matchbox" will become common. Distributed data processing will be widespread. Advances in symbolic languages, operating systems, and other programming aids will continue. Most important, techniques for managing computer applications, from inception to operation, will be improved. These techniques are called systems analysis. The person who applies these techniques is called a systems analyst. Hence, we can call the Maturing Era the era of the systems analyst.

THE DEVELOPMENT OF SYSTEMS ANALYSIS

To understand the development of the profession of systems analysis, we need first to define some systems concepts. We will also distinguish between levels of system complexity, explain some of the difficulties encountered in developing computer-based business systems, and emphasize the need for the synthesis of humans and machines to provide usable solutions to problems.

A system definition

Let us state what we mean by the term "system" and then describe three levels of system complexity. We define a *system* as a combination of personnel, materials, facilities, and equipment working together to convert inputs into outputs. This conversion process is depicted in the first part of FIGURE 1-6, *System concepts*. As the second part of the same figure illustrates, we can identify four

FIGURE 1-6. System concepts

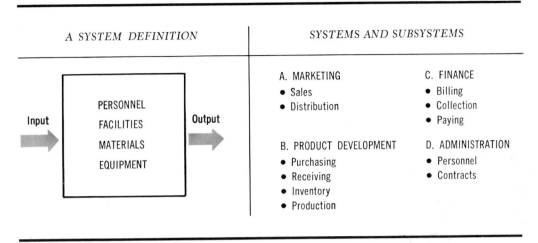

major business systems that are present in most enterprises. These are marketing, finance, product development, and administration. As is also indicated in this figure, these major systems are made up of subordinate systems, or subsystems, which perform specific functions. An example is a marketing system which is composed of sales and distribution subsystems. Typically, an input to a sales system is a sales order, and an output is a shipping order.

Levels of system complexity

The complexity of systems and subsystems varies greatly with the nature and size of business enterprises. However, we can distinguish between three general levels of computer applications. These levels are functional applications, integrated information systems, and management science. Functional applications are those that are self-contained and largely limited to a single activity or function. A payroll subsystem, for example, may be considered to be a functional computer application. Functional systems may be combined, or integrated, into more complex systems, called integrated information systems. For example, a payroll system and a personnel system may be combined to form an integrated personnel-payroll system.

An important characteristic of integrated information systems is the fact that their input data and output information needs do not necessarily conform to organizational boundaries. Rather, these systems rely upon the concept that data need be recorded only once and that, thereafter, it can be accessed and used for more than one purpose. Such data, when captured and stored in a suitable device, such as a magnetic disk, is said to comprise a "data base." This data base may be shared by related computer applications. There are many possible relationships between systems that can use shared data bases. The following are examples of integration within a major system and between major systems:

1. *Within a system:* Payroll and Cost Accounting (elements of a financial system) may share a data base because both applications have common data elements, such as employee number, job identification, regular hours worked, overtime hours worked, and pay rate.

2. *Between systems:* Personnel (an element of an administrative system) and Payroll (an element of a financial system) may share a data base because both use common data elements, such as employee number, number of dependents, department number, pay rate, and length of employment.

Management science applications relate to planning, control, and decision making. For example, management may be aided in making a sales forecast if data based upon past experience can be combined with estimates of general economic conditions. One scientific technique which might be used for this purpose is a mathematical model consisting of equations that represent economic and business relationships. A computer could be used to solve these equations and to answer questions of a "what if" nature.

The potential for management science applications of computers is virtually unlimited. Such applications may range from the more efficient scheduling of machines in a factory to strategic decisions such as the selection of new markets and the decision to acquire or to merge with another company. Management science systems that provide information needed by managers for the control of their operations often are called *management information systems.* We shall discuss this important management science application of computers in Chapter 4: System Concepts: A Business as an Information System.

In general, management science is related to a branch of mathematics known as decision theory. Decision theory attempts to use mathematical or logical techniques to aid executives in dealing with their decision problems. This is a relatively new field, and it requires considerable technical training. Although such training is now offered in many business schools, most business managers have not had it and hence are reluctant to explore management science techniques that depend heavily upon mathematics.

Difficulties in developing computer-based business systems

FIGURE 1-7, *Levels of computer applications,* shows the three levels of computer-based business systems: functional applications, integrated information systems, and management science. This figure indicates a trend in which functional applications are replaced by more complex and comprehensive applications. In the 1960s, one major reason for the frequent failures in applying computers successfully to the solution of business problems was an inability to distinguish between the levels of system complexity. Very unrealistically, in the early 1960s a time span of 1960–70 was assigned to the transition shown in Figure 1-7. With the advantage of hindsight, we can assign 1970–80 as a more reasonable time interval. In the past, greatest success was achieved with functional applications of the type listed in Figure 1-6. Of course, integrated data-base-oriented applications

FIGURE 1-7. Levels of computer applications

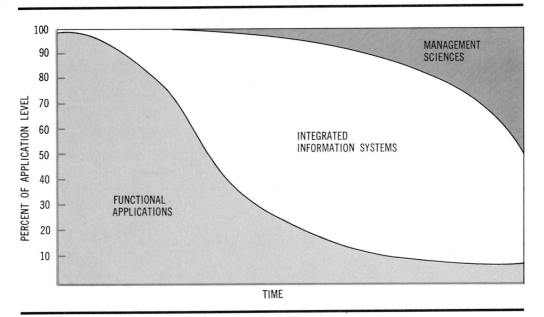

of computers were made in such areas as income tax accounting and social security record maintenance; airline and hotel reservation systems; life insurance records; stock market reporting and account recording; and computer-maintained mailing lists. However, progress in developing sophisticated computer applications in the 1960s and most of the 1970s must be evaluated from the viewpoint of the user rather than from that of the computer designer, the programmer, or the salesperson. Unfortunately, a consensus of most users of computer systems probably would have been that performance fell significantly short of promise.

Successes with all but the most basic functional applications, while noteworthy, usually were achieved only after an excessive expenditure of time and money. By no means were the difficulties due only to problems directly related to machines and to the interaction between programmers and machines. The significant reason for overexpectation and underachievement in the human-machine-problem environment was failure to discriminate between levels of application complexity. As a result, efforts were made to develop complicated management reporting systems that were not supported by functional systems. This was like trying to build a house by starting with the roof, and such applications seldom got off the ground.

Another major reason for failures during the Growing and Refining Eras was the lack of an organized procedure, or methodology, for controlling all the elements of the design of complex systems. This lack proved extremely costly. Few responsible studies were made of computer programming costs; however, such

FIGURE 1-8. Instruction productivity vs. application difficulty

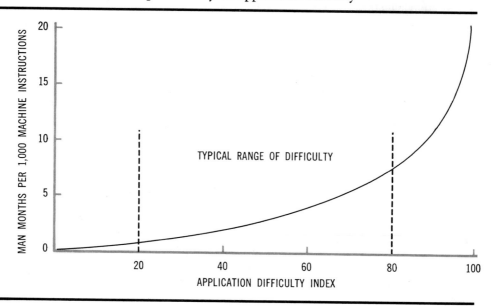

data as was developed was very alarming. One such study was made for the Air Force by E. A. Nelson of the Systems Development Corporation.[1] This study summarized the results of the statistical analysis of the cost factors associated with 169 computer-based systems. FIGURE 1-8, *Instruction productivity vs. application difficulty,* is based on Nelson's study. It illustrates the relationship between problem difficulty and the time required to produce 1,000 machine language instructions. For example, a problem with a difficulty rating of 80 percent required six man-months to produce 1,000 machine language instructions. This is approximately 8 machine language instructions per day (even fewer instructions if the computer program is written in a high level symbolic language). Difficulty, and hence programming inefficiency, was found to correlate most closely with the lack of an adequate problem definition and with the lack of techniques for planning and managing the computer programming effort.

In retrospect, these initial deficiencies in applying computers to the solution of business problems are not surprising. The language and technology involved were foreign to all but a few computer professionals. Existing systems and procedures groups generally were not trained in computer-oriented systems design. As a result, they frequently distorted the communication between the computer programmers and the users of the system. Users were similarly uneducated, and their responsibilities for systems design were poorly defined. Managers

---

1. Edward A. Nelson, *Management Handbook for the Estimation of Computer Programming Costs* (Santa Monica: Systems Development Corporation, 1967).

lacked the ability to communicate with computer programmers and so often abdicated their responsibilities. Programmers, on the other hand, frequently were forced to make systems decisions beyond the area of their responsibility and knowledge in order to get something "to run." The results often were "solutions" seeking "problems" and, as such, were sometimes catastrophic.

A list of additional reasons for the difficulties encountered in developing usable business systems in the Growing and Refining Eras would include these:

1. *Lack of management acceptance:* Computers were not accepted by management. At best they were tolerated.

2. *Lack of managerial knowledge:* The new technology was not understood, and there was a consequent reluctance to apply standard management techniques because of the EDP (Electronic Data Processing) "mystique."

3. *Lack of standards:* There were no historical standards by which computing efforts could be measured.

4. *Continual change:* The computer sciences, equipment, languages, and applications were rapidly changing.

Synthesis of humans and machines to solve problems

By the end of the Refining Era, however, there was an observable trend toward a more realistic approach to computer-based system development. Three factors accounted for this. First, there was growing management dissatisfaction with return on computer investment, forcing management education and participation. Second, project-control techniques that had been developed in high technology industries for the management of large computer projects became more widely available. Third, a higher place in the organization was created for computer-related activities because of their interaction with all business operations. The importance of this third factor was emphasized by a landmark study performed by the management consulting firm of McKinsey and Company, Inc.[2] It pointed out that the success of a computer-based system depended on the reporting level of the corporate computer executives.

In many companies the factors discussed above led to the integration of the computer center and the conventional systems and procedures activities. Individuals equipped with both a computer and an applications background began to emerge and to assume responsibility for all the activities associated with the analysis, design, and development of computer-based systems. These individuals were called systems analysts.

We have already noted that improvements in machine performance and in human-machine communications will continue throughout the Maturing Era, which will extend from 1980 to the end of the century. A study of data processing in the period 1980–1985 has concluded that the major tasks of the data processing industry will not be the design of more effective computers or computer programs. Rather, it will try to improve (1) the quality of data processing services as per-

---

2. *Getting the Most Out of Your Computer* (New York: McKinsey and Company, Inc., 1963).

FIGURE 1-9. Computer system responsibility

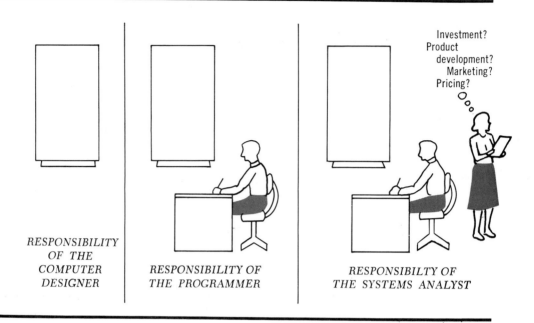

Investment?
Product
  development?
    Marketing?
      Pricing?

RESPONSIBILITY
OF THE
COMPUTER
DESIGNER

RESPONSIBILITY OF
THE PROGRAMMER

RESPONSIBILTY OF
THE SYSTEMS ANALYST

ceived by the users of such services; (2) the productivity of the end-users; and (3) the productivity of data processing systems and applications development efforts.[3] That is, in the future, emphasis will be on the *usability* of computer systems. The person who will be responsible for creating usable systems is the systems analyst.

As FIGURE 1-9, *Computer system responsibility*, indicates, the responsibility of the systems analyst is broader than that of the designer or the programmer. The systems analyst uses the products of the computer designer and the computer programmer to create computer-based business systems and to manage the changes that will occur throughout their operational lives. The Maturing Era may, indeed, become known as the era of the systems analyst.

KEY TERMS

Early Era	*systems analysis*	*integrated information system*
Growing Era	*subsystem*	*management information system*
Refining Era	*functional application*	*usability*
Maturing Era		

3. Dolotta, T.A., et al., *Data Processing in 1980-1985: A Study of Potential Limitations to Progress* (New York: John Wiley and Sons, 1976).

FOR DISCUSSION

1. Describe the responsibilities of the computer designer, the programmer, and the systems analyst. Can you relate these characteristics to the computer eras?

2. Define the term "system." What are some examples of systems and subsystems?

3. Distinguish between the three levels of computer applications and provide examples of each.

4. Discuss the principal reasons why difficulties were encountered in developing computer-oriented business systems in the 1960s.

5. Discuss the meaning of "usability" as it applies to computer-based business systems.

The Life Cycle of the Computer-Based Business System

2

Systems are characterized by a life cycle that has four distinct phases. The goal of this chapter is to define these phases and introduce a "top-down" methodology for performing, managing, and documenting the activities associated with each one. You will learn the major characteristics of each phase and come to understand why the systems analyst is called a life-cycle manager.

THE LIFE-CYCLE CONCEPT

Systems are created by a dynamic process which moves through a series of stages, or phases. The concept of a life cycle has evolved to describe the relationship between these phases. This concept includes not only forward (in time) motion, but also the possibility of having to return, i.e., cycle back, to an activity previously considered completed. This cycling back, or feedback, may occur as the result of the failure of the system to meet a performance objective or as the result of changes in or redefinition of system objectives.

Hardware and software end-products

Practical techniques for the management of relatively complex projects have been developed from the life-cycle concept. However, in the past, most such projects have had as their objective the creation of hardware end-products. These *hardware* end-products are described primarily by their physical, e.g., electrical or mechanical, attributes, which can be observed and measured as the hardware moves through the several stages of its development. Examples of complex systems that have been developed by the application of life-cycle techniques are rockets, communications networks, computer systems, and spacecraft.

The computer-based business system also contains hardware components; however, its most significant characteristic is a software end-product. *Software* may be defined as a collection of programs or routines that facilitates the use of a computer. This definition includes operating systems and application programs. The latter is the end-product associated with a computer-based business

Figure 2-1. Distinction between hardware and software end-products

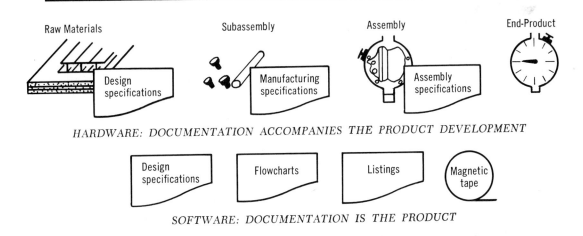

HARDWARE: DOCUMENTATION ACCOMPANIES THE PRODUCT DEVELOPMENT

SOFTWARE: DOCUMENTATION IS THE PRODUCT

system. Software, in contrast with hardware, does not possess attributes that can readily be observed and measured from concept to end-product. The software end-product is information. Although it may be stored or printed on a physical medium such as a magnetic disk, a reel of tape, or a sheet of paper, information is transient and fragile compared with hardware.

Many of the past difficulties in developing effective computer-based business systems stemmed not only from belated efforts to apply management controls, but also from failure to recognize that techniques applicable to the development of hardware end-products could not be applied without modification to the development of software end-products. However, as a result of experience gained from large government and commercial software projects in the latter part of the 1960s, the concept of life-cycle management was adapted to fit the development of computer-based business systems.

The key to modifying the life-cycle concept for the management of software projects was the observation that, although supporting documentation *accompanies* a physical product throughout its development, documentation *is* the software product. This distinction is made clear in Figure 2-1, *Distinction between hardware and software end-products.*

Life-cycle phases and the life-cycle manager
Like most systems, the life cycle of a computer-based system exhibits distinct phases. These are:

1. The Study Phase
2. The Design Phase
3. The Development Phase
4. The Operation Phase

As is discussed later in this chapter, all the activities associated with each phase must be performed, managed, and documented. Hence, we now define *systems analysis* as the performance, management, and documentation of the four phases of the life cycle of a business system. This is a significantly broader definition of systems analysis than might be associated with the meaning of the word "analysis." *Analysis* is the process of breaking something down into its parts so that the whole may be understood. The definition of "systems analysis" includes not only analysis, but also *synthesis,* the process of putting parts together to form a new whole. The systems analyst is, in reality, both an analyst and a synthesist. We can identify the *systems analyst* as the individual who is responsible for the performance of systems analysis for all, or a portion of, the phases of the life cycle of a business system. The analyst is, in effect, a life-cycle manager.

PERFORMANCE, MANAGEMENT, AND DOCUMENTATION OF THE PHASES OF A COMPUTER-BASED BUSINESS SYSTEM: AN OVERVIEW

The life-cycle flowchart

The principal focus of this book is on the operations associated with performing, managing, and documenting all the life-cycle activities of a computer-based business system. In order to view these life-cycle activities in perspective, let us consider FIGURE 2-2, *The life cycle of a computer-based business system.* This figure is a pictorial overview with which we will become increasingly familiar; we will refer to it to mark our progress through this book. The pictorial representation used in Figure 2-2 is called a flowchart. *Flowcharts* use predefined symbols to represent operations or information flow in a business system. The flowchart symbols used in Figure 2-2 will be defined in context as we discuss performance, management, and documentation of the life-cycle activities.

Performance of the life-cycle activities

The life-cycle methodology for developing complex systems is a modular, top-down procedure. In the Study Phase, modules that describe the major functions to be performed by the system are developed. The procedure is called "top-down" because in successive phases the major modules are expanded into additional, increasingly detailed, modules. Powerful graphic tools have been developed to structure the top-down design and development of systems. We shall learn about these as we study the Design and Development Phase activities in detail. For the present, we can summarize the principal activities associated with each of the phases of the life cycle of a computer-based business system as follows:

The Study Phase. This is the phase during which a problem is identified, alternate system solutions are studied, and recommendations are made about committing the resources required to design the system. Activities performed in the study phase are grossly analogous to (1) determining that a shelter from the elements is needed, and (2) deciding that a two-bedroom house is a more appropriate shelter than a palace, a cave, or other possible selections.

Figure 2-2. The life cycle of a computer-based business system

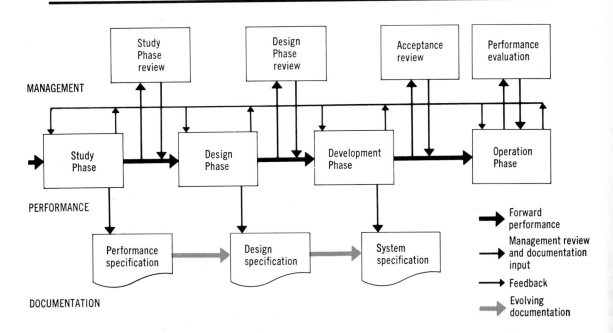

The Design Phase. In this phase the detailed design of the system selected in the Study Phase is accomplished. This is analogous to drawing the plans for the two-bedroom home decided on in the Study Phase. In the case of a computer-based business system, Design Phase activities include the allocation of resources to equipment tasks, personnel tasks, and computer program tasks. In the Design Phase, the technical specifications are prepared for the performance of all allocated tasks.

The Development Phase. This is the phase in which the computer-based system is constructed from the specifications prepared in the Design Phase. Equipment is acquired and installed. All necessary procedures, manuals, software specifications, and other documentation are completed. The staff is trained, and the complete system is tested for operational readiness. This is analogous to the actual construction of our two-bedroom house from the plans prepared in its Design Phase.

The Operation Phase. In this phase, there is a changeover from the old system (if a previous system or partial system existed) to the new system. The new system is operated and maintained. Its performance is reviewed, and changes in it are managed. This phase is analogous to living in the house which we have built. If we have performed the activities of the preceding phases adequately, the roof should not leak.

The symbol used in Figure 2-2 to represent the phases is called a "process" symbol. Processes are similar to systems because *processes* are operations that convert, or transform, inputs into outputs. Thus, the Study Phase consists of all the processes required to produce an output that is identified on the flow-chart of Figure 2-2 as a Performance Specification. The Performance Specification is represented by the symbol for a "document."

Management of the life-cycle activities

Management review of the life-cycle activities may occur at any time. However, the conclusion of each phase is a natural time for a major management review. The major management reviews are shown by the process symbols at the top of Figure 2-2. These are formal scheduled reviews which must occur before a phase can be considered complete. They are essential to a structured inter-action between the system analyst and the user, ensuring user involvement at critical decision points. Three types of decisions can be forthcoming at each review: (1) proceed to the next phase; (2) cancel the project; or (3) redo certain parts of a previous phase.

Activities that are redone must be reviewed before the project can proceed to a subsequent phase. Management review often is the mechanism that triggers "cycling back" (feedback) to an earlier state in the life cycle, to remedy per-formance deficiencies or to respond to changes in requirements. Each successful review is a renewal of management commitment to the project.

Documentation of the computer-based business system

The accumulation of documentation parallels the life-cycle performance and management review activities. Documentation is not a task accomplished as a "wind-up" activity; rather, it is continuous and cumulative. Cumulative docu-mentation is implied by the gray lines and arrowheads of Figure 2-2. The most essential documents are called "baseline" specifications (i.e., specifications to which changes can be referred). There are three baseline specifications:

1. *Performance Specification:* Completed at the conclusion of the Study Phase, and describing in the language of the user exactly what the system is to do. It is a "design to" specification.

2. *Design Specification:* Completed at the conclusion of the Design Phase, and describing in the language of the programmer (and others employed in actually constructing the system) how to develop the system. It is a "build to" specification.

3. *System Specification:* Completed at the conclusion of the Development Phase and containing all of the critical system documentation. It is the basis for all manuals and procedures, and it is an "as built" specification.

The Design Specification evolves from the Performance Specification, and the System Specification evolves from the Design Specification. And, since these documents are the only measurable evidence that progress is being made toward the creation of a useful software end-product, it is not possible to manage the life-cycle process without them. Thus, documentation is not only the "visible" software end-product, but also the key to the successful management of the life cycle of computer-based business systems.

KEY TERMS

hardware end-product	*life cycle*	*top-down*
software end-product	*Study Phase*	*Performance Specification*
systems analysis	*Design Phase*	*Design Specification*
synthesis	*Development Phase*	*System Specification*
	Operation Phase	

FOR DISCUSSION

1. Describe the life-cycle concept.

2. Distinguish between hardware and software end-products. How does this distinction relate to the development of computer-based business systems?

3. What are the four phases in the life cycle of a computer-based business system? Describe each.

4. How is systems analysis defined in this chapter?

5. Why is the life-cycle methodology a top-down approach to system design and development?

6. What is the meaning of the term "baseline document"? Identify and describe the three baseline documents.

7. What is meant by the term "cumulative documentation"?

3

The Role of the Systems Analyst

We have described the systems analyst as a life-cycle manager, the person who is responsible for performing systems analysis for all, or a portion of, the phases of the life cycle of a business system. The goal of this chapter is to examine in more detail the analyst's role in the development of computer-based business systems. You will find that the role of the systems analyst is changing, due to the increasing impact of computer-related technology. Furthermore, the systems analyst's role is greater in organizations that are developing computer-based systems than in those that continue to emphasize manual systems.

SYSTEMS AND PROCEDURES

The field of systems analysis has evolved from a profession that was known as "systems and procedures." Systems and procedures units dealt almost exclusively with manual systems. The basic functions of these professionals were these:

1. To analyze systems with problems and to design new or modified systems to solve those problems.

2. To design the various business forms used to collect data and to distribute information.

3. To perform records management, i.e., to administer the creation, use, and retention of forms.

4. To analyze the distribution and use of reports.

5. To participate in the measurement and simplification of work.

6. To prepare written procedures for various manual activities and to establish standards for those procedures.

Systems and Procedures reporting level

Systems and procedures activities were advisory staff functions, and the staff usually reported to a financial officer of the company, often the controller. This was a logical reporting point because the systems with which the group worked, such as accounting applications and "overhead" cost studies, were of prime concern in the area of finance.

FIGURE 3-1, *Typical organizational location of Systems and Procedures,* shows a typical business organizational structure with Systems and Procedures reporting to a financial executive. This reporting structure was predominant as recently as the early 1960s. It not only put the Systems and Procedures staff under the direct control of its primary user, but also isolated it from other potential users. Although the accounting and financial functions of a business were generally the first areas to come under the scrutiny of systems people, they were not the only areas that could benefit from an analysis of their procedures. Moreover, finance was not the only area within a business to be affected by accounting systems. All areas of the business are linked to the information flow necessary to handle the accounting functions. Thus, although systems and procedures activities had to cut across departmental boundaries, the staff was under the control of only one information user.

Systems and Procedures problems

The dual responsibility of designing and maintaining multidepartmental systems while reporting to only one of those departments created two major problems for the Systems and Procedures personnel and for the business in general. First, since their "boss" was in finance, systems problems relating most directly to matters of

FIGURE 3-1. Typical organizational location of Systems and Procedures

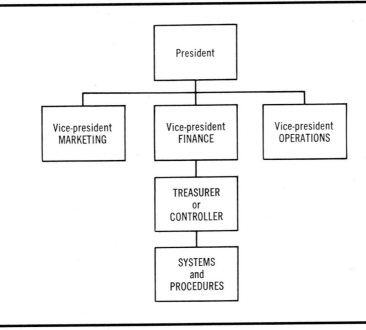

finance had first priority. Problems in marketing or in production were not as important to the controller as problems in finance. Second, Systems and Procedures personnel often had difficulty in collecting information and in investigating problems when systems crossed departmental lines. They were the "efficiency experts who came snooping around to cause trouble." They had to rely totally on voluntary cooperation. Finance often had no great influence on nonfinancial functions. The net effect of reporting to Finance was to confine the major efforts of Systems and Procedures to financial systems and to that department.

THE AUTOMATION OF SYSTEMS

In such an organization, there usually was no direct association between Systems and Procedures and Data Processing. The Systems and Procedures staff dealt primarily with manual systems. The data processing equipment with which they came into contact was unit record equipment, and the business systems were designed around manual operations. Most members of the Systems and Procedures staff did not need to be familiar with computers. In the 1970s, however, business systems became increasingly computer-oriented. The transition from manual systems to computer-oriented systems brought major changes into the methods for systems analysis and design.

Manual systems

Manual systems are business systems designed around a pattern of manual operations performed by people. Before the large-scale use of computers in business, this was the usual approach to the design of business systems. Even after their computers were installed, many businesses unfortunately attempted to automate manual systems simply by replacing people with a computer. When this was done without reorienting the system design, the result usually was an inefficient system, since placing a computer in a human's environment does not take advantage of the computer's capabilities. It is still not unusual to see the potential of modern computers wasted in systems that remain "manual" in concept.

Computer-oriented systems

Computer-oriented systems are those in which the capabilities of humans and computers have been blended to take advantage of the unique capabilities of each. This blending is more than simply getting a computer to do a person's work. While it is true that most tasks of an unvarying or repetitive nature can be performed by a machine, the computer can do much more. However a computer cannot adapt to an existing system; the system must be designed to take advantage of the machine's special capabilities.

Reasons for automation

Computer-oriented systems differ from manual systems in at least four important capabilities:

1. *Accuracy:* There is a greater potential for accuracy. Once the data is entered correctly into the system in a machine-readable format, it is not neces-

sary to reenter it again. This reduces the chances for error by reducing the number of times humans are involved. Of course, the computer system is highly vulnerable to the entry of invalid data.

2. *Data collection and communication:* Methods for collecting and communicating data are faster and more efficient. Modern computers allow data communication networks to be established to collect data and to respond to inquiries. An airline reservation system is an example of a network of data communication sites tied into a central data processing center. A reservation clerk may inquire about space availability on any flight and receive an almost immediate response. Seat reservations can be made and confirmed while the customer waits. The communication sites may be nearby or remote.

3. *Data storage:* Another way in which manual and human-machine systems differ is in the quantities of data that can be stored and accessed. In computer-oriented systems, data is kept in master files, usually magnetic, in a machine-readable format. A collection of related files forms a data base. Data bases allow for the centralized storage of data, thereby eliminating the need for a multiplicity of redundant files. Data base systems require special measures to prevent their contamination by bad data.

4. *Speed of response:* Speed of response—the time required for information to become available—can be greatly increased by use of computers. Retail operations provide an example of the capabilities of fast-response systems. Specially designed cash registers not only perform the functions of traditional cash registers, but also serve as data terminals. As terminals, they become part of a "real-time" system which can perform such functions as credit checks, search for lost credit cards, accounting for cash and credit transactions, and inventory management. These systems are able to make information available as needed rather than after the close of a traditional accounting period of perhaps weeks or months.

We can visualize "pure" machine-oriented systems that are capable of functioning without the active participation of humans. Such systems have not yet been developed; however, they do offer the potential for overcoming two major "bottle-necks" in the design of many current man-machine systems. These two problems are the mismatch between the operating speeds of people and machines and the tendency of humans to make mistakes. Getting humans out of the picture or at least into the background, will certainly be a great challenge to the systems analyst of the future.

SYSTEMS ANALYSIS

To make a distinction between systems and procedures and systems analysis, let us consider FIGURE 3-2, *Major systems activities.* This chart shows the percentage of systems units in more than 1,200 companies engaged in specific activities.[1] Note that the companies surveyed apparently do not agree which activities truly belong

---

1. *Profile of the Systems Professional* (Cleveland: Association for Systems Management Bookshelf Series, 1978).

FIGURE 3-2. Major systems activities

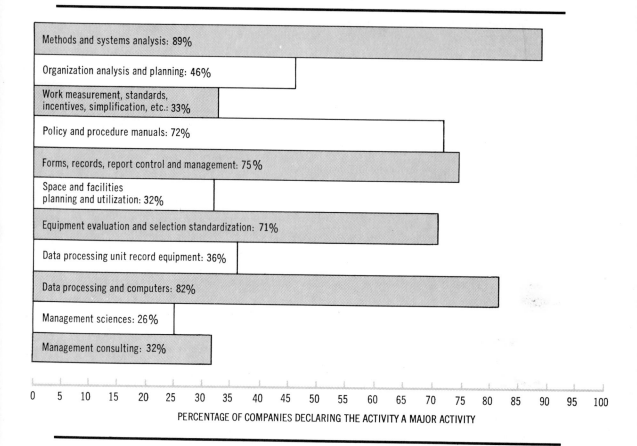

Methods and systems analysis: 89%

Organization analysis and planning: 46%

Work measurement, standards, incentives, simplification, etc.: 33%

Policy and procedure manuals: 72%

Forms, records, report control and management: 75%

Space and facilities planning and utilization: 32%

Equipment evaluation and selection standardization: 71%

Data processing unit record equipment: 36%

Data processing and computers: 82%

Management sciences: 26%

Management consulting: 32%

0   5   10   15   20   25   30   35   40   45   50   55   60   65   70   75   80   85   90   95   100

PERCENTAGE OF COMPANIES DECLARING THE ACTIVITY A MAJOR ACTIVITY

in the systems area. This discrepancy is due to differences in the size and nature of the businesses involved and in the attitudes of their management. Of particular significance are the high percentages of a common core of activities: methods and systems analysis; policy and procedure manuals; forms, records, report control, and management; equipment evaluation and selection standardization; and data processing and computers.

From this information, the basic functions of systems analysis can be described as:

1. To analyze systems with problems and to design new or modified systems to solve those problems.

2. To develop manuals to communicate company policy and procedures.

3. To design the various business forms used to collect data and distribute information.

4. To perform records management, including the distribution and use of reports.

5. To participate in the evaluation of equipment and to define standards for equipment selection.

6. To interface with data processing to coordinate the development of systems whenever computer-oriented systems have been selected.

What, then, are the real differences between systems analysis and systems and procedures? They are (1) the complexity and sophistication of computer-based systems; and (2) the expanded role the systems analyst plays in the analysis, design, development, and implementation of these systems.

The use of computers in business applications is more than the mechanization of manual activities. Computers make available vast amounts of data not available in manual systems, but at the same time require new techniques for systems design and data handling. Because these systems are more complex and technical, and have a greater impact on the business, changes were required in the traditional approaches of systems and procedures. These changes created the new profession we now call systems analysis.

The systems analysts who practice the new profession are not obsessed with computers. They do not feel that all business systems must be computer-oriented. They are able to evaluate alternate solutions without bias. The process·by which alternate solutions are selected and evaluated is described in Chapter 13: Feasibility Analysis.

Reporting level

One of the most important changes occurring in systems work is the organizational level to which the systems unit reports. The trend is away from Systems Analysis reporting to a financial officer and toward its reporting directly to higher management. FIGURE 3-3, *Systems unit reporting level,* shows a dramatic change in reporting level beginning in the early 1960s.[2] There is a marked decrease in the percentage of companies in which the systems unit reports to a financial manager. Also, in the companies in which Systems is the responsibility of a nonfinancial executive, this executive often reports directly to the president. This is illustrated in FIGURE 3-4, *Typical organizational location of Systems Analysis.* The Systems Analysis staff typically is headed by a director of corporate systems who reports directly to the vice-president of information systems. The director of corporate systems is on the same organizational level as the directors of the user areas of the company and has a direct line to top management.

Personal qualifications

What are the personal attributes of a successful systems analyst? In order to accomplish the task of analyzing current and potential systems, the systems analyst often forms a team of technical specialists. These specialists are selected from the operating personnel of the department involved with the system. They are familiar with the day-by-day operational problems and can help to fill in the

---

2. Ibid.

FIGURE 3-3. Systems unit reporting level

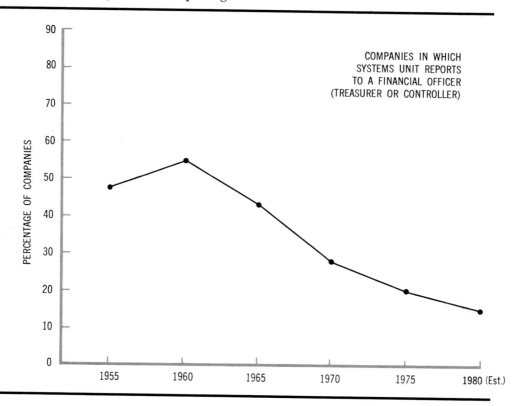

COMPANIES IN WHICH
SYSTEMS UNIT REPORTS
TO A FINANCIAL OFFICER
(TREASURER OR CONTROLLER)

more theoretical views of the systems analyst. In order to manage this team, the analyst must be a leader.

The systems analyst must be able to secure cooperation. Because this position is principally a staff or advisory one, the systems analyst cannot force people in other organizational areas to provide necessary information about their systems or their problems. Many people whom the analyst contacts feel threatened by probing and questioning and are reluctant to cooperate. The systems analyst must, therefore, have the ability to obtain the cooperation of others.

The systems analyst also must be creative. An important part of the job is to modify existing systems or to design new systems to eliminate problems that users are having. An almost limitless number of combinations of system components exists to produce desirable systems. Some will provide better solutions to the problem than others. The systems analyst must design a system that is the best solution possible with the limited resources, such as time and money, available. Within these constraints, the systems analyst must have enough creative imagination to develop and then evaluate feasible system solution candidates.

The systems analyst also must be able to speak and write well. After the analyst has defined the problem and selected a "best" system, management must be con-

FIGURE 3-4. Typical organizational location of Systems Analysis

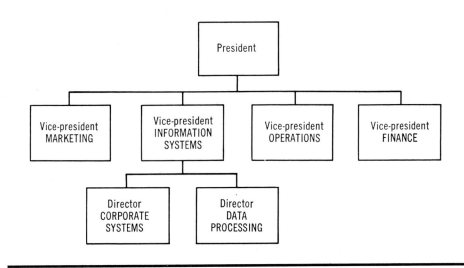

vinced that it is a good problem solution. Management also must be sold on the idea that the business should spend resources to design, develop, and put the system into operation. Selling management includes preparing effective written reports and verbal presentations. If management approves the project, the analyst must also convince the system users that the system will work. The new system will benefit the organization only if it is accepted and used. Unless the analyst has the ability to sell his ideas to others through the written and spoken word, all his work may be of little value.

Educational background

As computer-based business systems continue to increase in scope and complexity, the background required for systems analysis becomes more important and more demanding. Most systems analysts now entering the field have a bachelor's degree or higher. The most common college majors for systems analysts are business administration, accounting, computer science, and data processing. Obviously, the major field of study should be in areas that will contribute to the understanding of computer-based business systems.

A formal education is only the beginning of an educational background. Many companies hold in-house seminars and executive training programs to provide a specific knowledge of how their company operates and to broaden the backgrounds of their professional personnel. There are several professional organizations, such as the Association for Systems Management and the Data Processing Management Association, which provide an opportunity for a free exchange of ideas. These associations also hold seminars designed to help their members to discover new approaches to solving problems.

Work experience

Formal and informal education are very important contributors to the systems analyst's know-how, but there is no substitute for "having been there." Work experience separates theory from practice, the things that work from those that do not work. Anyone entering the field of systems analysis will have to serve an apprenticeship period to get on-the-job experience. When starting to work on projects, the new analyst should undertake small assignments, usually under the supervision of senior analysts. In this way, the analyst can gain experience, build personal confidence, and earn management's confidence.

Senior positions in systems analysis are management level positions. Most analysts get into systems analysis through promotion from other jobs. The most common "other job" has been computer programming. There are several reasons for selecting programmers for promotion to systems analysis. First, they are familiar with the details of the computer portion of many existing systems. Second, they know how to work with computers and speak the "language" of the computer. Third, as programmers, they have shown an ability for analysis and for thinking in a logical manner.

Programmers, of course, are not the only candidates for a systems analyst's position. Anyone who has demonstrated analytical ability and has a detailed knowledge of particular systems or their components is a potential candidate.

KEY TERMS

systems and procedures   *manual systems*   *computer-oriented systems*

FOR DISCUSSION

1. In what types of organizations have systems analysts achieved the greatest stature?

2. From what profession has systems analysis evolved? Describe this profession.

3. What is the trend in reporting level for the systems analysis group? Why has it changed during the past ten years?

4. Why shouldn't a manual system be put on a computer without modifying the system?

5. Describe four ways in which computer-oriented systems differ from manual systems.

6. What are the real differences between the systems analyst and the systems and procedures person?

7. What are the qualifications for a position as a systems analyst?

4

Systems Concepts: A Business as an Information System

A business is an information system that accepts inputs and produces outputs. The goals of this chapter are to define key system concepts that relate to businesses, to explain how organization charts are prepared and used, to describe the information structure of a business, and to summarize the "state of the art" in business information system design. You will acquire a background of concepts that will increase your understanding of the importance of the life-cycle concept and the emerging role of the systems analyst.

A BUSINESS: A SYSTEM OF SYSTEMS

Business goals and objectives

All businesses have goals and objectives. The goals of most businesses differ in kind and in scope. Their objectives differ in specific detail. Before discussing business goals and objectives, however, it is necessary to give some definitions.

A *business* may be defined as a combination of personnel, materials, facilities, and equipment to accomplish specific objectives and to achieve defined goals.

A *goal* is a very broadly stated purpose. Examples are the goal of making profit and the goal of educating students. *Objectives*, on the other hand, are concrete and specific accomplishments necessary to the achievement of goals. For example, an automobile manufacturer must have as an objective the production of a competitive product in order to achieve a profit goal; a college must have as an objective relevant curricula in order to achieve its educational goal. Major objectives are composed of lower order objectives. Accordingly, before a car can be made, subassemblies must be produced and, before that, proper tools must be designed. Goals are relatively long term, and objectives are relatively short term.

Most business enterprises fall into one of two broad categories: production or service. Examples of *production enterprises* are manufacturing, farming, construction, and agriculture. *Service enterprises* include transportation, communications, medicine, and education. Each enterprise, whether production or service, has its particular goals and objectives supporting them. However, certain system con-

FIGURE 4-1. Generalized system environment

SYSTEM ENVIRONMENT

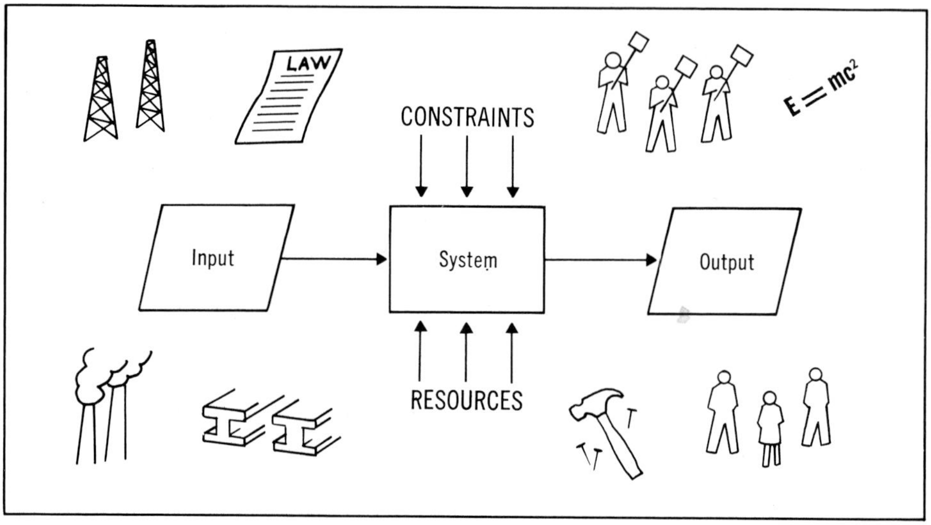

cepts are applicable to all business enterprises. The systems analyst must be familiar with these concepts because they enable him to understand how businesses are structured and organized.

Systems concepts: Systems and subsystems

Because of the multiplicity of objectives and subobjectives that must be achieved within an enterprise, a business is divided into major elements. These major elements are called systems. A generalized concept of a system is shown in FIGURE 4-1, *Generalized system environment*. This figure shows a system as a process that transforms, or converts, an input into an output. This transformation process occurs at many different points and levels within a business. Some combination of resources, i.e., personnel, materials, facilities, and equipment, is required to effect the conversion. Also, a business functions within a set of constraints, which generally it cannot alter significantly. Examples of such constraints are federal laws, social environment, total market, raw materials limitations, and scientific principles. The resources and constraints which affect the transformation of inputs into outputs also are shown in Figure 4-1.

Principal functional systems associated with most product-oriented enterprises are shown in the flowchart of FIGURE 4-2, *Functional business systems*. In order to emphasize the relationship between these functional systems, management and administrative systems, although present in all enterprises, are not included in

Figure 4-2. Customers, employees, and vendors, indicated by dashed-line rectangles, are shown to provide continuity to the illustration. The nine basic functional systems shown in this figure are:

1. *Purchasing:* procuring from the vendors the goods and materials needed by the business.

2. *Receiving:* inspecting and accepting delivered goods and materials.

3. *Inventory:* storing the received goods and materials.

4. *Production:* designing and manufacturing the goods to be sold.

5. *Sales:* marketing the goods produced.

6. *Distribution:* supplying the customer with the goods sold from a produced-goods inventory.

7. *Billing:* sending statements of the amount owed to customers.

8. *Collection:* receiving payments from customers.

9. *Paying:* making payments to those whom the business owes money, such as vendors and employees.

Each of these functional systems produces one or more outputs in the form of products or documents. These outputs establish the relationship of each system to other systems and to the business as a whole. Since systems are assigned their own necessary resources they are, to a degree, relatively independent elements of a business. This is why we have defined a *system* as a combination of personnel, materials, facilities, and equipment working together to convert inputs into out-

FIGURE 4-2. Functional business systems

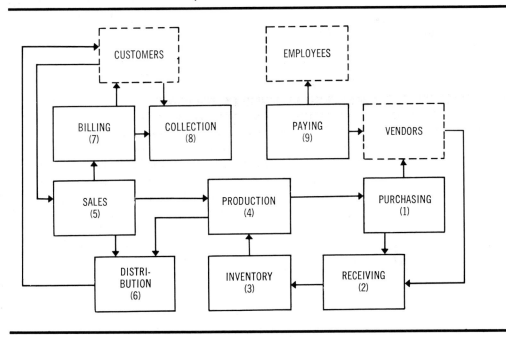

FIGURE 4-3. The business: a system of systems

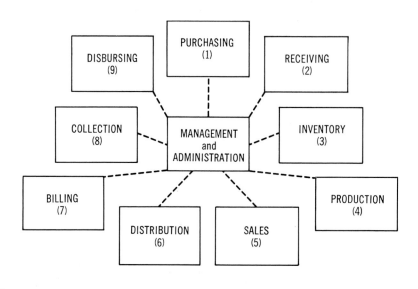

puts. Note that the definition of a system is similar to the definition of a business. However, whereas a system produces *outputs,* a business integrates the outputs of its component systems to accomplish objectives and to achieve goals. Often a system is thought of in terms of its mechanics, such as the methods, techniques, and procedures by which it achieves its purpose. The above definition of a system, by inference, includes such mechanics. For example, the distribution system is defined to include not only its functions, but also the associated written methods and procedures for processing shipping orders.

Because systems are its major elements, a business may be considered to be a "system of systems." This concept is illustrated in FIGURE 4-3, *The business: a system of systems,* which depicts the nine operational systems and a central complex of management and administration systems. By extension of this concept, most systems may be considered to be composed of subsystems with the same transformation characteristics as systems. For example, as is shown in the first part of FIGURE 4-4, *Systems and subsystems,* a production system may be composed of subsystems such as engineering, production planning, manufacturing, and quality control. In practice, the distinction between systems and subsystems is fluid. It depends on the size, field of enterprise, objectives, and goals of the particular business. Thus, the other example in Figure 4-4 shows the billing, collecting, and disbursing systems of Figure 4-3 assembled as subsystems of an accounting system.

The dependence of the detailed characteristics of systems and subsystems on the unique goals and objectives of a business reveals an essential characteristic of most business systems. This is the fact that systems and subsystems are not

Figure 4-4. Systems and subsystems

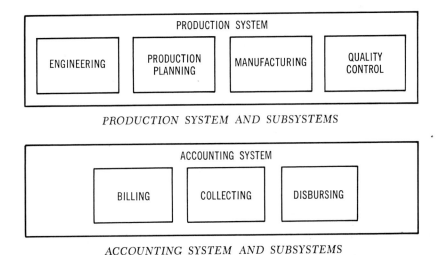

PRODUCTION SYSTEM AND SUBSYSTEMS

ACCOUNTING SYSTEM AND SUBSYSTEMS

readily transferred from one industry to another. Even systems used by one business within an industry seldom can be used by another business within the same industry. An analogy might be made, in one case, to transplanting the heart of a monkey into a human and, in the other, to transplanting a heart from one person into another person. Even in the latter case, the failure rate is high because in physiological detail the "systems" of host and donor are not the same. Thus, for example, it is highly unlikely that the production control system used by one automobile manufacturer could be used by another automobile company without "rejection" by the other systems in the "host" company. "Rejection" would be manifested by the inability to interface (i.e., exchange data elements between) the new system and the remaining old systems effectively.

The inability to pick up and use someone else's system has been one of the most costly lessons learned in the short history of modern computer-based business systems. It is the reason why many predesigned and "packaged" systems have not been successful. Careful analysis is required to determine whether or not it is more cost-effective to try to insert a "canned" system into a dynamic enterprise than to create one to meet the specific needs of the business. Such a decision can only be made after a thorough study of a particular problem, including an evaluation of alternative solutions. And, as is presented in Unit Three of this text, The Study Phase, this type of study is the essence of the methodological, phase-wise approach to the design of effective business systems. Otherwise, costly mistakes may be made by trying to make problems conform to preconceived solutions.

The functional business systems shown in Figure 4-3 require supervision and control in order to function as integrated elements of a business. The management and administration systems, also depicted in Figure 4-3, are the means for directing and controlling these activities. To effect direction and control, it is necessary to define responsibility and authority within a business organization and to disseminate this information. A flowchart used to convey such information is called an organization chart. To function effectively in a modern business, the systems analyst must understand the use and significance of organization charts.

THE BUSINESS ORGANIZATION CHART

Organization chart responsibility and use

The owners of a business decide on the organizational management and structure that best meet their goals and objectives. The owners, or their legal representatives, the board of directors, hire managers and other employees. Each employee, from the president on down, occupies a position that must be defined with respect to those of all other members of the organization. This definition is necessary to control activities and channel the flow of information within the business organization.

The *organization chart* is a flowchart that identifies the organizational elements of a business and displays areas of responsibility and lines of authority. It is the responsibility of top management to define and to update the organization chart. However, a continuing effort is required to prepare organization charts and to modify them as organizational plans are altered to cope with changes in the business environment. Hence, the responsibility for the preparation and maintenance of organization charts usually is delegated to the systems staff. This is an important systems activity because it stimulates management to keep its organizational plan up to date.

Management has many uses for current organization charts. These include (1) to review functions performed by major elements of the company; (2) to align the corporate structure with business opportunities; and (3) to compare salaries, authority, and organizational size at equivalent and subordinate levels.

As useful as they may be to management, organization charts are essential to the systems analyst. In all aspects of his work, the systems analyst deals with individuals who have a specific position in the organization. Therefore, the analyst must understand the organization chart—not only what is printed on it, but also the personalities who are behind it. Without an understanding of the latter, the analyst may be unaware of real but unwritten authority.

Organization chart structure

The structure of the typical modern business organization chart has evolved from concepts of authority and responsibility handed down from the governments of Greece and Rome and from the feudal period of history. These concepts have been formalized in more recent times by church and military organizations as a series of superior-subordinate relationships, as illustrated in FIGURE 4-5, *Basic*

FIGURE 4-5. Basic superior-subordinate relationship

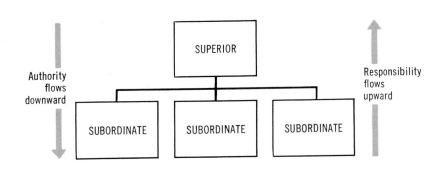

superior-subordinate relationship. The standard means for presenting an organization chart is a flowchart which uses lines to connect rectangles identifying individuals and functions. As is indicated in Figure 4-5, authority can be delegated downward, but responsibility must flow upward. When expanded, this type of organization chart displays vertical overlapping group linkages. FIGURE 4-6, *Overlapping organization chart,* is a segment of a typical organization chart for·a modern business enterprise. It clearly depicts the superior-subordinate relationship. It also displays the characteristic aspect of this type of organization— the expansion into successively subordinate levels, using the connecting elements as "link pins." Thus, to the extent that the organization is shown in Figure 4-6, the vice-president, Operations; the director, Research; and the manager, Chemical Research, are "link pins."

There is considerable recent evidence that an organization like the one in Figure 4-6 functions more effectively if its operating characteristics are participative rather than authoritarian.[1] For example, organizations in which departmental goals are established by group participation tend to have superior motivation and to outperform those in which goals are rigidly set by "orders from above." Also, in most organizations there are meaningful requirements for horizontal as well as vertical linkages. One area in which such a requirement is strikingly evident is systems analysis. Systems analysts work with information systems, and these systems often have needs which flow across organizational boundaries. Accordingly, the corporate systems organization, as shown in Figure 4-6, not only reports vertically to the director, Information Services, but also may link horizontally with operational elements, such as the Chemical Research department. Horizontal linkages permit the Systems department to cross organization chart boundaries to perform its functions. This need is particularly accentuated in the case of computer-based business systems because many of these generate outputs

1. Rensis Likert, *New Patterns of Management* (New York: McGraw-Hill Book Co., Inc., 1961).

FIGURE 4-6. Overlapping organization chart

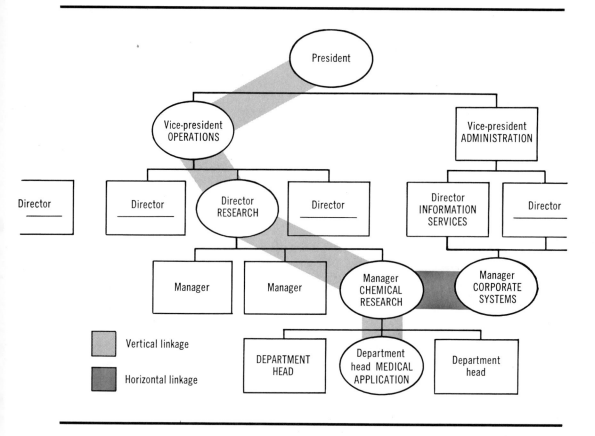

for the use of more than one organizational group and derive their inputs from many different groups.

Horizontal linkages imply a "staff" or "service" relationship rather than a "line" relationship, since no direct authority is indicated. A typical staff position is "assistant to" an executive. Some executives, for example, the President of the United States, have large staffs. A service organization provides assistance to other organizations and usually derives its authority from the nature of the service it performs. The Systems department is a service organization and has no direct authority over operational groups with which it interacts. However, it does derive authority indirectly from the specifics of its assignments, which are endorsed by a senior functional administrator, and from a "line of command" that, if necessary, leads to the president of the company.

Organization chartsmanship

There are no universal standards for the construction of organization charts. However, certain general principles apply. Above all, it is important, in consid-

FIGURE 4-7. Organization chart symmetry

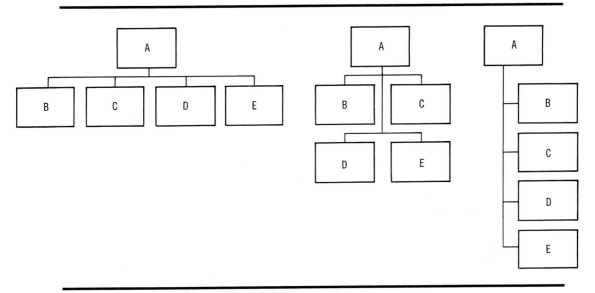

ering what to put on a chart and what to leave off, to realize that the organization chart is the picture of the company that is seen not only by its management and employees, but also by its general business environment. Therefore, this chart should properly reflect to important vendors, customers, and agencies the picture the company wishes them to see. With this in mind, some general guidelines for organization "chartsmanship" are suggested:

1. *Layout:* The layout of the chart should be attractive. The picture should be made up of rectangles and lines. It should be centered, with margins and white space selected to make the chart pleasing to the eye. The structure of the chart should be symmetrical. As FIGURE 4-7, *Organization chart symmetry,* illustrates, there is more than one way of displaying equivalent relationships. In the three sections of this figure, the same relationship is shown in different ways. In all cases B, C, D, and E are at the same level and report to A. A general guideline is to make balanced use of the space available.

2. *Title and approvals:* The organization chart should have a meaningful title. A standard position should be provided for approvals, date, and other identifying information.

3. *Scope:* One organization chart giving an overview of the organization's main elements is required. For example, for the business system shown in Figures 4-2 and 4-3, the overview organization chart would show the nine major operational elements and the principal administrative functions. This much detail should fit easily on an 8½ by 11-inch page, viewed from the 11-inch edge. This type of layout is common. The amount of information presented on an organization chart should not exceed that which can be shown conveniently placed on a

FIGURE 4-8. Information systems organization chart

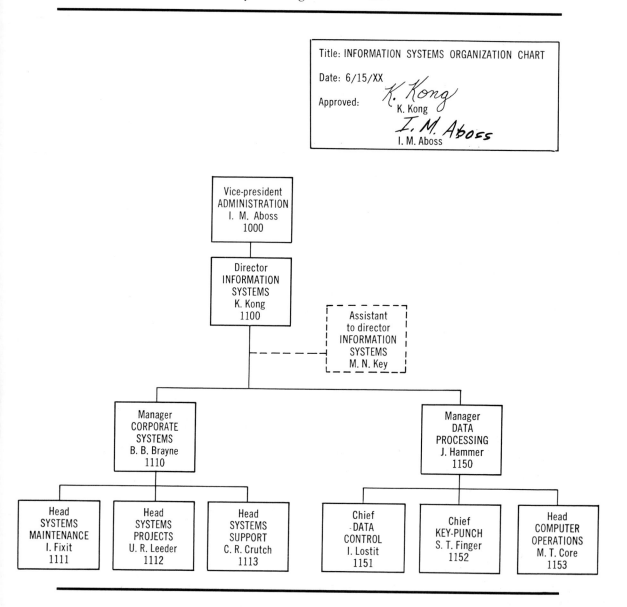

Title: INFORMATION SYSTEMS ORGANIZATION CHART

Date: 6/15/XX

Approved: *K. Kong*
K. Kong

I. M. Aboss
I. M. Aboss

Vice-president
ADMINISTRATION
I. M. Aboss
1000

Director
INFORMATION
SYSTEMS
K. Kong
1100

Assistant
to director
INFORMATION
SYSTEMS
M. N. Key

Manager
CORPORATE
SYSTEMS
B. B. Brayne
1110

Manager
DATA
PROCESSING
J. Hammer
1150

Head
SYSTEMS
MAINTENANCE
I. Fixit
1111

Head
SYSTEMS
PROJECTS
U. R. Leeder
1112

Head
SYSTEMS
SUPPORT
C. R. Crutch
1113

Chief
DATA
CONTROL
I. Lostit
1151

Chief
KEY-PUNCH
S. T. Finger
1152

Head
COMPUTER
OPERATIONS
M. T. Core
1153

standard page. The overview picture of the entire organization is like a long-range photograph. Some closer-range pictures are required also.

A medium-range picture should be prepared for each of the organizational elements shown on the overview organization chart. FIGURE 4-8, *Information systems organization chart,* is an example of a medium-range organizational picture.

Some close-up pictures also may be required for lower level organizational elements. For example, organization charts often are prepared in detail by managers responsible for particular projects or activities. Such charts are necessary for assigning and monitoring tasks. However, the systems group should exercise restraint with respect to the number of organization charts they prepare, because these charts must be maintained. In a dynamic company, this maintenance can be both costly and time consuming.

Restraint should be exercised also in deciding on the amount of detail to be presented on an organization chart. For example, Figure 4-8 shows only significant individual staff positions, such as the assistant to the person occupying the key position on the organization chart. An acceptable convention is to indicate a staff position by means of a dotted line.

4. *Organization chart distribution:* The overview organization chart should be distributed to top management and to all operating officers of the business. It should be available to customers and to employees who express an interest in the general organization of the company. Normally, new employees are provided with a copy of the top view organization chart as part of their indoctrination. Other organization charts should be distributed to the individuals who have the responsibilities shown on the chart, to their superiors, and to any other persons, such as systems analysts, who have a legitimate need for the information. Of course, a file should be maintained of all current and past organization charts. These should be available to the president and to other authorized persons upon request.

5. *Information provided:* The organizational rectangle on the chart should contain a title with functional significance (e.g., Vice-President, Engineering), the name of the individual in that position, and an identifying organization number. Figure 4-8 shows a typical format.

Other kinds of information, such as salaries and number of individuals supervised, can be added to charts for the use of managers who wish to review their organizational plan. This type of information usually is confidential and is not for general distribution. The organization chart identifies the major functions of the organizations shown. Additional details are supplied by supporting documents known as organization function lists.

The organization function list

An *organization function list* is a document that is prepared for each organization shown on an organization chart, to describe the specific major activities performed by that organization. It is keyed to the organization chart by use of the organizational titles and numbers shown on the organization chart. FIGURE 4-9, *Organization function list*, is a function list for the Systems Support department of the information systems organization shown in Figure 4-8. Note that the functions are described briefly in the present tense using action verbs (*controls, performs, etc.*).

The systems analyst who understands the organization chart and its associated function list is better equipped to improve the efficiency of business sys-

Figure 4-9. Organization function list

```
ORGANIZATION FUNCTION LIST
SYSTEMS SUPPORT DEPARTMENT
DEPARTMENT NUMBER:  1113
DATE:  6/15/XX
APPROVED:
              C. R. CRUTCH

              B. B. BRAYNE
```

1. Designs and Controls Forms

2. Manages and Retains Records

3. Performs Work Measurement Studies

4. Prepares and Maintains Organization Charts

5. Analyzes Reports

6. Writes Policies and Procedures

tems for which he is responsible. He can use the organization chart as a means of increasing his knowledge of both product and information flow.

THE INFORMATION STRUCTURE OF A BUSINESS

Product flow and information flow

The organization chart is only a one-dimensional picture of a business. Behind it there is a constant flow of information-oriented and product-oriented activities. All these activities involve individuals with differing levels of responsibility and authority. In order to examine the information structure of a business, let us start by distinguishing between information flow and product flow.

Product flow, which is relatively easy to visualize, is the flow of raw materials into subassemblies, then into assemblies, and finally into finished goods. *Information flow* consists of the creation and movement of the administrative and operational documentation necessary for product flow. Information flow is more difficult to visualize than product flow because its physical manifestation is a vast paper network. Yet it is this network that the analyst must understand. Although his actions must be governed by the physical reality of the goods which his company is producing, the systems analyst deals primarily with the creation and management of paper. Therefore, it is necessary that he know the information flow in those segments of the business for which he has assigned responsibilities.

To bring information flow into sharper focus, we can redraw Figure 4-2, which depicts functional business systems, to emphasize the distinction between product flow and information flow. This is done in FIGURE 4-10, *Product flow vs. information flow*. In this figure, the heavy flow lines trace the product flow path. The lighter lines indicate the paths by which information flows among the nine major functional business systems.

If we identify the principal documents associated with these information flow paths, the relative complexity of information flow can be depicted. This complexity is illustrated in FIGURE 4-11, *Principal information flow documents*. The documents shown in Figure 4-11 can be defined, in context, as follows:

1. The **purchase order** is prepared by Purchasing, which sends the original to the vendor, retains a copy, and sends a copy to Receiving.

FIGURE 4-10. Product flow vs. information flow

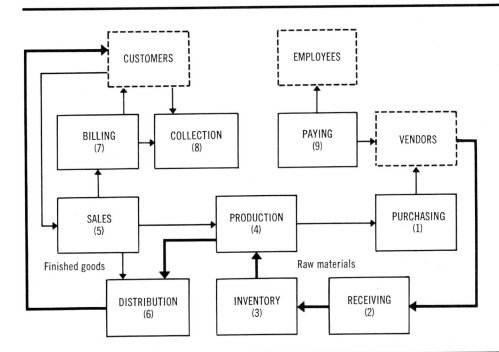

Figure 4-11. Principal information flow documents

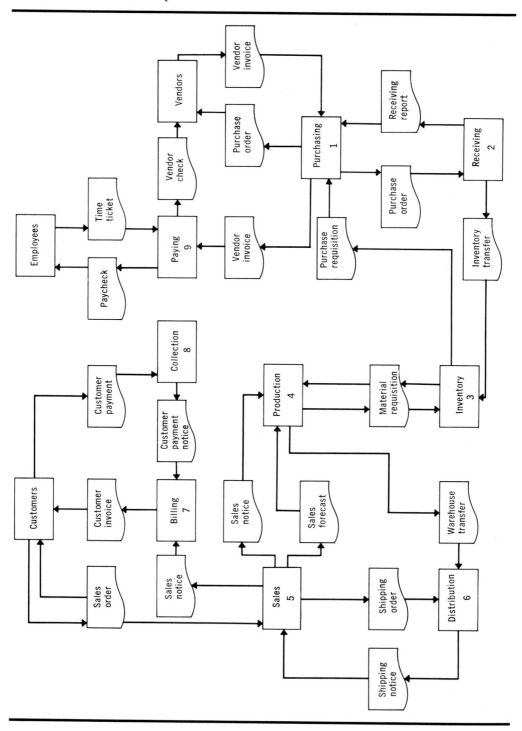

2. When the materials ordered arrive, Receiving verifies the order against its copy of the **purchase order,** inspects the material, and informs the Purchasing department of its arrival and acceptance by means of a **receiving report.** The material is transferred to Inventory accompanied by an **inventory transfer.**

3. By means of a **purchase requisition,** Inventory requests Purchasing to order those materials that are not on hand in sufficient quantity.

4. Production designs and develops the product. The components that are built in-house are combined with the components or subassemblies that are procured out-of-house. Production uses a **material requisition** to request needed materials from Inventory. Inventory notifies Production of the availability of the requisitioned materials by returning a copy of the **material requisition.**

5. Sales contacts the customer, sells the product, and prepares the **sales order.** The customer is provided a copy of the **sales order.** A copy of the **sales order,** entitled **sales notice,** is sent to Billing and to Production. An additional copy, the **shipping order,** is sent to Distribution.

6. Distribution receives the finished goods from Production accompanied by a **warehouse transfer notice.** Distribution ships the product to the customer and informs Sales by means of a **shipping notice.**

7. Billing prepares and mails the **customer invoice.**

8. Collection receives **customer payments** from the customer and sends updated information to Billing by means of a **customer payment notice.**

9. Paying makes payments to vendors by means of a **vendor check.** This check is prepared after the vendor has submitted a **vendor invoice** and after that invoice has been verified and forwarded by Purchasing. Paying also distributes **paychecks** to employees. The amounts of the **paychecks** are based upon **time tickets** submitted by employees.

As complicated as the information network shown in Figure 4-11 may appear, it is a necessary oversimplification of the real volume of paper flow in a typical corporation. Every major functional system is composed of complex subsystems, each of which has its documentation needs. Two other factors add to the complexity of the information network: (1) There are external as well as internal generators of information. (2) Information must be reported with different emphasis and formats according to the needs of different levels of management. Each of these factors requires discussion.

Information generators
A company must develop information systems to meet not only its internal reporting needs, but also the external reporting needs that arise from its general business environment. FIGURE 4-12, *Information generators,* distinguishes between these two information needs. The internal information needs are represented by the nine functional business systems discussed previously. Externally generated needs are represented by agencies such as federal, state, and local governments, shareholders, vendors, advertising, lenders, unions, and customers.

Not all the information generated externally is useful to the corporation. That which is useful is most likely to be of use to the upper levels of management.

FIGURE 4-12. Information generators

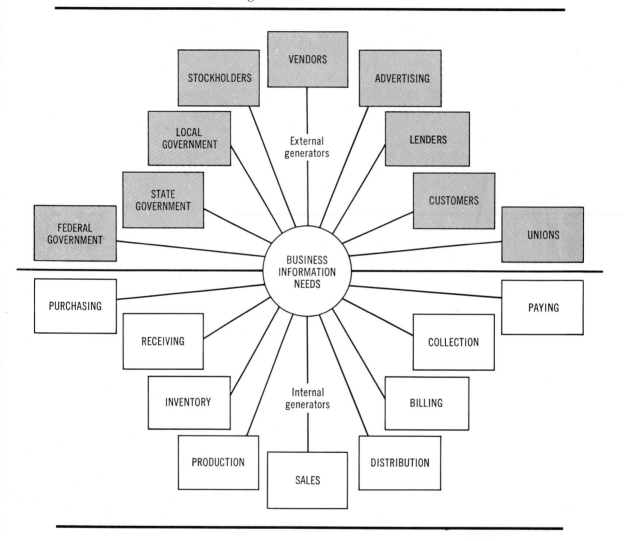

Also, in its "raw" form not all the internally generated information is useful at all levels within the corporation. Different types of reports must be prepared to meet the information needs of each level of user. Because of these differing user needs, we must identify levels of information systems.

Information system levels

FIGURE 4-13, *Information system levels,* depicts the four levels of information systems which exist in a typical business of moderate to large size. These are (1) operational; (2) lower management; (3) middle management; and (4) top management.

At the operational level, routine production or clerical operations are performed. Operational systems provide little feedback directly to the employee. For example, the materials clerk receives a material requisition, fills the requisition, and files a report of his action. A supervisor evaluates his performance. However, records of transactions occurring at the operational level constitute data that, when collected, organized, and processed, becomes the basis for higher level management actions.

Lower management performs supervisory functions that are short term relative to the higher levels of management. They deal with day-to-day job scheduling, checking the results of operations, and taking the necessary corrective actions.

Middle management functions are tactical in nature. This level is responsible for allocating and controlling the resources necessary to accomplish objectives that support the strategic goals of the business. Planning is performed; authority is delegated to the supervisory level; and performance is measured.

Top management functions are strategic. They include establishment of the goals of the business, long-range planning, new market and product development, mergers and acquisitions, and major policy decisions. Appropriate authority is delegated to middle management.

Figure 4-13 also shows that there are both horizontal and vertical information system structures. In this figure, for illustrative purposes, the nine func-

FIGURE 4-13. Information system levels

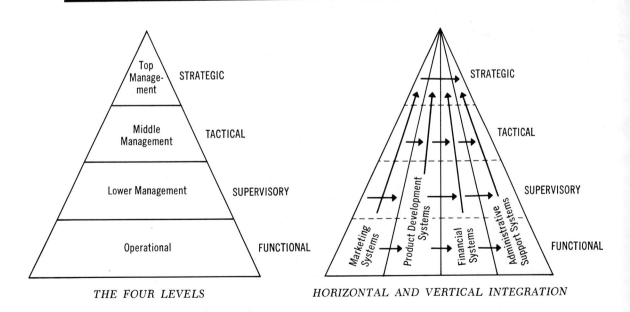

THE FOUR LEVELS   HORIZONTAL AND VERTICAL INTEGRATION

tional systems are collected, vertically, as major systems. Marketing systems include Sales and Distribution; product development systems include Purchasing, Receiving, Inventory, and Production. Financial systems include Billing, Collection, and Paying. Support operations, such as personnel and contracts, are grouped as administrative support systems.

Horizontal integration may occur within or between major systems. An example of horizontal integration, internal to a major system, is the combination of Purchasing, Receiving, and Inventory (within product development) into a procurement system on the basis of a shared data base. An example of horizontal integration, between major systems (in this case between finance and administrative support), is a personnel-payroll system based on employee-related data elements common to both Personnel and Payroll.

The following is an example of a possible vertical integration of an information system within Production.

1. Machine assignment and job time reporting—*functional.*
2. Machine scheduling—*supervisory.*
3. Make (in own shop) or buy (from vendor) decision—*middle management.*
4. New product decision—*top management.*

All management level positions require that decisions be made. These decisions range from the routine to the complex. However, all management decisions involve two elements:

1. A process that includes objectives, measurement of performance against objectives, and corrective action.
2. The availability of appropriate information on which to base decisions.

The first of these elements establishes management as a feedback and control process. The second leads to distinctions between the characteristics of information required at each management level. Feedback and control and management level information characteristics are described in the next sections.

Feedback and control

Feedback and control are essential to the design of any management system. *Feedback* is the process of comparing an actual output with a desired output for the purpose of improving the performance of a system. *Control* is the actions taken to bring the difference between an actual output and a desired output within an acceptable range. These concepts are illustrated in Figure 4-14, *Feedback and control.* Part A depicts a system in which there is no feedback and control. This system does transform an input into an output; however, because it lacks feedback, it is called an open loop system.

From part A of Figure 4-14, it is evident that the output depends solely on the characteristics of the input and of the system. If the output is not satisfactory, there is no provision for modifying either the input or the system. Operating such a system is analogous to driving a car while blindfolded. If, however, the driver compares the position of the car with the location of the white line in the middle of the road, corrective action is possible. In this case, the feedback is visual, and the corrective action is initiated by manually turning the steering

Figure 4-14. Feedback and control

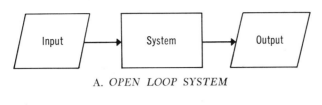

A. *OPEN LOOP SYSTEM*

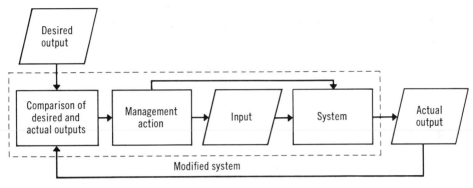

B. *CLOSED LOOP SYSTEM*

wheel. Because there is feedback, this type of a system is called a closed loop system. The elements of a closed loop system are shown in part B of Figure 4-14. This flowchart demonstrates that the comparison of desired and actual outputs results in management action which may modify the inputs, the system, or both. The result is a modified system that will produce altered outputs. Many operational systems are open loop systems. All true management systems are closed loop systems.

Because management information systems are feedback systems, they are more complex to design than are open loop operational systems. Feedback systems are effective only if they can respond quickly enough for the necessary corrective action to take place when needed. Otherwise, the time lapse may be so great that belated management action only makes the situation worse. Such systems are said to be unstable. Instability may also result if information is fed back at such a rate that it cannot be absorbed or if management action is premature.

Management information system characteristics

The term *management information system* is frequently encountered in business systems literature. Usually capitalized, a *Management Information System* (also called an *MIS*) can now be defined as an information system that displays these two characteristics: (1) at least one level of vertical integration; and (2) feedback and control.

FIGURE 4-15. **Management decision levels: information use and requirements**

MANAGEMENT LEVEL	INFORMATION USE	INFORMATION REQUIREMENTS

TOP MANAGEMENT	1. GOAL SETTING
	2. LONG-RANGE PLANS
	3. STRATEGY
	4. RETURN ON INVESTMENT
		1. EXTERNAL INFORMATION, e.g.
		   Competitor actions
		   Government actions
		   New markets
		   Resource availability
		2. INTERNAL INFORMATION, e.g.
		   Financial reports
		   Key exception reports
		3. LONG-TERM TRENDS
		4. "WHAT IF" INFORMATION

MIDDLE
MANAGEMENT
	1. OBJECTIVES DEFINITION
	2. MEDIUM-RANGE PLANS
	3. TACTICS
		1. INTERNAL INFORMATION, e.g.
		   Financial reports
		   Exception reports
		2. SHORT-TERM TRENDS
		3. SOME "WHAT IF" INFORMATION

LOWER
MANAGEMENT
	1. OBJECTIVES ATTAINMENT
	2. SHORT-RANGE PLANS
	3. SUPERVISION
		1. INTERNAL INFORMATION, e.g.
		   Recent historical information
		   Detailed operational reports
		   Appropriate exception reports

Of course, at each management level, the specific requirements for information, and hence for the design of the feedback system, vary significantly. The different uses and requirements for information at each management decision level are summarized in FIGURE 4-15, *Management decision levels: information use and requirements*. Note that all management systems rely upon exception reporting. The lower level exception reports are closely related to day-to-day operations. Some other significant observations are:

1. The higher the decision level, the greater the reliance on externally generated information and the less the reliance on internally generated information.

2. The higher the decision level, the greater the emphasis upon planning and the use of longer term trend information.

3. The higher the decision level, the greater the necessity to ask "what if" questions as part of the decision process.

Thus, at the higher decision levels in a company, information needs and uses are future-oriented and depend significantly upon external sources of information. This type of information is difficult to quantify and must be coupled with the experience and judgment of the decision maker. It is not surprising to find that such information systems are at the forefront of the art of information system design. The systems analyst, particularly when working with computer-based business systems, must know what is and what is not practical to attempt. Therefore, it is appropriate to describe briefly the "state of the art" in business information system design.

THE STATE OF THE ART IN BUSINESS INFORMATION SYSTEM DESIGN

Information systems at the operational level can provide immediate payback, usually measurable in dollars. The continuing development of such systems is a meaningful activity not only because they pay off in dollars, but also because they provide the necessary foundation on which to base higher level systems. Although the payoffs for higher level systems may be less tangible than dollars, there is increasing management acceptance of such other benefits. Intangible payoffs include (1) improved internal control; (2) better management awareness of problems and opportunities; (3) long-term profitability; and (4) faster response to changes in the business environment.

In seeking to devise solutions that both satisfy information needs and improve the efficiency of the business, the systems analyst must use appropriate tools and techniques. Basic tools and techniques, such as forms design, codes, flowcharts, and the use of tables and graphs are presented in Unit Two of this book. Some advanced techniques that are representative of the state of the art in computer-based information system design are discussed briefly here.

Data management

The successful application of computers in business depends on their ability to store, access, and manipulate large amounts of data. A problem commonly encountered is the need for the same data in many different applications programs. Without an effective method of data management, duplicate data would have to be stored in more than one file or be vulnerable to modification by different applications programmers. Efforts to avoid redundant files began in the Growing Era, were modified in the Refining Era, and are reaching maturity in the Maturing Era. FIGURE 4-16, *Progress in data management,* shows the successful return to an objective that was not possible with the hardware and software technologies of the earlier eras. As background to describing the state of the art in data management, we will examine briefly the stages in the cycle shown in the figure.

During the Growing Era of the 1960s and before the complexities of information system design were well understood, attempts were made to meet a corporation's information needs by trying to develop a total data base that could serve all its information needs. Unfortunately, the software needed to manage massive data bases and create "total information systems" was beyond the technology of that era. Each programmer had to know the location and structure of the data needed by each application. Maintaining the integrity of the data base was extremely difficult because many people had access to it and could modify it, affecting others' programs as well as their own. In addition, because of the magnitude of the effort devoted to redefining duplicate fields of data, programming projects were large, complex, and costly. Successes in creating a total information system were partial at best, and failures far outnumbered them.

A less ambitious approach to the management of data, using smaller, integrated data bases, was introduced and used with considerable success in the

FIGURE 4-16. Progress in data management

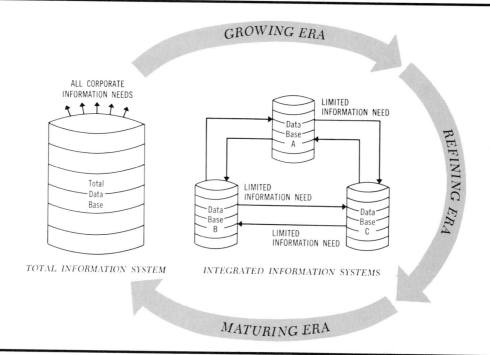

Refining Era of the 1970s. In contrast with the total information system approach of the Growing Era, the integrated data base technique is to use multiple linked data bases, each designed to meet a limited corporate information need. The personnel-payroll system mentioned in Chapter 1 as an example of an integrated system, is typical of the use of a common data base for more than one purpose. Integrated data bases can be linked together by allowing applications programs to supply data to or access it from more than one data base. The design of integrated data bases reduced the severity of the problem of redundant storage. However, programmers still had to expend much time and effort in locating, accessing, and structuring the data needed by applications that were continuing to grow in variety and scope.

Throughout the latter half of the Refining Era, that is, most of the 1970s, efforts continued to develop software programs to manage large data bases and to relieve the programmer of the need to do more than specify how the data needed by a particular application was to be structured. These systems, called *data base management systems* (DBMS's), organize and maintain data in a non-redundant structure that can be accessed for processing by more than one application. Data base management systems free the programmer from concern about the location and structure of data. Also, through special query languages, they provide a means for a nonprogrammer to generate needed reports. DBMS's are particularly effective as elements of management information systems because they provide access to large amounts of data that can be structured to meet individual managers' information reporting needs. We will consider data base management systems in greater detail in Chapter 19: File Design.

Structured design and development techniques

The life-cycle methodology stresses a top-down approach to the design of complex systems. As Study Phase and Design Phase techniques have evolved, they have tended to follow this methodology. The Development Phase activities of preparing computer software, however, traditionally have been a bottom-up procedure. The lowest level modules were completed first, tested, and then combined into higher level modules. Problems were often encountered in integrating these modules, either delaying the project or forcing high-level design changes that necessitated much rework. Top-down procedures, called *structured design and development techniques*, have been introduced to reduce such problems. Among the more significant of these techniques are Hierarchy plus Input Process Output (HIPO) charts, structured programming, and pseudocode.

HIPO charts resemble organization charts of the type presented in this chapter. They are a graphic Design Phase tool and are used to describe the functions to be performed by a system by proceeding from the general to the detailed level. *Structured programming* and *pseudocode* are compatible Development Phase techniques. Structured programming is a method for modularizing the logic of computer programs; pseudocode is a computer language independent method of describing unambiguously the logic to be performed by each program module. We will examine these techniques in more detail in later chapters.

Management science techniques

Management science techniques for the design of business systems are being applied with increasing frequency to the development of systems to meet the information needs of higher level decision makers. These techniques include simulation, linear programming, and critical path methods.

1. *Simulation:* It is expensive to create actual systems and to modify them by trial and error. Fortunately, there are techniques, usually involving a computer, for developing mathematical models of systems and for simulating their performance under a series of "what if" conditions. An adequate coverage of simulation techniques is beyond the scope of this text. However, their existence and continuing development are indicative of the potential for the systems analysis profession. The reader who is interested in large scale simulation may wish to read books or articles by Jay W. Forrester, professor of management at the Massachusetts Institute of Technology.[2] Professor Forrester has applied his knowledge of feedback and control systems to the simulation of industrial systems, of social systems, and of the dynamics of the world. His work has been widely quoted.

---

2. Jay Forrester, *Industrial Dynamics* (New York: John Wiley & Sons, Inc., 1961).

2. *Linear programming:* Another advanced technique, which often makes use of the power of the computer, is linear programming. Linear programming involves the use of a mathematical model in order to find the best combination of available resources to achieve a desired result. An example of this technique is the optimum routing of freight-carrying vehicles. The cost savings implicit in the use of this technique are obvious.

3. *Critical path methods:* These techniques make possible the determination of the most effective scheduling of time and resources when a complex product, such as a bridge, rocket, or computer system, is being developed. For complicated systems, a computer program is used. One such technique, PERT (Program Evaluation and Review Technique), is described in Chapter 22: Preparation for Implementation.

Life-cycle management

The life-cycle management process, previously described in Chapter 2, is a scientific method for the definition, design, development, and operation of effective computer-based business systems. Its methodology provides for the application of other tools and techniques as required throughout the life cycle of a business system. FIGURE 4-17, *The life cycle of a computer-based business system,*

FIGURE 4-17. **The life cycle of a computer-based business system**

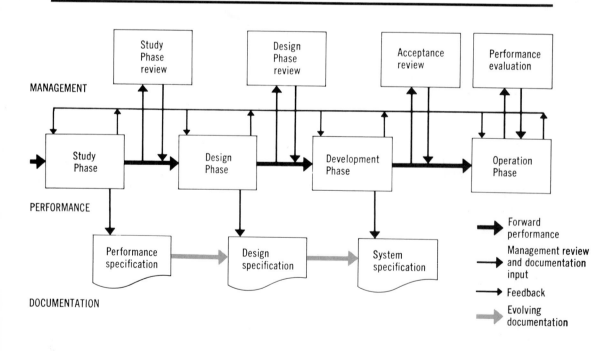

is the same as Figure 2-2. It is presented again in order to emphasize the information system concept aspects of life-cycle management.

First, the computer-based business system generally involves both horizontal and vertical integration at more than one level. Second, each phase is a systems process. Inputs are transformed into outputs, which, in turn, become the inputs for the next phase. Finally, feedback and control are evident throughout. Management reviews, obstacles internal to each phase, and externally caused changes in one or more baseline specifications are examples of events that may trigger feedback and corrective action.

Thus, the systems analyst is called upon to exercise many of the strategic, tactical, and operational management skills discussed in this chapter.

We have deliberately concluded the unit by returning to the central theme of this book: the life-cycle management process. In the next unit, we will describe some of the basic tools and techniques which the analyst uses throughout the entire life-cycle process. The remaining units describe, in time sequence, each of the four phases of the life cycle of computer-based business systems.

KEY TERMS

business	*information flow*
goal	*information generator*
objective	*feedback and control*
organization chart	*management information system* (MIS)
organization function list	*data base management system* (DBMS)
product flow	*structured design and development*

FOR DISCUSSION

1. Define a "business" and a "system." What are their similarities? Their differences?

2. Distinguish between goals and objectives. Name some businesses and identify typical goals and objectives.

3. Describe the generalized system environment concept. What are typical constraints and resources?

4. What is the principal function of an organization chart? Whose responsibility is the organization chart? Identify some management uses for organization charts.

5. Relate flow of authority and of responsibility to the superior-subordinate relationship.

6. Distinguish between authoritative and participative organizations.

7. Describe some guidelines for organization chart preparation. What is an organization function list? How does it relate to the organization chart?

8. Distinguish between product flow and information flow in a business.

9. Distinguish between internal and external information generators. What are some examples of each?

10. What are the differences between open loop and closed loop systems? Distinguish between feedback and control. How do they relate to the concept of exception reporting?

11. What are the identifying characteristics of a Management Information System (MIS)?

12. How does a data base management system compare with a Growing Era total data base system? With an integrated information system?

13. What is meant by "top-down structured design and development"?

14. What is meant by the term "management science techniques"? Identify and describe some management science techniques.

UNIT TWO

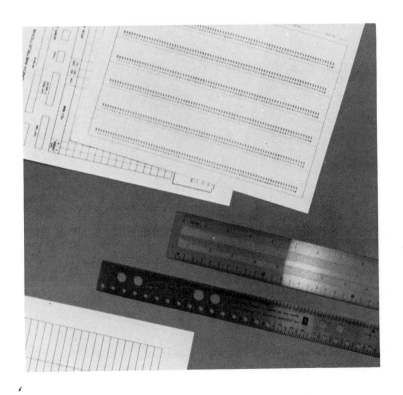

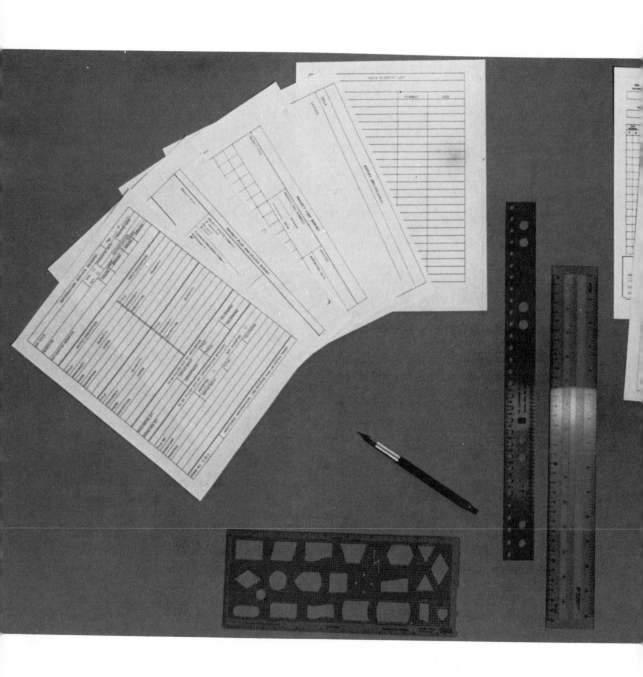

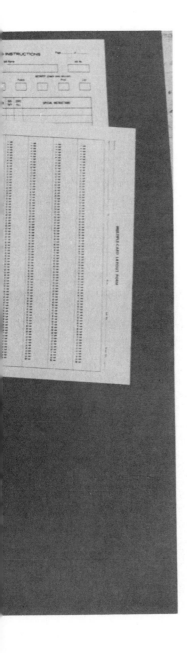

TOOLS AND
TECHNIQUES
OF SYSTEMS
ANALYSIS

5   Coding

In the previous chapter, we distinguished between
product flow and information flow, noting that
information flow takes place through the movement of
a large number of documents, which generally contain
many items of data. The goal of this chapter is to
show how a large number of data items can be uniquely
identified through the use of codes. You will learn how
businesses plan and use codes as brief, meaningful identifications of data items, replacing longer descriptions
that might be more awkward to store and to manipulate.

DEFINITION OF A CODE

When large volumes of data are being handled, it is important that the items be
identified, sorted, or selected easily and quickly. To accomplish this, each data
item must have a unique identification and must be related to other items of data
of the same type. Codes can provide brief identifications of data items and
replace longer descriptions that would be more awkward to store and to manipulate. We can define a *code* as a group of characters used to identify an item of
data and to show its relationship to other items of a similar nature.

For example, most businesses identify credit customers by numbers or letter-
number combinations, a code that is more concise than the customer's name.
It also is more precise because large businesses may have more than one customer with the same name. Also, a customer code may provide more information than just identification. It may contain a digit or letter that indicates such
information as geographic area, store through which credit was obtained, and
credit limits. Thus, the code can communicate data about the credit customer and
about his relationship to other credit customers.

Other examples of codes are all around us in our daily lives. The postal
service uses ZIP codes to identify delivery areas. We order merchandise through
catalog sales orders using inventory codes. We find library books by using their
call numbers, a form of code. Social Security numbers, form numbers, and bank
account numbers—all are examples of codes.

CODING CONSIDERATIONS

The need for a code

A knowledge of codes and coding techniques is essential to the systems analyst. He is called upon frequently to analyze or to create documents that contain codes. He needs to be able to interpret codes, to evaluate coding schemes, and to devise new or improved codes. He must be trained to evaluate the need for a code and to set up a plan if a code is required.

Some codes come to us from external sources. ZIP codes are required by the postal service for bulk mailings and are requested for all mail. Federal and state governments require us to use Social Security numbers as an identification code for employees in reporting taxes withheld, earnings, etc. The requirement for codes on external reports does not necessarily mean that we must use these codes for internal purposes. Many internal items and data elements that we deal with do not require a code to identify them efficiently, while other internal items can be handled more efficiently if they are coded.

To determine whether a code is needed, the systems analyst must find answers to questions related to the items to be coded. Typical questions include these:

1. Who uses the items or data that is to be coded?
2. How often will the coded items be retrieved or used?
3. What are the coded items used for?
4. How much data should the code contain about the coded items?
5. How many items are to be coded?
6. How will the codes be used?
7. How will expansion of the number of coded items be accommodated?
8. What system characteristics must be accommodated by the code?

After he obtains the answers to these questions, the analyst can decide upon the usefulness of a code in a particular system. If the specific benefits of using a code can be identified, he can proceed to establish a plan for the code.

The code plan

The code plan is based on the determination of what information about a specific item the code ought to include. Only information that makes possible efficient identification and retrieval of coded items should be included. For example, if an analyst were required to prepare a code for a business form, such as an organization chart, he would develop his code plan by selecting the characteristics of the form and its environment that are appropriate to the identification and retrieval of that form. Typical characteristics might include form identification, responsible department identification, revision number, and date of issue.

Characteristics that seem similar may be coded quite differently for unrelated items. For example, consider a tire code and a dress code. The code plan for each would specify an identification of size. In the case of a tire, size is expressed in terms of the ratio between the tire height and width, and of rim size. The size of a dress would, of course, be expressed quite differently.

After he has prepared a code plan identifying the particular characteristics of the item that must be contained in the code, the analyst selects an appropriate coding method. The method which he selects must meet these requirements:

1. *Expandable:* The code must provide space for additional entries that may be required.

2. *Precise:* The code must identify the specific item.

3. *Concise:* The code must be brief and yet adequately describe the item.

4. *Convenient:* The code must be easy to encode and decode.

5. *Meaningful:* The code must be useful to the people dealing with it. If possible, it should indicate some of the characteristics of the item.

6. *Operable:* The code should be compatible with present and anticipated methods of data processing—manual or machine.

To select the coding method that best meets these criteria, the analyst must be familiar with the common types of codes and must know how they are used separately or in combination.

COMMON TYPES OF CODES

There are five common types of codes: sequence codes, group classification codes, significant digit codes, alphabetic codes, and self-checking codes. In practice, combinations of these codes often are found.

Sequence codes

Simple Sequence Code. A sequence code has no relation to the characteristics of an item. Therefore, a directory—a list of items to which sequence numbers are assigned—is required. The assignment of consecutive numbers, e.g., 1, 2, 3, . . . , to a list of items as they occur is called a simple sequence code. FIGURE 5-1, *Simple sequence code,* is an example in which employees' names are listed alphabetically and then assigned an employee number in sequence as they appear on the list. The alphabetic order of the items is for the purpose of aiding in the decoding process. However, if a new item were added, it would be assigned the next sequential number. Thus, if "Allen, James" joined the company, he would be assigned the next available number, and the effectiveness of the alphabetic sequence would be diminished.

The advantage of the simple sequence is its ability to code an unlimited number of items with the least number of code digits. Its principal disadvantage is the limited amount of information it can convey. However, the simple sequence code often is used as a component of more complex codes.

Block Sequence Code. This code is a modification of the sequence code that makes possible a more homogeneous collection of related items. In a block sequence code, a series of consecutive numbers is divided into blocks, each one reserved for identifying a group of items with a common characteristic.

As in the simple sequence code, a list is prepared of items to be coded. The difference is that, in assigning the codes, "blocks" of sequence numbers are set

FIGURE 5-1.
Simple sequence code

Code	Employee name
1	ADDINGTON, HORACE R.
2	ANDERSON, BERTHA A.
3	CONRAD, ROBERT L.
4	CRANE, JAMES M.
5	CUSTER, GEORGE G.
6	DAWSON, PETER R.
7	DUNCAN, HENRY A.
8	ECKEL, GARY T.
*	* * * *
*	* * * *
*	* * * *

FIGURE 5-2.
Block sequence codes

Code	Employee name	Code	Data item
1	ADDINGTON, HORACE R.	1	CHAIR, WOOD—TABLE
2	ANDERSON, BERTHA A.	2	CHAIR, WOOD—FOLDING
20	CONRAD, ROBERT L.	3	CHAIR, WOOD—ROCKING
21	CRANE, JAMES M.		
22	CUSTER, GEORGE G.	10	CHAIR, PLASTIC—TABLE
30	DAWSON, PETER R.	11	CHAIR, PLASTIC—FOLDING
31	DUNCAN, HENRY A.	12	CHAIR, PLASTIC—ROCKING
40	ECKEL, GARY T.		
*	* * * *	20	CHAIR, CHROME—TABLE
*	* * * *	21	CHAIR, CHROME—FOLDING
*	* * * *	22	CHAIR, CHROME—ROCKING

aside for items with some common characteristics. As an example, the simple sequence codes assigned to employees in Figure 5-1 could be changed to a block sequence code in which the common characteristic of the items in a block is the first letter of the employee's last name. As shown in the first part of FIGURE 5-2, *Block sequence codes*, a "block" of numbers (1–9) is assigned to the A's, another block of numbers (10–19) assigned to the B's, and so on. With this block code, we can add new employees and assign them a code from their alphabetic block. Although we cannot maintain the original alphabetic sequence, we can keep the employees grouped by the first letter of their last name.

A common use of the block sequence code is shown in the second part of Figure 5-2. In this example of a furniture inventory, blocks of code numbers are assigned by basic characteristics—in this case, the material used in the furniture's construction. Note that, in this example, we could have used the type of chair as the major characteristic just as easily as the construction material. Table chairs could have been assigned numbers 1–10; folding chairs, numbers 11–19; rocking chairs, numbers 20–29; and so on. The characteristics the analyst should select are those that are most meaningful to the users of the code.

Like the simple sequence code, the block sequence code often appears as part of more complex codes.

Group classification code

Another common code type, the *group classification code*, designates major, intermediate, and minor data classifications by successively lower orders of digits. This code type is useful when the item or information to be coded can be broken down into subclassifications or subdivisions. The ZIP code is a familiar example

FIGURE 5-3. Group classification code

STORE DEPARTMENT SALESPERSON

XX   XX   XXXX

12070468   Store number 12 = Long Beach
Department 07 = Hardware
Salesperson 0468 = Linda East

26140301   Store number 26 = Santa Ana
Department 14 = Patio furnishing
Salesperson 0301 = Phil Harding

of a group classification code. For example, the ZIP code 91791 relates to major, intermediate, and minor classifications as follows:

9	17	91
Section of country	Region within section	Subdivisions of region

The code provides for 10 sections, 100 regions within each section, and 100 subdivisions within each region. Each element of the codes is a sequence code. Code directories are available for the interpretation of each sequence code.

In another example, shown in FIGURE 5-3, *Group classification code,* the primary objective is to identify uniquely a salesperson within a large department store chain. In addition to the identification of the individual, we want to be able to determine the store and the department where he works. The highest level of classification is the store, and so the store number becomes the "major" classification. The second subdivision is the department within the identified store; the department number becomes an "intermediate" classification. The number of the employee within an identified department is the "minor" classification. We form the group classification code by combining the numbers of the major, intermediate, and minor classifications. In this example of a code, each salesperson has a unique identification number. Furthermore, we have coded additional valuable data about the work station of the employee.

Note that the store, department, and salesperson numbers are probably simple sequence or block sequence codes. The code is called a group classification code, however, because the dominant part of the code plan is the use of major, intermediate, and minor classifications.

Significant digit code

A third common code is the significant digit code, a numeric code in which the numbers describe a measurable physical characteristic of the item. The characteristic may be weight, size, length, capacity, time, or any other physically measurable attribute that is part of the code plan. FIGURE 5-4, *Significant digit code,* gives as an example the code plan for tire size. It has three elements: the

FIGURE 5-4. Significant digit code

		TIRE SIZE DESIGNATION	
X XX - XX			E = 7.35 inches
└ Rim size (inches)			F = 7.75 inches
└ Ratio of tire height to its width			G = 8.25 inches
└ Tire profile (load carrying capacity)			H = 8.55 inches
			J = 8.85 inches
G78-15	G	Profile 8.25 inches	L = 9.15 inches
	78	Ratio: tire is 78% as high as it is wide	
	15	Rim 15 inches	

tire profile, the ratio of the tire height to its width, and its rim size. This code describes two of the elements as significant digits. These are "ratio of tire height to width" and "rim size." The tire profile is indicated by a letter rather than the actual numerical measurement. A dictionary is required to interpret the profile. As in this example, it is not unusual to see a mix of code types. However, in this case, the tire code is predominantly a significant digit code.

Significant digit codes and group classification codes are often confused with one another. Remember: In a significant digit code, the digits are a measurement of a physical characteristic.

Alphabetic codes

A fourth common type of code is the alphabetic code, which describes items by the use of letter and number combinations. There are two categories of alphabetic code: mnemonic codes and alphabetic derivation codes.

Mnemonic Codes. These are letter and number combinations obtained from descriptions of the coded item. A mnemonic, or memory aid, is a reminder of the name or description of an item. Often it is a severe abbreviation of the item's name. FIGURE 5-5, *Mnemonic codes,* shows two examples of mnemonic merchandise codes. With a little experience, most people using the code can decode it without reference to a dictionary.

FIGURE 5-5. Mnemonic codes

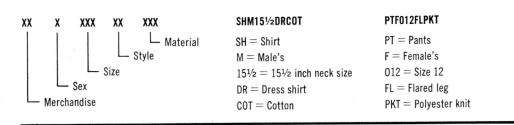

		SHM15½DRCOT	PTF012FLPKT
XX X XXX XX XXX		SH = Shirt	PT = Pants
└ Material		M = Male's	F = Female's
└ Style		15½ = 15½ inch neck size	012 = Size 12
└ Size		DR = Dress shirt	FL = Flared leg
└ Sex		COT = Cotton	PKT = Polyester knit
└ Merchandise			

FIGURE 5-6. Alphabetic derivation code

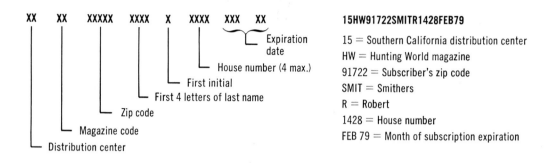

Mailing labels can be printed in ZIP code sequence within the distribution center for ease of handling for shipment.

Many computer language codes used by programmers are symbolic codes. As an example, consider the following assembler language instructions:

Mnemonic	Instruction
L	Load
A	Add
S	Subtract
ST	Store
DC	Define Constant

Alphabetic Derivation Codes. These codes are characters taken from the name or description of the coded item according to a set of rules. Alphabetic derivation codes are used to handle large volume lists that must be maintained and processed in sequence. These codes are used because it is not practical to encode and decode full descriptions or numeric codes. FIGURE 5-6, *Alphabetic derivation code,* is an example of a magazine subscriber's code. The code not only uniquely identifies the subscriber, but also provides information about the distribution center, the ZIP code, the magazine's name, and the expiration date of the subscription. Mailing labels can be printed in ZIP code sequence within the distribution center for ease of handling for shipment. Renewal notices can be sent within selected time periods based on the subscription's expiration date. The magazine name may identify special interests of the subscriber to which direct mail advertisers can appeal.

There are other forms of alphabetic derivation codes. These are based on relatively elaborate sets of rules for the use of consonants and phonetic characteristics of the item to be coded. An excellent reference for additional information about the codes which we have discussed and about more elaborate codes is provided in an IBM manual on coding methods.[1]

1. *Data Processing Techniques: Coding Methods,* Form F20-8093 (White Plains: IBM Technical Publications Department).

Self-checking codes

The fifth code type, which we will discuss briefly, is the self-checking code. It uses a check digit to check the validity of the code. This type of code is an important means of controlling the validity of data that is being processed. For this reason, it is important that an analyst have a knowledge of self-checking codes. These codes require the performance of a simple repetitive arithmetic operation. In computer-based systems, the checking operation can be performed rapidly on large volumes of data.

Figure 5-7, *Self-checking code,* is an example of how such a code can be developed and used. The method for developing the check digit is to double every other digit of the numeric portion, add up the digits, and use the units position of the resulting total as the check digit. If an error has occurred in recording or processing the coded item, the check digit will not "check." As a specific example, Figure 5-7 shows a code of 12463 with a check digit of 4. The complete code for the item is 12463-4. If the common error of transposition occurred and the second and third digits were reversed, the code would appear as 14263-4. To check the validity of the code, the computer program would double the second digit (4) and the fourth digit (6), add up the digits $(1+8+2+12+3=26)$, and compare the units position of the total (6) to the check digit of the code (4). Since they don't match, the program would reject the code as invalid. This method works well for most errors due to transposition.

More sophisticated self-checking codes, often statistical in nature, have been developed for checking the validity of large volumes of data. Often this data has to be transmitted over long distances and interpreted and evaluated by complex processing programs.

The reader should be aware that there is an entire field of mathematics, known as information theory, which deals with information and its validity. However, with respect to codes, our purpose has been only to introduce the analyst to the basic codes and to their uses in implementing effective code plans.

Figure 5-7. Self-checking code

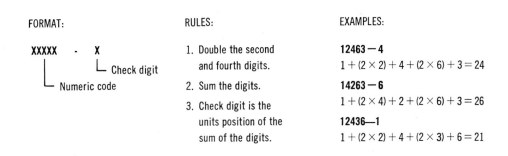

FORMAT:	RULES:	EXAMPLES:
XXXXX - X └ Check digit └ Numeric code	1. Double the second and fourth digits. 2. Sum the digits. 3. Check digit is the units position of the sum of the digits.	**12463 — 4** $1 + (2 \times 2) + 4 + (2 \times 6) + 3 = 24$ **14263 — 6** $1 + (2 \times 4) + 2 + (2 \times 6) + 3 = 26$ **12436—1** $1 + (2 \times 2) + 4 + (2 \times 3) + 6 = 21$

KEY TERMS

code	*simple sequence code*	*alphabetic codes*
code plan	*block sequence code*	*mnemonic code*
sequence codes	*group classification code*	*alphabetic derivation code*
	significant digit code	*self-checking code*

FOR DISCUSSION

1. Why are codes required in business?

2. What kinds of questions must an analyst consider in order to determine if a code is needed?

3. What is a code plan? Present an example of a code plan.

4. Identify the five common types of codes.

5. Distinguish between simple sequence and block sequence codes.

6. What is the essential characteristic of significant digit codes? Present an example.

7. What are the two types of alphabetic codes discussed in this text? Present an example of each.

8. Why should an analyst be familiar with self-checking codes?

9. Why are alphabetic derivation codes used for large volume mailings?

6   Forms Design

The collection of raw data and the distribution of processed information are two of the major costs of a system. Since most of the data that enters and leaves a system are recorded on forms (source documents and reports), careful forms design can greatly affect a system's cost effectiveness. The goal of this chapter is to introduce the principles of developing effective forms. You will learn the basic parts of a form, styles and types of forms, and principles of forms design. You will also be introduced to methods of forms control.

FORMS DESIGN RESPONSIBILITY

The task of drawing a detailed layout for a form is the responsibility of a forms specialist. Forms specialists are experts in types and styles of forms, sizes and styles of print, and details of preparing a form layout for reproduction. These specialists are available to the systems analyst from in-house reproduction centers or from the major forms manufacturers.

The only things the forms specialist does not know are (1) what data the user wants to collect with the form, and (2) how the form is going to be used in the system. The coordination of the forms design effort between the user and the forms specialist is the responsibility of the systems analyst. It is the analyst who must verify that proof copy of the form is exactly as required by the user and the system. The forms manufacturers can provide a wide variety of sample forms for ideas, but the analyst must select and check the final form.

To be able to evaluate a form intelligently, the analyst must be familiar with the function of each of its parts.

BASIC PARTS OF A FORM

Most forms have these five basic parts: title, instructions, heading, body, and conclusion.

FIGURE 6-1. A typical form

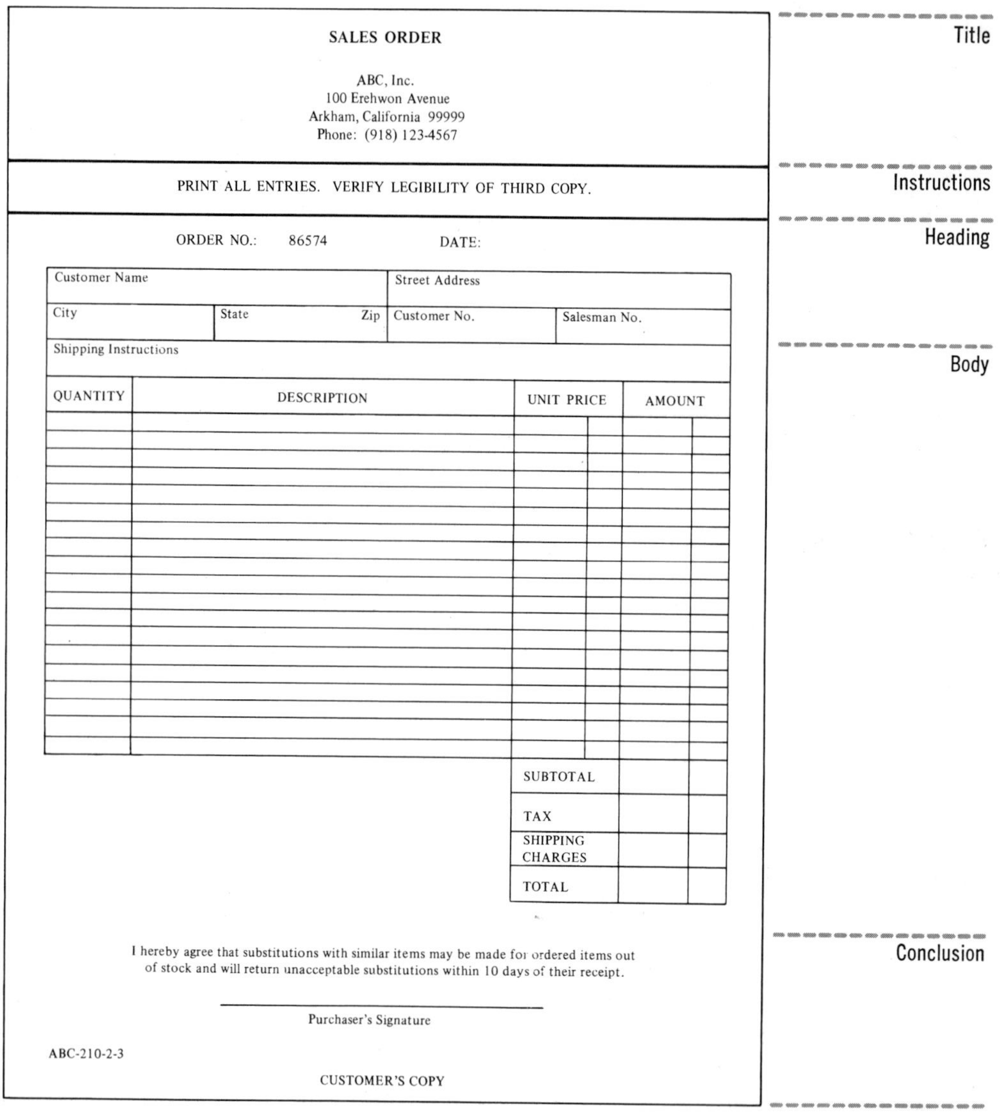

SALES ORDER	Title
ABC, Inc. 100 Erehwon Avenue Arkham, California 99999 Phone: (918) 123-4567	
PRINT ALL ENTRIES. VERIFY LEGIBILITY OF THIRD COPY.	Instructions
ORDER NO.: 86574 DATE:	Heading

The *title* identifies the form. It should be as descriptive and as brief as possible. Examples are "Purchase Order," "Memo," and "Sales Order." The title usually is centered at the top of the form.

Instructions tell how to complete or use the form. To be most useful, general instructions should be at the beginning of the form. Instructions should be placed so that they are seen before the form is completed. Forms that have multiple sections or parts may have a new set of instructions at the beginning of each section. Some forms are so commonly used and the instructions are so obvious to any user that general instructions are omitted. Instead, lines or boxes are labeled. Common examples are bank checks and receipts.

The *heading* contains all the general identification data. For example, it might include the date, form sequence number, name, and address. The heading data usually is not the information the form was designed to collect, but that which is necessary for record identification purposes. All data used for reference filing is contained in the heading. The heading often is separated from the remainder of the form by ruled lines or by a box drawn around it.

The specific data the form was designed to collect is called the *body* of the form. An example is a sales invoice which shows quantities, item descriptions, unit prices, and total prices. The body of the form should read from left to right and from top to bottom. This helps both those who must complete the form and those who must extract data from it. Since the body of many forms is numeric, it is common to see the body set up in columnar form. The appropriate use of columns groups similar data and is an aid in filling out the form.

The last part of a form is the *conclusion*. The conclusion contains the approvals, signatures, and summary data. It appears at the bottom of the form.

The basic parts described above are found on most forms, but exceptions are common. Forms design is a combination of skill and art, but do not allow considerations of art or "pretty forms" to override the principles of good forms design.

Figure 6-1, *A typical form*, illustrates the five basic parts of a form.

STYLES AND TYPES OF FORMS

Styles of forms

Two basic styles are used in the design of forms: the open style and the boxed style. The open style is the simplest. It consists of headings and open areas in which data can be entered. The boxed style allocates space to each data item. Each box is clearly identified by name or by a brief description.

Forms are seldom pure "open" or pure "boxed." They are usually described as predominantly open, predominantly boxed, or as a combination of boxed and open. Figures 6-2 through 6-5 illustrate four different styles of forms.

Figure 6-2, *Information service request*, is an example of a predominantly "boxed" form. The only open areas are the spaces for the description and remarks entries.

Figure 6-3, *Data element list*, is predominantly "open." The columns headed Description, Format, and Size divide the form into sections. However, the form is primarily designed for the unrestricted entry of an unspecified number of items.

Figure 6-4, *Flowchart worksheet*, is another example of an almost pure "open" form. The "boxes" on the form serve a function similar to that of ruled lines on a piece of notebook paper. In this case, the characters are flowchart symbols and

FIGURE 6-2. Information Service Request

INFORMATION SERVICE REQUEST				Page ___ of ___

JOB TITLE:

NEW ☐
REV. ☐

REQUESTED DATE: **REQUIRED DATE:**

AUTHORIZATION

OBJECTIVE:

	LABOR		OTHER	
	HOURS	AMOUNT	HOURS	AMOUNT

ANTICIPATED BENEFITS:

OUTPUT DESCRIPTION	INPUT DESCRIPTION
TITLE:	TITLE:
FREQUENCY: QUANTITY:	FREQUENCY:
PAGES: COPIES:	QUANTITY:
DESCRIPTION:	DESCRIPTION:
TITLE:	TITLE:
FREQUENCY: QUANTITY:	FREQUENCY:
PAGES: COPIES:	QUANTITY:
DESCRIPTION:	DESCRIPTION:

TO BE FILLED OUT BY REQUESTOR

REQUESTED BY:	DEPARTMENT:	TITLE:	TELEPHONE:
APPROVED BY:	DEPARTMENT:	TITLE:	TELEPHONE:

TO BE FILLED OUT BY INFORMATION SERVICES

FILE NO:	ACCEPTED ☐ NOT ACCEPTED ☐		
SIGNATURE:	DEPARTMENT:	TITLE:	TELEPHONE:

REMARKS:

FORM NO: C–6–1	ADDITIONAL INFORMATION: USE REVERSE SIDE OR EXTRA PAGES

FIGURE 6-3. Data element list

DATA ELEMENT LIST		
TITLE:		
DESCRIPTION	FORMAT	SIZE

Figure 6-4. Flowchart worksheet

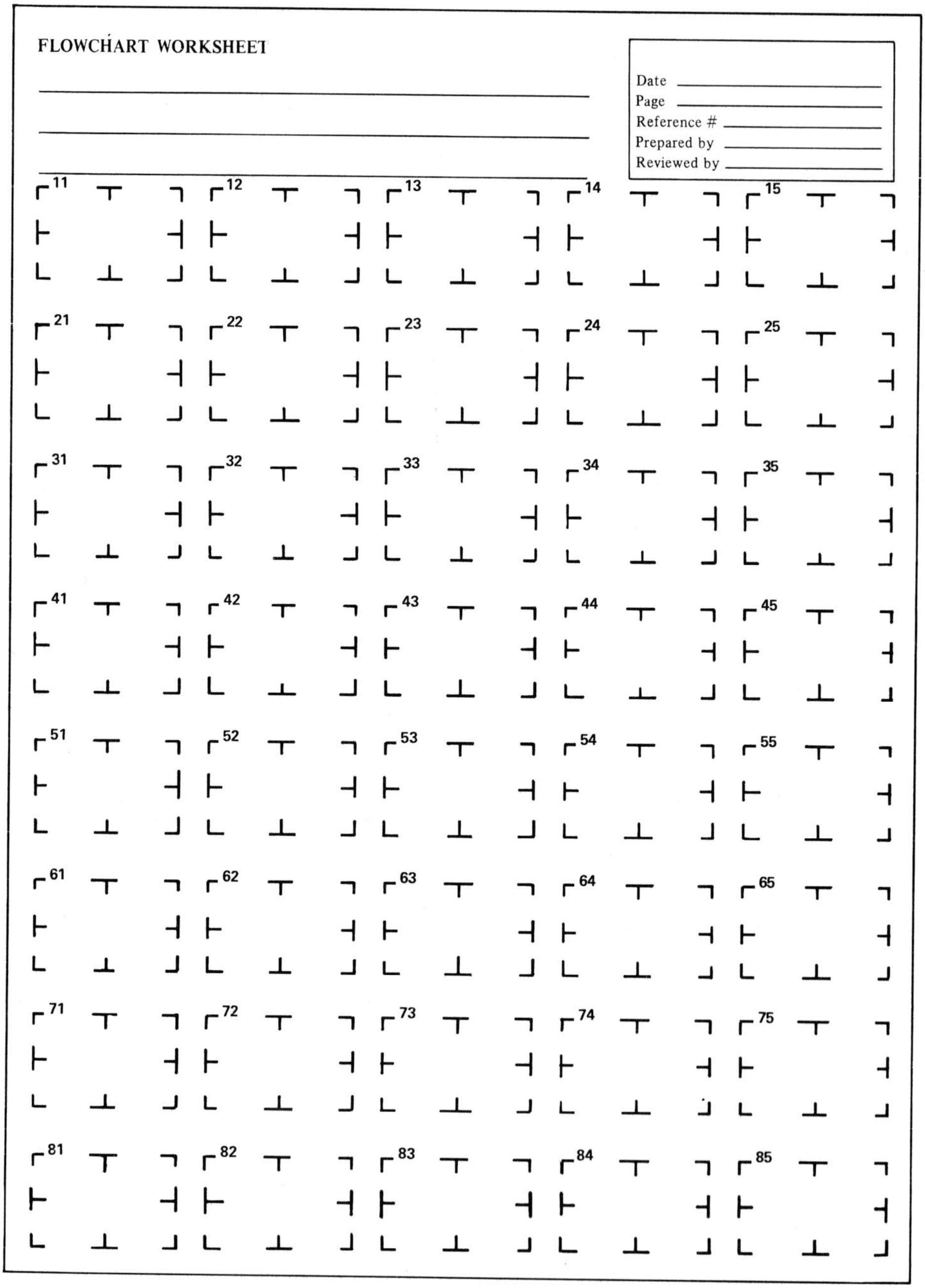

FIGURE 6-5. Report specification

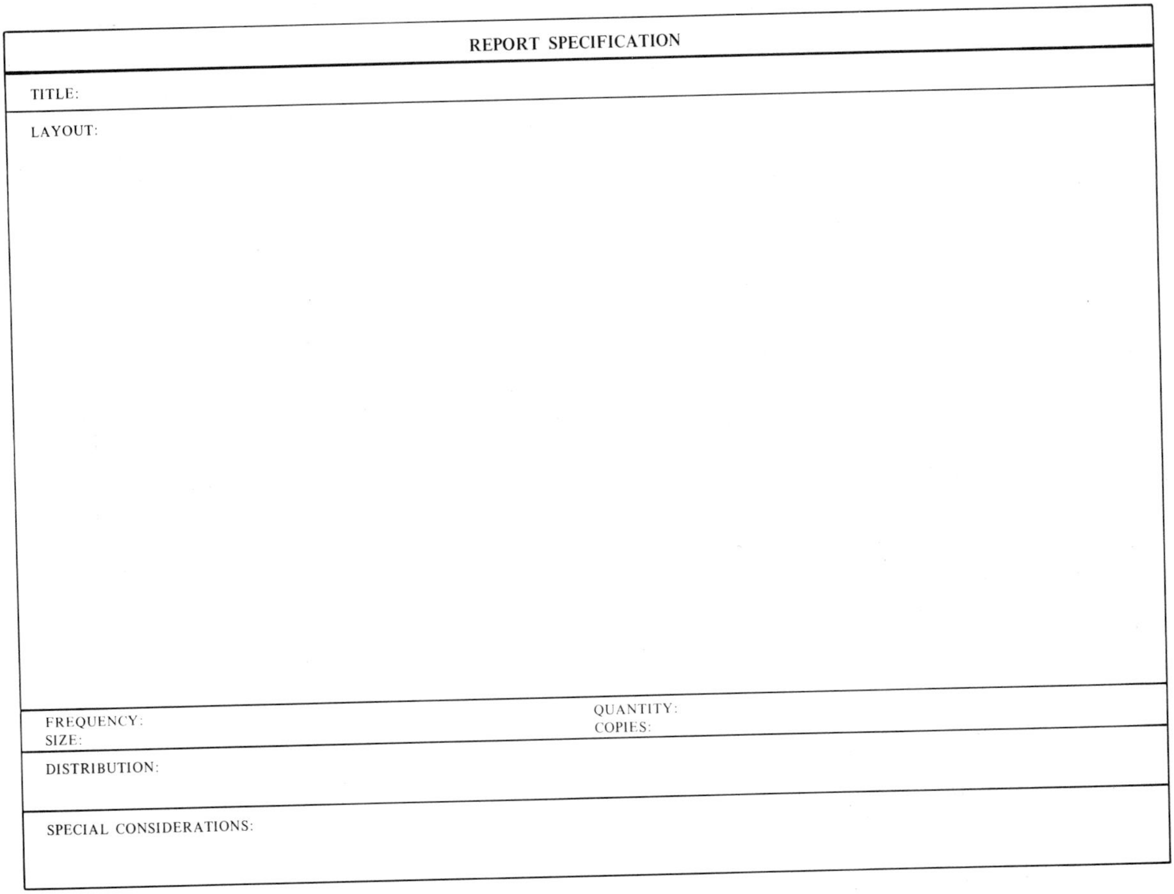

REPORT SPECIFICATION
TITLE:
LAYOUT:
FREQUENCY: QUANTITY:
SIZE: COPIES:
DISTRIBUTION:
SPECIAL CONSIDERATIONS:

not letters of the alphabet. The user of the form may place these symbols wherever he wishes.

FIGURE 6-5, *Report specification,* is an example of a combination boxed and open style. This form is divided into well-defined areas. However, the center area, labeled "layout," is completely open.

Types of forms

The type of form is determined by the complexity of its manufacture. The most common forms are printed single sheets of paper, called *cut forms.* Cut forms make up approximately 90 percent of all forms. Cut forms are usually designed by the user and printed in-house or by a local printer. Many ready-made stock forms carried by stationery dealers are also cut forms. Cut forms are often made into pads for convenience, and several copies may be made in one writing by the use of carbon paper.

Specialty forms are more complex. Examples are multiple copy forms, forms with special binding, and forms designed to be completed with the use of a machine. Specialty forms are complex enough in their construction to require special equipment for their manufacture or use. Most specialty forms are custom-designed by a forms manufacturer, usually a large printing firm that specializes in forms design and has equipment to produce specialty forms. Some specialty forms are designed to be used only with special equipment. Others are designed to be completed manually. Still others require both manual and machine operations. There are five principal types of specialty forms: (1) forms bound into books; (2) continuous forms—manual; (3) detachable stub set; (4) continuous forms—machine; and (5) mailers.

Examples of these five forms are shown in Figure 6-6, *Specialty forms.*

The simplest specialty forms are those that are *bound into books;* they are very similar to padded cut forms except for a stronger binding. They are designed to be completed manually. Examples are sales books and receipt books.

Continuous forms—manual are attached end-to-end in a long, continuous string. They are designed to be used with a counter-top machine. The machine is used only to feed and hold the forms, which are filled in by hand.

A type of specialty form that can be filled in by hand or by machine is the *detachable stub set,* which is an original and one or more carbon copies bound together. The set may either use carbonless paper or be bound complete with carbon paper. The binding may be on any of the four edges of the form, but is most often at the top edge. The bound portion of the set, or the stub, is perforated. Individual copies may be removed from the set, or the stub may be torn off to separate all the copies. These forms are very popular because of the ease and convenience of use. The form may be completed either manually or by machine. The individual using the form does not have to align the carbon paper and the multiple copies of the form. Also, because of the binding in each sheet, copies do not slip out of alignment as the form is written on or put into a machine. A very common example of the detachable stub set is the form used by credit card companies to record charge sales. Devices to record the information from a customer's Master Charge, Visa, etc., are found in many retail stores.

Continuous forms—machine are the forms used by computer printers. They may be single part (no carbons) or multiple part (with carbons) forms. Often forms to be completed by a computer will simply be blank continuous forms. In this case all titles, headings, etc., are printed as a function of the computer program. This process is almost as fast as using formated or printed forms. Using blank paper is much less expensive, and it eliminates the problem of keeping many different types of forms in inventory. Printed continuous forms also are designed for machine printing. The most common example is the paycheck. However, even printing the complete form by the computer does not eliminate the necessity for forms design. The output format must be designed, regardless

Figure 6-6. Specialty forms

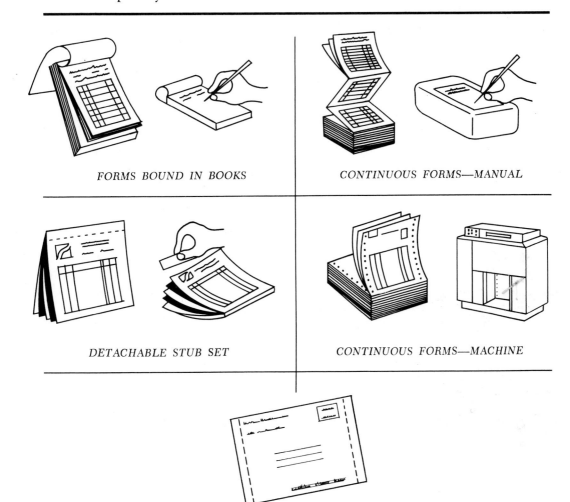

FORMS BOUND IN BOOKS   CONTINUOUS FORMS—MANUAL

DETACHABLE STUB SET   CONTINUOUS FORMS—MACHINE

THE MAILER

of how the form is printed. Computer output design and its special considerations are described in Chapter 18: Output Design.

The last general type is the *mailer*. It is a version of continuous forms designed to be filled in with a computer printer; however, its construction is different enough to classify it as a fifth type of specialty form. Mailers are blank forms sealed inside envelopes that are attached end-to-end as continuous forms and are covered by a "cover page." Selected areas of the cover page and the front of each envelope are backed by carbon paper. All the data to be printed, including the name and address, is printed on the cover page. Because of the positioning of carbon paper behind the cover page, only the mailing name and address print through on the envelope. Because of the carbon paper on the front inside of the envelope, the form inside the envelope also is printed. The cover page is usually retained as a file copy of the data being mailed; it may be printed with information that does not print on either the envelope or the form. Mailer forms are fairly expensive, but their use saves the cost of stuffing and sealing envelopes. Mailers are usually printed with postage permit information, so no postage needs to be added. The forms may be sent to the post office as soon as they are printed and separated.

PRINCIPLES OF FORMS DESIGN

Well-designed business forms can increase clerical efficiency, improve work flow, and lower system costs. To evaluate a form's effectiveness, the analyst should keep four principles in mind:
1. The form must be easy to fill out.
2. The completed form must be easy to use in the system.
3. The form should not collect data that will not be used in the system.
4. The form should not be unnecessarily expensive.

Ease of data recording
Business forms should be designed so that they can be filled out quickly and accurately.

It is important that the analyst avoid errors induced by the form's design. Design-induced errors can occur whenever the person completing the form is not sure what data is being requested. Whenever a form is used in more than one department or is used infrequently, it is usually wise to include appropriate instructions. The instructions should be placed on the form just before the section to which they apply. It should be noted, however, that including instructions where they are not required hinders clarity and adds to the expense of producing the form.

Data items should be grouped in a logical pattern. Grouping requires fewer instructions and results in fewer errors. Fewer errors will occur if all the logically related data is collected prior to changing the subject.

All data entry areas must be clearly labeled. Make sure that the user knows whether the label applies to the line above the label or the line below. If the form will be filled in using a typewriter, the data area label should appear above the data entry area so that the label is visible when the form is in the typewriter. Avoid uncommon abbreviations or uncommon words as labels. Although labels should be brief, they must be complete enough to communicate exactly what data is being requested.

Leave adequate space for the response. Common typewriter horizontal spacing is 10 or 12 characters per inch. Make sure that the data area is long enough to allow for reasonable responses. Remember, also, that handwritten entries require more space than typewritten responses. Vertical spacing also is important to forms design. Forms that are expected to be completed with handwritten responses should allow at least one-half inch of vertical spacing. Forms that may be completed using a typewriter should allow at least one-third of an inch and should be a multiple of one-sixth of an inch. (Most standard typewriters print six lines per vertical inch.) Avoid spacing that requires the typist to realign the typewriter for each line. The minimum of one-third inch would be equivalent to double spacing. If the form is always completed using a typewriter, leave out the horizontal lines to make alignment easier. Aligning the form can take as much of the user's time as actually entering the data.

Easy-to-use completed forms

Sequence the data on the form in the order in which it is to be used. This is especially true when the data is to be entered into a computer system through a key-stroking operation such as keypunching or data terminals.

The analyst should be aware of the effect of ink and paper color combinations on the legibility and readability of forms. Readability can be improved (or made worse) by the combination of ink color and background color. FIGURE 6-7, *Le Courier's legibility table*, ranks thirteen ink-background combinations in order of legibility. The common black on white combination ranks sixth, while black on yellow is at the top of the list. Colored paper can be used to distinguish the various copies of a form and to aid in form distribution. However, the use of colored paper should not be allowed to interfere with the legibility of the data. This is particularly problematic for copies at the bottom of a carbon stack.

FIGURE 6-7. Le Courier's legibility table

Order of Legibility	Color of Printing	Color of Background
1	BLACK	YELLOW
2	GREEN	WHITE
3	RED	WHITE
4	BLUE	WHITE
5	WHITE	BLUE
6	BLACK	WHITE
7	YELLOW	BLACK
8	WHITE	RED
9	WHITE	GREEN
10	WHITE	BLACK
11	RED	YELLOW
12	GREEN	RED
13	RED	GREEN

Many businesses input source data into computerized systems with optical scanners. If optical scanning of forms is to be used, the analyst must consider character size and vertical spacing requirements. It is the analyst's responsibility to verify that the form layout is compatible with the scanner hardware.

Collect required data

The analyst should verify that all the data items requested on a form are required and actually used in the system. Many times data is collected on a form simply because it was collected on previous versions of the form. Data items not actually required waste the time of the person completing the form and clutter the form for those who use the data. Wasting clerical time adds unnecessary expense to the system.

Avoid unnecessary costs

The costs of using a form are far greater than the costs of producing it. The area with the greatest potential for cost effectiveness is the efficiency of a form in use, rather than the cost of the form itself. Still, forms should not be unnecessarily expensive. If the company has in-house reproduction capability, there has to be a decision on whether to produce the form in-house or out-of-house. This decision must be based on the required quality and complexity of the form relative to in-house capability. For complex or high-quality forms, in-house production is not always the least expensive.

Design forms in a standard size, such as 8½″ x 11″ or 5½″ x 8½″. Printers buy their paper stock in standard sizes; if a form of an uncommon size is desired, it may be unnecessarily costly to produce because of the extra cutting or trimming of paper.

In general, *avoid forms larger than 8½″ x 11″*. Larger forms are often more expensive to store and require larger, more expensive, file storage.

Print forms in reasonable quantities. Bids for printing jobs include a basic set-up charge, which stays the same regardless of the quantity of forms produced. It is advantageous, therefore, to buy forms in as large a quantity as is reasonable considering the rate of use, the likelihood of modification, and the costs of storage. The larger the quantity, the lower the cost per form.

FORMS CONTROL

A form designed for efficient use is a major step toward controlling the cost of collecting data. However, an equally important consideration is the prevention of a flood of new and modified forms from each department of the company. Departments tend to act independently of other departments when it comes to forms. Departments rarely inquire of each other to find out if a form is already in existence. They just design a "new" one.

The solution to the problem is twofold: (1) Establish a central forms authority and (2) establish control files. The central authority should be an individual or a group with complete control over all company forms. The approval of the central authority must be obtained prior to the design or modification of any form. The advantage of this procedure is that this authority will have knowledge (and samples) of all forms currently in use or being designed. Since many forms may meet the needs of more than one department, the coordination of the design or modification of forms can be handled expediently by one authority. The use of one form rather than several similar forms can be a real cost saving in the production, storage, and distribution of forms.

Two control files are needed to keep track of the forms being used in the company: a numerical file and a functional file. The numerical file contains at least one sample of each form being used. The samples are filed by form number, creating a "catalog" of forms being used. Any form can be accessed by means of its coded form number. The functional file contains additional copies of each form. They are filed in order of subject, operation, or function. If a form has multiple uses or functions, it will be found more than once in the file. Whenever a new form is required, the functional file can be checked to determine whether a form already exists for that purpose. When the functional file is originally established, many forms usually can be eliminated or consolidated.

The two control files also aid in forms inventory control. Knowledge of which departments use any particular form and their approximate rate of use prevents the build-up of too large an inventory of forms and also is a timely reminder to reorder.

KEY TERMS

title	*body*	*boxed style*	*numerical file*
instructions	*conclusion*	*cut forms*	*functional file*
heading	*open style*	*specialty forms*	

FOR DISCUSSION

1. What are the forms design responsibilities of the user, the systems analyst, and the forms manufacturer?

2. What are the five basic parts of a form?

3. Describe the purposes of the title, heading, and body of a form.

4. What are the two basic styles of forms? Define each.

5. What are the two basic types of forms? Define each.

6. Name and discuss the four principles of forms design.

7. Discuss the "cost" of forms.

8. What are the advantages of formal forms control?

9. What two types of files are required for effective forms control? Why?

7   Charting Techniques

Charts are used by systems analysts to present complex data in a concise and meaningful manner. The goal of this chapter is to introduce the most commonly encountered charts and to explain how they are used. You will learn the best uses of bar charts, line charts, pie charts, step charts, and tables.

BASIC CHARTS

The complexity of modern business, coupled with the increasing use of computers, is producing a veritable avalanche of data that must be analyzed and simplified before it can be used. Charts are one effective means of compressing data into a concise, clear format. *Charts* are graphical or pictorial expressions of relationships or movement. This chapter introduces important basic charts as well as some specialized charts of particular significance in systems analysis. These include decision tables, charts for project management, and critical path networks. Another class of specialized chart, the flowchart, is so important that the next chapter is devoted to the discussion of this powerful pictorial tool.

Types of basic charts

Charts inform, compare, emphasize, and, in some cases, predict. Charts inform by relationships or changes in relationships. They compare by relating items of information to an index, or scale. They emphasize significant changes or patterns of movement by accenting them visually. To the degree that past performance is an indicator of future performance, charts can predict by displaying trends.

There are four types of basic charts: bar charts, line charts, pie charts, and step charts. Most of these charts can be used to display relationships and motion. However, some are more suitable than others for each type of display. Figure 7-1, *Best use of basic charts*, relates each basic chart to the display for which it is best suited. An alternate, less frequent use, is identified as "other use." Each of the four basic types of charts is described in the sections which follow.

FIGURE 7-1. Best use of basic charts

Display ＼ Type	Bar Chart	Line Chart	Pie Chart	Step Chart
RELATIONSHIP	✔	O	✔	O
MOVEMENT	O	✔		✔

✔ = Best use
O = Other use

Bar Charts. Bar charts depict relationships between elements better than any other type of chart. For this reason, and because they are easily understood in a variety of arrangements, bar charts often are used for management displays. When the bars are separated, the chart displays relationships. When they are spaced closely together, the chart creates an impression of a pattern of movement. FIGURE 7-2, *Bar charts*, depicts the appropriate use of bar charts to emphasize a relationship and to emphasize movement. The individual bars may be shaded to enhance the visual impact.

Line Charts. Line charts are the most common type of chart. Line charts often are called *graphs* because they usually are constructed by connecting a set of previously plotted points. Line charts communicate movement better than any other type of chart. They can display trends, curves, or any relationship where rate of change is important. Two or more lines may be used to compare trends. If more than one "line" is shown on a line chart, different types of lines (solid, broken, dotted, etc.), or colors may be used to provide contrast. However, care must be taken not to display too many lines. When more than three or four patterns of movement are indicated, the chart may confuse the viewer. FIGURE 7-3, *Line charts*, demonstrates both a good and a bad example of the use of line charts. Note that the first part of the figure not only compares the two lines, but

FIGURE 7-2. Bar charts

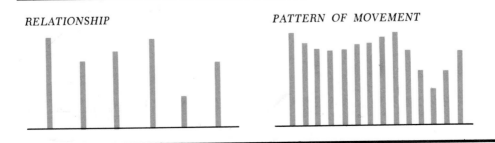

RELATIONSHIP　　　　　　　　　　PATTERN OF MOVEMENT

FIGURE 7-3. Line charts

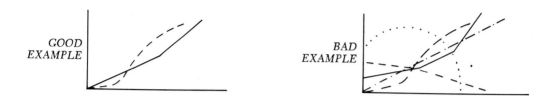

also lets the viewer extrapolate a change in relationship on the basis of the pattern of motion shown. The second part is too cluttered to be an effective graph.

Pie Charts. Pie charts are excellent charts for presenting relationships as percentages. In the first part ·of FIGURE 7-4, *Pie charts,* a single pie is divided up into slices of various sizes. Since the total number of degrees in a circle is 360°, each slice represents a percentage that is the ratio between the angle of its arc and 360°. Thus, slice A of this standard "pie" shown is 50 percent of the total, and slices B and C are each 25 percent of the total.

FIGURE 7-4. Pie charts

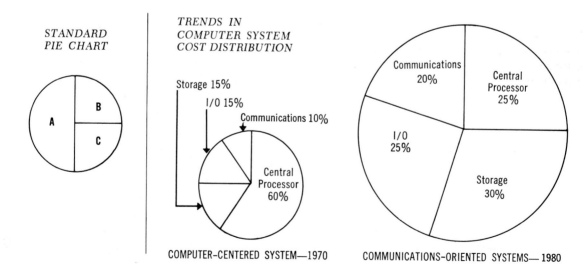

FIGURE 7-5. Step charts

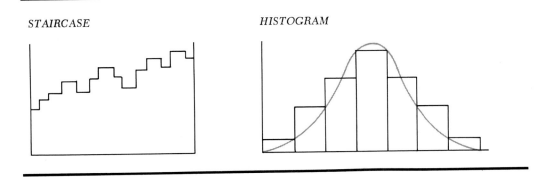

STAIRCASE   HISTOGRAM

Two pie charts also may be used to good effect for comparisons. Both charts should be the same size unless the total quantity that is sliced up has changed. For example, if the sources of funds for a fiscal year were presented on one pie chart, the applications of those funds could be presented on another pie chart of the same area. When the total quantity to be presented has changed in size, as might be the case at different points in time, the areas of the charts should be adjusted. When making this type of comparison, it is important to remember that the area increases as the square of the diameter. For example, if 10-year data for a "computer-centered system" and a "communications-oriented system" were presented as two pie charts, with the number of systems increasing by a factor of four in the interval, the representation would be as shown in the second part of FIGURE 7-4. Note that a 4:1 increase in surface area is obtained by doubling the diameter.

Step Charts. Step charts often can be used in the place of line charts to convey patterns of motion when relatively few points are plotted and when individual levels are to be emphasized. The first part of FIGURE 7-5, *Step charts*, is an example of a common type of step chart. This chart, sometimes called a "staircase chart," is an alternative to the line chart for showing movement. This chart does not convey a "flow" of movement to the same degree as does the line chart. However, it also possesses some of the characteristics of a bar chart. It can display even minor differences in relationships between small increments.

In many cases step charts can be used effectively in lieu of line charts. An interesting example, which brings together the step and line charts, is the histogram. The histogram is used by statisticians to plot the relative frequency of the occurrence of events over definite intervals. The step chart in the second part of Figure 7-5 is a typical histogram. The histogram can be used to develop a mathematical approximation to a continuous distribution. This is illustrated by the "equivalent" normal distribution curve which is superimposed on the pictured histogram.

FIGURE 7-6. Effect of scale selection

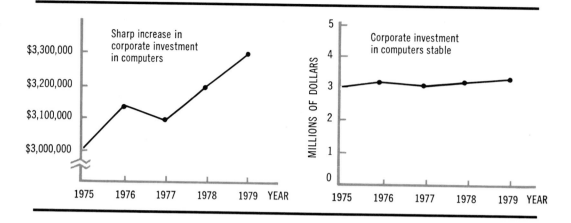

Development of effective charts

There are six basic rules for the development of effective charts.

1. Decide upon the message for the chart.

2. Decide upon the best type of chart (e.g., line, pie, bar, or step) to communicate the message.

3. Make an initial layout of the chart.

4. Analyze the layout to be sure that the chart stresses its message.

5. Modify the chart to eliminate unnecessary words and distracting detail.

6. Prepare the final chart.

This step-by-step procedure will result in the development of effective and useful charts.

An important thing to remember when preparing a chart is to "keep the chart honest." Charts can be misleading. For example, comparisons between quantities can be distorted by the improper selection of scales for the abscissa (horizontal axis) and the ordinate (vertical axis). FIGURE 7-6, *Effect of scale selection,* illustrates how the choice of scale can alter the emphasis of a graph. Both graphs present the same data about corporate computing costs. Each reveals a 10 percent increase in computing costs from 1975 to 1979. The first graph accents the increase in cost; the second graph deemphasizes it. Whether or not the increase is alarming depends upon factors that are not presented in either graph. However, an alert person would be suspicious of the motive behind such obvious "chartmanship." Recommended defensive reading for every analyst is Huff's classic book, *How to Lie with Statistics.*[1]

FIGURE 7-7, *Charts from the 1970 annual report of the Communications Satellite Corporation,* is an excellent example of the effective use of different types of charts within one report.

---

1. Darrell Huff, *How to Lie with Statistics* (W. W. Norton and Co., Inc., New York, 1954).

FIGURE 7-7. Charts from the 1970 annual report
of the Communications Satellite Corporation

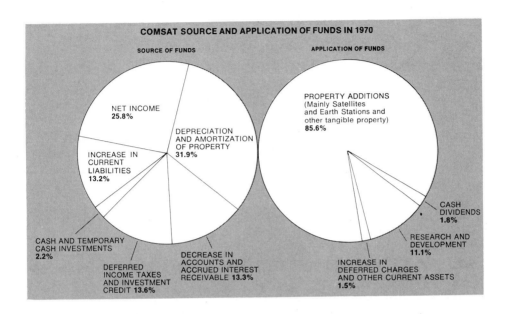

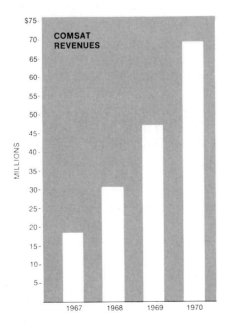
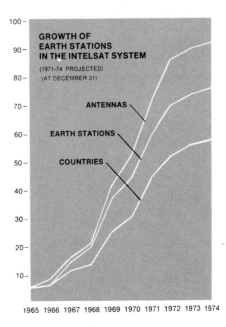

FIGURE 7-8. Examples of tables

N₁ \ N₂	0	1	10
0	0	0	0
1	0	1	10

QUANTITATIVE: BINARY MULTIPLICATION TABLE

Factor \ Processing system	Manual	Electro Mechanical	Small-medium computer	Medium-large computer
VOLUME OF DATA	Low	Medium	High	Very high
SPEED OF PROCESSING	Low	Low-medium	Medium-high	High-very high
ACCURACY OF PROCESSING	Low	Medium	High	Very high
FREQUENCY OF PROCESSING	Low	Low-medium	Medium-high	High-very high
COMPLEXITY OF PROCESSING	Low	Low	Medium	High
TOTAL COST	Low	Low-medium	Medium	High

QUALITATIVE: SELECTION OF A DATA PROCESSING SYSTEM

TABLES

Tables as an analytic tool

Tables are so commonplace that there is a tendency to overlook their usefulness as analytic tools. However, tables, sometimes called grid charts because they are made up of intersecting horizontal and vertical lines, are useful in all systems analysis activities. They provide an organized approach to decision making and are a handy reference for complex data. Setting up a table should be second nature to systems analysts; there is no more convenient method for expressing in summary form the relationships between two or more complex factors.

These relationships may be quantitative, qualitative, or a mixture of both. The first part of FIGURE 7-8, *Examples of tables,* is a segment of the binary multiplication table, and the product of two binary numbers always is a single quantity. The second part presents a qualitative relationship between factors which might be important to the choice of a data processing system in some business application. Although very superficial, this example illustrates one of the principal tasks the systems analyst is called upon to undertake. This task, known as a study of alternatives, involves the identification of potentially suitable systems and the selection of the most appropriate system after evaluation of all of the factors relevant to a particular application. This important process will be discussed in detail in Chapter 13: Feasibility Analysis.

Another particularly useful table for the systems analyst is the decision table, described in the following section.

Decision tables

Decision tables are a tabular technique for describing logical rules. Most people tend to associate decision tables with the logic of computer programs. However, decision tables also are an important tool of the systems analyst because they are an effective means of expressing the logic of administrative rules and procedures. The first part of FIGURE 7-9, *Decision tables,* depicts the basic format of a decision table. The table has four parts:

1. *Condition stub*—lists all conditions to be considered.
2. *Condition entries*—make up the rules to be followed.
3. *Action entries*—point to actions which may be taken.
4. *Action stub*—identifies the action to be followed.

The decision table is read in the direction indicated by the heavy line and arrowheads. The condition stub is read as an "if" statement, and the action stub is read as a "then" statement. These statements are connected by a rule, which is a combination of the condition entry, usually indicated by a Y(yes) or an N(no), and the action pointed to, usually indicated by X.

We will use a simple example to exhibit the use of a decision table to condense and display systems logic. Consider the following check-cashing policy in a supermarket:

> If the customer has a valid credit card, he may cash a check for the amount of the purchase plus $25.00. If a customer does not have a valid credit card but can show two other identifications, he may cash a check for the amount of the purchase, not to exceed $20.00. Otherwise, he must be referred to the store manager.

The "check-cashing policy" decision table appears in the second part of Figure 7-9. A typical rule reads: "If a customer does not have a valid credit card, and if his purchase is not greater than $20.00, and if he has two identifications, then allow his check for the amount of the purchase." Note that, in order to avoid redundancies, it is not necessary to fill in all the spaces in the condition entry section with Ys and Ns. In Rule 4, for example, if the amount of the purchase is greater than $20.00, the store policy is that the manager must approve the customer's check if the customer does not have a valid credit card. Therefore, it would not be necessary to include a Y or N entry corresponding to the condition stub "two identifications."

Systems analysts often use decision tables as a means of communicating the systems logic, embedded in policies and procedures, to the programmer. When this type of logic is made available to the programmer, he is able to do a more effective job of developing the detailed computer program logic. Decision tables, then, are a technique that is useful in eliminating one of the major pitfalls that has impeded past efforts to develop effective computer-based business systems. This is the pitfall of forcing programmers, through default, to develop logical

Figure 7-9. Decision tables

Heading	Rule numbers
CONDITION STUB	CONDITION ENTRIES
ACTION STUB	ACTION ENTRIES

BASIC FORMAT

	Check cashing policy	1	2	3	4
CONDITIONS	Valid credit card	Y	N	N	N
	Purchase > $20.00		N	N	Y
	Two identifications		Y	N	
ACTIONS	Allow purchase + $25.00	X			
	Allow purchase amount		X		
	Call store manager			X	X

EXAMPLE: CHECK CASHING POLICY

rules that may not reflect the true policy the computer program is intended to implement.

In summary, the decision table has the following major values for the systems analyst:

1. The structure of the table lends itself to a concise and correct statement of decision logic.

2. The table is an effective means of communicating with the computer programmer because it is easily understood.

The above examples are the barest introduction to the uses of tables. We have encountered and will continue to encounter many kinds of tables in this text. What must be emphasized here is the value of tables as powerful tools for collecting, analyzing, and reporting relationships between data.

CHARTS FOR PROJECT MANAGEMENT

Project planning and status reporting

All projects are made up of significant events, or milestones, that must occur in some time sequence in order for the project to be completed. A project plan is a schedule of milestones over the duration of the project. Charts are an effective means of depicting a project schedule and of reporting progress (or lack of progress) as it occurs. The type of chart most often used for this purpose is a horizontal bar chart, sometimes called a Gantt chart. Figure 7-10, *Gantt-type chart,* illustrates the principles of a project planning and reporting chart. In this chart six activities are scheduled over a time period of seven weeks. The length of the horizontal bar corresponds to the duration of the activity. Initially, activities are scheduled by means of an open bar. Then, the bar is "filled in" to

FIGURE 7-10. Gantt-type chart

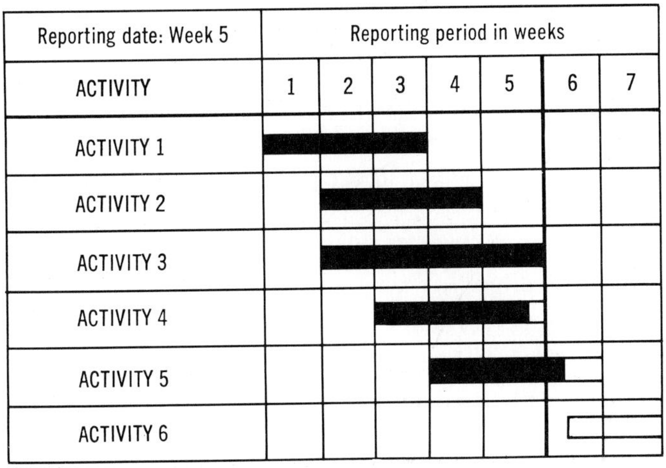

Reporting date: Week 5	Reporting period in weeks						
ACTIVITY	1	2	3	4	5	6	7
ACTIVITY 1	███	███					
ACTIVITY 2		███	███				
ACTIVITY 3		███	███	███			
ACTIVITY 4				███	██		
ACTIVITY 5					███	██	
ACTIVITY 6						▭	

show how much of the activity has been completed. In the example of Figure 7-10, the reporting date is the end of the fifth week. Activities 1, 2, and 3 have been completed at this point in time. Activity 4 appears to be lagging about one-half week behind schedule. Activity 5 is slightly ahead of schedule, and Activity 6 has not yet been started.

There are many techniques for managing projects. Among the more innovative and effective of these is "management by objectives." This technique depends on the development of a psychological environment within which the individual participates in defining his responsibilities and has the opportunity to achieve results and to earn recognition and advancement. Within such an environment, the individual responsible for a project (or for a phase of a project), in a joint discussion with his superior, arrives at mutually understood and accepted objectives, results, and criteria for measuring results.

FIGURE 7-11, *Project plan and status report,* is an example of a Gantt-type chart that can be used to manage projects in this type of an environment. This chart reports:

1. *Project title:* The name of the project.
2. *Programmer/analyst:* The name of the responsible individual.
3. *Committed date:* The date the project is scheduled for completion.
4. *Completed date:* The date the project actually is completed.
5. *Status date:* The date of the status report.
6. *Activity/document:* A line entry for each major activity or document to be completed.
7. *Percent complete:* The analyst's interpretation of the percentage already completed of a scheduled line entry.

8. *Status:* The analyst's evaluation of the status of each line entry. Status is reported by means of the following symbols:

○ Project status satisfactory.

□ Caution: problem encountered but not considered critical.

△ Critical condition: completion of project could be endangered.

9. *Period ending:* The end dates of selected reporting intervals (e.g., weeks or months).

10. *Project planning progress symbols:*

▭ Scheduled progress.

▬ Actual progress to date.

∨ Scheduled or rescheduled completion date.

▼ Actual completion date.

FIGURE 7-11. Project plan and status report

PROJECT PLAN AND STATUS REPORT																				
PROJECT TITLE	PROJECT STATUS SYMBOLS ○ Satisfactory □ Caution △ Critical																			
	PLANNING/PROGRESS SYMBOLS ▭ Scheduled Progress ∨ Scheduled Completion ▬ Actual Progress ▼ Actual Completion		PROGRAMMER/ANALYST																	
			COMMITTED DATE			COMPLETED DATE				STATUS DATE										
ACTIVITY/DOCUMENT	PERCENT COMPLETE	STATUS	PERIOD ENDING																	

FIGURE 7-12. **Study Phase plan and status report**

ACTIVITY/DOCUMENT	PERCENT COMPLETE	STATUS
STUDY PHASE	45	□
Initial Investigation	100	O
Project Directive	100	O
Performance Definition	100	O
Feasibility Analysis	50	□
Performance Specification	0	O
Study Phase Report	0	O
Study Phase Review	0	O

FIGURE 7-12, *Study Phase plan and status report,* is an example of the use of this management technique. In this figure the principal activities that constitute the Study Phase for a computer-based business system appear as line entries. The report, which has a status date corresponding to the eighth week of the project, is interpreted as follows:

1. *Initial investigation:* 100 percent complete; completed one week ahead of schedule (as indicated by the appearance of the actual completion date, ▼, ahead of the scheduled completion date, ∨); status is satisfactory.

2. *Project directive:* 100 percent complete; completed approximately one-half week ahead of schedule; status is satisfactory.

3. *Performance definition:* 100 percent complete; completed on schedule; status is satisfactory.

4. *Feasibility analysis:* 50 percent complete; approximately one-half week behind schedule; rescheduled for completion a week later; status is caution because slippage has occurred.

5. *Performance specification, Study Phase report, and Study Phase review:* not started, but all have slipped a week because of the rescheduled completion date for the feasibility analysis.

6. *The Study Phase:* The overall project is 45 percent complete; status is caution because the completion date has been rescheduled. (In this reporting scheme a major line entry, e.g., Study Phase, must not be given a more satisfactory rating than its least satisfactory element, in this case, the feasibility analysis.)

The percentage complete and status ratings shown in Figure 7-12 represent the analyst's personal evaluations. For example, even though the shaded-in part of the Study Phase bar is more than 50 percent of the total area, the analyst feels that only 45 percent has been completed. This could be due to the fact that he has scheduled additional resources for the latter part of the project. The evaluation of caution and the analyst's apparent acceptance of a week's lag in completion of the project may not be concurred with by his supervisor. However, in a psychological environment in which it is "safe" for an individual to report openly, many possible actions may be taken before temporary difficulties become insurmountable problems. We also should realize that plans and schedules will change because no one can forecast the future without error. A major advantage of a plan, however, is that it provides a good reference on which to base necessary changes.

Project cost reporting

Project status reporting, as described in the previous section of this chapter, does not by itself provide a complete status picture. Cost must be reported as well as progress. All projects operate within the constraints of a budget. A project might be on schedule performance-wise, but at the same time be seriously overexpended. Therefore, a project cost report is required as well as a project plan and status report. FIGURE 7-13, *Project cost report,* is an example of a report that might accompany the project plan and status report of Figure 7-12.

In this example the project is approximately $1,700 overexpended at the end of the eighth week. This overexpenditure, coupled with the schedule slippage, is reason for a reappraisal meeting now between the analyst and his supervisor. As a matter of fact this meeting should have taken place at least one week earlier. When appropriate, as in this instance, the analyst should submit an explanatory memorandum along with his project plan and status report and project cost report.

Performance indices

The project plan and status report and the project cost report always present a current picture of project performance. They do not present historical or trend information. Although this type of information can be obtained by referring to previous reports, it is more desirable to extract the required information from reports as they are presented and to maintain a management control chart. This chart should contain only the data essential to summarizing past performance and to predicting future performance. An excellent "Cost vs. Achievement"

FIGURE 7-13. **Project cost report**

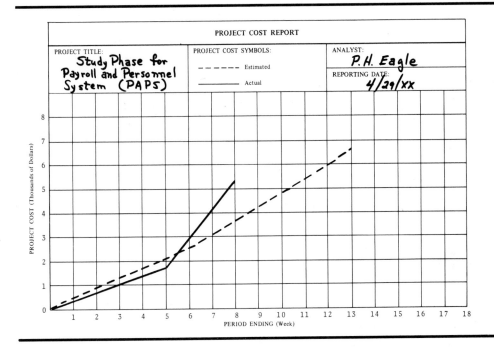

technique for this purpose has been described by L. I. Krauss.[2] The following discussion of performance indices is based upon this technique.

We can define three performance indices:

1. *Cost Index* (CI): The ratio of actual costs to planned costs.

$$CI = \frac{\text{actual costs}}{\text{planned costs}}$$

2. *Achievement Index* (AI): The ratio of actual achievement to planned achievement.

$$AI = \frac{\text{actual achievement}}{\text{planned achievement}}$$

3. *Status Index* (SI): The ratio of the Achievement Index to the Cost Index.

$$SI = \frac{AI}{CI}$$

The Cost Index measures the expenditure of money. The information for calculating Cost Index is obtainable from the project cost reports. A value of CI greater than 1.00 represents overexpenditure.

2. L. I. Krauss, *Administering and Controlling the Company Data Processing Function* (Englewood Cliffs: Prentice Hall, 1969), pp. 130-135.

The Achievement Index measures results. It can be calculated from the project plan and status report as the ratio between the estimates of actual percentage complete and planned percentage complete. A value of AI less than 1.00 represents underachievement.

The Status Index is a single measure of effectiveness that is calculated from the other two indices. It may be viewed as a "rate of return" on expenditure. Note that the Status Index alone cannot indicate schedule slippage or cost overrun. We still have to refer to either the Achievement Index or the Cost Index for this information. For example, a project with an Achievement Index of 0.80 and cost index of 0.60 would have a Status Index of 1.33. This means that the rate of return on dollars expended is very high. However, the Achievement Index indicates that accomplishment is behind schedule.

Let us make some sample calculations showing the value of the three performance indices in reporting trends. Let us assume that the data summarized in FIGURE 7-14, *Project trend summary data*, was extracted from the status and cost

FIGURE 7-14. Project trend summary data

WEEK	COST ($)		ACHIEVEMENT (%)		PERFORMANCE INDICES		
	ACTUAL	PLANNED	ACTUAL	PLANNED	CI	AI	SI
1	450	500	7	5	0.90	1.40	1.55
2	800	900	13	10	0.89	1.30	1.46
3	1,100	1,300	18	15	0.85	1.20	1.41
4	1,500	1,700	23	20	0.88	1.15	1.31
5	1,850	2,050	25	25	0.90	1.00	1.11
6	3,000	2,500	35	35	1.20	1.00	0.83
7	4,200	3,100	40	45	1.35	.89	0.66
8	5,450	3,750	45	50	1.45	.90	0.62
9							
10							
11							
12							
13							
14							
15							
16							
17							
18							

PROJECT SUMMARY STATUS REPORT WORKSHEET

FIGURE 7-15. Performance indices for a typical out-of-control project

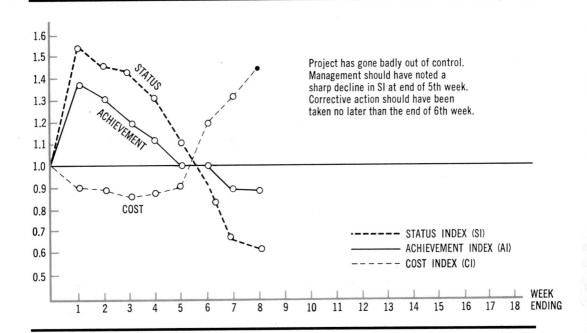

reports as they were received by management. Note that the cost and achievement entries are cumulative and relate to the overall project. The last entry (Week 8) corresponds to the data shown in Figures 7-12 and 7-13. Note that we were able to obtain all of the cost data from Figure 7-13; however, we would have to rely on previous status reports for the historical achievement information. FIGURE 7-15, *Performance indices for a typical out-of-control project,* is a graph of the three indices summarized in Figure 7-14.

As Figure 7-15 dramatically illustrates, costs begin to increase and achievement decreases rapidly by the end of the fifth week. Management action should have been triggered by the declining SI and AI no later than the end of the sixth week. By the end of the eighth week the project is badly out of control.

Status Index graphs for some potential performance situations are shown in FIGURE 7-16, *Illustrative Status Index graphs.* The left part of this figure shows a project that is going out of control; the center part a project that "appears" to be outperforming the plan; and the right part a project that "appears" to be performing consistently as planned. We say "appears" because we must remember to check the Achievement Index or Cost Index also.

The following "rules of thumb" apply to the use of the Status Index:

1. SI between .9 and 1.1: normal range.

2. SI between 1.1 and 1.3 or between .7 and .9: management attention, perhaps action.

FIGURE 7-16. **Illustrative Status Index graphs**

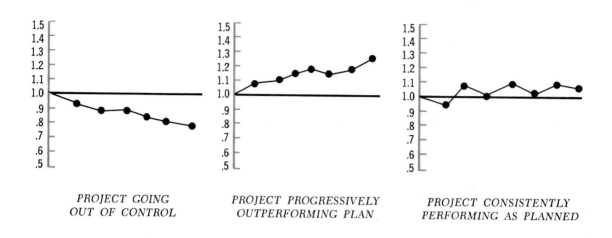

PROJECT GOING
OUT OF CONTROL

PROJECT PROGRESSIVELY
OUTPERFORMING PLAN

PROJECT CONSISTENTLY
PERFORMING AS PLANNED

3. SI greater than 1.3 or less than .7: management action usually required.

The project management techniques we have discussed thus far usually can be applied without the aid of a computer. More sophisticated techniques are available, but they usually require the assistance of a computer. Among the more powerful and widely used of these techniques are critical path networks.

Critical path networks

Critical path networks are planning and management tools that use a graphical format to depict the relationship between tasks and schedules. They differ from conventional scheduling methods in two major respects: (1) they do not use a single time scale; and (2) they facilitate the analysis of many interdependent tasks, some of which must be performed in sequence and some of which should be performed parallel with other tasks.

The two most common critical path network techniques, which are the same in all essential aspects, are CPM (Critical Path Method) and PERT (Program Evaluation Review Technique). FIGURE 7-17, *Critical path network*, is a simplified example illustrating the principles that underlie this powerful management tool. A network such as that shown in Figure 7-17 is constructed from two basic elements:

1. *Activity:* the application of time and resources to achieve an objective. Activities are measured in units of time, usually weeks.

2. *Event:* the point in time at which an activity begins or ends.

Network management techniques are based upon calculation of the time required to proceed from start (S) to finish (F) along each possible path in order to determine the path that requires the longest overall time.

Figure 7-17. Critical path network

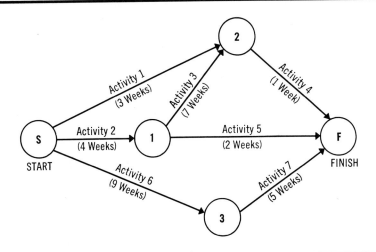

The longest network path from start to finish is called the *critical path*. In Figure 7-17, all the possible paths from start to finish and their respective times are:

Path	"S" to "F" Time
S-1-F	6 weeks
S-1-2-F	12 weeks
S-3-F	14 weeks

Note that S-2-F is not an allowable path because the activities along S-1-2, which take 11 weeks, must be completed before it is possible to proceed from 2 to F. The critical path is S-3-F.

Events along paths other than the critical path can be delayed without causing the time from start to finish to exceed the critical path time. Critical path information is valuable to the project manager because he has an opportunity to shift resources from activities associated with events not on the critical path to activities that are.

As is apparent from inspection of Figure 7-17, a critical path network could become quite complex for even a moderate-sized project. Computer programs that perform critical path network analysis are available. As a matter of fact, computer programs have been devised to relate network schedules and cost; an example is PERT/COST. Nevertheless, the manual construction of critical path networks is of value on small projects or on segments of larger projects.

Critical path networks have been used most successfully on applications for which all the tasks are well understood and where estimates of times can be based upon valid past experience. For example, the construction industry makes excellent use of critical path techniques. As another example, networks are useful in scheduling the flow of work through computer centers. They also are of value in scheduling the many activities in the process of converting from an old system to a new, computer-based system. We will examine the use of a critical path network in considerable detail in Chapter 22: Preparation for Implementation.

We shall encounter additional applications of charts throughout this text. Flowcharts, another important class of charts, are powerful pictorial tools which are described in the next chapter.

KEY TERMS

chart	*grid chart*	*Achievement Index*
pie chart	*decision table*	*Status Index*
line chart	*Gantt-type chart*	*critical path network*
step chart	*Cost Index*	

FOR DISCUSSION

1. Name and relate each of the four basic types of charts to its best use.

2. Discuss Figure 1-1 and Figure 1-2 (of Chapter 1).

3. Compare Figure 1-4 and Figure 1-5 (of Chapter 1).

4. Why are tables useful as systems analysis tools?

5. Why are decision tables used by systems analysts as well as by programmers?

6. What is meant by "management by objectives"?

7. What elements of the project plan and status report are most dependent upon the relationship between the analyst and his supervisor? If this were a poor relationship, what might happen?

8. What correlations should be made between the project status and project cost reports? Explain the use of the performance indices.

9. How do critical path networks differ from Gantt-type charts?

10. What is the critical path, and what is its significance to a project manager?

8   Flowcharting

The previous chapter introduced charts as a means of
compressing large amounts of data into a concise,
clear format. The goal of this chapter is to introduce the
application of charting techniques to the description
or documentation of systems. You will learn how
to use standardized flowcharting symbols to describe
information flow and processing in a system. In
addition, you will learn how to draw HIPO charts
to describe system functions and procedure analysis
charts to describe manual activities.

INTRODUCTION TO FLOWCHARTING

Definition of a flowchart

Flowcharting is a graphical technique specifically developed for use in data
processing. A *flowchart* is a pictorial representation that uses predefined symbols
to describe data flow in a business system or the logic of a computer program.

The system flowchart stresses "what" as contrasted with the program logic
flowchart which stresses "how." FIGURE 8-1, *System flowchart*, is an example of a
simple system flowchart. The symbols shown in this figure are "predefined";
their shapes identify data and communicate what is happening to it. In this
example the top and bottom symbols represent input or output data. The middle
symbol on the left is the process symbol; it represents the operation performed
on input data to convert it into meaningful output. The symbol to the right of
the process symbol depicts on-line storage that is available to the computer
program. The words within each symbol provide additional information about
each step. There are other important symbols that the systems analyst must know
in order to make effective use of flowcharts. We will present these after introducing the principal uses of flowcharts .

Uses of flowcharts

Flowcharts help the analyst to describe and to communicate complex sets of data in three principal ways. He uses flowcharts (1) to analyze existing systems; (2) to synthesize new systems; and (3) to communicate with others.

The flowchart of an existing system enables the analyst to visualize the parts of the system and to record their functions. A system flowchart can compress many pages of written description into one informative picture.

Flowcharts help the analyst synthesize new systems. Each "candidate" system can be described quickly and effectively by an appropriate flowchart. As he studies systems, the analyst must be able to communicate effectively with users, with programmers (if computer programs are required), and with other analysts. Flowcharts are a powerful method for efficient internal communication because all persons involved can grasp their meaning quickly.

Flowcharts also are an effective method for communication with groups outside of the company. External communication is most often accomplished through professional journals, seminars, or meetings with user groups. The user groups may be composed of companies in the same or related industries, or of companies with problems of a similar nature. Knowledge of what other companies have done to solve similar problems often is of great aid to the analyst in solving his company's problems.

FLOWCHARTING SYMBOLS

Standardization of symbols

For communication to be improved by the use of symbols, the meaning of the symbols must be understood by all their users. Several groups have contrib-

FIGURE 8-1. **System flowchart**

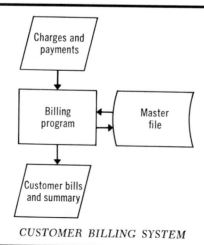

CUSTOMER BILLING SYSTEM

uted to the standardization of flowchart symbols. The history of flowcharting and the definition of symbols is described by Chapin.[1] National and international efforts to develop standard flowcharting symbols began in the early 1960s. The effort in the United States resulted in the set of symbols adopted by the American National Standards Institute (ANSI). The ANSI standard was developed through the combined efforts of professional associations, including the Association for Communication Machinery (ACM) and the Data Processing Management Association (DPMA). These symbols are a subset of those adopted as a result of the parallel efforts of an international group. This more extensive set of symbols is called the International Standards Organization (ISO) flowchart symbols.

The ANSI-ISO standards are conformed to widely by the systems and programming professions. However, they have been augmented in areas in which additional symbols could improve clarity. In particular the IBM Corporation has developed some additional symbols. Through the production and distribution of a useful plastic "template," IBM has achieved widespread acceptance of its set of symbols.[2] Hence, we use the IBM set of flowcharting symbols in this text.

IBM flowcharting symbols

Symbol Groups. FIGURE 8-2, *IBM flowchart symbols,* illustrates the outlines of the flowcharting symbols as they appear on the IBM template. Some of these symbols are used only in systems flowcharts; some are used only in computer program flowcharts; and some are used in both types. We will describe each group, with particular stress on those symbols used to prepare system flowcharts.

Basic Symbols. FIGURE 8-3, *Basic flowcharting symbols,* shows the basic symbols, which are common to both systems and programming flowcharts. The two symbols in the upper left-hand corner (process and input/output) were introduced in Figure 8-1. The process symbol is a rectangle. In a systems flowchart, the "process" depicted can range from a single manual activity to a computer program component to a complete computer program. The amount of "processing" the process symbol represents depends on the intended detail of the flowchart. In program flowcharts the processes are relatively specific, usually representing arithmetic operations or data movement.

The other three basic symbols shown in Figure 8-3 are the onpage connector, offpage connector, and arrowheads. All are used to connect, or to link, other flowchart symbols. The use of these symbols, along with flowlines (a line drawn to connect symbols) is illustrated in FIGURE 8-4, *Flowlines and connectors.* The normal flow is downward and from left to right. As shown in this figure, connectors are used in pairs. The connector with the "A" at the bottom of the left column is considered to be "connected" to the "A" at the top of the middle column. The

---

1. Ned Chapin, *Flowcharts* (New York: Auerbach Publishers, 1971), pp. 27–29.
2. *Flowcharting Template,* Form GX20-8020 (White Plains: IBM Corporation).

Figure 8-2. IBM flowchart symbols

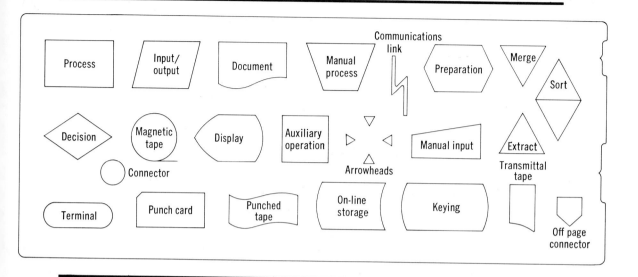

connectors at the bottom of the flowchart columns are called exit connectors. Connectors that "depart" from the normal downward flow also are called exit connectors. Connectors at the top of the flowchart columns and connectors that

Figure 8-3. Basic flowcharting symbols

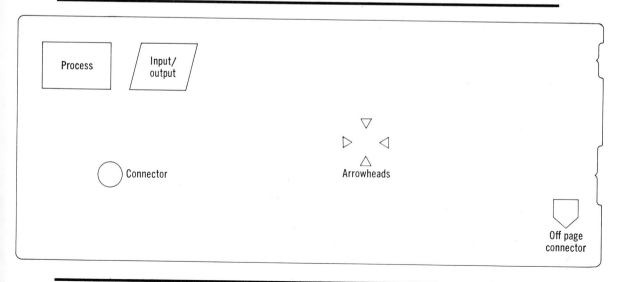

FIGURE 8-4. Flowlines and connectors

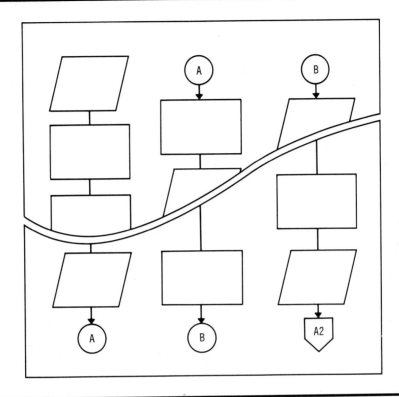

"join" the downward flow are called entry connectors. If a flowchart is continued on another page, the IBM standard provides for a special offpage connector symbol. The offpage connector appears at the bottom of the right-hand column in Figure 8-4. Arrowheads are connected to flowlines anywhere there might be confusion about the direction of flow. Since the normal direction of flow is down, flowlines that continue down the chart normally do not have arrowheads.

Symbols Related to Systems. Fifteen symbol outlines are shown in FIGURE 8-5, *Systems flowcharting symbols.* Additional symbols can be formed by combining or modifying the symbols shown in this figure. For ease of discussion, we will split the symbols into three groups, shown in separate figures:
 1. Symbols for equipment (Figure 8-6)
 2. Specialized input/output symbols (Figure 8-7)
 3. Specialized processing symbols (Figure 8-8)
 FIGURE 8-6, *Symbols for equipment,* illustrates three symbols used to show specific types of equipment.

FIGURE 8-5. Systems flowcharting symbols

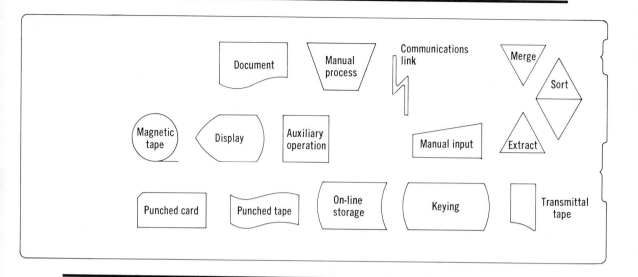

1. The *communications link* is used in place of a normal flowline to indicate that remotely located equipment is tied into the system through telephone lines, microwave transmitters, or other media.

2. *Off-line storage* is used to show storage that is not accessible to the computer. For example, it is the symbol used to show the manual filing of data in a storage or file cabinet. It is a modification of the merge symbol.

3. *On-line storage* is storage that is accessible by a computer program as data is being processed. Examples of on-line storage devices are the magnetic disk and magnetic drum. This symbol is a generalized symbol and does not identify specific media.

When a specific input or output device or media is known, it usually is helpful to indicate what it is. FIGURE 8-7, *Specialized input/output symbols,* contains nine

FIGURE 8-6. Symbols for equipment

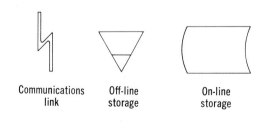

FIGURE 8-7. Specialized input/output symbols

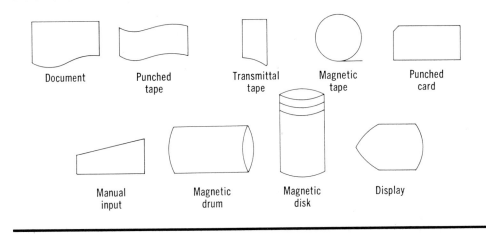

specialized symbols that may be used in place of the basic input/output symbol (parallelogram).

1. The *document symbol* is used to describe any input or output that is a paper document. It includes source documents and printed reports.

2. *Punched tape* often is produced by attachments to cash registers and book-keeping machines.

3. A *transmittal tape* is a proof or other control total produced by a device such as an adding machine.

4. The *magnetic tape* symbol represents the use of magnetic tape as an input, output, or auxiliary storage device.

5. *Punched cards* may be used as input, output, or storage media. Some punched cards also serve as source documents.

6. The *manual input* symbol indicates inputs to computer systems by means of on-line keyboards, switches, or buttons. It is not used to indicate keying processes such as keypunching or verifying.

7. *Magnetic drum* and *magnetic disk* are specific replacements for the general on-line storage symbol. Both of these symbols are constructed from the on-line storage outline.

8. The *display* symbol shows visual outputs from on-line devices, such as CRT (cathode ray tube) terminals, console printers, and plotters.

Symbols used to replace the basic process symbol (rectangle) are illustrated in FIGURE 8-8, *Specialized processing symbols.*

1. *Manual off-line operations* are operations that are performed by humans without the aid of equipment. An example is filling in a source document.

2. The *auxiliary off-line operations* symbol represents off-line operations. These are performed with equipment, but they are not under the control of a computer.

Figure 8-8. Specialized processing symbols

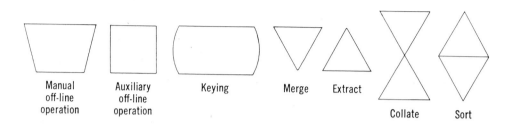

3. The *keying* symbol indicates keypunching, verifying, and other key-driven operations.

4. The *merge, extract, collate,* and *sort* operations are represented by special symbols. The collate and sort symbols are constructed by combining the merge and extract outlines. These symbols are used to represent unit record operations rather than computer operations.

Symbols Related to Programming. Figure 8-9, *Program flowcharting symbols,* shows the special symbols most commonly used to prepare flowcharts for computer programs:

Figure 8-9. Program flowcharting symbols

Figure 8-10. The predefined process symbol

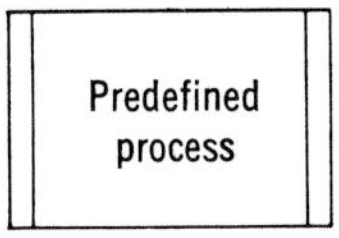

1. The *preparation* symbol shows the setting of a program switch, the modification of an index register, or the initialization of a routine in a computer program.

2. The *decision* symbol is used for operations that determine which of two or more alternative paths will be followed in the program.

3. The *terminal symbol* indicates a start, stop, halt, pause, or interrupt in a computer program.

In addition to these three unique programming symbols, a fourth symbol called the predefined process is commonly used. The *predefined process symbol* is a composite symbol drawn by combining the basic process symbol with two vertical lines drawn near the left and right edges. Figure 8-10, *The predefined process symbol*, illustrates this symbol. It is used to show the execution of a function that is defined elsewhere in the flowchart or on a separate flowchart. Examples are title-column heading routines, data movement routines, calculation routines, and total routines.

Symbol sets

The basic symbols, the symbols related to systems, and the symbols related to programming are combined into two ways:

1. System flowcharting is performed using both the basic and systems-related symbols.

2. Computer program flowcharting is performed using both the basic and programming-related symbols.

Note: It is not good practice to use programming-related symbols for system flowcharting or to use systems-related symbols for computer program flowcharting.

Because we are primarily concerned with system flowcharting, we next will examine the primary uses of the system flowcharting symbols.

SYSTEM FLOWCHARTS

Types of system flowcharts

The purpose of systems flowcharts is quite different from that of computer program flowcharts. These flowcharts describe "what," while computer program flowcharts describe "how." There are three types of "what" flowcharts: information-oriented system flowcharts, process-oriented system flowcharts, and HIPO

FIGURE 8-11. Information-oriented flowchart

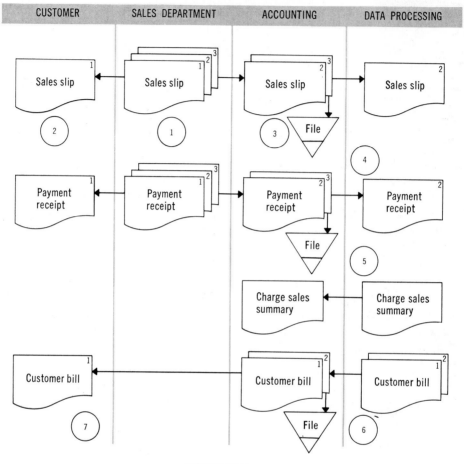

CUSTOMER BILLING SYSTEM

1. Charge sales slips and payment receipts are made out in triplicate.

2. The original copies of sales slips and payment receipts are given to the customer.

3. The second and third copies of sales slips and receipts are sent to accounting where the third copies are retained in files.

4. The second copies of charge sales slips and payment receipts are sent to data processing.

5. A charge sales summary is produced and sent to accounting.

6. Two copies of customer bills are produced and sent to accounting where the carbon copies are filed.

7. The original copies of the customer bills are mailed to the customers.

charts. Each of these has a specific use. *Information-oriented flowcharts* show information flow through an organization. *Process-oriented flowcharts* identify the sequence of operations that are performed upon data. *HIPO charts* (Hierarchy plus Input Process Output) graphically show system functions.

Information-oriented system flowcharts

Information-oriented flowcharts use a grid structure to trace the flow of data. They identify input data and follow its flow until its subsequent appearance as output information. They do this by identifying specific forms. Usually they do not identify processing operations. Hence, the document symbol is predominant in information-oriented flowcharts. An example is shown in FIGURE 8-11, *Information-oriented flowchart.* This figure shows how data, i.e., filled-out forms, flows across organizational boundaries. The storage of data is indicated by use of the off-line storage symbol.

It is customary to accompany information-oriented system flowcharts with a narrative description. One technique for doing this is to number the significant information flow steps and to describe them by a narrative on an accompanying sheet of paper. The numbers encircled on the flowchart in Figure 8-11 key the symbols in this figure to the narrative shown below the flowchart. Another technique is to describe the inputs and outputs for each labeled column on separate sheets.

Process-oriented system flowcharts

Levels of System Flowcharts. Process-oriented flowcharts commonly are referred to as "system flowcharts." They show which data processing operations are converting inputs into outputs. These flowcharts can be drawn to any appropriate level of detail. The highest level, and least detailed, flowchart is called a high-level system flowchart. Lower levels of detail are represented by expanded flowcharts, which are referred to by names such as "intermediate level" and "detailed level."

FIGURE 8-12, *High-level system flowchart—basic symbols,* is an example of the highest level of a process-oriented system flowchart. It uses the basic symbols to give an overview of the system.

Structure of System Flowcharts. System flowcharts have a characteristic "sandwich" structure, so called because the chart is made up of alternating layers of input/output identifiers and process identifiers. Figure 8-12 exhibits the basic sandwich structure. Charges and Payments is the "bread" of the input data; the Billing Program is the "filling" of the processing operation; and Customer Bills and Summary is the "bread" of the output data. Note that this chart does not explain how processing is performed; it only identifies what processing is done. Also, note that the output "bread" of one step may become the input "bread" of a successive step.

Flowcharts should be accompanied by a narrative. The flowchart of FIGURE 8-13, *Flowchart and narrative,* is the same as Figure 8-1; however, it also illustrates the use of an accompanying narrative.

FIGURE 8-12. High-level system flowchart—basic symbols

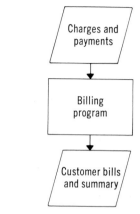

CUSTOMER BILLING SYSTEM

FIGURE 8-13. Flowchart and narrative

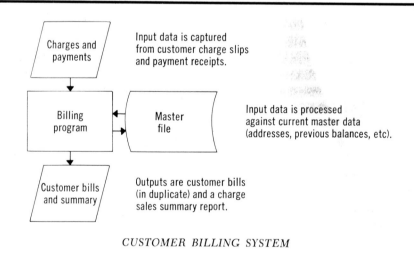

CUSTOMER BILLING SYSTEM

Many flowcharts are too complex and too detailed to accommodate the narrative on the same page. Either there is not enough room or the flowchart would appear confusing. FIGURE 8-14, *Flowchart and separate narrative*, illustrates the use of a separate page for the narrative.

FIGURE 8-14. Flowchart and separate narrative

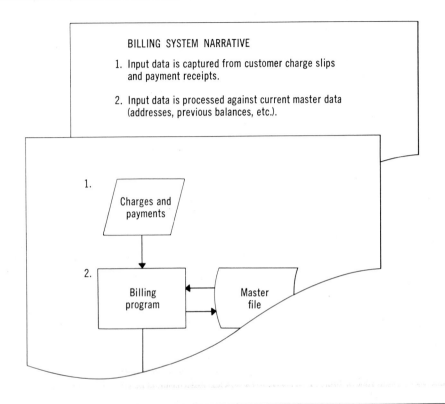

BILLING SYSTEM NARRATIVE

1. Input data is captured from customer charge slips and payment receipts.

2. Input data is processed against current master data (addresses, previous balances, etc.).

1. Charges and payments

2. Billing program   Master file

The process flowcharts we have examined so far have been high-level flowcharts. These flowcharts are expanded in detail as the computer-based business system proceeds through its life cycle. The flowchart levels are associated with certain life-cycle phases:

1. *High-level system flowcharts: Study Phase.* These flowcharts are very valuable at Study Phase reviews. The participants in these reviews usually are not data processing professionals. Elimination of confusing detail in the flowchart helps to highlight the user-oriented characteristics of the system. If we present management with systems flowcharts that are too detailed, we become "confusers" instead of "simplifiers." FIGURE 8-15, *High-level system flowchart—basic and system symbols,* illustrates a system flowchart suitable for a management presentation.

2. *Intermediate-level system flowcharts: Design Phase.* These flowcharts identify the specific inputs, outputs, and processes in considerable detail. FIGURE 8-16, *Intermediate-level flowchart and narrative,* is an example of this type. The accompanying narrative is shown below the flowchart.

Figure 8-15. High-level system flowchart—basic and system symbols

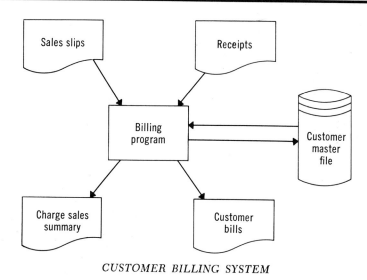

CUSTOMER BILLING SYSTEM

As we will discuss in Chapter 16: System Design, major input, processing, and output controls also can be indicated on intermediate-level flowcharts.

3. *Detailed-level system flowcharts: Development Phase.* These flowcharts precede the construction of computer program flowcharts by programmers. They identify the inputs, outputs, and processing operations for each of the computer program components. Detailed control operations also are shown. The use of this type of flowchart is described in Chapter 23: Computer Program Development.

HIPO charts

HIPO charts are designed to document functions. The functions may be those of a system or a computer program.

HIPO stands for Hierarchy plus Input Processing Output. Actually, two types of charts make up a HIPO package. One shows the hierarchy; the other depicts the input, processing, and output. The first presents the functional modules of a system (or computer program) as a hierarchy of functions. Levels of hierarchy were shown on an organization chart in Chapter 4. The hierarchy of functions can be presented in the same way as the hierarchy of positions is shown on organization charts. Figure 8-17, *Customer billing system hierarchy,* illustrates the concept of hierarchy of functions. The system is the top level. The second level is made up of the major functions of the system. For the third level, each of the major functions is then broken down into its subfunctions. "Breaking down" functions into smaller, more detailed, subfunctions can continue until the chart shows as much detail as desired or until a basic function

FIGURE 8-16. Intermediate-level flowchart and narrative

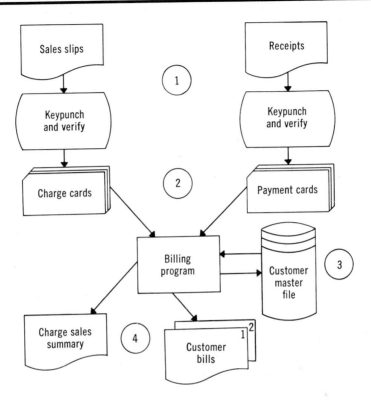

CUSTOMER BILLING SYSTEM

1. Charge sales slips and receipts are keypunched and verified.

2. Charge and payment cards are inputs as a transaction file.

3. An online customer file supplies master data to the program and is updated by the program.

4. Program outputs are a charge sales summary and two copies of customer bills.

Figure 8-17. Customer billing system hierarchy

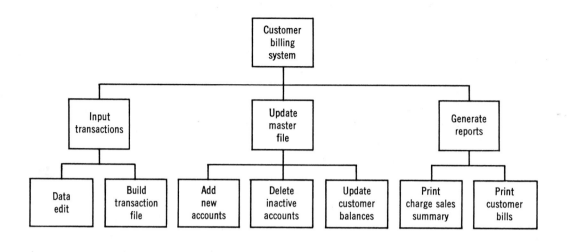

is reached. Note that the hierarchy chart is more detailed than the high-level system flowchart of Figure 8-15. The hierarchy chart is a Design Phase tool with a detail level about equal to intermediate-level system flowcharts.

The second of the HIPO package charts is a detail-level chart listing the inputs, processing steps, and outputs of each functional module of the hierarchy chart. These charts are commonly referred to as IPO charts. They do not show hierarchy. Figure 8-18, *IPO detail chart for data edit function,* is an example.

It should be noted that HIPO charts may be used for the top-down planning of programs as well as the planning of systems. The hierarchy of functions charted would be the functions of the program. The program HIPO chart is a common planning tool in a top-down approach to programming called *structured programming.* The drawing of HIPO charts for a program would be done during the Development Phase.

Figure 8-18. IPO detail chart for data edit function

INPUTS	PROCESSING	OUTPUTS
1. Sales data	1. Verify account numbers	1. Transaction file (magnetic disk)
2. Payment data	2. Validate all numeric fields	2. Error report
3. New accounts	3. Check for valid transaction code	
4. Inactive accounts		

COMPUTER PROGRAM FLOWCHARTS

The definition of a flowchart included the phrase: "uses predefined symbols to describe . . . the logic of a computer program." In this definition, "logic" refers to the types of instructions that business computers normally execute, e.g., arithmetic, conditional, and data movement.

This book will not present techniques of computer program logic flowcharting, for these flowcharts are the special tools of programmers and are more properly covered in programming texts.

Computer logic programming takes place during the Development Phase of the life cycle of a computer-based business system. We will consider a computer program flowchart in Chapter 23: Computer Program Development.

PROCEDURE ANALYSIS FLOWCHARTS

Another type of flowchart with which the systems analyst should be familiar is a *procedure analysis chart,* used to record the details of manual procedures in pictorial form. A special set of symbols used with procedure analysis flowcharts is shown in FIGURE 8-19, *Procedure analysis flowchart symbols.*

Procedure analysis flowcharts are a particularly useful means of making a "step-by-step" analysis of procedures. FIGURE 8-20, *Procedure analysis sheet,* is an example of a procedure analysis flowchart. The details of present (and proposed) procedures can be recorded. Time and distance measurements also can be entered in the analysis sheet. A carefully prepared procedure analysis sheet will point out duplications of effort, time delays, backtracking, and excessive inspection and transportation times. In this example, the procedure analysis sheet reveals several steps that might be modified, such as the walks to and from the A/R ledger files and the searches for customers' cards.

A procedure analysis of an existing system also can stimulate an analyst to conceive of major system changes. Some of these might be of an organizational nature. For example, in this case, the analyst might consider a computer-based credit checking system which could lead to the consolidation of the credit and accounts receivable functions into a single department.

FIGURE 8-19. Procedure analysis flowchart symbols

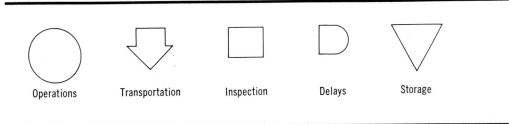

| Operations | Transportation | Inspection | Delays | Storage |

FIGURE 8-20. Procedure analysis sheet

No. ______ **PROCEDURE ANALYSIS SHEET** Page ____ of ____

SUMMARY

	PRESENT		PROPOSED		DIFFERENCE	
	NO.	TIME	NO.	TIME	NO.	TIME
OPERATIONS	7	6:37				
TRANSPORTATIONS	5	1:17				
INSPECTIONS	2	3:05				
DELAYS	1	:02				
STORAGES	1	:30				
DISTANCE TRAVELLED	140	FT.		FT.		FT.

JOB CREDIT CHECK PROCEDURE

☐ MAN OR ☐ MATERIAL ______

CHART BEGINS ______ CHART ENDS ______

CHARTED BY ______ DATE ______

	Details of Present/Proposed Method	Operation / Transport / Inspection / Delay / Storage	Distance in feet	Quantity	Time	Analysis Why? What?	Where?	When?	Who?	How?	Notes	Action Change Eliminate	Combine	Seque.	Place	Person	Improve
1	Select next sales order	● ⇨ □ D ▽			:02												
2	Check salesman's math	○ ⇨ ■ D ▽			3:00												
3	Walk to A/R ledger file	○ ➡ □ D ▽	50		:30												
4	Find customer's card	● ⇨ □ D ▽			:30												
5	Record customer's balance	● ⇨ □ D ▽			:10												
6	Walk to credit memo file	○ ➡ □ D ▽	20		:12												
7	Note unprocessed memos	● ⇨ □ D ▽			5:00												
8	Return to desk	○ ➡ □ D ▽	40		:25												
9	Subtract memos from balance	● ⇨ □ D ▽			:30												
10	Add sale amount to adjust balance	● ⇨ □ D ▽			:20												
11	Compare new balance to limit	○ ⇨ ■ D ▽			:05												
12	Approve or disapprove credit	● ⇨ □ D ▽			:05												
13	Place 3 copies of order in out tray	○ ⇨ □ ◗ ▽			:02												
14	Take copy 4 to order file	○ ➡ □ D ▽	15		:05												
15	File by customer	○ ⇨ □ D ▼			:30												
16	Return to desk	○ ➡ □ D ▽	15		:05												
17		○ ⇨ □ D ▽															
18		○ ⇨ □ D ▽															
19		○ ⇨ □ D ▽															
20		○ ⇨ □ D ▽															
21		○ ⇨ □ D ▽															
22		○ ⇨ □ D ▽															

KEY TERMS

flowchart	*process-oriented system flowcharts*
system flowchart	*HIPO charts*
basic symbols	*hierarchy charts*
system symbols	*IPO charts*
programming symbols	*procedure analysis flowchart symbols*
information-oriented system flowcharts	*procedure analysis flowcharts*

FOR DISCUSSION

1. What is a flowchart?

2. What is the principal difference between system flowcharts and computer program flowcharts?

3. Discuss the three principal uses of flowcharts.

4. Why is it important to standardize flowchart symbols? Distinguish between the ANSI, ISO, and IBM standards.

5. Relate the IBM basic symbols, the IBM symbols related to programming, and the IBM symbols related to systems to the preparation of system and computer program flowcharts.

6. What is an information-oriented system flowchart?

7. What is a process-oriented system flowchart?

8. What are the two types of charts in a HIPO package?

9. Relate the levels of system flowcharts to the phases of the life cycle of a computer-based business system.

10. What is a procedure analysis flowchart? How is it used?

9

Communications: Technical Writing and Presentations

A systems analyst must be able to communicate effectively. The goal of this chapter is to describe the communication process and to present two types of communication that are important tools in the development of computer-based systems. You will be able to identify the types of technical writing used by systems analysts and will learn techniques for making effective presentations.

THE ELEMENTS OF COMMUNICATION

The communication process

Communication is the process of transferring information from one point to another. This transfer may involve both people and machines. In this chapter, however, we are not concerned with the machine aspects of data communication. Our purpose is to present the elements of effective person-to-person communication and to relate them to technical writing and presentations, two of the most essential ways in which systems analysts must be trained to communicate.

Communication consists of sending and receiving messages. Effective communication requires that the sender send the message accurately and that the receiver receive it without distortion. Distortion may occur because of the characteristics of the transmission medium or because of "filtering" by the receiver. FIGURE 9-1, *The communication process*, illustrates the dynamics of communication. Note that feedback is included in this communication model. All the elements of the communication process must function; if not, information will not be transferred without error. Here are some examples of defective communication elements which the analyst should avoid:

1. The sender's message is not clear because his vocabulary is not understood by the receiver.

2. The transmission medium is incorrect because the situation calls for a face-to-face meeting instead of a memorandum.

3. The receiver has "tuned out" the message because he is preoccupied with another matter.

4. There is no feedback because the sender only "gives orders."

The ability to communicate is an essential skill that the systems analyst must acquire because he is sending and receiving information constantly as he interacts with managers, programmers, users, and fellow team members. The analyst should, therefore, work continuously toward more effective communication.

Toward more effective communication

Communication becomes more effective if the sender and the receiver are sensitive to each other, if an effort is made to seek feedback, and if the appropriate transmission media are selected. FIGURE 9-2, *Tips for senders and receivers,* lists some simple guidelines for the transfer of information.

The sender should organize his thoughts by arranging his main ideas so as to stress the purpose of his message. The message should be receiver-oriented, not sender-oriented. The sender should gauge the ability of the receiver to understand the message. He should be sensitive to the status of the user in the organization and to his attitudes. The sender should use facts and evidence to support the objectives of the message; he should avoid the use of unsupported opinions.

The receiver should try to remain alert and attentive. He should adjust his attention span to the requirements of the message. He should analyze the message and note its main points as it is presented. The receiver should set aside his own attitudes and be open-minded in order to comprehend the sender's objectives.

In previous chapters we have emphasized the importance of feedback in information systems. Examples are the life cycle of computer-based business systems, Management Information Systems, and project planning and status

FIGURE 9-1.
The communication process

FIGURE 9-2.
Tips for senders and receivers

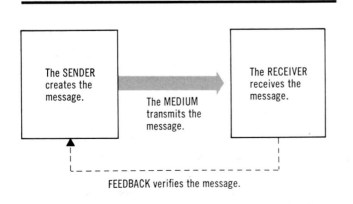

TIPS FOR THE SENDER	TIPS FOR THE RECEIVER
Organize your thoughts	Be alert and attentive
Know your receiver	Analyze the message
Use facts and evidence	Be open minded

FIGURE 9-3. Communications and managerial effectiveness

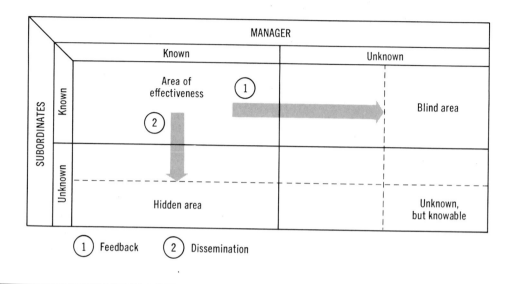

reporting. On a person-to-person basis, the analyst not only reports to a supervisor, but also often finds himself supervising the work of others. The analyst should be aware that if he encourages and reacts positively to feedback, he will increase his own effectiveness as a manager.

FIGURE 9-3, *Communications and managerial effectiveness,* depicts the importance of feedback and dissemination (of information) in managerial effectiveness. Four areas are shown, each representing an information-based relationship between a manager and subordinates:

1. *Area of effectiveness*—Known both to the manager and to the subordinates.
2. *Blind area*—Known to subordinates, but not known to the manager.
3. *Hidden area*—Known to the manager, but not known to the subordinates.
4. *Unknown, but knowable area*—Not known to the manager or to the subordinates, but potentially knowable.

By encouraging feedback, the manager is able to reduce the size of the blind area, and by disseminating information he is able to reduce the size of the hidden area. As shown by the dashed lines in Figure 9-3, the result of these actions is an enlargement of the manager's area of effectiveness and a reduction of the area representing information not known to either the manager or the subordinates. Thus, communication is not an event in time, but a continuous process. The effectiveness of this process depends on both present communication and past actions.

As Figure 9-1 shows, the remaining element of the communication process is the medium. It should be selected with both the message and the receiver in mind. The two primary media for transferring information are audio and visual. Effective communicators both "show and tell." All the tools of the systems analyst that we have discussed in this text (e.g., forms, codes, and charts) can be used to enhance communication. Let us now consider the two formal communication-oriented activities that systems analysts perform most often: technical writing and presentations.

TECHNICAL WRITING

Definition of technical writing

The written word is the most common conveyor of business information. For example, we have identified cumulative documentation as the key to the successful development of computer-based information systems. Throughout the life cycle of a business system, the systems analyst writes many different types of technical documents. Technical writing, as contrasted with many forms of nontechnical writing, is direct and to the point. Its purpose is to communicate facts. Therefore, easily understood words and short sentences are used to transmit information from the sender to the receiver. Some of the more important technical documents are policies and procedures, narratives, specifications, manuals, and reports.

As the list implies, the analyst must be qualified to prepare many types of documents. Brief descriptions of these documents illustrate their use as communication media. Examples of the first three types of documents (policies, procedures, and narratives) are included in this chapter because, although we will encounter and use them, we will not describe them in further detail in this book. The remaining three documents (specifications, manuals, and reports) are described in this chapter; however, examples are not provided at this time. In later chapters we will discuss in more detail the specifications, manuals, and reports that are of particular importance to the process of developing computer-based business systems.

Types of technical writing

Policies and Procedures. Policies are broad written guidelines for conduct or action. They are the result of top level decision making. Policies should be readable; that is, they should use clear sentences, tell who has authority, and state any exceptions. (Occasionally the systems analyst will encounter—and so should be sensitive to—"unwritten" policies.)

Procedures are subordinate to policies. *Procedures* are specific statements that tell how policies are to be carried out. They provide the series of logical steps by which repetitive business operations are performed. They state the necessary action, who is to perform it, and when it is to be performed.[1]

---

1. A network of related procedures for a significant business activity, e.g., payroll processing, is called a system. This is within the context of our use of the word "system"; however, it is not the primary meaning of "system" in this text.

FIGURE 9-4. Policy and procedure statement

THE ABCDEF CORPORATION	POLICY AND PROCEDURE	
SUBJECT: COMPUTER-BASED BUSINESS SYSTEMS: STUDY PHASE	DATE: 3/17/XX	NUMBER: CS-300-0
	PAGE: __1__ of __1__	SUPERCEDES: NEW
	APPROVED: *G. Washington* PRESIDENT	

POLICY:

     All Study Phase Activities for computer-based business systems shall be completed prior to the authorization of a Design Phase.

RESPONSIBILITY:	ACTION:
User	1. Prepares a Service Request, Form C-6-1.
Information Service	2. Performs an initial investigation.
	3. Prepares a Modified Service Request, Form C-6-1.
User	4. Reviews Modified Service Request.
	5. Issues a Project Directive, Form C-6-1.
Information Service	6. Prepares a formal definition of system performance.
	7. Performs a feasibility analysis.
	8. Prepares a Performance Specification, Form No. C-9-3.
	9. Prepares a Project Plan and Status Schedule, Form C-9-1.
	10. Prepares a Project Cost Estimate, Form C-10-0.
	11. Prepares a Study Phase Report, Form No. C-10-1.
User	12. Reviews Study Phase Report.
	13. Issues Approval to Proceed, Form C-10-1.

Policies are collected in manuals called policy manuals; procedures are collected in procedure manuals. Since procedures relate to policies, a common practice is to include the policy statement in the procedure. When this is done, the policy appears at the top of the first page and is followed by the procedure, as shown in FIGURE 9-4, *Policy and procedure statement*. The particular format in which the example policy and procedure statement is laid out is called play-script. Although other formats, such as outlines and narratives, are used for policy and procedure statements, playscript is one of the most effective formats. The actors (i.e., the doers) are shown clearly on the left side of the page; the steps of the procedure are numbered in sequence; and the actions are expressed in simple sentences using action verbs. The allowance for white space adds to the statement's readability.

Narratives. The narrative tells a story and is the most informal type of technical writing. Technical reports frequently contain many passages which are best communicated in a storytelling fashion, for example, introductions, summaries, problem statements, and background discussions. The narrative technique also may be used to describe flowcharts and to define words or concepts in context. Thus, in Chapter 4, the description of Figure 4-2 is a type of narrative. The paragraph you are reading is an example of a narrative description.

Specifications. Specifications are reference documents that contain basic detailed data. They are the most formal and rigid type of technical document and may even include technical drawings. Specifications may accompany procedures or narratives. For example, if we consider the step-by-step process for rebuilding an automobile engine to be a procedure, the technical description of the engine and its component parts is a specification.

As was illustrated in Figure 2-2 of Chapter 2, the process of managing the life cycle of computer-based business systems depends upon the creation of three critical specifications: the Performance Specification, the Design Specification, and the System Specification. We shall describe these specifications in Chapters 14, 20, and 24, respectively.

Manuals. Manuals are printed and assembled pages of instructional material. Manuals usually are written for the use of a homogeneous group of people, and so most corporations have many different manuals. However, they are of four basic types:

1. *Employee manuals:* introduce the employee to the company, to its rules, and to his benefits.

2. *Policy and procedure manuals:* used to collect policies and procedures.

3. *Organization manuals:* contain organization charts and organization function lists.

4. *Specialty manuals:* prepared to meet the needs of different occupational groups.

The manuals with which we will be most concerned are the three types of specialty manuals required before a computer-based business system can be considered operational. These are (1) the programmer's reference manuals; (2) the operator's reference manuals; and (3) the users' reference manuals. We shall discuss the format and content of these reference manuals in Chapter 22: Preparing for Implementation.

Reports. A report is a formal communication of results and conclusions due to a particular set of actions; it summarizes work that has been performed. The types of reports of most importance to us are the decision-oriented reports prepared at the conclusion of each phase of the computer-based business system life cycle. In particular, these are the Study Phase report, the Design Phase report, and the Development Phase report. These reports are described in Chapters 14, 20, and 24 respectively.

PRESENTATIONS

Preparing for the presentation

Presentations of plans or results are made in order to influence people and to obtain decisions. Because they are decision-oriented, presentations are a form of selling. Analysts are expected to do more than just present facts; they are expected to have opinions. After all, by the time that an analyst has immersed himself at length in a problem, he has to have developed some conclusions and recommendations that he believes to be in the best interest of the company. They are what he must "sell."

All the principles of good communications discussed in this chapter should be applied to the preparation of presentations. The analyst should use both verbal and visual techniques. Some pointers are:

1. *Participate in the selection of people to attend the presentation.* Attempt to have there the individuals who will benefit most from the project and who are most involved in it at present.

2. *Know the names, titles, and attitudes (prejudices?) of all of the attendees.* Prepare to counter anticipated objections. *Above all, know which person is the decision maker.*

3. *Select a title for your subject* that is easy to remember. For example, call it the "Inventory Cleanup Project" instead of "Project 13A."

4. *Keep your presentation simple.* Use words that will be understood. Organize your main points step-by-step so that they lead to your conclusion.

5. *Make the intangible tangible.* "Before" and "after" comparisons are effective. Examples are comparisons of the number of required inventory items; reductions in out-of-inventory items; reductions in cost, time, and personnel.

6. *Use visual aids.* Visual aids that can be used in most conference rooms are flip charts (large sheets of paper which can be clipped together and "flipped" over to accompany a verbal presentation), chalkboards, and overhead projectors.

7. *Keep an eye on the clock.* Do not overstay your welcome. Complete your presentation within the allocated time. Allow approximately 25 percent of your time for discussion.

8. *Rehearse your presentation.* Almost nothing is more disconcerting than not being able to operate equipment. Be particularly aware of unintentional nonverbal communication. You will be communicating to the audience by your dress and manners, by your vocabulary, by your posture, by your sense of humor, and by your enthusiasm.

Scheduling the presentation

Frequently, the analyst is faced with the prospect of presenting material to several different groups. These groups may have different interests and represent different levels of management. The analyst must decide whether to start the presentations at the top level or at a lower level. The top level is determined by the scope of the application. A department head is the top level manager for systems affecting only his department; the president of the company may be the top level manager for a system with corporate-wide impact. It is advantageous if the material to be presented is familiar to top management and if there is genuine top level interest in the system. A top level presentation can result in formal management backing, giving the analyst an aura of authority. Also, if the project is rejected at the top management level, there is no need to schedule other meetings.

The advantage of starting at lower levels is the opportunity to inform and to "sell" the system to operational people. Often managers consult with their subordinates after hearing a presentation and before making a decision. A subordinate who feels that he has been left out can "poison" the mind of his supervisor against a good system. Most managers are realists; they know that a poor system may be made to work if accepted and that a good system will not work if not accepted.

A recommended approach is to work with the supervisor who is most directly involved with the system and who has the most to gain from its success. He can assist the analyst in gaining the support of his subordinates and can help to pre-sell his own management. He and the analyst, jointly, can decide when and how to present the project to top management.

Sometimes it is desirable to make informal presentations. These provide opportunities to pre-sell and to get valuable feedback without actually seeking a decision. Informal presentations, particularly to senior management, are valuable. However, a word of caution is in order. The analyst should plan for an informal presentation no less carefully than for a formal one. Because an informal presentation is less structured than a formal one, he must be prepared to be responsive to a broad range of topics and questions.

The presentation outcome

There are many possible outcomes from a management level presentation. Some typical outcomes are:

1. The analyst's recommendations are accepted.
2. The analyst's recommendations are accepted with modification.
3. Some recommendations are accepted and others are rejected.
4. A decision is deferred on all recommendations.
5. The project is terminated.

In the case of the first two, the analyst is free to move forward. The second two usually mean that he has additional work to do and must schedule another presentation. These outcomes are not necessarily bad. The analyst can have received valuable feedback and direction, and, in any event, many system projects have to be "sold" in increments.

One of the most important storm signals that an analyst can sense during a presentation is lack of user identification with the system. If he hears the managers who will be most affected by the system referring to it as "your (their)" system and not as "my (our)" system, the analyst knows that the system will not be accepted or successful until those attitudes are changed. This is the most important reason why it is necessary to work with a user-manager who has identified himself with the system.

If the project is terminated, the action the analyst should take is clear. He should update his documentation and file the project, analyze (and rationalize) his failures, smile, and look forward to his next assignment.

Within the context of this book, the outcomes of certain presentations are critical. These are the outcomes of the reviews held at the conclusion of each of the first three major phases of the computer-based business system life cycle: (1) the Study Phase review; (2) the Design Phase review; and (3) the Development Phase review. These reviews are critical because they are a structured inter-action with management for the purpose of obtaining a renewed commitment to the system.

Management interest normally is highest when a project is launched and when the system first becomes operational. (Of course, problems encountered as the system is being designed and developed may result in periods of intense management interest.) The interim reviews are a means of reminding management that a significant activity is underway. They also are a means of sustaining interest and support during periods when large expenditures of resources are being made for activities that are not wholly comprehensible to management because of their detailed or technical nature. The importance of these reviews is portrayed in FIG-URE 9-5, *Management interest and commitment patterns*. In this figure, the phases of the computer-based business system life cycle are spaced to simulate realistic time spans. Note that management interest is high at the onset of a program and then tends to decay as the project enters the Design and Development Phases. It is

FIGURE 9-5. Management interest and commitment patterns

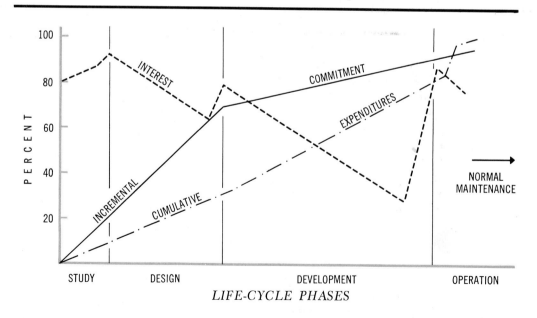

FIGURE 9-6. Incremental commitment and cumulative documentation in the life cycle of a computer-based business system

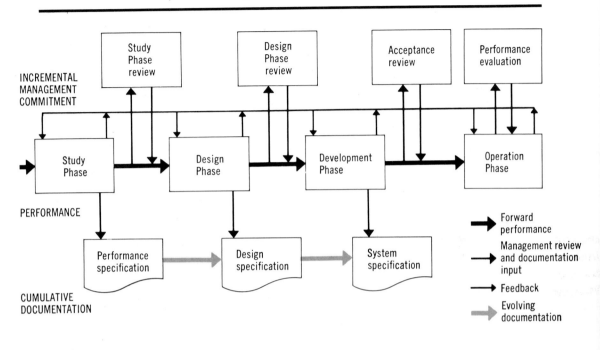

high again as the system approaches operational status and drops off after the initial operational problems have been overcome and the system qualifies for normal maintenance. The peaks shown in the graph of management interest are due to the scheduled Study, Design, and Development Phase reviews. As the commitment and expenditure graphs indicate, commitment tends to outstrip expenditure. Note that at the end of the Study Phase, when the cumulative expenditures are only 10 percent, the commitment is 25 percent. Similarly, the commitment is 70 percent at the beginning of the Development Phase, when expenditures are only 30 percent. Thus, the key management reviews rekindle and peak management interest and generate a new increment of management commitment at the end of each phase.

The communications-oriented concepts of "cumulative documentation" and "incremental commitment" are related in FIGURE 9-6, *Incremental commitment and cumulative documentation in the life cycle of a computer-based business system*. This figure is our familiar life cycle. In addition, the incremental commitment and cumulative documentation are identified to the ongoing processes of management and documentation.

Having returned to the life cycle of the computer-based business system, we conclude our discussion of communication. We will proceed to study each of the four life-cycle phases in the next four units of this text.

KEY TERMS

communication	*narrative*	*report*
policy	*specification*	*incremental commitment*
procedure	*manual*	

FOR DISCUSSION

1. Give an example of communication and identify each of the four elements (or lack thereof). Why is feedback necessary for effective communication?

2. Why do the authors state that "communication is not an event in time, but a continuous process"?

3. It has been estimated that communication is 80 percent visual. What visual communication processes were described in this chapter? Can you name some others?

4. Distinguish between policies and procedures. What purposes do narratives, specifications, manuals, and reports serve?

5. Discuss different approaches to scheduling presentations. How can an analyst sense a lack of user identification?

6. What are the differences and similarities between formal and informal presentations?

7. What is meant by the terms "cumulative documentation" and "incremental commitment"? How do they relate to effective communication? To the life cycle of computer-based business systems?

UNIT THREE

THE
STUDY
PHASE

10 Study Phase Overview

The Study Phase is the phase in which a problem is
identified, alternate solutions are evaluated, and the most
feasible solution is recommended. The goal of this
chapter is to introduce the major Study Phase activities
and show the relationships between them. You will
gain an overview and a perspective of the Study Phase
that will provide you with a reference and guide
as you study the specific topics in the chapters in
this unit.

STUDY PHASE ACTIVITIES

The Study Phase is the first phase of the effort to create a computer-based
business system, either a new one or a modification of an existing system. During
the Study Phase a preliminary analysis is carried out in sufficient depth to permit
a technical and economic evaluation. of the proposed system. At the conclusion
of the Study Phase, a decision is made whether or not to proceed with a Design
Phase. A formal project may not be established until a Design Phase is initiated.
However, the Study Phase is conducted in an organized, project-like manner. The
principal Study Phase activities, as depicted in the flowchart of FIGURE 10-1,
Study Phase activities for the computer-based business system, are these:

User Need. The creation of a computer-based business system begins with a
stated user need. This need may be a requirement for new information or for the
solution of a problem. The statement of need is a written request for systems
analysis service, which we shall refer to as an *information service request.* The
information service request may define the user's needs completely and may be
sufficient for an analyst to proceed with the system design. In this case, it would
be accepted as a "contract" between the sponsor and the analyst. However,
normally an initial investigation must be completed before a fully informed
response can be made. When this is the case, the request for service is identified

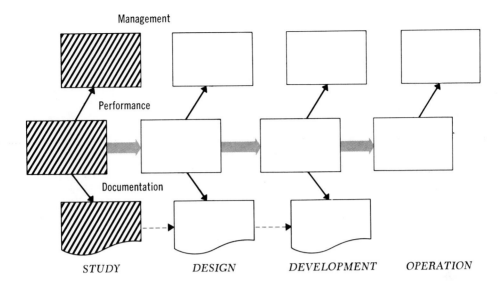

as a limited information service request, and an analyst is assigned to conduct an initial investigation.

Initial Investigation. The first steps in the initial investigation are directed toward clarifying the problem assignment and strengthening the analyst's background in the problem area. If there is an existing system, either manual or computer-based, which is performing some or all of the functions the new system is to perform, the analyst must study this system. After he becomes familiar with the system, he can investigate specific operations, particularly problem areas, in detail.

The analyst begins the initial investigation by studying the organization responsible for the current system, identifying product flow and information flow. Such a study of the existing organization provides the analyst with a background knowledge of the problem environment. The identification of product flow familiarizes him with the physical processes involved in making the product. The identification of information flow deals with the documents, such as forms, tapes, cards, and other data carriers, that control the operation of the current system. He studies information flow by finding and analyzing facts. Fact-finding activities include reviewing existing manuals and procedures, preparing questionnaires, and conducting personal interviews. Fact analysis is accomplished by techniques such as data element analysis, input-output analysis, recurring data analysis, and report use analysis.

After completing the initial investigation, the analyst organizes and summarizes the results of his fact-finding and fact-analysis activities. He now has a current information file and a comprehensive knowledge of the existing system. He can relate the cost and performance of the present system to the stated objectives of the study; he has identified the performance requirements for the

Figure 10-1. Study Phase activities for the computer-based business system

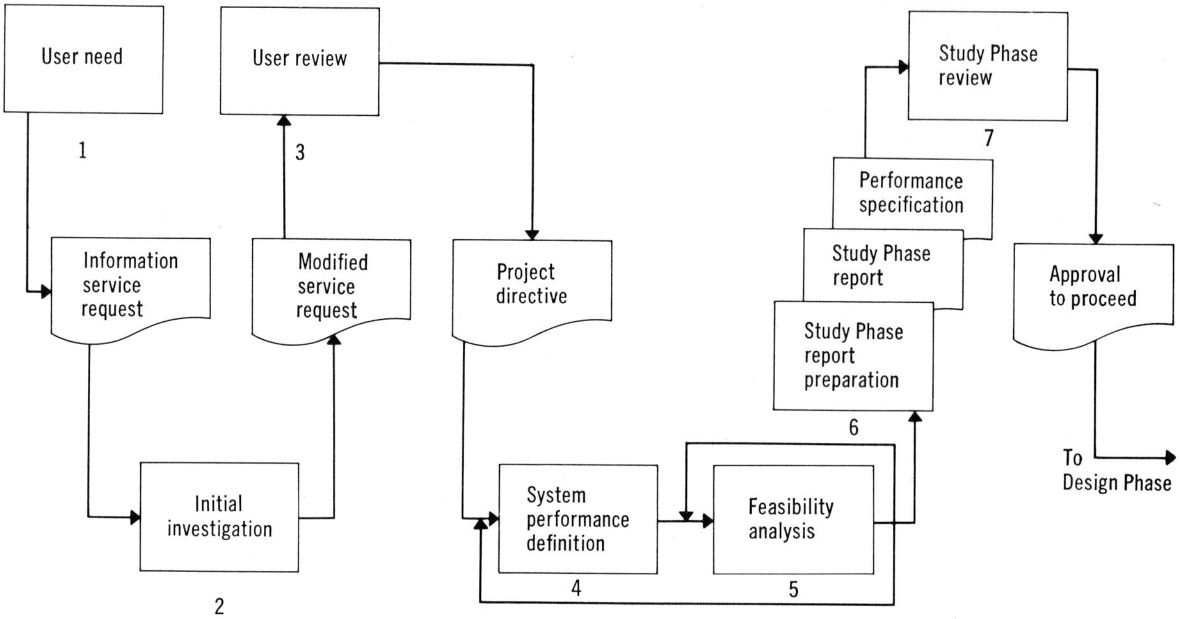

new or modified system and has identified problem constraints. He has reached some conclusions about discarding, modifying, or continuing the present system or some of its elements. He then summarizes and presents the results of the initial investigation to the user in the form of a modified Information Service Request.

User Review. The modified Information Service Request reflects the analyst's understanding of the problem and states his understanding of the system's objectives. The modified request is discussed with the user-sponsor, and additional revisions are made if necessary. With the concurrence of the user, the modified service request becomes the formal "contract" between the user-sponsor and the analyst. This "contract" is called a project directive. The project directive authorizes the analyst to proceed to define the formal, user-oriented performance requirements for the "new" system and to complete the Study Phase.

The Study Phase proceeds in two major sequences:

1. System performance definition: (a) statement of general constraints; (b) identification and ranking of specific objectives; and (c) description of outputs.

2. Feasibility analysis: (a) selection and description of candidate systems, including flowcharts, specific constraints, inputs, processing, and storage; and (b) selection (from the candidates) of the most feasible system.

System Performance Definition. The performance of the new system is defined by listing its specific objectives in order of priority and describing in detail the outputs to be produced. The outputs must be described in terms meaningful to potential users, not in "computerese." Typically, there are external and internal constraints which will limit the number of possible problem solutions the analyst can consider. He must take these into account as he relates outputs to objectives.

Feasibility Analysis. The feasibility of designing the system is determined by evaluating alternate methods of converting available input data into the required outputs to fulfill the system objectives. Each of these alternate methods is termed a "candidate" system. For each "candidate," an information-oriented flowchart is drawn. This flowchart traces information flow from input to output by identifying all data carriers (reports, forms, punched cards, etc.) required by the system. Then, a high-level system flowchart is prepared. It identifies the system data base and the major processing operations that must be performed on the input data to produce the desired outputs.

The constraints unique to each candidate are stated. Both the unique and general constraints are taken into account as each "candidate" system is evaluated.

"Candidate" systems are evaluated by identifying factors that significantly affect system cost and performance and by ranking each candidate in terms of these factors. Typical factors are cost, response time, development time, accuracy, and reliability. The feasibility study is concluded by the selection of the most suitable candidate.

As shown in Figure 10-1, two major feedback loops can occur during the Study Phase. The loop around the feasibility analysis block indicates the consideration of more than one system variation, or candidate. The loop around the system performance definition block indicates that the process of selecting a feasible system could include modification of the initially desired outputs.

Study Phase Report Preparation. After the feasibility study has been completed, a Study Phase report is prepared for the user-sponsor of the system. It contains a summary of the feasibility study and presents recommendations related to proceeding with the Design Phase. An essential part of the Study Phase report is a user-oriented Performance Specification. This specification is the first of the three major baseline specifications. If the recommendation is to proceed with a Design Phase, a project plan and a cost schedule are prepared, and they are included as part of the Study Phase report. These schedules provide detailed estimates for the Design Phase and gross estimates for the Development Phase of the system project. They also serve as bases for continuing and expanding project control.

Study Phase Review. The Study Phase report is reviewed with the user-sponsor and other affected management. If the recommendations of the report are accepted, the user issues a written approval to proceed. This approval includes an authorization for manpower and other resource expenditures required for the Design Phase.

FIGURE 10-2. Study Phase project plan and status report

PROJECT PLAN AND STATUS REPORT																				

PROJECT TITLE

PROJECT X

PROJECT STATUS SYMBOLS
O Satisfactory
□ Caution
△ Critical

S. A. Nallist

PROGRAMMER/ANALYST

PLANNING/PROGRESS SYMBOLS
□ Scheduled Progress   V Scheduled Completion
■ Actual Progress   ▼ Actual Completion

COMMITTED DATE 8/15/xx

COMPLETED DATE

STATUS DATE 3/1/xx

ACTIVITY/DOCUMENT	PERCENT COMPLETE	STATUS	PERIOD ENDING																	
			2	4	6	8	10	12	14	16	18	20	22	24	26				
STUDY PHASE	0	0												▼					
Initial Investigation	0	0		▼															
User Review	0	0		▼															
Project Directive	0	0																	
Sys. Perf. Definition	0	0				▼													
Feasibility Analysis	0	0						▼											
Performance Spec.	0	0							▼										
Study Phase Report	0	0							▼										
Study Phase Review	0	0									▼								

FIGURE 10-3. Study Phase project cost report

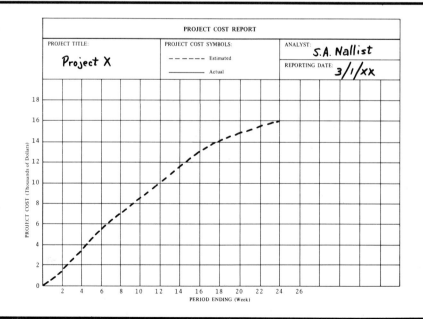

PROJECT COST REPORT

PROJECT TITLE:
Project X

PROJECT COST SYMBOLS:
– – – – – Estimated
————— Actual

ANALYST: S.A. Nallist
REPORTING DATE: 3/1/xx

PROJECT CONTROL

As stated in the preceding section, a project plan and a cost schedule are prepared before the Design Phase is initiated. It is good professional practice to introduce project control at the onset of the Study Phase if more than a minimal effort is contemplated. The elements of project control are (1) a project file, in which pertinent documents and working papers are organized and stored; (2) a project plan and status report chart; and (3) a project cost report chart.

FIGURE 10-2, *Study Phase project plan and status report,* displays a typical project plan. In this example the Study Phase is of twenty-four weeks duration. FIGURE 10-3, *Study Phase project cost report,* is a typical estimate of accompanying costs. These charts conform to the format presented in Chapter 7: Charting Techniques. The activities projected in Figure 10-2—the principal Study Phase activities—will be discussed in additional detail in the next chapters of this unit. As we proceed, we shall make use of an example accounts receivable system to provide a coherent and continuous thread between related life-cycle activities.

11

Initial
Investigation

After the need for a new system has been identified, the systems analyst makes an initial investigation to define the problem in detail. The goal of this chapter is to explain the major steps in performing an initial investigation. You will learn how an Information Service Request (ISR) is used as a method of communication between the user and the analyst; specific techniques for fact finding and fact analysis; and the importance of identifying the principal user.

PROBLEM IDENTIFICATION

Need identification

Either a user or a systems analyst may identify the need for a new or improved system. The user must react to external environmental conditions, such as government regulations; he must respond to his own management's request for additional information; he may become aware of the unsatisfactory performance of systems for which he is responsible. For instance, the manager of an Accounts Receivable department may become concerned about the repeated late billing of customers or about an increase in the percentage of delinquent accounts.

Similarly, a systems analyst who is familiar with an operational or administrative area may suggest improvements. Frequently a systems analyst is able to view systems and their interactions with a perspective that individuals involved in daily operations lack. Often problems come into focus after joint discussions between a user and an analyst, each of whom provides his own expertise and viewpoint.

The Information Service Request

For illustrative purposes, we will assume a typical industrial systems environment, one in which the Systems Analysis department is part of a larger information organization, which we will call the Information Services division. This division also is responsible for programming support and for computer operations. We will identify the formal request for systems support as an Information

Service Request (ISR). FIGURE 11-1, *Information Service Request,* is our ISR form. As a typical document of this type, it provides for:

1. *Job title:* Name assigned by user to the work requested.
2. *New or rev:* Identifies the request as a new job or a revised job.
3. *Requested date:* Date the request is submitted.
4. *Required date:* Date the job should be completed.
5. *Objective:* Briefly states the principal purposes of the job.
6. *Labor:* Authorization to expend labor hours and dollars (amount).
7. *Other:* Authorization to expend nonlabor (e.g., computer time) hours and dollars (amount).
8. *Anticipated benefits:* Lists the principal benefits (e.g., cost savings, faster response) the company will derive from the system.
9. *Output descriptions:* For each principal output:
   frequency—how often the output is required.
   quantity—number of distinct outputs (volume).
   pages—number of pages per report.
   copies—number of sets of output.
   description—pertinent output information,
      e.g., distribution, special paper, controls.
10. *Input description:* For each principal input:
    frequency—how often the input will be received.
    quantity—number of source documents.
    description—pertinent input information,
       e.g., location, availability, controls.
11. *To be filled out by requestor:*
    Requested by—name, department, title, telephone.
    Approved by—name, department, title, telephone.
12. *To be filled out by Information Services:*
    File number—identifier assigned to request by Information Services.
    Accepted or not accepted—explained, as necessary, in remarks.
    Signature—name, department, title, telephone.
    Remarks—filled in by Information Services as appropriate, e.g., explanation of nonacceptance, indication of limits on the ISR, request for additional information, or identification of an analyst assigned to the job.
13. *Additional information:* The requestor may use the reverse side of the form, additional pages of the form, or other supplemental pages, as appropriate, to describe more fully any part of the Information Service Request.

Normally, a substantive ISR is not submitted until after discussions have taken place between representatives of the user organization and the Computer Service division.

There are two types of affirmative responses to an ISR. The first response is a "can do" response. If all the data and other resources required to perform the task within the authorized expenditure and time limits are available, the ISR can be accepted without modification as a project directive. This means that work can commence on the entire job.

FIGURE 11-1. Information Service Request

INFORMATION SERVICE REQUEST	Page ___ of ___

(Form reproduced below)

```
┌─────────────────────────────────────────────────────────────────────────────┐
│        INFORMATION SERVICE REQUEST              Page ___ of ___              │
├──────────────────────────────┬──────┬─────────────────┬─────────────────────┤
│ JOB TITLE:                    │NEW □ │ REQUESTED DATE: │ REQUIRED DATE:      │
│                              │REV.□ │                 │                     │
├──────────────────────────────┴──────┴─────────────────┴─────────────────────┤
│                                            AUTHORIZATION                     │
│ OBJECTIVE:                              LABOR          │     OTHER           │
│                                   HOURS │ AMOUNT │ HOURS │ AMOUNT            │
├─────────────────────────────────────────────────────────────────────────────┤
│ ANTICIPATED BENEFITS:                                                        │
├──────────────────────────────┬──────────────────────────────────────────────┤
│      OUTPUT DESCRIPTION       │           INPUT DESCRIPTION                  │
│ TITLE:                        │ TITLE:                                       │
│ FREQUENCY:     QUANTITY:      │ FREQUENCY:                                   │
│ PAGES:         COPIES:        │ QUANTITY:                                    │
│ DESCRIPTION:                  │ DESCRIPTION:                                 │
│                               │                                              │
│ TITLE:                        │ TITLE:                                       │
│ FREQUENCY:     QUANTITY:      │ FREQUENCY:                                   │
│ PAGES:         COPIES:        │ QUANTITY:                                    │
│ DESCRIPTION:                  │ DESCRIPTION:                                 │
├─────────────────────────────────────────────────────────────────────────────┤
│              TO BE FILLED OUT BY REQUESTOR                                   │
│ REQUESTED BY:        │ DEPARTMENT: │ TITLE: │ TELEPHONE:                     │
│ APPROVED BY:         │ DEPARTMENT: │ TITLE: │ TELEPHONE:                     │
├─────────────────────────────────────────────────────────────────────────────┤
│           TO BE FILLED OUT BY INFORMATION SERVICES                           │
│ FILE NO:             │ ACCEPTED □  NOT ACCEPTED □                            │
│ SIGNATURE:           │ DEPARTMENT: │ TITLE: │ TELEPHONE:                     │
│ REMARKS:             │                                                       │
│                                                                             │
├──────────────────────┬──────────────────────────────────────────────────────┤
│ FORM NO: C-6-1       │ ADDITIONAL INFORMATION: USE REVERSE SIDE OR EXTRA PAGES│
└──────────────────────┴──────────────────────────────────────────────────────┘
```

However, if the job is new, if the system is large, or if many factors are unknown, another type of response usually is made. The ISR is identified as "limited" in the remarks section of the Information Service Request. Typically, a limited ISR authorizes an initial investigation so that the analyst can study the problem and develop a more definitive ISR before major expenditures are authorized for the remainder of the Study Phase. Often, the limited ISR cannot identify or define all the outputs and inputs of the system under study. In this case preliminary best estimates are made or a "to be determined" (T.B.D.) entry is made. After the initial investigation has been completed, a modified ISR is prepared by the analyst and reviewed with the user-sponsor. The modified ISR is the project directive suggested by the analyst. During the review of the modified ISR with the user, additional changes may be made. If the result of the review is to proceed with the job, a final ISR is drafted. When approved by the appropriate user and Information Service managers, the final ISR becomes a "contract" between the user and the analyst.

This "contract," the *project directive,* as distinguished from less comprehensive or intermediate Information Service Requests, is the formal, mutual commitment that binds the user and the analyst throughout an information system project. After identifying and describing the principal elements of an initial investigation, we will conclude this chapter with a discussion of the project directive.

THE INITIAL INVESTIGATION

Project initiation

The analyst commences an initial investigation armed with a limited ISR. FIGURE 11-2, *Limited Information Service Request—partial,* is an example of one page of a limited ISR. This ISR authorizes an initial investigation for an accounts receivable system. Unknown items (e.g., number of copies) are identified as "to be determined" (T.B.D.). When he starts the initial investigation, the systems

FIGURE 11-2. Limited Information Service Request—partial

| INFORMATION SERVICE REQUEST | Page 1 of 3 |

| JOB TITLE: Initial Investigation of a Modified Accounts Receivable System | NEW ☒ REV. ☐ | REQUESTED DATE: 9/1/xx | REQUIRED DATE: 9/22/xx |

AUTHORIZATION

OBJECTIVE: To improve the efficiency of customer billing and account collection	LABOR		OTHER	
	HOURS	AMOUNT	HOURS	AMOUNT
	120	$1200	0	0

ANTICIPATED BENEFITS: 1. Faster customer billing.
2. Reduction in Delinquent Accounts.

OUTPUT DESCRIPTION	INPUT DESCRIPTION
TITLE: Customer Monthly Statement	TITLE: Billing Notice
FREQUENCY: Monthly QUANTITY: 7,000	FREQUENCY: Daily
PAGES: 1 COPIES: T.B.D.	QUANTITY: 300
DESCRIPTION: To be printed on a multi-part form.	DESCRIPTION: Generated as a copy of the Sales Order.
TITLE: A/R Transaction Register	TITLE: Payment/Credit Memorandum
FREQUENCY: Daily QUANTITY: 1	FREQUENCY: Daily
PAGES: T.B.D. COPIES: T.B.D.	QUANTITY: 1,000 min.
DESCRIPTION: For use of A/R and Credit Departments	DESCRIPTION: Prepared by Credit Department to enter customer payments and credits.

TO BE FILLED OUT BY REQUESTOR

| REQUESTED BY: J. Davis | DEPARTMENT: 310 | TITLE: Head A/R Dept. | TELEPHONE: X3250 |
| APPROVED BY: Ben Franklin | DEPARTMENT: 300 | TITLE: Manager Accounting Div. | TELEPHONE: X3208 |

TO BE FILLED OUT BY INFORMATION SERVICES

| FILE NO: ISR-310-1 | ACCEPTED ☒   NOT ACCEPTED ☐ |
| SIGNATURE: C. Hampton | DEPARTMENT: 200 | TITLE: Manager Info. Ser. Div. | TELEPHONE: X2670 |

REMARKS: This is a limited ISR. All output and input descriptions are tentative. J. Herring, Senior Systems Analyst, is assigned to conduct an Initial Investigation.

| FORM NO: C–6–1 | ADDITIONAL INFORMATION: USE REVERSE SIDE OR EXTRA PAGES |

FIGURE 11-3. Information memorandum

MEMORANDUM

TO: All Department Heads and Supervisors, Accounting Division.

COPIES TO: Vice President, Finance; Vice President, Sales; Division
           Managers; Head, Systems Analysis Department, J. Herring; File.

FROM: Manager, Accounting Division

SUBJECT: Study of a Modified Accounts Receivable System (MARS)

DATE: September 1, 19XX

I have requested that the Systems Analysis department of our Information
Services Division initiate a study of the feasibility of modifying our
present manual accounts receivable system. As you are aware, we are currently experiencing difficulties in billing customers promptly and in
identifying and collecting delinquent account payments. An additional
reason, stemming from our business success, is an anticipated acceler-
ated growth in the number of new accounts and in the daily volume of
invoices.

Ms. J. Herring has been assigned the responsibility for conducting an
initial investigation related to MARS. She will be working most closely with Mr. G. Davis, Head of the Accounts Receivable Department.
However, I have asked that Ms. Herring visit with each Accounting
Division department head preparatory to beginning her investigation
in order to explain her approach to this assignment. I will appreciate
your cooperation in aiding her to familiarize herself with all of the
current accounting operations and documentation related to accounts
receivable.

Please inform your personnel of Ms. Herring's assignment and solicit
their participation in an area which can contribute significantly to the
profitability of our corporation.

Ben Franklin

Ben Franklin
Manager, Accounting Division

Approved:

Alex Hamilton

Alex Hamilton
Vice President, Finance

---

analyst must contact individuals in the user's organization and in other organizations that may be affected by the system. These individuals will be concerned
(and often with cause) about the analyst's activities. Therefore, it is a good practice for a senior user-manager to issue an information memorandum stating the
general purpose of the investigation and establishing the identity and responsibilities of the systems analyst. This memorandum should originate at the managerial level, where responsibility lies for all activities the system may affect.
FIGURE 11-3, *Information memorandum*, shows an information memorandum related to an initial investigation of a modified accounts receivable system. This
system has been given the acronym of MARS.

The scope of the initial investigation may vary from a brief one-person effort to an extensive series of activities requiring the participation of many individuals. Regardless of the size of the initial investigation, the analyst should perform the investigation within a project management framework. This framework should include (1) a project file; (2) a project plan and status report chart; and (3) a project cost report chart.

A project file is essential to the management of systems projects because of the volume of data that must be collected, digested, and summarized. The major elements of a project file are:

1. The Information Service Request and other directives and memoranda received by the project.
2. Plans and schedules.
3. Collected documentation and working papers.
4. Memoranda and reports produced by the project.

Of course, the scope and depth of the initial investigation and of the project management framework must be scaled to the size of the assignment. However, effective project management is required in order to provide documentation of completed work and a sound basis for continuing the Study Phase.

The principal activities managed and performed during an initial investigation are background analysis, fact finding, fact analysis, and the organization and presentation of results.

Background analysis

The analyst makes background analyses related to the proposed application in order to familiarize himself with the organization environment and with the physical processes related to the new or revised system. The analyst must understand the structure of the organization within which the current system is operating and within which (often after considerable alteration) the new system will be expected to operate. He must determine the interactions between procedures and organization. Often, complex procedures are the result of inefficient organization. The analyst may have occasion to recommend organizational changes. He should, therefore, (1) obtain or prepare organization charts; (2) obtain or prepare organizational function lists; and (3) learn the names and duties of the people shown in the organization charts.

Since product flow deals with the movement of material and with the physical operations performed upon that material, the analyst observes these physical processes to acquire a "feel" for them. This "feel" is important if he expects to conceive and implement systems that will perform in an actual working environment. As an example, the manufacturing processes for producing a large volume of small components, such as integrated circuits, are quite different from those for producing a relatively low volume of large items, such as computers, although each computer contains large quantities of integrated circuits. The systems for controlling each of these types of operations are different. The former may be highly repetitive and component-oriented, while the latter may be nonrepetitive and system-oriented.

After he has acquired the necessary background knowledge, the analyst investigates the information environment in which the proposed system is to operate. To do this, he finds and analyzes facts and then organizes and summarizes them.

Fact-finding techniques

The analyst collects data from two principal sources: written documents and personnel who are knowledgeable about or involved in the operation of the system under study. The analyst selects the fact-finding techniques he judges to be most appropriate to the situation. Some systems are well documented; others are not. In some instances, interviewing all operating personnel may be effective; in others, interviews should be conducted on a very selective basis.

A list of fact-finding techniques that analysts often employ includes (1) data collection, (2) correspondence and questionnaires, (3) personal interviews, (4) observation, and (5) research.

Data Collection. In this first fact-finding step, the analyst gathers and organizes all the documents that are data carriers for the system under investigation. Examples of data carriers are forms, records, reports, manuals, and procedures. The analyst must be cautious in relying upon the validity of collected documents. Procedures, for example, may not have been updated to include recent changes to the system. Day-to-day problems may have introduced changes that are not reflected in the system documentation. And, of course, some people have a tendency to ignore procedures. Therefore, unless he has a recent familiarity with the system and with its operating personnel, the analyst needs current information. He can obtain this information through correspondence, including questionnaires; through personal interviews; and by direct observation.

Correspondence and Questionnaires. One method by which the analyst can determine if a particular procedure is current and is being followed is to request that the individuals responsible for specific activities verify the procedure. The analyst may accomplish this by marking or reproducing appropriate sections of manuals or procedures and sending them to the responsible persons along with an explanatory letter.

Correspondence enables the analyst to explain the purpose of his activities and to inform people of what he expects from them. It is particularly important that interviews be preceded by correspondence defining the subject area and the specific topics to be reviewed.

The questionnaire is an important and often effective type of correspondence. For example, it may be the only efficient method of obtaining responses from a large number of people, particularly if they are widely scattered or in remote locations. Questionnaires should be brief in order to increase the promptness and probability of response. The questionnaire also can be used to solicit responses to specific questions from individuals. However, because of the possibility of misinterpretation, questionnaires should be followed up by personal interviews

FIGURE 11-4. A questionnaire

TO: P. Levier, Manager, Credit Department

FROM: Judy Herring

SUBJECT: Modified Accounts Receivable System (MARS)

DATE: October 1, 19XX

I have used the manuals and procedures which you sent me to
prepare a grid flowchart. This flowchart reflects my understanding of the flow of documents between the customer, the
Shipping department, the Accounts Receivable department, and
the Credit department. A copy of my flowchart and accompanying
input-output analysis sheets are attached to this memorandum.
I would like to discuss the chart with you and will call you
for an appointment in a few days. I also would appreciate
it if, at the same meeting, you could provide me with answers
to the following questions:

1. How many days after the end of the month did you
   receive your most recent customer statements?

2. Have you observed an increasing delay in receipt of
   your copies of the customer statements? If so, to
   what do you attribute the delay?

3. Do the customer statements contain all of the information you need to send out delinquent account notices?
   If not, what changes would you suggest?

4. Are there alternatives to monthly billing, such as
   cycle billing, which would improve the efficiency
   of monthly . . .

---

whenever possible. FIGURE 11-4, *A questionnaire,* is an example of question-oriented correspondence between an analyst and an individual, in this case, a Credit department manager. Note that an effort has been made to make the questions straightforward and unambiguous.

Personal Interview. The personal interview is one of the most fruitful methods of obtaining information. An interview is a person-to-person communication. Hence, the guidelines for effective presentations described in Chapter 9: Communications should be observed. However, the analyst is more of a receiver than a sender when he is conducting an interview. Although it is valid for the analyst to use the interview to explain his project and to "sell" himself, he primarily is seeking information. Therefore, he must remember to be a good listener.

Interviews are critical because people are the most important ingredient of any system. The success or failure of a system often depends upon the acceptance of the analyst by the personnel who are affected by the system. The following are some interview guidelines:

1. Plan the interview just as carefully as you would plan a presentation.

2. Adhere to your plan by keeping the interview pertinent. However, be flexible. Do not "force" the interview to follow a preconceived pattern.

3. Be informed, but do not attempt to present yourself as "the expert."

4. Arrange for a meeting time and place free from interruptions and other distractions.

5. Be punctual.

6. Know the name and position of the person you are interviewing.

7. Be courteous at all times.

8. Avoid the use of potentially "threatening" devices, such as tape recorders and cameras.

These guidelines are intended to help the analyst to create an atmosphere of cooperation, confidence, and understanding. This type of atmosphere is conducive to effective communication; however, it is difficult to create. The difficulty often is explained by describing the types of "personalities" that the interviewer may encounter. Typical descriptions are caricatures that classify people as "worriers," "snoopers," "old timers," etc. These caricatures are demeaning to the interviewer and the interviewee. Individuals deserve respect. The factors by which they are motivated are complex. Abraham Maslow defined a widely accepted ascending hierarchy of the needs of individuals in his classic book, *Motivation and Personality*.[1]

1. Physiological needs.
2. Safety needs.
3. Belonging and love needs.
4. Need for self-esteem and the esteem of others.
5. Self-actualization needs.
6. Cognitive needs.
7. Aesthetic needs.

Except for self-actualization and cognitive needs, the list is self-explanatory. Self-actualization refers to a self-started growth that encourages people to be what they are best suited to be. Cognitive needs refer to one's impulse to understand and to explain. Higher order needs usually emerge only after the lower order needs are satisfied. Thus, it is unlikely that cognitive needs could be gratified by an individual who perceived himself to be deprived of physiological or safety needs.

When it is likely that the solution to a problem will involve the use of a computer, many individuals become fearful. They sense a threat to the gratification of basic needs, such as physiological needs and safety needs. Unfortunately, their fears often are justified because computers can introduce major changes. However, most companies do not want to lose the services of skilled and loyal employees. Very often these employees are or can become qualified to perform important functions in the new system. Also, it usually is less expensive (and more humanitarian) to retrain employees of proven worth to the company than it is to recruit and indoctrinate new employees.

---

1. Abraham Maslow, *Motivation and Personality* (New York: Harper and Brothers, 1954).

TEST

As an analyst, you should attempt to motivate individuals to work toward the success of the new system. Frederick Herzberg,[2] a psychologist who has devoted many years to the study of motivation, developed insights which should be of value to the analyst. Professor Herzberg distinguishes between *motivating* factors and *hygiene* factors. The motivators are the primary cause of job satisfaction; they relate to job content. The hygiene factors do not motivate, but cause dissatisfaction if they are absent. They relate to job environment. Motivators include achievement of something useful, recognition of achievement, meaningful work, responsibility for decisions, advancement, and growth.

Hygiene factors include relationship with supervisors, salary, status, security, and working conditions. Unhappiness results if these factors are not present. However, their presence does not contribute nearly as much to job satisfaction as the presence of motivators does. Hence, a systems analyst should describe the roles of individuals in the new system in terms of motivators whenever he can.

It is good professional practice for the analyst to schedule his first interviews with management personnel. He should solicit their aid in scheduling interviews with employees under their supervision. The analyst should attempt to enlist user-managers as his allies in quieting the concerns of their subordinates and in encouraging support for the new system.

If the analyst is successful in the conduct of interviews, he will have not only obtained information, but also gained the support and confidence of the people who can make his project succeed or fail. He needs this support throughout all the phases of the life cycle of the business system.

Observation. In the course of data collection, interviewing, and other fact-finding activities, an experienced analyst observes the operation of the ongoing system. He begins to formulate questions and to draw conclusions on the basis of what he sees going on around him. A skilled analyst is able to discipline his powers of observation and recall. By "walking through" operations and seeing for himself, he is able to correlate work flow and data flow and to identify anomalies.

Observation is a continuous process. It usually is informal. However, there also are formal observation techniques the analyst may employ. For example, he may sample operations at predetermined or random times. He may perform statistical analyses. One observation technique that often is effective with manual systems is the construction of procedure analysis charts of the type described in Chapter 8: Flowcharting. Such a flowchart might show that a clerk in the Credit department makes frequent, lengthy trips to the Accounts Receivable department to check ledger cards to locate specific items for which payment may have been made. From this observation the analyst might conclude that he had identified one possible reason for delays in account collections.

Research. The final fact-finding technique we will mention is research. Research is of particular importance when a new application is being considered

---

2. Frederick Herzberg, "One more time: How do you motivate employees?" *Harvard Business Review* (Jan.-Feb. 1968).

because it is a means of stimulating creative approaches to problem solving. All the fact-finding methods we have discussed are forms of in-house research. However, there are many out-of-house sources of information. These include trade and professional publications, such as the *Journal for Systems Management,* published by the Association for Systems Management (ASM), and the *Journal of Data Management,* published by the Data Processing Management Association (DPMA). Other organizations, such as the American Management Association, also publish books and reports that provide detailed information in specific applications areas.

Computer-oriented news publications, such as *Datamation* and *Computer World,* provide current articles to help an analyst to keep informed about hardware, software, and application developments.

Government publications often are pertinent, particularly as a means of obtaining background information. And, of course, libraries not only are sources of information, but also contain indexes to a large volume of periodical literature.

A major problem with much of the literature available to an analyst is that it may be out of date by the time it is in print. Two relatively time-current research resources are vendors and personal contacts. Vendors, such as the IBM Corporation, have found that by providing "applications" assistance to their customers, they can increase the effectiveness of and enlarge the market for their products. An analyst who can distinguish between his real needs and the possible overenthusiasm of a vendor can tap this rich research resource.

Analysts should establish and maintain contacts with their counterparts in other companies. One highly recommended method for making such contacts is membership and active participation in a professional society, such as the Association for Systems Management or the Data Processing Management Association. These organizations conduct many professional seminars related to current topics. Also, visits to companies with similar problems and the exchange of ideas with their analysts can be rewarding.

Fact-analysis techniques

Fact finding and fact analysis are related activities. As he collects information, the efficient analyst organizes it, analyzes it, and uses it to identify additional information needs. There are many useful techniques for the organization and analysis of collected documents. These techniques provide the analyst with insight into the interaction between organizational elements, personnel, and information flow. Four techniques we will discuss are:

1. Data element analysis
2. Input-output analysis
3. Recurring data analysis
4. Report use analysis

Data Element Analysis. Through this technique the analyst assures himself that he understands the meaning of the data names and the codes which appear in the manuals, procedures, charts, and other forms of documentation he has collected. One method of data element analysis has two steps:

1. Assign a number to each data element or code that appears upon a document.

2. Head a separate piece of paper with the title or other identification of the document, and write the meaning of each numbered data element or code.

FIGURE 11-5, *Document numbered for data element analysis*, is an example of a document, in this case a customer monthly statement, taken through the first step. FIGURE 11-6, *Data element analysis*, is a partial analysis of the same document.

The analyst employs his knowledge of code classification and construction in data element analysis. He must be able not only to understand the codes and their elements, but also to recommend meaningful improvements.

Similarly, he uses his knowledge of forms analysis and design to determine whether a form is adequate. Very often he will recommend the redesign of forms as a means of reducing error and improving information flow.

FIGURE 11-5.
Document numbered for data element analysis

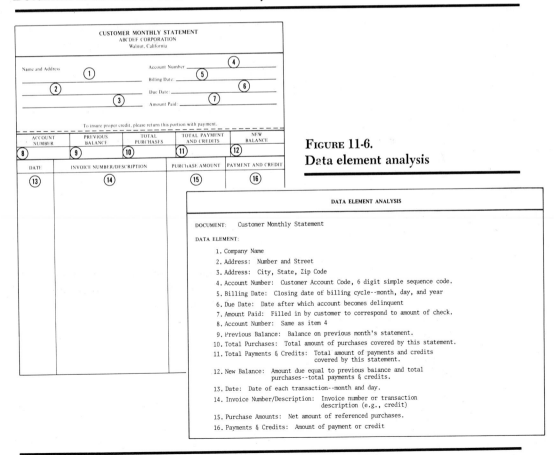

FIGURE 11-6.
Data element analysis

DATA ELEMENT ANALYSIS

DOCUMENT: Customer Monthly Statement

DATA ELEMENT:

1. Company Name
2. Address: Number and Street
3. Address: City, State, Zip Code
4. Account Number: Customer Account Code, 6 digit simple sequence code.
5. Billing Date: Closing date of billing cycle--month, day, and year
6. Due Date: Date after which account becomes delinquent
7. Amount Paid: Filled in by customer to correspond to amount of check.
8. Account Number: Same as item 4
9. Previous Balance: Balance on previous month's statement.
10. Total Purchases: Total amount of purchases covered by this statement.
11. Total Payments & Credits: Total amount of payments and credits covered by this statement.
12. New Balance: Amount due equal to previous balance and total purchases--total payments & credits.
13. Date: Date of each transaction--month and day.
14. Invoice Number/Description: Invoice number or transaction description (e.g., credit)
15. Purchase Amounts: Net amount of referenced purchases.
16. Payments & Credits: Amount of payment or credit

Input-Output Analysis. This is a general term for analysis techniques based on the concept of a system as a process that converts inputs into outputs. Flowcharts, for example, are excellent input-output analysis tools. The systems analyst constructs a grid-type information-oriented flowchart as soon as he feels that he has a sufficient understanding of the system to do so. This accomplishes two things. First, he acquires meaningful "pictures" of connections between the information elements of the system. Second, the effort to draw flowcharts pinpoints areas in which his understanding may not be complete. FIGURE 11-7, *Information-oriented*

FIGURE 11-7. Information-oriented flowchart for a manual accounts receivable system

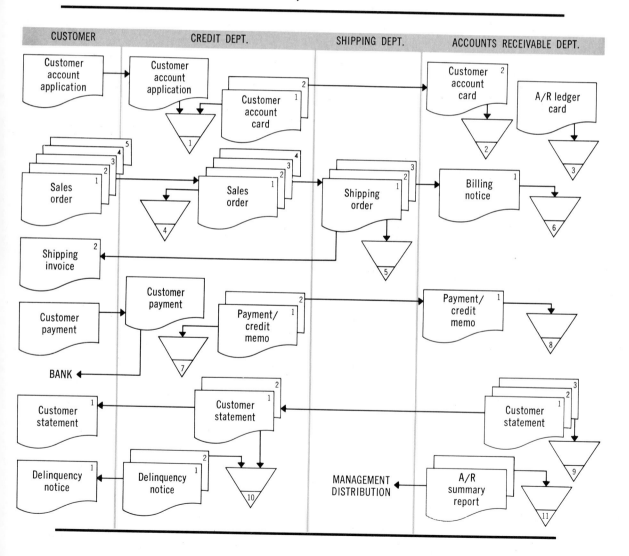

FIGURE 11-8. Input-output analysis sheet

INPUT-OUTPUT ANALYSIS SHEET		
ORGANIZATION: Credit Department	SYSTEM: Accounts Receivable	DATE: 9/3/XX
INPUT	**FUNCTION/FILES**	**OUTPUT**
Customer Account Application	Approves Credit. Enters Credit Limit on Application. Orders Credit Card. Prepares Customer Account Card in duplicate. Forwards duplicate of Customer Account Card to A/R Dept. Staples Customer Account Application to back of original Customer Account Card and stores in Customer Account File. (File No. 1)	Customer Account Card
Sales Order	Confirms customer credit. Files Copy 4 of the Sales Order (File No. 4) and forwards copies 1, 2, and 3 to the Shipping Department.	Sales Order (Copies 1, 2, and 3)
Customer Payments	Checks amount of payment against total due and indication of amount enclosed. Transmits checks (accompanied by a check listing) to the bank. Prepares a Payment/Credit Memo in duplicate. Files duplicate (File No. 7) and forwards original to A/R Department	Payment/Credit Memo
Customer Statement	Checks customer statement for delinquent accounts and prepares delinquency notices. Mails customer statement (with delinquency notice if required). Files duplicate copies. (File No. 10)	Delinquency Notice

flowchart for a manual accounts receivable system, is an example of this type of forms-oriented flowchart. Input-output analysis sheets can then be prepared for each organization, or entity, listed on the flowchart. These sheets identify the input, output, processing, and filing functions the organization performs. FIGURE 11-8, *Input-output analysis sheet,* is an example of one page of a sheet prepared to correspond to the Credit department column on the flowchart of Figure 11-7. If such sheets are prepared, an additional narrative need not be written to accompany the flowchart.

It is usually helpful for the analyst to prepare system flowcharts showing the principal information-processing operations and the sequence in which they occur. These are called high-level system flowcharts. An example of such a flowchart, along with the narrative that should be prepared to accompany it, is shown in FIGURE 11-9, *System flowchart for a manual accounts receivable system.*

A dramatic input-output analysis technique which analysts sometimes employ is to mount actual forms and reports on the wall of a room. Information flow can be displayed by colored tape or string. The values of this technique are that it provides the analyst with a "life-size" model; it keeps all the data carriers in view; and it provides "impact" for presentations and group discussions.

Recurring Data Analysis. After the analyst becomes familiar with the content and meaning of the principal system documents, he usually analyzes recurring

Figure 11-9. System flowchart for a manual accounts receivable system

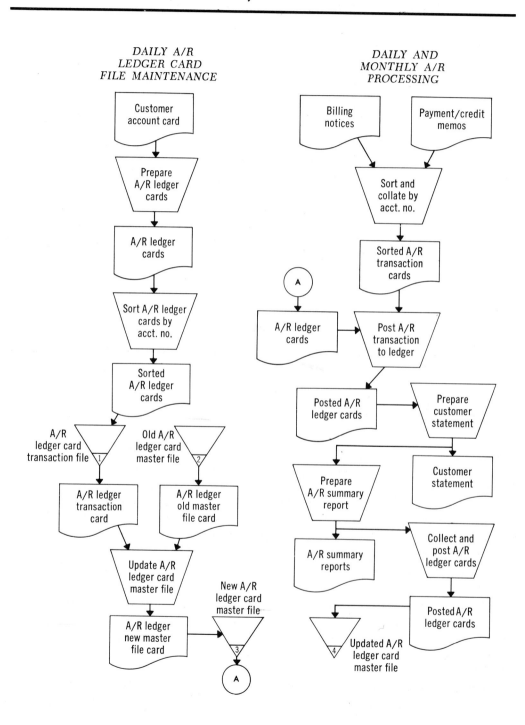

NARRATIVE DESCRIPTION OF SYSTEM FLOWCHART
FOR MANUAL A/R SYSTEM

1.0   DAILY A/R LEDGER CARD FILE MAINTENANCE

1.1   New or changed Customer Account Cards, (received from the Credit Department) are used to prepare header information for the new A/R Ledger Cards.

1.2   The A/R Ledger Cards are sorted by Customer Account Number, and the sorted A/R Ledger Cards become the A/R Ledger Card Transaction File (File No. 1).

1.3   The A/R Ledger Card Transaction File is used to update the old A/R Ledger Card Master File (File No. 2) producing an updated A/R Ledger Card Master File (File No. 3)

2.0   DAILY A/R PROCESSING

2.1   Billing Notices (forwarded, as copies of Sales Orders, from the Shipping Department) and Payment/Credit Memos, (received from the Credit Department) are sorted and collated by Customer Account Number, producing sorted A/R Transaction Cards.

2.2   The A/R Ledger Cards are posted from the sorted A/R Transaction Cards.

2.3   At the same time that entries are posted to the A/R Ledger Cards, transactions are entered on the Customer Statement.

3.0   MONTHLY A/R PROCESSING

3.1   The A/R Ledger Card entries are totaled and the totals are transcribed to an A/R Summary Report.

3.2   The totals are posted on the A/R Ledger Cards, producing a monthly update of A/R Ledger Card File (File No. 4)

3.3   The Customer Statements are prepared by totaling the daily entries.

---

data. For this purpose a form is prepared like the one in FIGURE 11-10, *Recurring data analysis sheet.* Document names and identifying numbers are entered across the top of the sheet. All the data elements associated with the first form are listed in the column headed Data Element. This process is continued for each form, moving from left to right across the sheet. Only previously unlisted data elements are added to the Data Element column. A check mark is entered at the intersection of corresponding forms and data elements. The analyst must be familiar with the forms he is analyzing so that he is not deceived by the same name appearing with different meanings. An example might be the term "quantity," which could mean quantity ordered on a sales order and quantity shipped on an invoice. Similarly, the analyst should be able to distinguish between different names with the same meaning. For example, "employee number" and "badge number" might have the same meaning.

The significance of an analysis of recurring data is twofold: (1) Unnecessary input and output data duplication can be detected. This leads to form simplification, consolidation, and elimination. (2) Redundant files can be located. This leads to more efficient use of file media and may suggest the use of shared data bases.

Report Use Analysis. Reports and copies of reports tend to proliferate. Many individuals are collectors of reports, more because of fear of being left out than

FIGURE 11-10.
Recurring data analysis sheet

RECURRING DATA ANALYSIS SHEET											
DATA ELEMENT / **FORM NAME**	Sales Order	Shipping Order	Shipping Invoice								
Customer Name	✓	✓	✓								
Customer Address	✓	✓	✓								
Invoice No.	✓	✓	✓								
Account No.	✓	✓	✓								
Date	✓	✓	✓								
Quantity Ordered	✓	✓	✓								
Description	✓	✓	✓								
Unit Price	✓		✓								
Amount	✓		✓								
Customer Signature	✓										
Sales Person	✓										
Total Amount	✓		✓								
Ship to		✓									
How Shipped		✓									
Quantity Shipped			✓								

FIGURE 11-11.
Report use analysis sheet

REPORT USE ANALYSIS SHEET

REPORT DESCRIPTION: Customer Monthly Statement

DATA ELEMENT / **USER NAME/FUNCTION**	Customer	Customer Account Credit Clerk	Accounts Receivable Department (File copy)			
Customer Name	✓					
Customer Address	✓					
Account No.	✓	✓				
Billing Date	✓	✓				
Due Date	✓	✓				
Amount Paid	✓	✓				
Previous Balance	✓	✓				
Total Purchase	✓	✓				
Total Payments & Credits	✓	✓				
New Balance	✓	✓				

because of any legitimate need for information. A useful technique for dealing with reports that are suspect because of a lengthy distribution list is a report use analysis. A form of the type shown in FIGURE 11-11, *Report use analysis sheet,* is prepared, and the data elements are associated with identified users of the report. A completed report use analysis sheet can be correlated with information obtained from other sources, such as user interviews. It may disclose data elements (and possibly entire reports) not required by many of the individuals on the distribution list. It is not unusual to find reports that no one uses. The report use analysis sheet can provide insight into the true information needs of an organization and can help the analyst to develop more meaningful reports for the new or revised system.

At this point, the analyst, having concluded his fact finding and fact analysis, is prepared to organize and summarize the results of these activities.

Results of analysis

The systems analyst usually collects and analyzes large amounts of data. In the course of his initial investigation, he has to discard data that is irrelevant and organize and summarize that which is relevant. When he has completed the process of organizing and summarizing data, the analyst should have a file of current information and a thorough knowledge of the current system. His information file should include:

1. Updated system documentation, including copies of all pertinent forms and reports.

2. Correspondence and completed questionnaires.

3. Interview records.

4. Results of fact analysis, including flowcharts prepared during the investigation.

The file should document the knowledge which the analyst has acquired in the course of the initial investigation. This knowledge should include:

1. A comprehensive understanding of how the current system operates, including its cost.

2. Familiarity with the names, positions, and personalities of personnel operating in or affected by the system.

3. Identification of the good and bad features of the current system.

4. Correlation of actual system problems with the problems listed on the ISR that initiated the investigation.

With respect to correlation between actual system problems and those listed in the ISR, the analyst should be able to distinguish between those problems that can be solved by a new or revised system and those that cannot. For example, a new system might be completely ineffective if the problem is an "uncontrollable" executive personality.

The single most important result of the initial investigation is the identification of the principal user. We will discuss the significance of this in the following section.

Identification of the principal user

Identification of the principal user is critical to the success of the computer-based business system. As he organizes the results of the initial investigation and considers the anticipated benefits of the system, the analyst should remember that these benefits are not measured by his value system, but by the value systems of users. In particular, he should identify the principal user and be sure that the anticipated benefits are "meaningful" in the value system of that user. The *principal user* is the person who, in practice, will accept or reject the computer-based business system. The principal user may be the individual who issues the project directive; usually he is. However, he also may be a superior or a subordinate of that individual. In some cases he may be a member of a different organization. For example, the head of the Purchasing department may request a report which identifies vendors by amount of money subcontracted and by geographic location. This report may not be used by the Purchasing department, but by the director of Contracts to demonstrate to the federal government that the company subcontracts a certain percentage of its work with small local businesses.

The analyst must be sure that his own concepts of meaningful benefits are compatible with those of the principal user. As a responsible professional, the analyst should seek to modify the principal user's concept of "meaningful" when it is, in his judgment, important to the cost or performance of the computer-based business system. For example, the principal user may have in mind instantaneous access, via a desk-top terminal, to a data base which is always time-current. The analyst may know that the volatility of the data base is so low that a relatively inexpensive weekly report would be adequate. Further, he may know that the activity on the terminal would not be high and that its use would be no more convenient than consulting a computer print-out. Under such circumstances, he should try to persuade the user to forego the "glamour" of a terminal (which may be operated only by the user's secretary after a few weeks) in favor of a well-organized weekly report and a brief daily change listing.

The analyst may or may not succeed in influencing the principal user's expectations of system performance. However, he should not knowingly undertake the development of a system that will produce outputs contrary to the principal user's expectations. Many of the failures of computer-based systems can be traced to analyst attitudes such as "He doesn't know what he needs" and "When he sees how good it is, he will buy it."

Before spending corporate resources to produce a doubtful system, a mature analyst invests the personal time and effort required to persuade the principal user to follow a reasonable course of action. We call this type of persuasion "ethical" pre-selling. Some methods of "unethical" pre-selling, which a true professional avoids, are taking advantage of the user's credulity about computers to sell him glamorous, but unneeded features; and climbing on the bandwagon and suggesting that the user request even more of something that he doesn't need. Unethical pre-selling can, in the short term, lead to fancy systems and large computer centers. In the long run, however, such practices seldom are successful. These systems do not pay their own way and often collapse from their own weight. In addition, they leave behind a stigma that affects the development of other, legitimate computer-based systems.

Identifying the principal user aids the analyst in another important way. It helps him to establish the scope of the project, which should not extend beyond the level of responsibility of the principal user. Thus, if the individual who is to accept or reject the system is the manager of the Accounts Receivable department, the scope of the system is different than it might be if it were to be used by the manager of Accounting. In the one case, the scope would be limited to the Accounts Receivable department and its immediate interfaces. In the other case, the scope might include several accounting departments and might interface with many other elements of the company.

Finally, armed with the results of the initial investigation, the analyst prepares for a formal user review.

USER REVIEW

Modified Information Service Request

The analyst presents the results of the initial investigation and his recommendations to the user-sponsor. (We will assume that the user-sponsor is the principal user. If he is not, it is vital that the principal user also attend the review.) If the analyst has concluded that the project should be continued, he includes a modified Information Service Request in his presentation. The modified ISR may suggest modifications to the objectives, benefits, output descriptions, and input descriptions from those put forth in the original ISR. FIGURE 11-12, *Modified Information Service Request—partial* is an example of a modified ISR for an accounts receivable system. It is identified as a modified ISR in the "remarks" section of the bottom of the form. Some of the differences from the limited Information Service Request of Figure 11-2 are:

1. Expansion of anticipated benefits.

2. Change in quantity of customer statements—because of a recommendation that there be three billing cycles, one for each region.

3. Additional detail on the number of pages and copies of the A/R transaction register.

However, the initial investigation produced no essential changes in the anticipated benefits of the system.

The analyst should provide all those invited to his presentation with copies of the modified ISR and of other pertinent written material beforehand. This affords them a chance to familiarize themselves with the material and to prepare questions. The user review typically includes the user-sponsor, the analyst, the analyst's supervisor, and other appropriate management and operational personnel.

The analyst should discuss the key elements of his initial investigation. He should be able to support his recommendations, whatever their nature. If his recommendation is to proceed with the Study Phase, he should identify the resources he will require, and he should present a project plan and a cost schedule for the remainder of the Study Phase.

As a result of the user review, the project may be terminated, modified, or continued. If the decision is to proceed, it is documented by the issuance of a project directive.

Project directive

The modified ISR really is a draft of a proposed project directive. The project directive is an authorization document issued by the user after the review of the

Figure 11-12. Modified Information Service Request—partial

INFORMATION SERVICE REQUEST	Page 1 of 3

JOB TITLE: Study Phase for the Modified Accounts Receivable System (MARS)	NEW ☒ REV. ☐	REQUESTED DATE: 10/30/xx	REQUIRED DATE: 12/7/xx

OBJECTIVE: To improve the efficiency of customer billing and account collection

	AUTHORIZATION			
	LABOR		OTHER	
	HOURS	AMOUNT	HOURS	AMOUNT
	560	$5600	0	0

ANTICIPATED BENEFITS:
1. Faster Billing
2. Reduction in Delinquent Accounts
3. Improved Controls
4. Improved A/R Reports

OUTPUT DESCRIPTION	INPUT DESCRIPTION
TITLE: Customer Monthly Statement	TITLE: Billing Notice
FREQUENCY: Monthly QUANTITY: 3,000/cycle	FREQUENCY: Daily
PAGES: 1 COPIES: 3	QUANTITY: 300
DESCRIPTION: Includes Late Account Finance Charge. Three billing cycles. Multi-part form.	DESCRIPTION: Generated as a copy of the Sales Order
TITLE: A/R Transaction Register	TITLE: Payment/Credit Memorandum
FREQUENCY: Daily QUANTITY: 1	FREQUENCY:
PAGES: 20 max. COPIES: 6	QUANTITY: 1,000 max.
DESCRIPTION: Listing for use of Credit and A/R Departments	DESCRIPTION: Prepared by Credit Dept. to enter customer payments and credits.

TO BE FILLED OUT BY REQUESTOR

REQUESTED BY:	DEPARTMENT:	TITLE:	TELEPHONE:
APPROVED BY:	DEPARTMENT:	TITLE:	TELEPHONE:

TO BE FILLED OUT BY INFORMATION SERVICES

FILE NO: ISR-310-1A	ACCEPTED ☒ NOT ACCEPTED ☐		
SIGNATURE: *C. Hampton*	DEPARTMENT: 200	TITLE: Manager	TELEPHONE: X2870

REMARKS:
This is a Modified Information Service Request prepared for Requestor Acceptance as a Project Directive. J. Herring is designated as Project Leader

FORM NO: C-6-1	ADDITIONAL INFORMATION: USE REVERSE SIDE OR EXTRA PAGES

initial investigation has been completed; it reflects the results of discussions and decisions made during that review. It may or may not be identical to the modified ISR prepared by the analyst.

When the project directive is signed by the user and accepted by Information Services, it becomes a "contract" under which both organizations are accountable for performance. The format and content of the project directive are similar to those of the ISR. Often the same form is used for both. This is the practice that we will follow in this book. Figure 11-13, *Project directive*, is based on the modified ISR of Figure 11-12. Note the following changes: The requested date and required date have been advanced, and the labor allocation has been increased slightly. In the course of the user review it was decided to specify a shared data base for credit and accounts receivable processing. In the remarks section, this

FIGURE 11-13. Project directive

INFORMATION SERVICE REQUEST			Page 1 of 3	

JOB TITLE: Study Phase for the Modified Accounts Receivable System (MARS)

NEW ☑ REV. ☐

REQUESTED DATE: 11/7/xx   **REQUIRED DATE:** 12/19/xx

AUTHORIZATION

OBJECTIVE: To improve the efficiency of customer billing and account collection

LABOR		OTHER	
HOURS	AMOUNT	HOURS	AMOUNT
600	$6,000	0	0

ANTICIPATED BENEFITS: 1. Faster Billing
2. Reduction in Delinquent Accounts
3. Improved Controls
4. Shared A/R Credit Dept. Data Base
5. Improved A/R Reports

OUTPUT DESCRIPTION	INPUT DESCRIPTION
TITLE: Customer Monthly Statement	**TITLE:** Billing Notice
FREQUENCY: Monthly **QUANTITY:** 3,000/cycle	**FREQUENCY:** Daily
PAGES: 1 **COPIES:** 3	**QUANTITY:** 300 max.
DESCRIPTION: Three billing cycles. To include late account finance charge. Multi-part form.	**DESCRIPTION:** To be generated as a copy of the Sales Order
TITLE: A/R Transaction Register	**TITLE:** Payment/Credit Memorandum
FREQUENCY: Daily **QUANTITY:** 1	**FREQUENCY:** Daily
PAGES: 20 max. **COPIES:** 6	**QUANTITY:** 1,000 max.
DESCRIPTION: Listing for use of A/R and Credit Departments	**DESCRIPTION:** Prepared by Credit Dept. to enter customer payment and credit transactions.

TO BE FILLED OUT BY REQUESTOR

REQUESTED BY: *H. Davis*	DEPARTMENT: 310	TITLE: Head A/R Dept.	TELEPHONE: X3250
APPROVED BY *Ben Franklin*	DEPARTMENT: 300	TITLE: Manager Account. Div.	TELEPHONE: X3208

TO BE FILLED OUT BY INFORMATION SERVICES

FILE NO: ISR-310-1B	ACCEPTED ☒ NOT ACCEPTED ☐		
SIGNATURE: *C. Hampton*	DEPARTMENT: 200	TITLE: Manager Info. Ser. Div	TELEPHONE: X2670

REMARKS: This is a Project Directive. J. Herring is appointed Project Leader. Advise requestor when authorized funds are 90% expended.

FORM NO: C–6–1	ADDITIONAL INFORMATION: USE REVERSE SIDE OR EXTRA PAGES

ISR is designated a project directive. Also, the requestor is to be informed when 90 percent of the authorized funds have been spent. This is a safeguard against an unauthorized cost overrun.

The project directive is the first of many incremental commitments made by management in the course of the life cycle of a computer-based business system. At this time, the project directive may authorize all the resources required to develop the new system. Usually it authorizes only the resources required to complete the Study Phase. Additional resources are authorized after successful reviews of the Study Phase and of subsequent phases. In Figure 11-13, as the job title indicates, the analyst is authorized to complete the Study Phase.

The project directive initiates a comprehensive study of the feasibility of the proposed system. The feasibility analysis is preceded by the development of a detailed user-oriented definition of expected new system performance. The process by which the expected system performance is arrived at is described in Chapter 12: System Performance Definition. The feasibility analysis itself involves the evaluation of alternative systems and the selection of the one that best meets the detailed system performance requirements. This process is discussed in Chapter 13: Feasibility Analysis.

KEY TERMS

Information Service Request (ISR)
motivating factor
hygiene factor
data element analysis
input-output analysis sheet

recurring data analysis sheet
report use analysis sheet
principal user
project directive

FOR DISCUSSION

1. Describe several ways in which a business system information problem might be identified.

2. Distinguish between the terms Information Service Request, modified Information Service Request, and project directive.

3. Why should an information memorandum be issued at the time an analyst begins an initial investigation?

4. What are the elements of project control that aid in the management of an initial investigation?

5. Why does an analyst perform a background analysis? Under what conditions might such an analysis not be necessary?

6. What tentative conclusions can you draw from the recurring data analysis and report use analysis sheets of Figure 11-10 and Figure 11-11?

7. How does an analyst apply his skills in coding and forms design during an initial investigation?

8. Discuss "motivators" and "hygiene factors" as they relate to personal interviews.

9. What should an analyst's information file contain and what knowledge should he have at the conclusion of an initial investigation?

10. Discuss the importance of identifying the principal user.

12

System
Performance
Definition

The process of system performance definition results
in a user-oriented definition of the outputs of a system.
The goal of this chapter is to describe the three steps
in the performance definition process. You will learn how
to state general constraints; how to identify and rank
specific objectives; and how to describe outputs,
using report specification sheets and data element lists.

PERFORMANCE DEFINITION

Overview

The performance required of a system is defined by the description of its outputs in a user-oriented format. Chapter 10: Study Phase Overview listed five
steps in which the Study Phase proceeds after the completion of the initial
investigation. The first three of these steps result in the definition of the performance of the new system. They are:

1. Statement of general constraints.
2. Identification and ranking of specific objectives.
3. Description of outputs.

These steps are described in this chapter. The final two steps:

4. Selection and description of candidate systems.
5. Selection of the most feasible system. _most difficult step_

relate to the analysis of feasibility, and they are discussed in Chapter 13:
Feasibility Analysis.

Throughout the Study Phase, the description of system performance is user-
·oriented. System performance definition follows the initial investigation, a user
review, and the issuance of a project directive.

In general, the initial investigation will have eliminated extraneous factors
and identified the major system problems. Similarly, the project directive will
have meaningful (to both the user and analyst) statements about constraints,
objectives, and outputs. The purpose of defining system performance is to de-

scribe the system outputs at an additional level of detail. At this level, the analyst is able to make sketches of all system outputs and to prepare accompanying data element lists. Sometimes all the required information is available to the analyst from the initial investigation and the project directive. Other times he may have to conduct additional investigative activities.

In this chapter, we will use the modified accounts receivable system (MARS) of the ABCDEF Corporation as an illustrative example of the procedure for defining system performance. We will continue to use the MARS example in subsequent chapters. Therefore, we will begin this chapter by presenting additional detail about the current accounts receivable system.

Example system: Additional information

Let us again consider the ABCDEF Corporation's current accounts receivable system (A/R system) presented in Chapter 11: Initial Investigation. In that chapter, we described a variety of techniques for fact finding and fact analysis. Elements of the A/R system were used for illustrative purposes throughout that chapter. Now, we will present some additional information about the ABCDEF Corporation and its accounts receivable system. This will enable us to use this system as a coherent example.

The ABCDEF Corporation is a small corporation (300 employees) which designs and manufactures specialty household items. It does not sell to the public, but is a nationwide wholesale and retail supplier. It has three regional sales divisions through which merchandise is supplied to its customers.

Currently, the ABCDEF Corporation has 1,000 customer accounts distributed over the three regional divisions. It has problems with accounts receivable and with related credit operations. All customer orders are sent to the Credit department for approval prior to shipment. After the customer's order is approved, a copy of the sales order is sent to the Shipping department as the shipping order. After filling the order, the Shipping department forwards another copy of the sales order, the billing notice, to the Accounts Receivable department. At the end of the month, customer accounts are processed and billing statements mailed.

Due to the month-end work load, billing statements are delayed an average of 5 days. In addition, in spite of credit agreements calling for payment of the net amount due within 30 days, the average payment time is 60 days. It is estimated that late billing and late payments together cause the company to allocate $200,000 continually to meet current expenses. If this money were borrowed at a rate of 9 percent it would represent an annual cost of $18,000. In addition, late billings and late payments are increasing more rapidly than sales. Therefore, it is anticipated that these problems will become more severe in the future.

Because the Credit department does not receive timely copies of current customer statements and because clerks must correlate account numbers and credit limits manually, many accounts have outstanding balances in excess of their credit limits. A significant number of these accounts are delinquent.

Also, although payments are received by the Credit department, they are accumulated and processed by the A/R department. Consequently, lacking a timely knowledge of a customer's outstanding balance, the Credit department often must delay the processing of new orders which might cause the customer's account to exceed the credit limit until a credit clerk has searched through the Accounts Receivable department's file of unprocessed payment/credit memos or checked the ledger card.

In addition, the number of customer billings in error is increasing. This increase is due to the above problems, to management pressure to get customer billings out earlier, and to an increasing month-end processing workload. It is estimated that at least 20 percent of the workload in the Credit and Accounts Receivable departments is caused by errors in customer statements.

Sales are estimated to double within the next year, and the number of customer accounts is expected to increase proportionately. The company expects to have 10,000 accounts in five years. Therefore, there is a well-founded concern that the manual A/R system will prove to be wholly inadequate in the future.

The ABCDEF Corporation has a small computer, an IBM System/3. The major business applications for which the computer is now being used are production control and inventory control. Mr. Alex Hamilton, vice-president, Finance, has asked Mr. Ben Franklin, manager of the Accounting division, to explore the feasibility of using a computer, preferably the in-house IBM System/3, to alleviate the problem.

Accordingly, Mr. Franklin instructed Mr. G. Davis, head of the A/R department, to ask the Information Services division to study the feasibility of a modified accounts receivable system. This system would include the use of a computer, if warranted. The initial request for service (presented in Chapter 11 as Figure 11-1) was accepted as a limited Information Service Request. Ms. J. Herring was assigned the responsibility for conducting the initial investigation.

We shall review and elaborate on the results of that investigation as an "example system" as we proceed to discuss the steps involved in system performance definition.

GENERAL CONSTRAINTS

Statement of general constraints

General constraints are those limiting all problem solutions that the systems analyst may consider. Typically, these are constraints which have been imposed upon him from the outset of the project or which he has identified in the course of his initial investigation and discussed with the user-sponsor. There are many possible general constraints. Among the most common are management policy, legal requirements, equipment and facilities, e.g., an existing computer center, audit and internal control requirements, fixed organizational responsibilities, cost, and time.

With respect to the cost and time constraints, it is important for the analyst to realize that management often is willing to accept something less than an optimum system provided that it meets basic needs, that its development cost is not excessive, and that it will be available when needed. The analyst who is not able to appreciate the realities of the corporate environment will not enjoy a long and rewarding career. Incidentally, this is one reason why it is often a good strategy, when possible, to segment large systems so that some elements can be installed and can begin to "pay their own way" while the development of other elements continues.

Example system: General constraints

For the example system, the ABCDEF Corporation's MARS, some general constraints might be as follows:

1. The system must be implemented within six months.
2. MARS must have a growth potential to handle 10,000 customer accounts.
3. Company policy states that use of the in-house IBM System/3 computer is to be given priority consideration.
4. MARS is to interface with the existing perpetual inventory system.

After the system constraints are established, the analyst proceeds to identify specific performance objectives.

SPECIFIC OBJECTIVES

Identification and ranking of specific objectives

The objective stated in the project directive is the major system objective. However, this objective is usually a general statement of purpose. The systems analyst must derive from this general statement specific objectives to which he can relate each system output. He starts by analyzing the anticipated benefits stated in the project directive. These benefits, in association with the general system objective, help him to formulate specific objectives. As he proceeds, the experienced analyst does not lose sight of the fact that the benefits of a system must be meaningful and measurable in the value system of the principal user.

The anticipated benefits may be tangible or intangible. FIGURE 12-1, *System benefits*, lists six categories of system benefits. They range from the very tangible, e.g., cost reduction, to the very intangible, e.g., "spring cleaning" (which means change for the sake of change). Historically, management has tended to emphasize tangible benefits. More recently, many companies have progressed to the use of computer-based systems to achieve competitive advantages and to provide information that aids in policy and planning decisions. These benefits may be visible only in the corporation's profit and loss statement.

FIGURE 12-1. System benefits

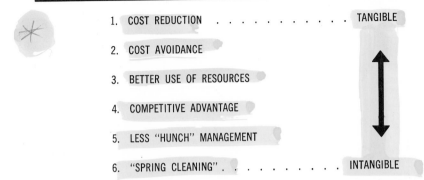

1. COST REDUCTION . . . . TANGIBLE

2. COST AVOIDANCE

3. BETTER USE OF RESOURCES

4. COMPETITIVE ADVANTAGE

5. LESS "HUNCH" MANAGEMENT

6. "SPRING CLEANING" . . . . INTANGIBLE

Whenever possible, benefits must be translated into specific objectives that can be stated in measurable terms. For example, "To improve customer service," a general objective and statement of purpose, might be supported by the following specific objectives:

1. To increase the percentage of goods shipped on schedule from 40 percent to 80 percent within six months and to 95 percent within a year.

2. To reduce the number of order cancellations from 35 percent to 5 percent within six months.

3. To reduce the number of back orders from 25 percent to 5 percent at a rate of 5 percent per month.

As illustrated above, percentage improvements are an effective means of comparing the performance of a new system with that of the existing system. However, the analyst should be careful not to use the present system's performance as the only reference for establishing the new system's objectives. The analyst should focus also on new needs, some of which may not be related to elements of the current system. Frequently, in the course of developing specific objectives, both tangible and intangible, the analyst has to extend fact finding and analysis to areas or depths not covered in the initial investigation.

Example system: Specific objectives

Let us again consider the ABCDEF Corporation's MARS. As the first step in identifying and ranking specific objectives, we shall review the salient results of the initial investigation. Figures 12-2 through 12-11 summarize and suppplement the information presented in Chapter 11. The material is presented as follows: manual system flowcharts, manual system outputs and inputs, manual system costs, new system project directive, and new system specific objectives.

Manual system flowcharts. FIGURE 12-2, *ABCDEF Corporation—partial organization chart,* depicts the reporting relationships between the major organizations affected by the A/R system. This is a working chart

FIGURE 12-2. ABCDEF Corporation—partial organization chart

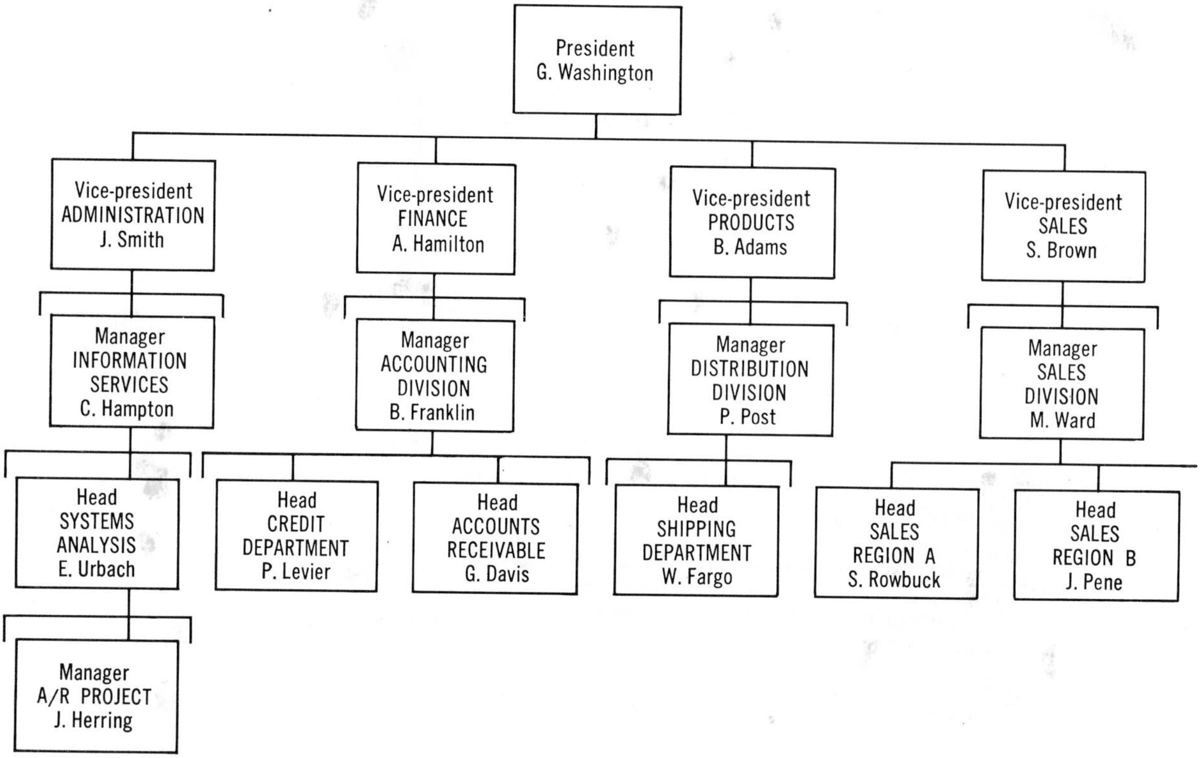

used by the analyst to record background information pertinent to the organizational environment. Other useful information, such as department numbers and telephone numbers, also can be indicated.

To show additional detail, such as the organizational breakdown within the Credit and Accounts Receivable departments, the analyst can prepare additional charts.

These charts should identify by name and function the individuals with whom he expects to come into contact. He should also develop organizational function lists for each department shown on the organization chart. This additional detail is not included as part of the example; however, it is implicit to the development of the detail presented in the subsequent figures that describe the example company's existing A/R system.

FIGURE 12-3, *Information-oriented flowchart for manual A/R system,* is the same as Figure 11-7 of the preceding chapter. It identifies the flow of data from the customer through the Credit, Shipping, and Accounts

Figure 12-3. Information-oriented flowchart for manual A/R system

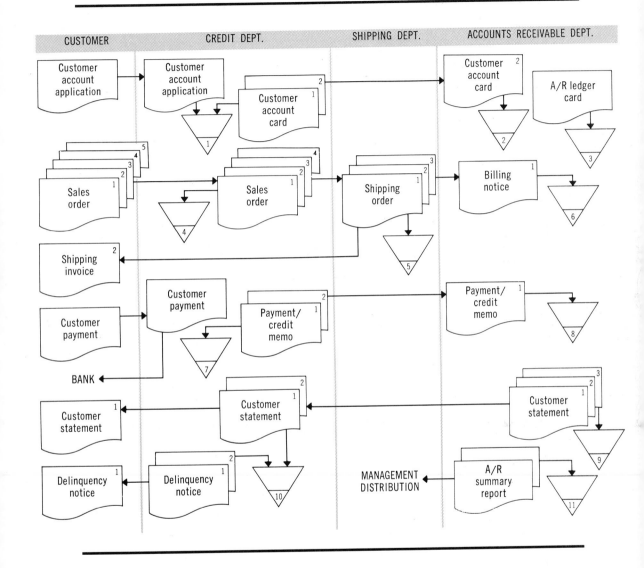

Receivable departments and back to the customer. Figure 12-4, *Credit department input-output analysis sheet,* is an accompanying document for the Credit department. The narrative content was prepared from organizational background information (e.g., flowcharts and organization function lists) and from information gathered during fact finding and analysis. It is the same as Figure 11-8. Figure 12-5, *Accounts Receivable input-output analysis sheet,* is similar to the sheet prepared for the Credit department.

FIGURE 12-4. Credit department input-output analysis sheet

INPUT-OUTPUT ANALYSIS SHEET		
ORGANIZATION: Credit Department	SYSTEM: Accounts Receivable	DATE: 9/3/XX
INPUT	**FUNCTION/FILES**	**OUTPUT**
Customer Account Application	Approves Credit. Enters Credit Limit on Application. Orders Credit Card. Prepares Customer Account Card in duplicate. Forwards duplicate of Customer Account Card to A/R Dept. Staples Customer Account Application to back of original Customer Account Card and stores in Customer Account File. (File No. 1)	Customer Account Card
Sales Order	Confirms customer credit. Files Copy 4 of the Sales Order (File No. 4) and forwards copies 1, 2, and 3 to the Shipping Department.	Sales Order (Copies 1, 2, and 3)
Customer Payments	Checks amount of payment against total due and indication of amount enclosed. Transmits checks (accompanied by a check listing) to the bank. Prepares a Payment/Credit Memo in duplicate. Files duplicate (File No. 7) and forwards original to A/R Department	Payment/Credit Memo
Customer Statement	Checks customer statement for delinquent accounts and prepares delinquency notices. Mails customer statement (with delinquency notice if required). Files duplicate copies. (File No. 10)	Delinquency Notice

FIGURE 12-5. Accounts Receivable input-output analysis sheet

INPUT-OUTPUT ANALYSIS SHEET		
ORGANIZATION: A/R Department	SYSTEM: Accounts Receivable	DATE: 9/4/XX
INPUT	**FUNCTION/FILES**	**OUTPUT**
Customer Account Card	Transfers header information from Customer Account Card to A/R Ledger Card. Files Customer Account Card (File No. 2) and A/R Ledger Card (File No. 3).	Updated A/R Ledger Cards. Customer Statement. (Header Information)
Billing Notice*	Transfers invoice data from Billing Notice to A/R Ledger Card and to Customer Statement Files Billing Notice (File No. 6); files A/R Ledger Card (File No. 3); and files Customer Statement (File No. 8).	Updated A/R Ledger Cards. Posted Customer Statements.
Payment/Credit* Memo	Transfers invoice data from Payment/Credit Memo to A/R Ledger Card and to Customer Statement. Files Payment/Credit Memo (File No. 8); files A/R Ledger Card (File No. 3); and files Customer Statement (File No. 9).	Updated A/R Ledger Cards. Posted Customer Statements.
*Monthly Processing of Billing Notice and Payment/Credit Memo Data	Summarizes data on A/R Ledger Cards and prepares monthly A/R Summary Report. Files A/R Ledger Cards (File No. 3) and A/R Summary Report (File No. 11). Totals data on Customer Statement and files one copy (File No. 9).	Monthly A/R Summary Report. Monthly Customer Statements.

Figure 12-6. System flowchart for the manual A/R system

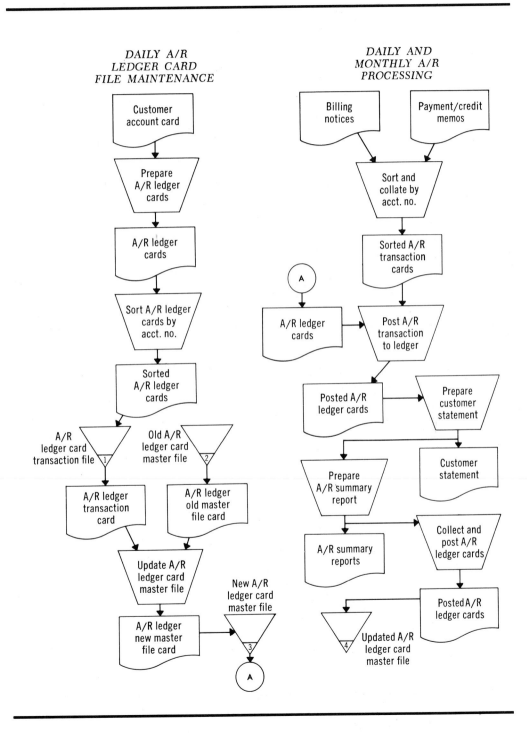

Figure 12-7. Narrative description of manual A/R system flowchart

NARRATIVE DESCRIPTION OF SYSTEM FLOWCHART
FOR MANUAL A/R SYSTEM

1.0 DAILY A/R LEDGER CARD FILE MAINTENANCE

    1.1 New or changed Customer Account Cards, (received from the Credit Department) are used to prepare header information for the new A/R Ledger Cards.

    1.2 The A/R Ledger Cards are sorted by Customer Account Number, and the sorted A/R Ledger Cards become the A/R Ledger Card Transaction File (File No. 1).

    1.3 The A/R Ledger Card Transaction File is used to update the old A/R Ledger Card Master File (File No. 2) producing an updated A/R Ledger Card Master File (File No. 3)

2.0 DAILY A/R PROCESSING

    2.1 Billing Notices (forwarded, as copies of Sales Orders, from the Shipping Department) and Payment/Credit Memos, (received from the Credit Department) are sorted and collated by Customer Account Number, producing sorted A/R Transaction Cards.

    2.2 The A/R Ledger Cards are posted from the sorted A/R Transaction Cards.

    2.3 At the same time that entries are posted to the A/R Ledger Cards, transactions are entered on the Customer Statement.

3.0 MONTHLY A/R PROCESSING

    3.1 The A/R Ledger Card entries are totaled and the totals are transcribed to an A/R Summary Report.

    3.2 The totals are posted on the A/R Ledger Cards, producing a monthly update of A/R Ledger Card File (File No. 4)

    3.3 The Customer Statements are prepared by totaling the daily entries.

Figure 12-6, *System flowchart for the manual A/R system,* displays the daily and monthly A/R processing operations. The A/R system flowchart is supported by the narrative of Figure 12-7, *Narrative description of manual A/R system flowchart.* These examples are the same as those shown in Figure 11-9 of the preceding chapter.

Manual system outputs and inputs. Figure 12-8, *Outputs from manual A/R system,* shows the three outputs of the existing system. These are the accounts receivable ledger card, the accounts receivable summary report, and the customer monthly statement. Figure 12-9, *Inputs to manual A/R system,* illustrates the inputs to the existing system. These are the customer account card, the payment/credit memorandum, and the billing notice.

Manual system costs. The direct operating costs of the current A/R system were found to be primarily the clerical costs in the Accounts Receivable and Credit departments. These costs are summarized in Figure

FIGURE 12-8. Outputs from manual A/R system

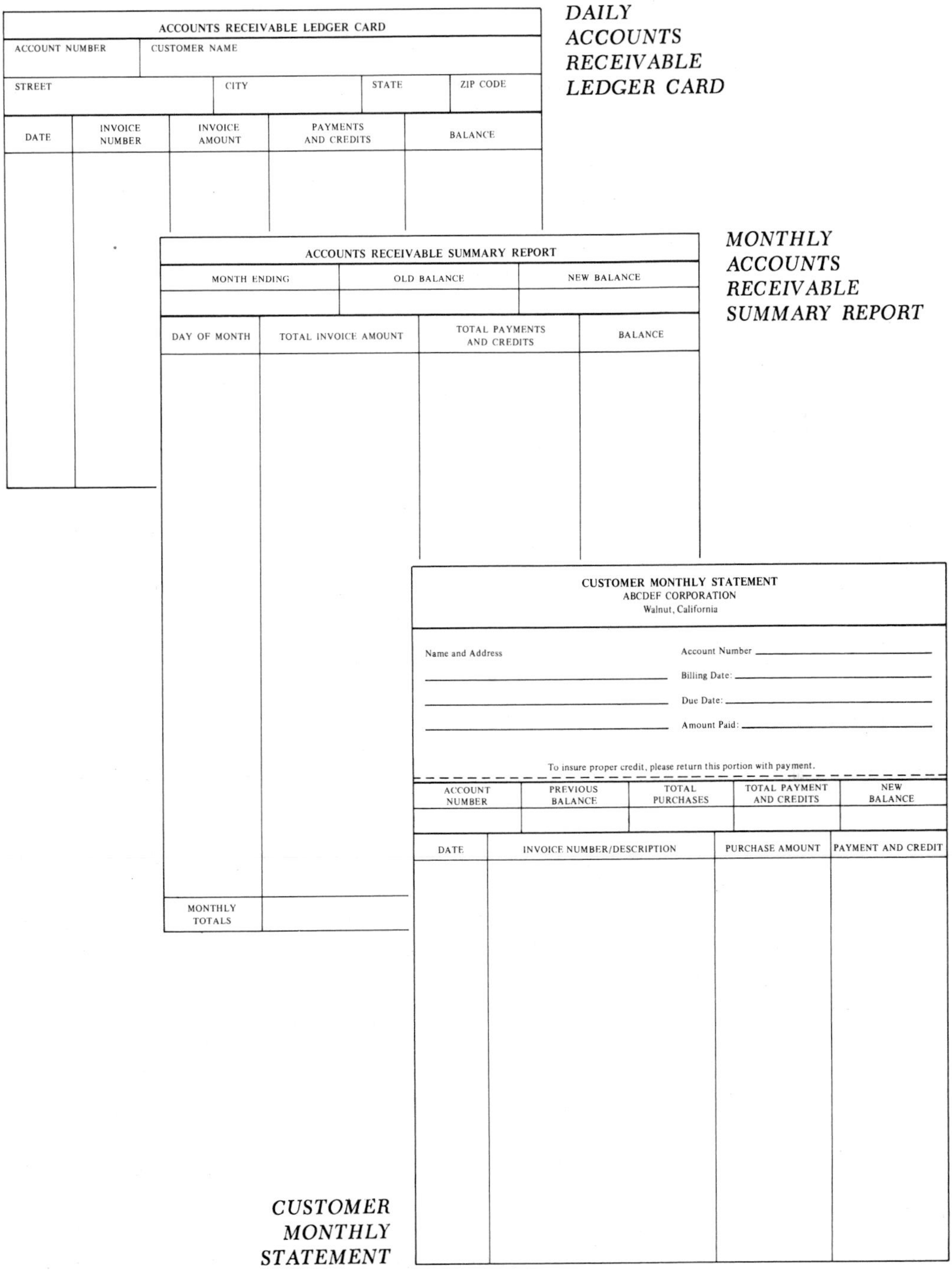

ACCOUNTS RECEIVABLE LEDGER CARD

ACCOUNT NUMBER	CUSTOMER NAME		

STREET	CITY	STATE	ZIP CODE

DATE	INVOICE NUMBER	INVOICE AMOUNT	PAYMENTS AND CREDITS	BALANCE

DAILY ACCOUNTS RECEIVABLE LEDGER CARD

ACCOUNTS RECEIVABLE SUMMARY REPORT

MONTH ENDING	OLD BALANCE	NEW BALANCE

DAY OF MONTH	TOTAL INVOICE AMOUNT	TOTAL PAYMENTS AND CREDITS	BALANCE

MONTHLY ACCOUNTS RECEIVABLE SUMMARY REPORT

MONTHLY TOTALS

CUSTOMER MONTHLY STATEMENT
ABCDEF CORPORATION
Walnut, California

Name and Address

Account Number _____
Billing Date: _____
Due Date: _____
Amount Paid: _____

To insure proper credit, please return this portion with payment.

ACCOUNT NUMBER	PREVIOUS BALANCE	TOTAL PURCHASES	TOTAL PAYMENT AND CREDITS	NEW BALANCE

DATE	INVOICE NUMBER/DESCRIPTION	PURCHASE AMOUNT	PAYMENT AND CREDIT

CUSTOMER MONTHLY STATEMENT

FIGURE 12-9. **Inputs to manual A/R system**

CUSTOMER
ACCOUNT CARD

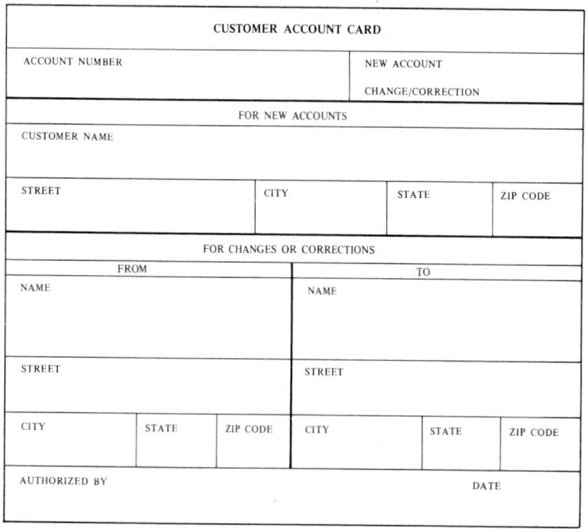

CUSTOMER ACCOUNT CARD			
ACCOUNT NUMBER		NEW ACCOUNT	
		CHANGE/CORRECTION	
FOR NEW ACCOUNTS			
CUSTOMER NAME			
STREET	CITY	STATE	ZIP CODE

FOR CHANGES OR CORRECTIONS

FROM		TO	
NAME		NAME	
STREET		STREET	
CITY	STATE	ZIP CODE	CITY	STATE	ZIP CODE
AUTHORIZED BY		DATE	

BILLING NOTICE

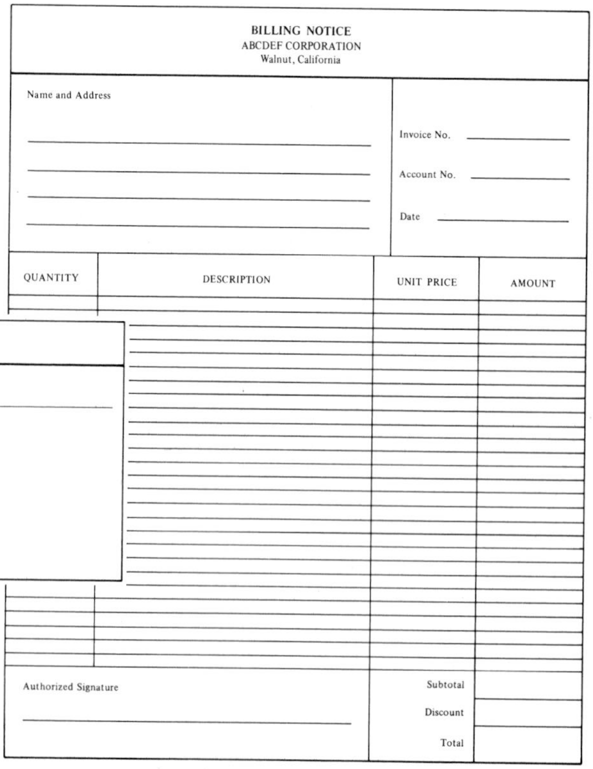

BILLING NOTICE
ABCDEF CORPORATION
Walnut, California

Name and Address

Invoice No. _____

Account No. _____

Date _____

QUANTITY	DESCRIPTION	UNIT PRICE	AMOUNT

Authorized Signature

Subtotal	
Discount	
Total	

PAYMENT/CREDIT
MEMORANDUM

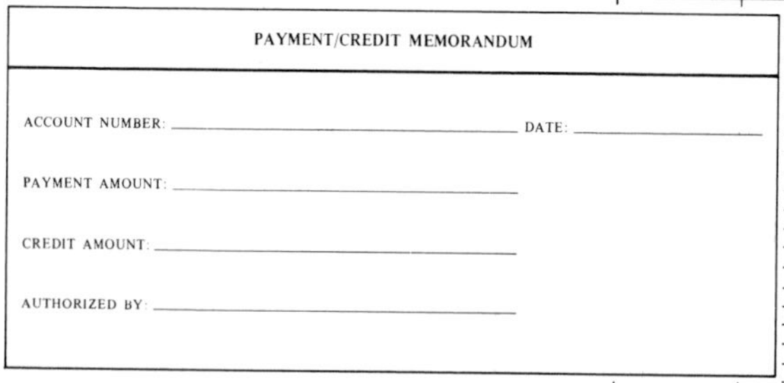

PAYMENT/CREDIT MEMORANDUM

ACCOUNT NUMBER: _____ DATE: _____

PAYMENT AMOUNT: _____

CREDIT AMOUNT: _____

AUTHORIZED BY: _____

FIGURE 12-10. Operating cost of current
                accounts receivable system

ACCOUNTS RECEIVABLE COST SUMMARY		
ITEM	NO.	COST/MONTH
1. Personnel: A/R Department		
Head of A/R Department	1	$1,600
A/R Clerks	2	1,000
A/R Typist	1	700
A/R Bookkeeping Machine Op.	1	800
SUBTOTAL		$4,100
2. Personnel: Credit Department		
Head of Credit Department	1	$1,500
Credit Clerks	2	1,000
Credit Typist	1	700
SUBTOTAL		$3,200
3. Supplies -	-	
Forms, Paper, and		200
Miscellaneous Supplies		
TOTAL		$7,500/MO.

12-10, *Operating cost of current accounts receivable system.* The total
current operating cost is $7,500 a month.

    New system project directive. The most significant conclusion reached
by J. Herring as a result of the initial investigation was that serious consideration should be given to a computer-based A/R system. Her conclusion is reflected in the project directive, which appears as FIGURE 12-11,
Project directive for MARS (modified accounts receivable system). This
figure completes the example project directive, the first page of which
was shown in the preceding chapter as Figure 11-13. Two additional
pages are used to complete the identification of the six outputs for the
new system. These are:
    1. Customer monthly statement
    2. A/R transaction register
    3. A/R summary report
    4. Aged accounts receivable report
    5. Customer account list
    6. Overcredit notice
    Tentatively, the inputs for the new system are the same as for the
manual system, except that the customer account card is no longer used.
Data will be taken directly from the customer account application.

FIGURE 12-11. **Project directive for MARS**
(modified accounts receivable system)

New system specific objectives. We will assume that, after a review of the project directive and of the results of the initial investigation, J. Herring prepared the following list of specific objectives for the modified accounts receivable system (MARS). They are ranked in order of importance.

1. To establish three billing cycles per month—one for each region.
2. To mail customer statements no later than two days after the close of each billing cycle.
3. To provide a daily list of A/R transactions.
4. To provide weekly and monthly A/R summary reports.
5. To initiate a finance charge of 1 percent per month on accounts that are overdue more than 30 days.
6. To identify accounts that have exceeded their credit limit prior to order processing.
7. To introduce controls to reduce the customer monthly statement error rate by 90 percent—a reduction in errors from 1 percent to 1/10 of 1 percent.
8. To provide a capability for listing customer accounts by region.

OUTPUT DESCRIPTION

Output identification and description

As the final step in performance definition, the analyst must describe the outputs as they will appear to the user. For example, if the system outputs are to be in report format, he prepares a layout and a data element description for each output. At this point in the life cycle of a system, it is not necessary to design the output report form. The report layout may be a neat sketch which the user can understand and comment upon. However, the sketch should conform to the general rules for good form design.

To prepare an effective output layout, the analyst has to make an initial judgment of the most likely output medium. The analyst should never undertake an assignment with a prejudgment that the solution requires a computer or computer-produced outputs. However, if, as a result of the initial investigation and the identification of specific objectives, he judges that the outputs are most likely to be computer-produced, he prepares his sketches with the characteristics of the output device in mind. Thus, if he were preparing a layout of a printed report, he would take the characteristics of line printers into account.

If a computer is to be considered, the analyst's flexibility in output presentation may be increased because a variety of output media are available. Figure 12-12, *Typical computer output devices,* displays examples of computer output media. In this figure, the flowchart symbol most appropriate to each output medium is indicated. Some of the output devices also can serve as input devices.

Printed reports are the most common computer outputs. These may be actual paper print-outs, called "hard-copy" reports, or they may be displays on cathode

FIGURE 12-12. Typical computer output devices

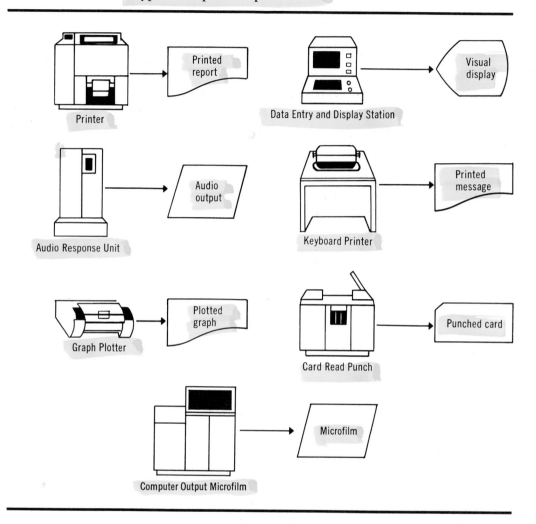

ray tubes (CRT's), called "soft-copy" reports. This discussion of report specifications and data element lists is, in general, applicable to both types of printed outputs.

The initial specification of output formats and media is necessary not only to complete the system performance definition, but also to "trigger" the process of selecting the "best" of alternative systems. This selection process is described in Chapter 13: Feasibility Analysis. The initially chosen outputs and media may or may not be those selected at the conclusion of the feasibility study. For the remainder of this section and throughout the discussion of MARS, which follows, we will assume that an initial decision was made to present the system output in the form of computer-printed reports.

FIGURE 12-13, *Report specification,* is a form that may be used to describe computer-printed output. It includes:

1. Report title.

2. A layout, i.e., a sketch or sample of the output form.

3. An estimate of the frequency, size (number of pages), quantity (number of unique reports), and number of copies of the output.

4. A distribution list, including the location of feasible distribution points.

5. Special considerations, including identified constraints and controls.

FIGURE 12-14, *Data element list—typical entry,* is an example of a form that should accompany the report specification. The data element list contains infor-

FIGURE 12-13. Report specification

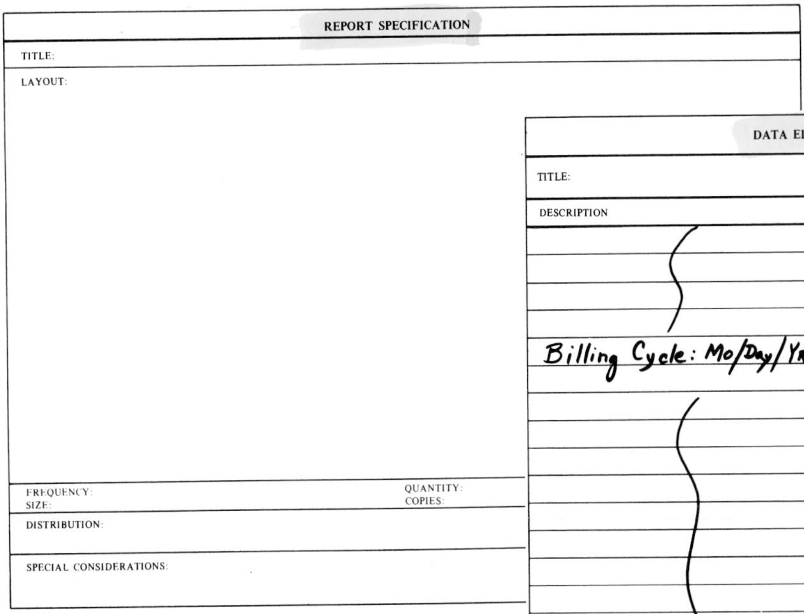

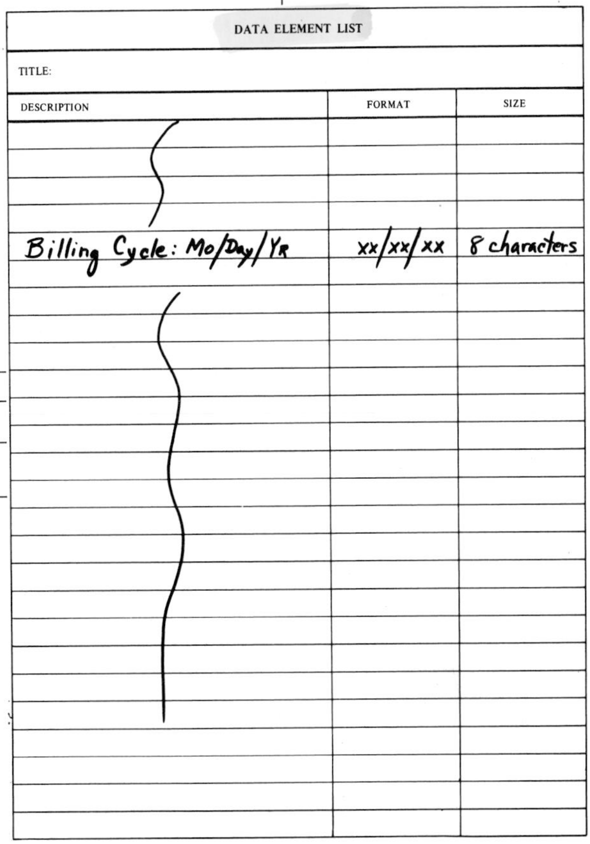

FIGURE 12-14.
Data element list—typical entry

mation describing each data element on the specified report. We will use this "typical entry" to illustrate the meaning of the column headings.

1. *Description* is the name plus any other significant description of the report:

Billing Cycle: Mo/Day/Yr

2. *Format* is an indication of the appearance of the output on a printed report. *X*'s are used to represent numbers and characters. Editing symbols are used if they are to be part of the output:

xx/xx/xx

3. *Size* indicates the number of characters to be printed:

8 characters

By specifying exactly how an output item will appear, the data element list clarifies communication. It leads to an estimate of storage requirements in the Study Phase. In subsequent phases, it is a basis for file design and for a description of computer program report output.

Example system: Output description

Sample outputs for the example A/R system are shown in Figures 12-15 through 12-20. The first part of each figure is a report specification, the second, a corresponding data element list.

> FIGURE 12-15, *Sample customer monthly statement,* is similar to the manually produced customer statement shown as part of Figure 12-8. However, provision has been made for including a finance charge. Also, it is intended that a delinquent account message be printed at the bottom of the statement, if required.
>
> FIGURE 12-16, *Sample A/R transaction register,* displays the output that replaces the entries made to the accounts receivable ledger cards of Figure 12-8. The old balance, new balance, and amount over credit are shown.
>
> FIGURE 12-17, *Sample A/R summary report,* replaces the summary report shown in Figure 12-8. This is a weekly report. Both current and cumulative weekly totals are reported for each accounting month.
>
> FIGURE 12-18, *Sample aged A/R report,* is a monthly report produced at the end of each billing cycle when the customer statements are prepared. Current amounts, and 30, 60, 90, and over 90 days past due amounts are shown.
>
> FIGURE 12-19, *Sample customer account list,* is a report prepared on demand in account number sequence. Each sales region receives a listing of its own accounts. If requested, this report can be run in customer name sequence.
>
> FIGURE 12-20, *Sample overcredit notice,* is prepared daily for each account which has exceeded its credit limit. This report is sent to the Credit department, which either approves the customer's credit and returns the notice with an approval to fill the order or returns the sales order to the customer.

FIGURE 12-15. Sample customer monthly statement

REPORT SPECIFICATION

TITLE: Customer Monthly Statement

LAYOUT:

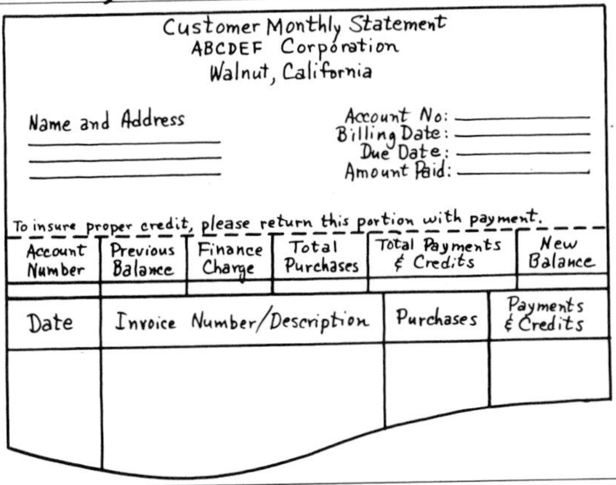

Customer Monthly Statement
ABCDEF Corporation
Walnut, California

Name and Address

Account No: _____
Billing Date: _____
Due Date: _____
Amount Paid: _____

To insure proper credit, please return this portion with payment.

Account Number	Previous Balance	Finance Charge	Total Purchases	Total Payments & Credits	New Balance
Date	Invoice Number/Description			Purchases	Payments & Credits

FREQUENCY: Monthly
SIZE: 1 to 5 pages
QUANTITY: 3,000
COPIES: 3

DISTRIBUTION: 1. Customer   3. A/R Department File
2. Credit Department

SPECIAL CONSIDERATIONS: A delinquent Account message will be printed o
than 30 days overdue at the beginning of a bil

DATA ELEMENT LIST

TITLE: Customer Monthly Statement

DESCRIPTION	FORMAT	SIZE
Name		26 characters
Address:		
Street		20 "
City		18 "
State		2 "
Zip Code		5 "
Account No: Region No.—Sequence No.	XX-XXXXXXX	10 "
Billing Cycle Date: Mo/Day/Year	XX/XX/XX	8 "
Due Date: Mo/Day/Year	XX/XX/XX	8 "
Amount Paid	XXX,XXX.XX	10 "
Previous Balance	XXX,XXX.XX	10 "
Finance Charge	X,XXX.XX	8 "
Total Purchases	XXX,XXX.XX	10 "
Total Payments & Credits	XXX,XXX.XX	10 "
New Balance	XXX,XXX.XX	10 "
Date: Date of Purchase, e.g., Jun 15	XXX XX	6 "
Invoice Number/Description		30 "
Purchases	XXX,XXX.XX	10 "
Payments & Credits	XXX,XXX.XX	10 "

FIGURE 12-16. Sample A/R transaction register

REPORT SPECIFICATION

TITLE: **Accounts Receivable Transaction Register**

LAYOUT:

Accounts Receivable Transaction Register				Date _____	
Account Number	Purchases	Payments & Credits	Old Balance	New Balance	Amount Overcredit
TOTALS					

FREQUENCY: **Daily**
SIZE: **20 pages, max.**
QUANTITY: **1**
COPIES: **6**

DISTRIBUTION: 1. Credit Department (3)   3. A/R File (1)
2. A/R Department (2)

SPECIAL CONSIDERATIONS: **Account number sequence**

DATA ELEMENT LIST

TITLE: **Accounts Receivable Transaction Register**

DESCRIPTION	FORMAT	SIZE
Date: Mo/Day/Year	xx/xx/xx	8 characters
Account No: Region No.–Sequence No.	xx-xxxxxxx	10 "
Purchases	xxx,xxx.xx	10 "
Payments & Credits	xxx,xxx.xx	10 "
Old Balance	xxx,xxx.xx	10 "
New Balance	xxx,xxx.xx	10 "
Amount overcredit	xx,xxx.xx	9 "
Totals	xx,xxx,xxx.xx	13 "

Figure 12-17. Sample A/R summary report

REPORT SPECIFICATION

TITLE: Accounts Receivable Summary Report

LAYOUT:

Accounts Receivable Summary Report					Week Ending ___		
Account No.	Name	PURCHASES		CREDITS		BALANCE		
		Current	Month to Date	Current	Month to Date	Old	New	Change
TOTALS								

FREQUENCY: Weekly
SIZE: 60 pages, max.
QUANTITY: 1
COPIES: 4

DISTRIBUTION: 1. Credit Dept. (1) 3. Manager, Accounting Division (1)
2. Accounts Receivable Dept (2)

SPECIAL CONSIDERATIONS: Weekly totals are accumulated for each accounting month.

DATA ELEMENT LIST

TITLE: Accounts Receivable Summary Report

DESCRIPTION	FORMAT	SIZE
Week Ending Mo/Day/Year	xx/xx/xx	8 characters
Account No.: Region No.-Sequence No.	xx-xxxxxxx	10 "
Name		26 "
Purchases		
Current	xxx,xxx.xx	10 "
Month to Date	xxx,xxx.xx	10 "
Credits		
Current	xxx,xxx.xx	10 "
Month to Date	xxx,xxx.xx	10 "
Balance		
Old	xxx,xxx.xx	10 "
New	xxx,xxx.xx	10 "
Change: + or −	±xxx,xxx.xx	11 "
Totals	xx,xxx,xxx.xx	13 "

FIGURE 12-18. Sample aged A/R report

REPORT SPECIFICATION

TITLE: **Aged Accounts Receivable Report**

LAYOUT:

Aged Accounts Receivable Report					Date _____		
Account Number	Name	Balance	Current Due	Past Due			
				30 Days	60 Days	90 Days	Over 90
	TOTALS						

FREQUENCY: **Monthly**

SIZE: **20 pages, max.**

QUANTITY: **1**

COPIES: **2**

DISTRIBUTION: **1. Credit Dept. (1)**
2. Accounts Receivable Dept. (1)

SPECIAL CONSIDERATIONS: **Run by region on billing cycle date.**

DATA ELEMENT LIST		

TITLE: **Aged Accounts Receivable Report**

DESCRIPTION	FORMAT	SIZE
Date: Billing Cycle Date: Mo/Day/Yr.	xx/xx/xx	8 characters
Account No.: Region No.-Sequence No.	XX-XXXXXXX	10 "
Name		26 "
Balance	XXX,XXX.XX	10 "
Current Due	XXX,XXX.XX	10 "
Past Due		
30 days	XXX,XXX.XX	10 "
60 days	XXX,XXX.XX	10 "
90 days	XXX,XXX.XX	10 "
Over 90	XXX,XXX.XX	10 "
Totals	XX,XXX,XXX.XX	13 "

FIGURE 12-19. Sample customer account list

REPORT SPECIFICATION

TITLE: **Customer Account List**

LAYOUT

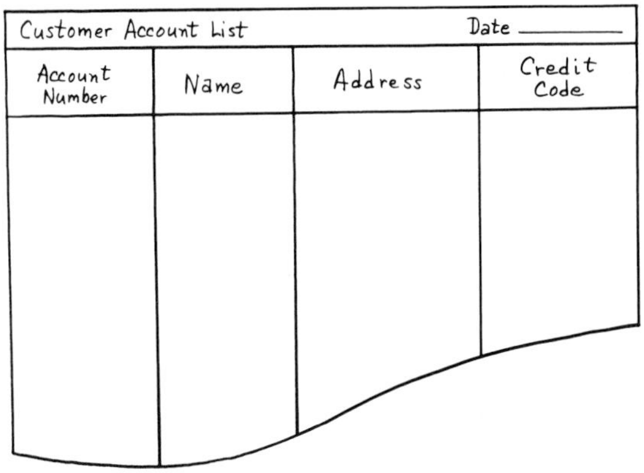

Customer Account List			Date _____
Account Number	Name	Address	Credit Code

FREQUENCY: On demand
SIZE: 100 pages, max.

QUANTITY: 1
COPIES: 5

DISTRIBUTION: 1. Region No. 01 (2)   3. Region No 03 (2)   5. Credit Depr̶t̶m̶ent (1)
2. Region No. 02 (2)   4. A/R Department (1)   6. Vice-Presi̶

SPECIAL CONSIDERATIONS: 1. Each region receives list of its own accounts
2. Also run on demand in customer name sequ̶

DATA ELEMENT LIST

TITLE: **Customer Account List**

DESCRIPTION	FORMAT	SIZE
Date: Mo/Day/Yr.	xx/xx/xx	8 characters
Acct. No.: Region and Seq.	xx-xxxxxxx	10 "
Name		26 "
Address:		
Street		20 "
City		18 "
State		2 "
Zip Code		5 "
Credit Code	xx	2 "
01 500 Limit		
02 2500 Limit		
03 10,000 Limit		
04 25,000 Limit		
05 Special		

FIGURE 12-20. Sample overcredit notice

REPORT SPECIFICATION

TITLE: Overcredit Notice

LAYOUT

Overcredit Notice

Sales Order No. _____
Sales Order Date _____
Account Number _____
Name and Address _____
_____
_____

Current Balance _____
Sales Order Amount _____
Total _____
Credit Limit _____
Amount Overcredit [_____]

☐ Overcredit Approved
☐ Return Sales Order

AUTHORIZATION

FREQUENCY: Daily
SIZE: 1 page
DISTRIBUTION: 1. Credit Dept. (2)

QUANTITY: 40 max.
COPIES: 2

SPECIAL CONSIDERATIONS

DATA ELEMENT LIST

TITLE: Overcredit Notice

DESCRIPTION	FORMAT	SIZE
Sales Order Number	XXXXXXXX	8 characters
Sales Order Date	xx/xx/xx	8 "
Account No: Region No.—Sequence No.	XX-XXXXXXX	10 "
Name		26 "
Address		
Street		20 "
City		18 "
State		2 "
Zip Code		5 "
Current Balance	XXX,XXX.XX	10 "
Sales Order Amount	XXX,XXX.XX	10 "
Total	XXX,XXX.XX	10 "
Credit Limit	XX,XXX.XX	9 "
Amount Overcredit	XX,XXX.XX	9 "

At this point, the analyst has identified the specific objectives of the system and has described the outputs required to meet those objectives. He is now ready to evaluate the feasibility of alternative systems that might produce these outputs.

KEY TERMS

general constraints	*specific objectives*	*data element list*
specific constraint	*report specification*	

FOR DISCUSSION

1. What are the three steps that result in the definition of system performance?

2. What is a general constraint? A specific constraint?

3. What is a specific objective?

4. In what ways does the system performance definition process extend the information contained in the project directive?

5. What is the reason for ranking specific objectives in order of importance?

6. Why must the analyst make a tentative selection of output media?

7. What are the values of the data element list in the Study Phase? In subsequent phases?

13 Feasibility Analysis

In the preceding chapter, the required performance of the new system was defined and documented. The next step in the life cycle is to find the best system that will produce the desired performance. The goal of this chapter, therefore, is to demonstrate the process of identifying the best system candidate. You will learn the purposes of a feasibility analysis and the steps necessary to find the best system.

PURPOSES OF A FEASIBILITY ANALYSIS

Several activities have now been completed in the Study Phase:

1. A user has recognized a need.
2. An initial investigation has been completed to study the existing system and uncover problem areas.
3. The user and the analyst have cooperatively defined the problem and identified the general objectives, required outputs, and general constraints of the new system. This resulted in the project directive.
4. The system performance has been defined by ranking specific objectives in order of their importance, and by preparing detailed descriptions of the outputs.

At this point both the user and the analyst know what the problems are and the general characteristics of the system that will solve those problems. The feasibility analysis activities will lead them, if they are successful, to a system that they have the capability to develop, that will work in their environment, and that the company can afford. The specific purposes of the feasibility analysis are (1) the selection and description of candidate systems; and (2) the selection of the "best" (i.e., the most feasible) system.

The specific objectives of the new system have been identified through the system performance definition activities. The system that meets those objectives, at the lowest cost within the general constraints, is the "best" system.

STEPS IN A FEASIBILITY ANALYSIS

The most difficult parts of a feasibility analysis are the identification of candidate systems and the evaluation of their performances and costs. This process is a highly creative one that requires imagination, experience, and a share of good luck. As with most tasks, however, this one can be proceduralized. There are nine identifiable steps in performing a feasibility analysis:

1. Form the system team.
2. Develop generalized system flowcharts.
3. Develop the system candidates.
4. Perform preliminary evaluation of candidates.
5. Prepare detailed descriptions of candidates.
6. Identify meaningful system characteristics.
7. Determine performance and cost for each candidate.
8. Weight the system performance and cost characteristics by importance.
9. Select the "best" candidate.

In the following discussion of the nine steps of the feasibility analysis, the examples presented are a continuation of the development of the modified accounts receivable system (MARS) of the ABCDEF Corporation.

Step 1: Form the system team

The first step is to enlist qualified participants for the system team. The team should be a group of involved, interested people who can represent their respective areas to help define system problems and develop methods of solution. Typically, user organizations, management, and data processing should be represented on the team. The inputs from team members and their reactions to the inputs of others can tell the analyst much about what they really consider important in the system. Often, this information-gathering technique is the only way for the analyst to get the whole picture. In addition, team members usually supply excellent ideas for consideration.

Another benefit of the system team is that the involvement of users and management in planning a system makes the system "their" system. When the people who are going to use the system and/or pay for the system refer to it as "their" system rather than "your" system, the analyst has saved himself from potential problems at system reviews and during system conversion.

Step 2: Develop generalized system flowcharts

The second step of the feasibility analysis is to develop generalized information-oriented and process-oriented flowcharts for the system. The information-oriented flowchart is a grid-type flowchart. The process-oriented flowchart is a high-level system flowchart. The value of the high-level system flowchart, at this point, is that it draws attention to the system inputs and outputs rather than to detailed processing operations. The use of the basic input/output symbol will also help the team keep an open mind about potential input/output media or devices.

Developing the generalized system flowchart usually proceeds without difficulty. The team has sketches and data element lists of all outputs identified during the system performance definition. System inputs were identified on the Information Service Request used as the project directive.

Returning to the example project, the ABCDEF Corporation's MARS, let us assume the following:

> In the course of team discussions, a representative of the Shipping department brought out the point that the shipping invoice and the shipping order are carbon copies of the sales order in the present system. The sales order consists of one original copy and four carbon copies. The carbon copies are often difficult to read. They cause some errors in shipping and are inconvenient to use in out-of-stock situations. He asked, "Would it be possible to interface our MARS with the existing inventory control system and/or produce better copies of the shipping invoice and shipping order?"
>
> Additionally, it was suggested that the Accounts Receivable department and the Credit department be combined in order to better coordinate their efforts and develop a shared data base for the two departments.
>
> These recommendations were taken to Mr. Franklin, manager of the Accounting division. Mr. Franklin gave tentative approval of the combined departments and indicated that the consolidation had already been discussed among Mr. Jones, vice-president, Finance; Mr. Levier, Credit department head; Mr. Davis, Accounts Receivable department head; and himself. In addition, he approved the adding of a seventh output, shipping invoice/shipping order, to the project directive of the MARS.
>
> Figure 13-1, *Shipping invoice*, depicts the specification and data element list for the daily output of shipping invoices as approved. The invoices, together with shipping orders, are to be forwarded to the Shipping department. Shipping orders and shipping invoices are to be produced simultaneously on multipart paper. The price information is suppressed on the shipping order.
>
> At this point the team is prepared to develop generalized flowcharts. Figure 13-2, *Information-oriented flowchart and narrative—MARS*, is a flowchart that reflects the recommendations made by the system team and approved by Mr. Franklin, manager of the Accounting division.
>
> Figure 13-3, *Generalized high-level system flowchart*, is a process-oriented flowchart which focuses on the data processing column of the flowchart in Figure 13-2.

Step 3: Develop the system candidates

The third step of the feasibility analysis is to develop candidate systems that could produce the outputs identified in the generalized flowcharts. This includes a consideration of hardware devices able to accomplish each of the four basic system functions of input, processing, storage, and output.

FIGURE 13-1. Shipping invoice

REPORT SPECIFICATION

TITLE: **Shipping Invoice**

LAYOUT:

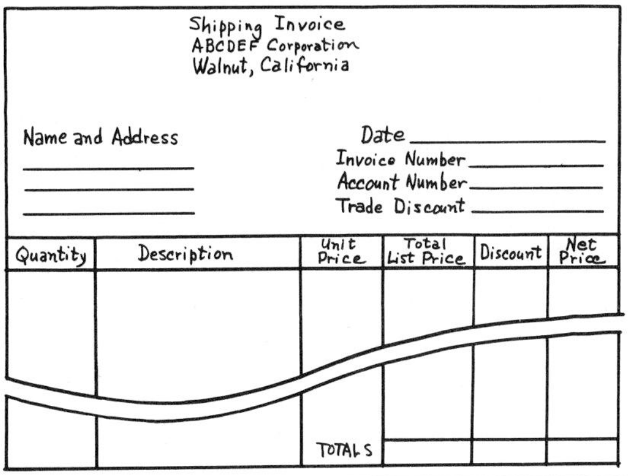

> Shipping Invoice
> ABCDEF Corporation
> Walnut, California

Name and Address

Date _____
Invoice Number _____
Account Number _____
Trade Discount _____

Quantity	Description	Unit Price	Total List Price	Discount	Net Price
			TOTALS		

FREQUENCY: **Daily**
SIZE: **8 pages, max.**
QUANTITY: **200**
COPIES: **3**

DISTRIBUTION: **Shipping Department (3)**

SPECIAL CONSIDERATIONS: Second and third copies are to be labeled S... price information is to be suppressed on the...

DATA ELEMENT LIST

TITLE: **Shipping Invoice**

DESCRIPTION	FORMAT	SIZE
Name		26 characters
Address:		
Street		20 "
City		18 "
State		2 "
Zip Code		5 "
Date: Mo/Day/Year	xx/xx/xx	8 "
Invoice Number		6 "
Account No: Region No.-Sequence No.	XX-XXXXXXX	10 "
Trade Discount: Wholesale %-Retail %	XX-XX	5 "
Quantity	X,XXX	5 "
Description		23 "
Unit Price	X,XXX.XX	8 "
Total List Price	XXX,XXX.XX	10 "
Discount	XX,XXX.XX	9 "
Net Price	XXX,XXX.XX	10 "
Totals:		
Total List Price	XXX,XXX.XX	10 "
Discount	XX,XXX.XX	9 "
Net Price	XXX,XXX.XX	10 "

FIGURE 13-2. Information-oriented flowchart and narrative—MARS

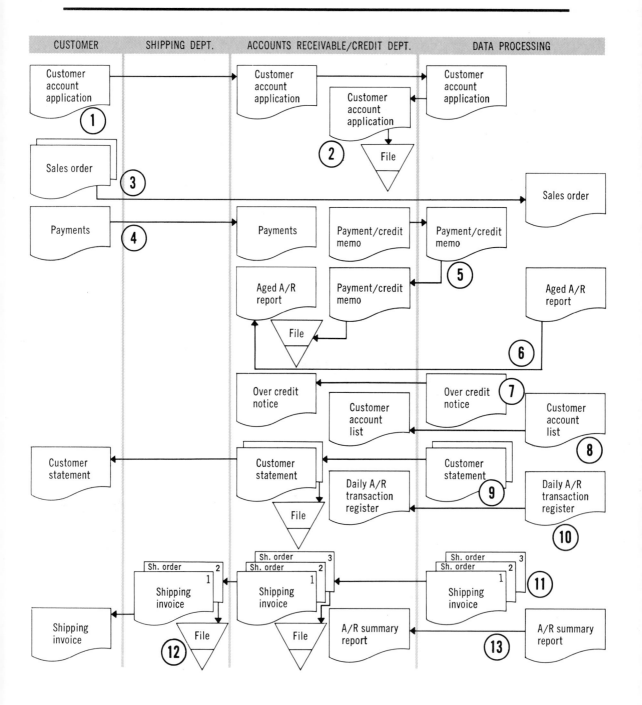

INFORMATION-ORIENTED FLOWCHART NARRATIVE

1. Customers submit account applications which are processed by the Accounts Receivable/Credit department.

2. If an application is accepted, it is sent to Data Processing for entry into the system. Data Processing returns the application for filing.

3. Sales orders are sent directly to Data Processing for order processing. The customer retains the carbon copy.

4. Payments are sent to the Accounts Receivable/Credit department.

5. A payment/credit memo is generated and sent to Data Processing. Data Processing returns the memo for filing.

6. An aged A/R report is sent to the Accounts Receivable/Credit department from Data Processing each month.

7. Data Processing sends overcredit notices to a credit clerk whenever a new order would exceed the customer's credit limit. If the additional credit is approved, the notice is returned to Data Processing with an authorization to process the order. If the additional credit is disapproved, the order and the notice are returned to the customer.

8. Customer account lists are produced on demand and sent to the Accounts Receivable/Credit department for distribution.

9. Customer statements are sent to Accounts Receivable/Credit in duplicate. The original copy is sent to the customer; the duplicate is filed. One-third of the statements are produced each ten days of the month, i.e., on the 1st, 10th, and 20th.

10. A daily A/R transaction register is sent to the Accounts Receivable/Credit department.

11. Three copies of the shipping invoice/shipping order are sent to the Accounts Receivable/Credit department. The original copy is entitled shipping invoice; the two carbon copies are entitled shipping order. The third copy is filed by A/R.

12. The shipping invoice and the first copy of the shipping order are sent to the Shipping department. The shipping order is used to "pick" inventory items for shipment and is then filed. The shipping invoice is packed with the merchandise and is sent to the customer.

13. The accounts receivable summary report is prepared weekly and sent to the Accounts Receivable/Credit department for distribution.

FIGURE 13-3. Generalized high-level system flowchart

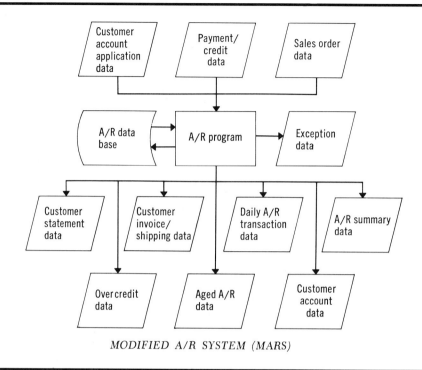

MODIFIED A/R SYSTEM (MARS)

Here again, the system team will be valuable to the systems analyst. The system team's task is to do some "brainstorming" by trying various hardware combinations for each of the four basic functions mentioned above. If some team members are not familiar with some of the potentially suitable devices, other members with knowledge of equipment, e.g., the data processing representative, can make a presentation to the team.

FIGURE 13-4, *Candidate system matrix format*, is an example of a table which can be used in the development of system candidates. The table is an effective means of presenting and comparing the basic functions of each candidate.

We can illustrate the use of a candidate system matrix by continuing with our example system.

In the ABCDEF Corporation's MARS, the output medium initially chosen for all outputs was computer-printed reports. This choice was made by the analyst, Ms. J. Herring, during the system performance definition activities because she judged it the most likely output medium. That initial assumption was made so that sketches of the outputs could be made with the characteristics of the output device in mind. That initial assumption, however, does not now prevent the system team from con-

FIGURE 13-4. Candidate system matrix format

CANDIDATE SYSTEM FUNCTIONS	I	II	III	IV	V	VI
OUTPUT						
INPUT						
STORAGE						
PROCESSING						

sidering other media. Since a computer is being considered as a likely tool to be used, output media choices should again be investigated. These were illustrated in Figure 12-12 in the preceding chapter.

In the case of the MARS, two alternatives to printer output are data display stations for visual output on a cathode ray tube (CRT) or an audio response unit for low volume output such as customer balances or credit status. Punched card output might be a choice for overcredit notices.

Possible input media are depicted in FIGURE 13-5, *Typical computer input devices.*

In the MARS example, one input is the sales order. Should that input be through punched cards, magnetic tape, magnetic disk, optical character readers, or a portable terminal keyboard carried by the salesperson? If the medium seems reasonable, it should be considered.

FIGURE 13-6, *Typical computer storage devices*, displays examples of storage media to be considered for the system's data base and for intermediate storage.

FIGURE 13-5. Typical computer input devices

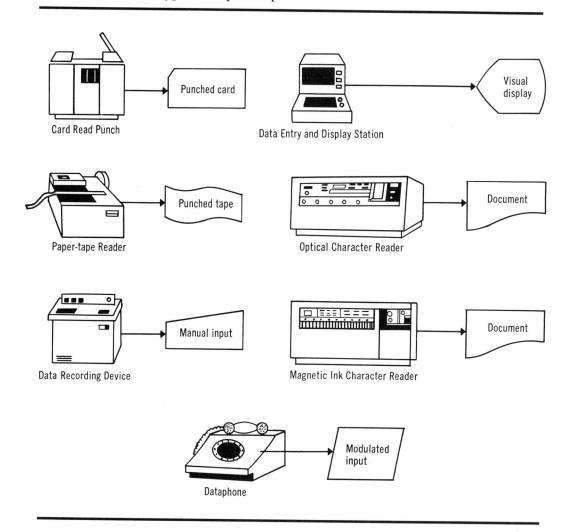

Each of these potential media has performance and cost advantages and disadvantages.

The last function to be considered is processing. The general processing choices are manual processing and computer processing. Methods of manual processing can range from pencil and paper to desk calculators to manually operated equipment such as bookkeeping machines. If a potential processing medium is a computer, there are a large number of computers with differing processor capabilities, processor speeds, main storage size ranges, auxiliary storage handling capabilities, and levels of software support. Computer vendors will be more than happy to provide the system team with information on their equip-

Figure 13-6. Typical computer storage devices

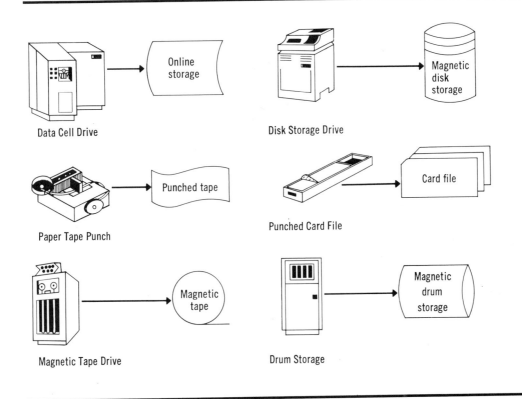

Data Cell Drive → Online storage

Disk Storage Drive → Magnetic disk storage

Paper Tape Punch → Punched tape

Punched Card File → Card file

Magnetic Tape Drive → Magnetic tape

Drum Storage → Magnetic drum storage

ment and to make recommendations. Representatives of the team, however, should always make it a point to verify data from vendors by making visits or con-tacts with other users or user groups. Each potential processor has its own advan-tages and disadvantages. Compromise may be necessary; however, know what you are giving up for what you are getting.

Step 4: Perform preliminary evaluation of candidates

Usually the analyst and his team have far too many candidates to evaluate in detail. Hence, the fourth step in the feasibility analysis is to make a preliminary evaluation of the system candidates and thus narrow down the number of can-didates to a manageable number.

In developing system candidates, the idea is to "brainstorm" as many candi-dates as possible. In the preliminary evaluation, any system that would not be practical because of its obvious high cost or its "overkill" for the task at hand is eliminated. Candidate systems that would require technical knowhow beyond that available to the company or that do not fit the overall personality of the company should also be dropped from consideration.

Figure 13-7. Candidate system matrix

CANDIDATE SYSTEM / FUNCTIONS	I In-house	II In-house	III In-house	IV Out-house	X Out-house
OUTPUT	Printer: all outputs	Printer: all outputs	Printer: all outputs	Printer: all outputs (carried by courier)	Printer: all outputs via in-house printer
INPUT	Punched cards: all inputs	Punched cards: all inputs	Punched cards: acct. app. and payments — — — — — —→ Terminal keyboard: sale orders	Punched cards: all inputs (punched in-house)	Punched cards: all inputs via in-house card reader
STORAGE	Data base on mag disk	Data base on mag disk	Data base on mag disk	Data base on mag disk	Data base on mag disk
PROCESSING	In-house S/3	Medium-size computer, e.g., S/370 Model 138	Medium-size computer, e.g., S/370 Model 138	Medium-size computer, e.g., S/370 Model 138	Medium-size computer, e.g., S/370 Model 138

The process of elimination should continue until the number of candidates is down to a manageable size. The actual number of systems to be considered in detail is, of course, a function of the amount of time and the resources available to the analyst and his team.

For example:

> The system team for the MARS project, headed by Ms. J. Herring, generated the system candidates depicted in part in Figure 13-7, *Candidate system matrix.* Some of the candidates utilize a small computer, most a medium-sized computer. Some involve an in-house computer, and some involve purchased time at a computer service bureau.

Step 5: Prepare detailed descriptions of candidates

The fifth step in the feasibility analysis is to prepare detailed descriptions of the remaining system candidates. The detailed descriptions should include flowcharts and narratives, specific constraints, identified inputs, processing requirements, and storage requirements.

The MARS project illustrates this step with the following assumed situation:

> In the MARS project, Ms. Herring and the system team have reduced the number of candidates for detailed study to three: (1) a computer system utilizing an in-house computer of medium size; (2) a computer system utilizing the current in-house IBM System/3; and (3) the current manual system. Both computer systems use punched-card input and computer-printed output. The medium-sized computer would have to be acquired, and no study has been made of particular manufacturers or specific model of a computer. If this computer acquisition is recommended, vendor proposals will be solicited and evaluated early in the Design Phase, assuming the analyst gets approval from the users and management to proceed.

> Parts A through D of FIGURE 13-8, *MARS Candidate I description*, illustrate the type of description which the team prepared for each candidate. The information-oriented flowchart for this candidate is the one shown in Figure 13-2. Part A of Figure 13-8 is an intermediate-level system flowchart with its accompanying narrative. It is the generalized high-level flowchart in Figure 13-3, modified to reflect specific media to be used in the input, storage, and output functions. The information-oriented flowchart of Figure 13-2 shows the source of input documents, the number of required copies of each document, the path of each document through the company, and the generation and distribution of all outputs. This flowchart and the high-level process-oriented flowchart of Figure 13-8 present a comprehensive overview of the candidate system.

Specific constraints are unique to each candidate. They must either be consistent with the general constraints of the project directive or must identify areas where the candidate does not meet the general constraints. If the specific constraints are too restrictive, the candidate will be eliminated or the general constraints of the project directive will have to be modified.

> Part B of Figure 13-8 lists the specific constraints for MARS Candidate I. Part C identifies the three major MARS inputs and specifies, in general, the equipment to be required by the system. In this case, the equipment required is a computer system.

> Part D presents the estimated number of characters of storage for each master record in the data base, the number of characters for the master file at current customer levels, and the size of the master file at the end of a five-year projection of customer growth. A general constraint affecting the storage estimates was the capacity to process 10,000 customers within five years.

The gross storage estimates can be developed from a worksheet like the form used in the MARS example, shown in FIGURE 13-9, *Output data element source*

FIGURE 13-8. MARS Candidate I description

PART A

SYSTEM FLOWCHART
MODIFIED A/R SYSTEM (MARS)

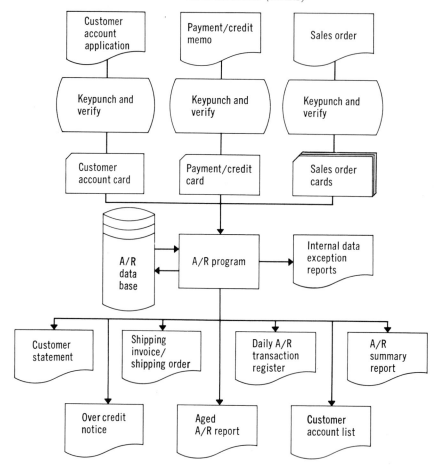

SYSTEM FLOWCHART NARRATIVE

1. Customer account applications, payment/credit memos, and sales orders are the three major system inputs.

2. Each source document is keypunched and verified.

3. The A/R program inputs the transaction data cards and reads/updates the master file on magnetic disk. Program edit routines produce exception reports whenever invalid input data is detected.

4. The seven major outputs of the system are the customer statements, invoice/shipping order, A/R transaction register, A/R summary report, overcredit notice, aged A/R report, and a customer account list.

PART B   SPECIFI CONSTRAINTS

1. This candidate does not give priority to the existing
   in-house IBM System/3 computer.

2. Implementation of this candidate would probably result
   in giving up the in-house System/3 and transferring its
   current load, i.e., production control and inventory
   control, to the larger machine. This may involve program
   modification and testing costs.

3. To be economical, the larger computer with this candidate
   will have to handle more applications than the current
   System/3 load plus the MARS. A study will be required
   to determine this utilization.

4. The original implementation schedule for MARS allows only
   four months from the end of the Study Phase. An in-house
   installation could not be made in time for the Development
   Phase programming, testing, and training activities. Using
   off-site equipment while awaiting installation should
   be investigated.

5. An order for the computer equipment required would have
   to be placed with a vendor or leasor as soon as possible.
   This will restrict the time available for configuration
   study and bids for equipment.

PART C
                            IDENTIFIED INPUTS

Title	Frequency	Quantity	Notes
1. Billing Notice	daily	300 max.	Sales Order Copy
2. Payment/Credit Memo	daily	1000 max.	from Credit Department
3. Customer Account Application	daily	4-10	can be batched

                       PROCESSING REQUIREMENTS

1. A medium-size CPU with a main storage of approximately
   144 K bytes. (e.g., IBM System/370, Model 138,
   or equivalent)

2. 1 ≈ 600 line-per-minute line printer

3. 1 ≈ 1000 card-per-minute reader

4. 1 ≈ 500 card-per-minute punch

5. 2 disk spindles, each with a removable disk pack
   of ≈ 70 million bytes

6. 1 tape transport, 9 track, 1600 bpi, low speed acceptable

7. 1 console keyboard/printer

8. Channels and controllers to support the above.

PART D
                        STORAGE REQUIREMENTS

1. Each master record consists of 15 data fields for a total
   of 167 characters.

2. Assuming approximately 8,000 characters of data per disk
   track and 696 tracks per disk pack:
   a. 24 tracks will be required for the current 1,000
      customers.
   b. 213 tracks will be required for the expected 10,000
      customers in five years.

3. In five years the master file will utilize less than 3
   percent of one disk pack on an IBM 3340 disk system,
   or its equivalent.

analysis. The purpose of this worksheet is to help determine the source of the data elements in the outputs of a system. The data element lists developed to accompany each output sketched during the system performance definition activities are referred to. The completed worksheet identifies the origin of the output data elements as master file, transaction file, or calculated result. In addition, it provides an overview of the output documents and their data element relationships.

These are the steps in using the output data element source analysis:

1. Complete the heading information.

2. List all output data elements found on the data element lists. Do not list a data element more than one time. Watch for single data elements listed by two or more different data element names. The names used on the data element lists are names that were appropriate and meaningful to that particular output. A slightly different name for the same data element might have been more meaningful on a different output. For example, in Figure 13-9 the data element "previous balance" is shown as being used in five of the seven outputs. The data element lists refer to the same data element as "previous balance" on one output, as "old balance" on two outputs, as "balance" on one output, and as "current balance" on one output. It is obviously the same field in each case regardless of its name on any one data element list.

3. In the column below each output document, place a check mark opposite each data element appearing on the document. The frequency of check marks opposite the data elements will be valuable information when designing the master record layout.

4. With the frequency-of-use information from above, decide which data elements should be maintained in a master file or a transaction file, or which ones are to be calculated by the computer program. In the appropriate Source of Data Element column, enter the number of characters for the data element. Data in the master file must originate either in transaction files or as calculated results. Such data is entered in two columns. The number of characters for each data element can be found in the appropriate data element list. Watch for inconsistent data element sizes on the data element list and make adjustments to the lists where required. Note that the numbers of characters entered in the Source of Data Element columns do not include editing symbols, i.e., dollar signs, commas, and decimal points, as these would not be stored in the master file or transaction file records.

5. Total each Source of Data Element column. The master file total is a usable estimate of the master record size. It does not take data formats, e.g., zoned or packed decimal, into consideration, but it is adequate for Study Phase planning.

Step 6: Identify meaningful system characteristics

Step six of the feasibility analysis is to select the criteria for evaluating the candidate systems. The candidates are evaluated by two major categories of criteria: performance characteristics and costs.

FIGURE 13-9. Output data element source analysis

The performance evaluation criteria relate to the satisfaction of specific objectives identified and ranked in the process of system performance definition. Typical criteria are accuracy, control capability, flexibility, growth potential, reliability, speed, and storage capacity. Often these characteristics do not lend themselves to quantitative measurements and must be described qualitatively. In any event, qualitative measurements (i.e., best, good, bad, worst) can be used to measure the relative performance of candidate systems.

The total cost of a system includes the costs of developing the system and operating it after its implementation. Cost factors that may be particularly important in evaluating a system are those for equipment, facilities, and training. Equipment costs are important when additional equipment, such as computers and bookkeeping machines, must be acquired or existing equipment must be modified. Existing equipment costs usually need not be considered in the evaluation of a system if these costs would remain the same whether or not the system was adopted. Facility costs reflect the costs of additional buildings or rooms, or the modification of existing facilities. Computer installations requiring additional air conditioning, subflooring to allow for cables, alterations to fire sprinkler systems, or installation of security devices are examples of such costs. Training costs are usually not collected unless they can be easily identified. They can be identified if employees must be sent to equipment vendor schools or if classes are to be held in-house with overtime being paid to either the employee attending classes or to his substitute on the job. However, normal training on the job is usually too difficult to separate from regular job duties to be counted as system costs.

Figure 13-10, *Candidate evaluation matrix,* depicts the system evaluation criteria to be used to evaluate the three remaining MARS candidates. In the MARS example, the manual system candidate is not a viable candidate. It is being retained as a candidate only because it will provide a standard against which the other two candidates can be measured. The requirements of the system's specific objectives would otherwise have eliminated it from further consideration.

2 major characteristics of evaluating candidates

Step 7: Determine performance and cost for each candidate
The next step in the feasibility analysis is to develop the data entries for the candidate evaluation matrix. Although the performance entries are often subjective, the analyst must be fair in making his appraisals of performance.

The "accuracy" of a candidate refers not to the accuracy of the equipment, but of the system. One computer is not likely to be more accurate than another, but a system using one computer can be more accurate than another system using the same computer. Accuracy, therefore, relates to the steps involved in getting source data into the system and the steps that are taken to keep the data as error free as possible. No system will be free of bad data. "Control capability" relates to the security of the system. It provides for auditing of the system. It also provides protection from mistakes made by humans and from fraud or

FIGURE 13-10. Candidate evaluation matrix

CANDIDATE SYSTEM / EVALUATION CRITERIA	CANDIDATE I Medium-size (S/370 138)	CANDIDATE II Current IBM S/3	CANDIDATE III Manual System
PERFORMANCE:			
Accuracy			
Control capability			
Flexibility			
Growth potential			
Reliability			
Speed			
Storage capacity			
COSTS:			
System development			
System operation			
Equipment			
Facilities			
Training			

illegal data manipulation. "Flexibility" refers to the ease of making adjustments to the system, such as modified or new outputs. "Growth potential" is a measure of how much the system can continue to grow without extensive modification to the system or a major component, such as a computer. Such changes are often costly. A system should be expandable for at least a few years. The analyst's confidence that the system can produce the desired outputs cycle after cycle is the "reliability" rating. Weak points in the system, or in equipment utilized within the system, which could bring the operation to a halt, should be reflected in the reliability rating. A system's "speed" is its ability to meet time requirements. It includes the system activities of data collection and output distribution as well as time required to process the data. The time required for processing must be estimated and is usually the basis for the speed rating. "Storage capacity" refers to computer-based systems. It refers to both main storage size and available auxiliary storage.

Costs can be developed most easily when the system benefits are relatively tangible. The most tangible cost comparisons are related to their actual cost savings. The next most tangible comparisons are those related to cost avoidance, usually the case when large growth factors are involved.

FIGURE 13-11. Account projection

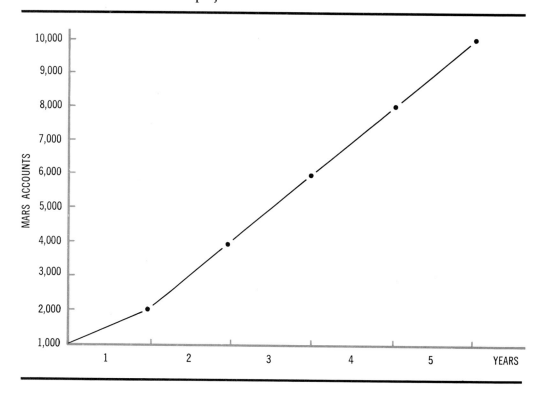

For the example MARS, it has been stated that the growth in the number of A/R accounts will be increased by a factor of 10 over the next five years. An estimate was made that sales and accounts would double within one year and continue to grow to an expected 10,000 accounts within five years. FIGURE 13-11, *Account projection*, depicts this estimated growth. Using this projection, the number of accounts can be estimated for any point in time over the next five years. Knowing the number of accounts to be processed, the analyst can break the total costs down into a "per account" cost for comparison purposes.

The MARS example cost calculations that follow are for MARS Candidate I only. Similar calculations were made for the other candidates, and the results are tabulated.

MARS Candidate I utilizes a medium-size computer. If this computer is acquired, the rental or lease costs will be the same if used eight hours per day, five days per week, or if it is not used at all. Some estimate must be made of the utilization of the computer. The cost per job or per hour will depend upon the number of jobs or hours that share fixed monthly costs.

Ms. J. Herring, the A/R project manager, contacted Mr. C. Hampton, manager of Information Services, to collect data for a computer utilization projection. She indicated to him that she was aware of the current IBM System/3 being used for production control and inventory control applications. She asked if there had been inquiries about adding other computer applications being considered by management in its planning. He answered that other applications were being considered, that it was almost certain that additional applications would be developed following implementation of MARS, but that no priorities had been set. Based on this and other information, Ms. Herring estimated that the initial computer utilization would be approximately 2.0 hours per day for the current production control and inventory control applications, 1.2 hours per day for MARS with 1,000 accounts, and approximately 2.6 hours per day for new application development for a total of 5.8 hours per day or 122 hours per month. In addition, she estimated that with new applications and the projected growth in the number of A/R accounts, a full 8-hour shift per day, or 175 hours per month, will be required within five years. FIGURE 13-12, *Candidate I—total computer utilization*, reflects this estimate. The hourly computer cost will be determined by dividing the monthly cost of the computer by the number of hours the computer is utilized.

FIGURE 13-12. Candidate I—total computer utilization

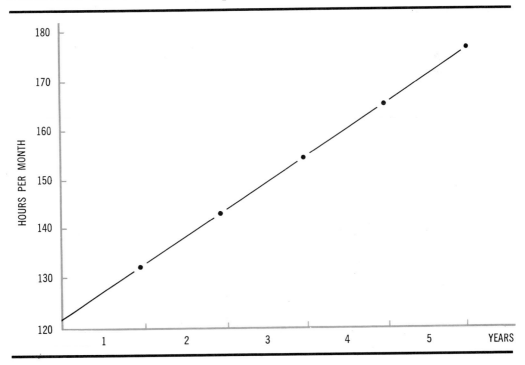

FIGURE 13-13, *Candidate I—cost calculations*, illustrates the calculations required to determine the MARS Candidate I cost of operation on a per account basis as the number of accounts and the computer utilization increase. Print time was determined by dividing the estimated volume of output lines by 600. This assumes a 600-line-per-minute printer running at full speed. The set-up and nonproductive time is the time used for changing printer forms and carriage control tapes, changing disk packs, loading the tape transport, logging jobs in and out on the console log, and other nonproduction activities, including time lost due to reruns. This time was estimated as 52 minutes per day or 18.2 hours per month. It was further estimated that the set-up time would be constant and independent of the number of accounts being processed. Computer time charged to MARS is based on print time plus a constant for set-up time.

Current personnel costs with the manual A/R system are $7,300 per month. It is company policy not to lay off computer-displaced personnel; therefore, personnel costs for MARS will remain at $7,300 per month. It is estimated that no new clerical personnel will be required with the expected growth to 10,000 accounts over the next five years. It was further determined that existing personnel would not be suitable as keypunch or verifier operators. The keypunch costs in Figure 13-13 allow for one full-

FIGURE 13-13. Candidate I—cost calculations

YEAR ENDING	Current	+1 Year	+2 Years	+3 Years	+4 Years	+5 Years
Number of Accounts	1,000	2,000	4,000	6,000	8,000	10,000
Print Time @ 600 1.p.m.	6.1 hrs.	12.2	24.5	36.7	48.9	61.0
Set-up & Nonproductive Time	18.2	18.2	18.2	18.2	18.2	18.2
Computer Time	24.3	30.4	42.7	54.9	67.1	79.2
Total Computer Usage/Month	122 hrs.	133 hrs.	143 hrs.	154 hrs.	164 hrs.	175 hrs.
Computer Cost/Month	$9,000	$9,000	$9,000	$9,000	$9,000	$9,000
Operator Cost	625	625	625	625	625	625
Total Computer Cost	$9,625	$9,625	$9,625	$9,625	$9,625	$9,625
Hourly Rate @ Usage	$78.90	$72.40	$67.30	$62.50	$58.70	$55.00
MARS Computer Cost	$1,917	$2,200	$2,874	$3,431	$3,938	$4,356
MARS Personnel Cost	$7,300	$7,300	$7,300	$7,300	$7,300	$7,300
Keypunch Cost/Month	$787.50	$787.50	$787.50	$1,575	$1,575	$1,575
Computer Cost/Account	$1.92	$1.10	$ .72	$ .57	$. 49	$ .44
Personnel/Account	$7.30	$3.65	$1.83	$1.22	$ .91	$ .73
Keypunch Cost/Account	$ .79	$ .39	$ .20	$ .26	$ .20	$ .16
Supplies/Account	$ .20	$ .20	$ .20	$ .20	$ .20	$ .20
Total Cost/Account	$10.21	$5.34	$2.95	$2.25	$1.80	$1.53

FIGURE 13-14. Candidate I—operating costs per account

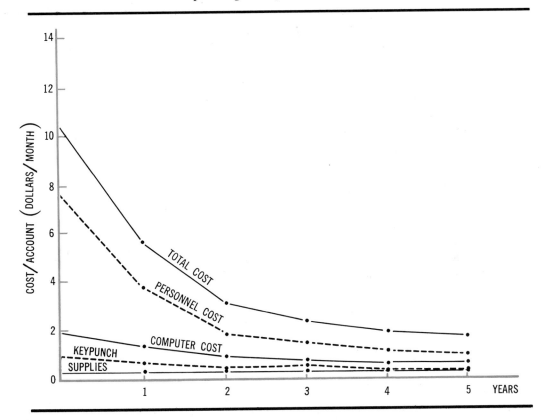

time keypunch operator at $4.50 per hour until there are 5,000 accounts. At 5,000 accounts one additional keypunch operator will be hired. FIGURE 13-14, *Candidate I—operating costs per account*, depicts the estimated operating costs in chart form. It can be seen that all the operating costs per account are reduced by increases in volume with the exception of supplies, which is a constant 20 cents per account. The operating costs will range from $10.21 per account at a volume of 1,000 accounts down to $1.53 per account at a volume of 10,000 accounts.

The estimated cost to design and develop the MARS Candidate I is shown in FIGURE 13-15, *Candidate I—project cost estimate*. This cost is the total of the Design and Development Phase costs. Study Phase costs are not included because they are "sunk" costs, already spent. Since the Study Phase cost is not affected by the acceptance or rejection of any candidate, it is not meaningful in an evaluation of candidates. FIGURE 13-16, *Candidate I—project cost estimate chart*, depicts the rate of spending and the cumulative cost of the Design Phase and Development Phase over a twenty-six week period.

FIGURE 13-15. Candidate I—project cost estimate

DESIGN PHASE: (8 WEEKS)

	Per Week	Total
Senior Analyst	$340	$2,720
Analyst	300	2,400
Senior Programmer	285	2,280
		$ 7,400

DEVELOPMENT PHASE: (18 WEEKS)

	Per Week	Total
Senior Analyst	$340	$6,120
Analyst	300	5,400
Senior Programmer	285	5,130
5 Programmers	225 each	20,250
200 Hours Computer Time @ 73.00 (off site)		14,600
200 Hours Keypunch @ 4.50		900
		52,400
Total Development Cost		$59,800

FIGURE 13-16. Candidate I—project cost estimate chart

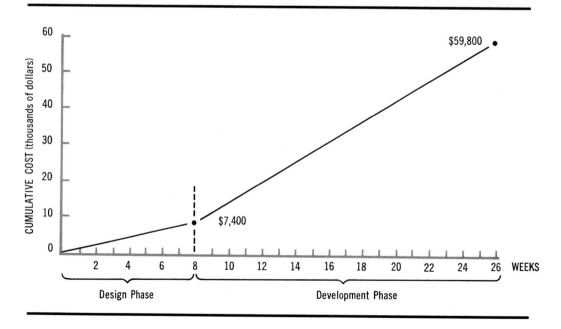

FIGURE 13-17. Operating cost of current A/R system

ACCOUNTS RECEIVABLE COST SUMMARY		
ITEM	NO.	COST/MONTH
1. Personnel: A/R Department		
Head of A/R Department	1	$1,600
A/R Clerks	2	1,000
A/R Typist	1	700
A/R Bookkeeping Machine Op.	1	<u>800</u>
SUBTOTAL		$4,100
2. Personnel: Credit Dept.		
Head of Credit Department	1	$1,500
Credit Clerks	2	1,000
Credit Typist	1	<u>700</u>
SUBTOTAL		$3,200
3. Supplies -		
Forms, Paper, and		
Miscellaneous Supplies		<u>200</u>
SUBTOTAL		$7,500/MO.
Interest Cost on $200,000 @ 9%		<u>1,500</u>
TOTAL		$9,000/MO.
Cost per Account @ 1,000 Accounts		$9.00

For the purpose of comparison, the cost of operating the current A/R system must be determined. FIGURE 13-17, *Operating cost of current A/R system,* is the same as Figure 12-10, except for the added cost of overdue accounts. The current system is allowing outstanding accounts to remain unpaid 30 days beyond their normal due date. It was estimated that this created a need to borrow $200,000 on a continuous basis at 9 percent interest. This interest cost of $1,500 per month was added to the current system's operating cost. With 1,000 accounts, the cost per account is $9.00 per month. The manual system was assumed to be operating at or near its maximum capacity with its current staff. In addition, it was estimated that the manual system would not increase in efficiency as the volume of accounts increased. Therefore, the rate of $9.00 per account was assumed to be the cost per account regardless of the volume of accounts handled.

FIGURE 13-18, *Candidate cost calculations,* depicts the costs for each candidate. The "savings" for Candidates I and II represent costs which can be avoided by *not* expanding the current system to handle the anticipated volume. They do not represent reductions in costs over the current expenditures.

FIGURE 13-18. Candidate cost calculations

CANDIDATE	YEAR	AVG. NO. OF ACCTS.	AVG. COST PER ACCT.	MONTHLY COST	*MONTHLY SAVINGS	*YEARLY SAVINGS	*CUMULATIVE YEARLY SAVINGS
I	1	1,500	$7.78	$11,670	$ 1,830	$ 21,960	$ 21,960
(Utilizing	2	3,000	4.15	12,450	14,550	174,600	195,560
medium-size							
computer)	3	5,000	2.60	13,000	32,000	384,000	580,560
	4	7,000	2.03	14,210	48,790	585,480	1,166,040
	5	9,000	1.67	15,030	65,970	791,640	1,957,680
II	1	1,500	$6.72	$10,080	$ 3,420	$ 41,040	$ 41,040
(Utilizing	2	3,000	3.53	10,590	16,410	196,920	237,960
current IBM							
System/3 +	3	5,000	2.18	10,900	34,100	409,200	647,160
upgrade)							
	4	7,000	1.70	11,900	51,100	613,200	1,260,360
	5	9,000	1.39	12,510	68,490	821,880	2,082,240
III	1	1,500	$9.00	$13,500	-	-	-
(Expanded	2	3,000	9.00	27,000	-	-	-
manual							
system)	3	5,000	9.00	45,000	-	-	-
	4	7,000	9.00	63,000	-	-	-
	5	9,000	9.00	81,000	-	-	-

*Savings relative to Candidate III, an expansion of the current system

The data for Figure 13-18 was determined as follows:

1. The average number of accounts for each year was taken from the mid-year account projection in Figure 13-11.

2. Candidate I average cost per account is from the mid-year total cost per account in Figure 13-14.

3. Monthly cost is calculated by multiplying average number of accounts times average cost per account.

4. Monthly savings is the difference between the monthly cost and the Candidate III (manual system) monthly cost.

5. The yearly savings is equal to twelve times the monthly savings.

6. The cumulative yearly savings is the total of the yearly savings and the previous cumulative yearly savings.

FIGURE 13-19, *Candidate I—payback analysis,* is a graph of the estimated development cost from Figure 13-15 and the cumulative yearly savings from Figure 13-18. The cumulative savings line crosses the development cost line—that is, payback occurs—in 15 months.

The performances and costs of each candidate are summarized in FIGURE 13-20, *Candidate evaluation matrix.* As the analyst proceeds

FIGURE 13-19. Candidate I—payback analysis

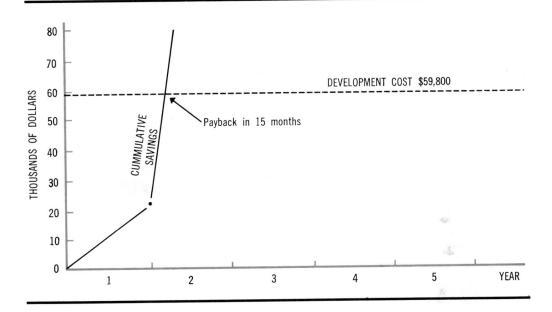

FIGURE 13-20. Candidate evaluation matrix

EVALUATION CRITERIA \ CANDIDATE SYSTEM	CANDIDATE I Medium-size (S/370 138)	CANDIDATE II Current (S/3)	CANDIDATE III Manual system
PERFORMANCE:			
Accuracy	Very good	Very good	Fair
Control capability	Very good	Very good	Poor
Flexibility	Very good	Good	Fair
Growth potential	Very good	Limited to 3-year growth without performance degradation	Very poor
Reliability	Good	Good	Fair
Speed	Very good	Good	Can't make schedule
Storage capacity	Good	Good	No problem
COSTS:			
System development	$59,800	$42,370	-0-
System operation	$10.21-$1.53 per account	$8.85-$1.27 per account	$9.00 per account
Payback period	15 months	12 months	N.A.

through the feasibility·analysis, additional system evaluation criteria may be identified, and/or criteria identified previously may be discarded. In this figure, costs of equipment, facilities, and training have been dropped from the evaluation matrix because no significant costs in these areas were identified for any of the candidates. The payback period was identified and added as an evaluation criterion.

Step 8: Weight the system performance and cost characteristics

In some cases the performance and cost data collected for each candidate will show one candidate as the obvious choice. When this occurs, the task of the feasibility analysis is completed. Many times, however, the "best" candidate is still not clearly identified. The eighth step of the feasibility analysis is to weight the system performance and cost characteristics by their importance.

Weighting the characteristics is accomplished in five steps:

1. Divide the evaluation criteria into categories of importance, e.g., very important, moderately important, important.

2. Assign a weighting factor to each category. The weighting factors should be in proportion to each criterion's effect on the success of the selected candidate system.

3. Rate each candidate for each criterion relative to the other candidates. This relative rating is often with a scale of 1 to 5, with 5 being the best and 1 the lowest.

4. Calculate the candidate's score for each criterion by multiplying the relative rating by the weight assigned to the category.

5. Add the score column for each candidate to determine its total score.

Figure 13-21, *Weighted candidate evaluation matrix*, depicts the relative criteria ratings and weighting of the MARS example. The importance categories and their relative weights were determined cooperatively by the system team. The relative criteria ratings were developed from the data summarized in Figure 13-20.

Step 9: Select the "best" system

The last step is to select the best candidate system. If the analyst has been objective and has judged each of the evaluation criteria for each candidate without prejudice, the weighted candidate evaluation matrix summarizes the facts collected as well as the subjective "impressions" about each candidate. The candidate with the highest total score *probably* is the best system. The analyst must select a candidate to present to the users and to management for their acceptance or rejection. If the total scores of two or more candidates are close, the analyst should reevaluate those criteria ratings that differ the most or in which he has the least amount of confidence. Finally, the analyst should select the candidate with the highest total score that is consistent with his confidence in the data. The analyst usually should not present several candidate choices to management for their selection, for they do not have the background to evaluate system per-

FIGURE 13-21. Weighted candidate evaluation matrix

CANDIDATE / EVALUATION CRITERIA	CANDIDATE I Medium-size (S/370 138)		CANDIDATE II Current S/3		CANDIDATE III Manual system	
	RATING	SCORE	RATING	SCORE	RATING	SCORE
PERFORMANCE:						
Very Important (Weight:5)						
Accuracy	4	20	4	20	3	15
Control Capability	5	25	5	25	2	10
Growth Potential	5	25	2	10	1	5
Speed	5	25	4	20	1	5
Important (Weight:3)						
Flexibility	5	15	5	15	3	9
Reliability	4	12	4	12	2	6
Storage Capacity	4	12	4	12	5	15
COSTS:						
Very Important (Weight:10)						
System Operation	4	40	4	40	2	20
Important (Weight:5)						
System Development	3	15	4	20	5	25
Payback Period	4	20	4	20	5	25
TOTAL SCORE		209		194		135

formance as well as the analyst. The analyst has just completed a period of concentrated study of the candidates and is therefore in the best position to make a selection.

In the example ABCDEF Corporation MARS, the criterion with the biggest effect on the total scores was the system growth potential. Candidate I, with a medium-sized computer, was considered to have adequate potential to accommodate the needs of the corporation for the foreseeable future. Candidate II, utilizing the current IBM System/3, was not expected to be able to grow with the corporate needs for more than three years. In addition, the System/3 would require immediate upgrading from its current 200 c.p.m. card reader, 200 l.p.m. printer, limited disk storage, and its 16k of main storage. Therefore, Candidate I was selected for presentation to management and the users.

The number of candidates that could be considered in the preceding example was necessarily limited. Actual situations usually are more complex, and choices are more difficult. However, there is one important practical guideline which the systems analyst always should keep in mind: The "best" system usually is the system that meets the performance requirements at the least cost.

This "best" system is not necessarily the system that provides the best performance, or even the best performance-to-cost ratio, if cost is a serious consideration. Overdesign frequently disguised as "the most bang for the buck" is liable to be an expensive luxury in a competitive, cost-conscious business environment. For example, a medium- to large-scale computer may have a better performance-to-cost ratio than a small computer. However, if a small computer will meet the performance requirement at a lower cost, the additional dollars might be more effectively utilized elsewhere in the corporation.

KEY TERMS

"best" system	*matrix*	*payback analysis*
system team	*system performance*	
system candidates	*system costs*	

FOR DISCUSSION

1. What general Study Phase activities have been completed prior to the feasibility analysis?

2. What are the two specific purposes of the feasibility analysis?

3. What is the purpose of the systems team? Who should be on the team?

4. Why should the high-level system flowchart emphasize inputs and outputs rather than processes?

5. What are the four basic functions to be performed by any system candidate? How does considering these functions aid in developing candidates?

6. Why is it necessary to perform a preliminary evaluation of system candidates prior to preparing detailed descriptions?

7. What should be included in a detailed description of a system candidate?

8. What is the purpose of the output data element source analysis worksheet?

9. Is the feasibility analysis in the Study Phase the only study of alternatives in the life cycle? Explain.

10. Discuss the statement: "The system that meets all the performance criteria at the least cost is the best' system."

14 Study Phase Report and Review

At the conclusion of the Study Phase, the analyst prepares a report and reviews it with the user of the system. The goals of this chapter are to describe the structure and content of the Study Phase report and the purpose of the Study Phase review. You will learn how to organize a Study Phase report.

PERFORMANCE SPECIFICATION

The Study Phase is concluded by a Study Phase review. Prior to this review, the Performance Specification is completed and a Study Phase report is prepared. The Performance Specification is contained in the Study Phase report. This specification is the first major baseline document. It is a complete, stand-alone specification which can be extracted from the Study Phase report as visible evidence of life-cycle progress.

The Performance Specification is the system performance communication link between the user and the analyst. FIGURE 14-1, *Performance Specification outline*, illustrates the content of this specification. It is divided into two parts. The first part describes the interaction of the system with its operating environment, i.e., inputs, outputs, interfaces with other systems, and resource needs. The resource needs include personnel, facilities, and equipment. These interactions are external to the computer program around which the computer-based business system is built. For this reason, this part of the specification is called the external performance description.

The second part of the Performance Specification, the internal performance description, describes the internal environment of the system. It includes a high-level system flowchart and describes the related data processing operations and storage requirements.

The Performance Specification is the central element of the Study Phase report. It is a user-oriented document, written in the language of the user. In subsequent phases of the system life cycle, both the external and internal parts of

FIGURE 14-1. Performance Specification outline

PERFORMANCE SPECIFICATION

A. EXTERNAL PERFORMANCE DESCRIPTION:
1. Information-oriented flowchart
2. System output description
3. System input description
4. System interface identification
5. System resource identification

B. INTERNAL PERFORMANCE DESCRIPTION:
1. System flowchart
2. Data processing description
3. Data storage description

the Performance Specification are expanded. The greatest expansion in documentation occurs in the internal part of the specification. This part becomes more technical and more comprehensive as the system moves through the Design and Development Phases.

STUDY PHASE REPORT

Structure and content

The Study Phase report is a carefully prepared document. It is a management-oriented report which must be free of computer jargon so that it can be understood by senior managers who may not have a data processing background. The structure and content of the Study Phase report are shown in FIGURE 14-2, *Study Phase report outline.*

The discussion of system scope is based on the project directive and on the performance definition activities by which specific objectives were identified. The problem statement and purpose section is a brief discussion of the problem and a statement of the system's general objective and anticipated benefits. The results of the initial investigation, which preceded the formulation of the project directive, may be referred to here.

The constraints are of the type referred to in Chapter 12 as general constraints. They are "ground rules" that apply to all the alternative means by which the general objective of the system may be accomplished.

The specific objectives are derived from the general objective and anticipated benefits. They should be complete and quantitative wherever possible. The method of evaluation should describe how the accomplishment of the specific objectives is to be measured during the Operation Phase of the life cycle.

The conclusions and recommendations are presented next in the report in order to emphasize them and to accommodate the executive who may not need to read the entire report. However, the conclusions and recommendations must be substantiated in the other sections of the Study Phase report. The conclusions

FIGURE 14-2. Study Phase report outline

STUDY PHASE REPORT

I. SYSTEM SCOPE:	A. System title B. Problem statement and purpose C. Constraints D. Specific objectives E. Method of evaluation
II. CONCLUSIONS AND RECOMMENDATIONS:	A. Conclusions B. Recommendations

III. PERFORMANCE SPECIFICATION:	A. External performance description
	  1. Information-oriented flowchart
	  2. System output descriptions
	  3. System input descriptions
	  4. System interface identification
	  5. System resource identification
	
	B. Internal performance description
	  1. System flowchart
	  2. Data processing description
	  3. Data storage description

IV. PLANS AND COST SCHEDULES:	A. Detailed milestones—Study phase B. Major milestones—all phases C. Detailed milestones—Design Phase
V. APPENDICES:	As appropriate

---

reflect the significant results of the system performance definition and feasibility analysis activities. The recommendations relate to the user's decision either to proceed with a Design Phase or to terminate the project.

The Performance Specification follows the conclusions and recommendations. Major elements of this baseline document were outlined in Figure 14-1.

The plans and cost schedules prepared at the onset of the Study Phase are updated to report actual progress and cost versus schedule for the entire Study Phase. The report also includes two additional sets of project plans and cost schedules. A chart of major milestones is prepared for the entire project. The purpose of such a chart is to make "visible" to the reviewers the key activities to be completed and the costs to be incurred in order for the proposed system to become operational. FIGURE 14-3, *Major milestones in the Design and Development Phases,* is a list of "key" Design Phase and Development Phase activities which are common to the life cycle of most computer-based business systems. A cost schedule is prepared to accompany the major milestone project plan.

A detailed milestone project plan also is prepared for the Design Phase. This plan is required because, after a successful Study Phase review, the authorization to proceed applies to the entire Design Phase. There is another review at the end of the Design Phase, when similar detail is given for the Development

FIGURE 14-3. **Major milestones in the Design and Development Phases**

MAJOR MILESTONES

DESIGN PHASE: Allocation of functions
Computer program functions
Test requirements
Design Specification
Design Phase report
Design Phase review

DEVELOPMENT PHASE: Implementation plan
Equipment acquisition
Computer program development
System tests
Personnel training
Changeover plan
System Specification
Development Phase report
Development Phase review

FIGURE 14-4. **Detailed milestones for the Design Phase**

DESIGN PHASE—DETAILED MILESTONES

ALLOCATIONS OF FUNCTIONS

MANUAL FUNCTIONS: Task definition
Reference manual identification

EQUIPMENT FUNCTIONS: Function definition
Equipment Specification

COMPUTER PROGRAM FUNCTIONS: Data base design
Computer program component
Design (for each component)

TEST REQUIREMENTS: System test requirements
Computer program test requirements

DESIGN SPECIFICATION

DESIGN PHASE REPORT

DESIGN PHASE REVIEW

Phase. FIGURE 14-4, *Detailed milestones for the Design Phase,* lists the milestones that will be described in Chapter 15. A cost schedule is prepared to accompany the plan.

Appropriate appendices are included in the Study Phase report. Typically, they contain the project directive, the significant results of the initial investigation, the feasibility analysis, and pertinent memoranda.

Example Study Phase report

Exhibit 1 on the following pages shows the Study Phase report that might be prepared for the example MARS. It includes all the features outlined in Figure 14-2. However, many illustrations that have already been presented in the text are not repeated here but simply referred to. In addition, the content of the appendix is limited to a listing of items typically included.

STUDY PHASE REVIEW

The Study Phase review is held to present the user with the results of the Study Phase activities and with recommendations for future action. If the recommendation of the analyst is to proceed with the design of the system, he should remember that the user will be making a commitment that transforms the system effort from a study to a formal project.

The analyst should be factual; however, he should not hesitate to "sell" his recommendation. After all, he has been working on the Study Phase for weeks, or even months. He *is* knowledgeable about the system, and he would be less than human if he had not formed some strong convictions. If he is enthusiastic, he should let his enthusiasm show.

The Study Phase review should be attended not only by the principal user, but also by senior representatives of other affected organizations and of the information services organization. All attendees should be provided with a copy of the Study Phase report in advance of the review meeting.

If the outcome of the Study Phase review is a decision to proceed with the Design Phase, the user-sponsor issues a written approval to proceed. This approval is an example of the renewed, or incremental, commitment that occurs at the end of each life-cycle phase. It extends the project directive by authorizing the expenditure of resources for the Design Phase.

KEY TERMS

external performance description   *internal performance description*

FOR DISCUSSION

1. What is the purpose of the Study Phase report?

2. What is the content of the Study Phase report?

3. Discuss the importance of the Performance Specification.

4. How many sets of project plans and schedules are presented at the Study Phase review? How do they differ?

5. What is the purpose of the Study Phase review? Who should attend?

EXHIBIT 1

MARS STUDY PHASE REPORT

I. SYSTEM SCOPE

   A. System Title
      Modified Accounts Receivable System (MARS)

   B. Problem Statement and Purpose
      The ABCDEF Corporation's manual accounts receivable system currently handles 1,000 accounts each month. This number is expected to double within one year and to reach 10,000 in five years. The manual system is not able to meet this projected growth. Serious problems have already been encountered in processing the current volume of accounts. Specific problems that have been identified are:

      1. A significant increase in late customer billings.
      2. An accompanying increase in billing errors.
      3. An increase in delinquent accounts.
      4. Inadequate control of credit limits.
      5. An inability to access current accounts receivable information.

      Therefore, the purpose of the MARS project is to replace the present accounts receivable system with one that can eliminate the problems enumerated above and meet the company's growth requirements. The use of a computer-based system is to be considered.

   C. Constraints
      The MARS constraints are:

      1. Design and development of the system are to be completed within six months.
      2. MARS is to have a growth potential to handle 10,000 customer accounts.
      3. The use of the current in-house IBM System/3 computer will be considered.
      4. MARS is to interface with an existing perpetual inventory system.

   D. Specific Objectives
      The specific objectives of MARS are:

      1. To establish three billing cycles per month--one for each region.
      2. To mail customer statements no later than 2 days after the close of each billing cycle.
      3. To provide a daily list of A/R transactions.
      4. To provide weekly and monthly A/R summary reports.
      5. To initiate a finance charge of 1% per month on accounts more than 30 days overdue.
      6. To identify accounts that have exceeded their credit limit prior to order processing.

   7. To introduce controls to reduce the customer monthly
      statement error rate by 90%--a reduction in errors
      from 1% to 1/10 of 1%.
   8. To provide a capability for listing customer accounts
      by region.

E. Method of Evaluation
   After MARS has been operational from 60 to 90 days:

   1. A statistical analysis will be made of customer bill-
      ings in order to verify elapsed time between the close
      of the billing cycle and the mailing of customer state-
      ments.
   2. Errors in monthly statements will be recorded for a
      30-day period, and the percentage of errors will be
      calculated.
   3. The processing of any overcredit accounts without
      authorization will be determined by an audit of one
      month's transactions.
   4. The timeliness and accuracy of the daily and weekly
      accounts receivable reports will be verified by an
      audit of one week's transactions.
   5. A random sample of the customer account lists for
      each region will be audited for validity.
   6. Personal evaluations of the effectiveness of the
      system will be obtained from its principal users.

II. CONCLUSIONS AND RECOMMENDATIONS

A. Conclusions
   The feasibility analysis of the Modified Accounts Receivable
System (MARS) has led to the conclusion that the best system
would be one utilizing a medium-sized computer, e.g., IBM
System/370 Model 138. The input data for this system is to be
punched into cards, and all outputs will be produced on a computer line printer.
   The selected system meets all performance requirements to
satisfy the MARS specific objectives listed above. Efficient
data handling will require the consolidation of the Credit and
Accounts Receivable departments.
   The projected system operation cost varies from $10.21 per
account at a volume of 1,000 accounts to $1.53 per account with
a volume of 10,000 accounts. The current manual system costs
$9.00 per account at a volume of 1,000 accounts with no antici-
pated efficiency improvements at higher volumes.
   The projected MARS development cost is $59,800. The savings
in the computer system operation cost over that of an expanded
manual system at projected account volumes would recover the
development cost in approximately 15 months of operation.
   The in-house IBM System/3 was not selected because the current configuration of the System/3 would require immediate
upgrading to higher capacity input, output, and storage devices.
In addition, it cannot grow to meet future requirements.
The selected medium-size computer will replace the System/3.

B. Recommendations
   It is therefore recommended that the MARS project be approved
for the Design Phase.

III. PERFORMANCE SPECIFICATION

   A. External Performance Description

      1. <u>Information-oriented flowchart</u>. Figure E1-1, "MARS
         information-oriented flowchart," displays the flow of
         data in the recommended modified system. The accompany-
         ing narrative appears as Figure E1-2, "MARS information-
         oriented flowchart narrative."

      2. <u>System output descriptions</u>. The seven MARS outputs are:
         a. Customer monthly statement
         b. Accounts receivable transaction register
         c. Accounts receivable summary report
         d. Aged accounts receivable report
         e. Customer account list
         f. Shipping invoice
         g. Overcredit notice
         A report specification and a data element list for an
         output are presented as Figure E1-3.

      3. <u>System input descriptions</u>. The three MARS inputs are:
         a. Customer account application
         b. Billing notice
         c. Payment/credit memo
         A description of the system inputs is included as
         Figure E1-4.

      4. <u>System interface identification</u>. The MARS must interface
         with (i.e., transfer data to and from) the existing in-
         ventory system. Inventory must be on hand for shipment
         prior to billing the customer, and inventory quantities
         should be reduced as merchandise is committed for shipment.

      5. <u>System resource identification</u>. The current IBM System/3
         will be replaced by a medium-size computer system with
         the following characteristics:
         a. A medium-size CPU with main storage of approximately
            144 K positions of memory.
         b. 1 ≈600 line-per-minute line printer.
         c. 1 ≈1000 card-per-minute reader.
         d. 1 ≈500 card-per-minute punch.
         e. 2 disk spindles, each with a removable disk pack
            of ≈70 million characters.
         f. 1 tape transport, 9 track, 1600 bpi--low speed
            acceptable.
         g. 1 console keyboard/printer.
         h. Channels and controllers to support the above.

The existing computer facilities will be adequate for the replacement computer. Three additional programmers will be required prior to the development of programs. No other increases or changes in personnel are anticipated.

B. Internal Performance Description

1. System flowchart. This flowchart is shown in the first part of Figure E1-5.
2. Data processing description. This narrative description of the system flowchart is also shown in Figure E1-5.
3. Data storage description. Each master record consists of 15 data elements for a total of 167 characters. The file will require from 17 tracks (1,000 customers) to 194 tracks (10,000 customers) out of 8,352 available on a disk pack. Thus, in five years the master file will utilize just over 2 percent of one disk pack.

IV. PROJECT PLANS AND SCHEDULES

A. Study Phase
   The Study Phase was scheduled for a six-week period, beginning 11/7/xx (this year) and ending 12/19/xx. The funding authorized for the Study Phase was $6,000. As shown in Figure E1-6, "Project plan and status report--MARS Study Phase," the project is on schedule. Only the Study Phase review remains to be completed.
   As shown in Figure E1-7, "Project cost report--MARS Study Phase," expenditures are slightly under budgeted cost.

B. Major Milestones--All Phases
   Figure E1-8, "Project plan and status report--major milestones," is a schedule for the entire project. The Design Phase is scheduled for 8 weeks, and the Development Phase is scheduled for 18 weeks. If we proceed as planned, the Design Phase will be completed 2/13/xy (next year), and the Development Phase will be completed on 6/19/xy.
   The estimated cumulative cost for the entire project (Study, Design, and Development Phases) is graphed in Figure E1-9, "Project cost report--total project." The total cost is estimated to be $65,800.

C. Detailed Milestones--Design Phase
   Since the next phase to be undertaken is the Design Phase, detailed projections are presented for that phase. Figure E1-10, "Project plan and status report--Design Phase," displays the specific milestones to be achieved in the course of an 8-week Design Phase effort.
   Figure E1-11, "Project cost report--Design Phase," presents the accompanying cumulative cost estimate. The total Design Phase cost is estimated to be $7,400.

V. APPENDICES

NOTE: The appendices include all supporting data for the conclusions of the study. For purposes of this exhibit,
such detail is not included. However, the following is
a list of typical appendices, with in-text references.

	Figure
Project directive	12-11
Account projection	13-11
Computer utilization--Candidate 1*	13-12
Cost calculations--Candidate 1*	13-13
Candidate operating costs--Candidate 1*	13-14
Candidate project cost--Candidate 1*	13-15
Current system operating cost	13-17
Candidate cost calculations	13-18
Payback analysis--Candidate 1*	13-19
Candidate evaluation matrix	13-20
Weighted candidate evaluation	13-21

*Calculations (not developed in the text) should also be
included for other candidates as well as for Candidate 1.

FIGURE E1-1. MARS information-oriented flowchart

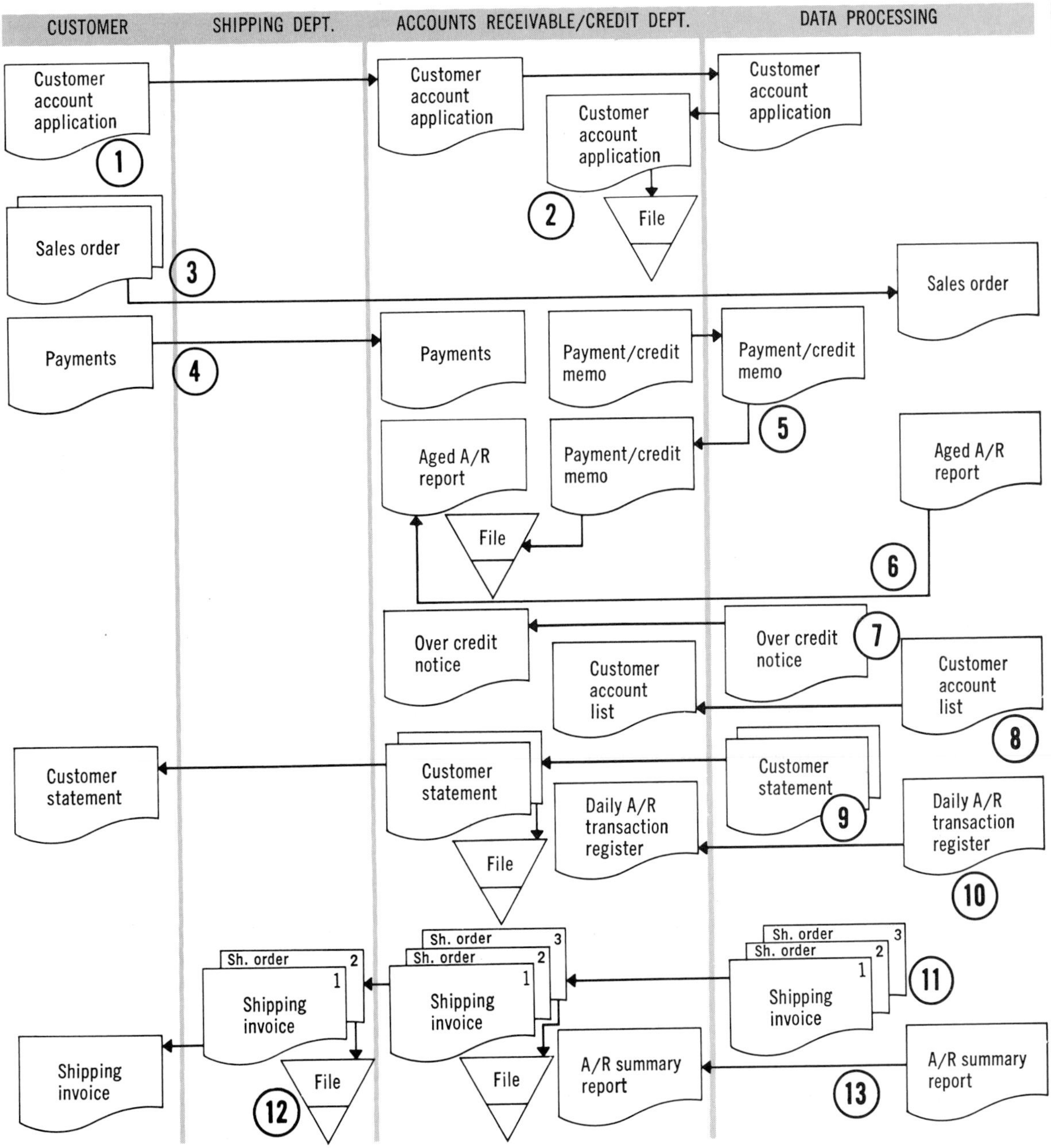
CUSTOMER
SHIPPING DEPT.
ACCOUNTS RECEIVABLE/CREDIT DEPT.
DATA PROCESSING
Customer account application
Customer account application
Customer account application
Customer account application
1
2
File
Sales order
3
Sales order
Payments
4
Payments
Payment/credit memo
Payment/credit memo
5
Aged A/R report
Payment/credit memo
Aged A/R report
File
6
Over credit notice
Over credit notice
7
Customer account list
Customer account list
8
Customer statement
Customer statement
Customer statement
9
Daily A/R transaction register
Daily A/R transaction register
File
10
Sh. order 3
Sh. order 2
Shipping invoice 1
11
Sh. order 2
Shipping invoice 1
Shipping invoice
File
12
File
A/R summary report
A/R summary report
13

FIGURE E1-2. MARS information-oriented flowchart narrative

<u>INFORMATION-ORIENTED FLOWCHART NARRATIVE</u>

1. Customers submit account applications which are processed by the Accounts Receivable/Credit department.

2. If an application is accepted, it is sent to Data Processing for entry into the system. Data Processing returns the application for filing.

3. Sales orders are sent directly to Data Processing for order processing. The customer retains the carbon copy.

4. Payments are sent to the Accounts Receivable/Credit department.

5. A payment/credit memo is generated and sent to Data Processing. Data Processing returns the memo for filing.

6. An aged A/R report is sent to the Accounts Receivable/ Credit department from Data Processing each month.

7. Data Processing sends overcredit notices to a credit clerk whenever a new order would exceed the customer's credit limit. If the additional credit is approved, the notice is returned to Data Processing with an authorization to process the order. If the additional credit is disapproved, the order and the notice are returned to the customer.

8. Customer account lists are produced on demand and sent to the Accounts Receivable/Credit department for distribution.

9. Customer statements are sent to Accounts Receivable/Credit in duplicate. The original copy is sent to the customer; the duplicate is filed. One-third of the statements are produced each ten days of the month, i.e., on the 1st, 10th, and 20th.

10. A daily A/R transaction register is sent to the Accounts Receivable/Credit department.

11. Three copies of the shipping invoice/shipping order are sent to the Accounts Receivable/Credit department. The original copy is entitled shipping invoice; the two carbon copies are entitled shipping order. The third copy is filed by A/R.

12. The shipping invoice and the first copy of the shipping order are sent to the Shipping department. The shipping order is used to "pick" inventory items for shipment and is then filed. The shipping invoice is packed with the merchandise and is sent to the customer.

13. The accounts receivable summary report is prepared weekly and sent to the Accounts Receivable/Credit department for distribution.

FIGURE E1-3. MARS output descriptions: overcredit notice

REPORT SPECIFICATION

TITLE: **Overcredit Notice**

LAYOUT:

Overcredit Notice

Sales Order No. _____	Current Balance _____
Sales Order Date _____	Sales Order Amount _____
Account Number _____	Total _____
Name and Address	Credit Limit _____
_____	Amount Overcredit [_____]

☐ Overcredit Approved
☐ Return Sales Order

AUTHORIZATION

FREQUENCY: **Daily**   QUANTITY **40 max.**
SIZE: **1 page**   COPIES: **2**
DISTRIBUTION: **1. Credit Dept. (2)**

SPECIAL CONSIDERATIONS:

NOTE: The MARS outputs were presented
earlier in this text. Rather than repeat
them here, only the overcredit notice
is shown for illustrative purposes.
The remaining outputs include:

Customer monthly statement
Accounts Receivable transaction register
Accounts Receivable summary report
Aged Accounts Receivable report
Customer account list
Shipping invoice

DATA ELEMENT LIST

TITLE: **Overcredit Notice**

DESCRIPTION	FORMAT	SIZE
Sales Order Number	xxxxxxx x	8 characters
Sales Order Date	xx/xx/xx	8 "
Account No: Region No.—Sequence No.	xx-xxxxxxx	10 "
Name		26 "
Address		
Street		20 "
City		18 "
State		2 "
Zip Code		5 "
Current Balance	xxx,xxx.xx	10 "
Sales Order Amount	xxx,xxx.xx	10 "
Total	xxx,xxx.xx	10 "
Credit Limit	xx,xxx.xx	9 "
Amount Overcredit	xx,xxx.xx	9 "

FIGURE E1-4. MARS input description: sketch
of customer account application

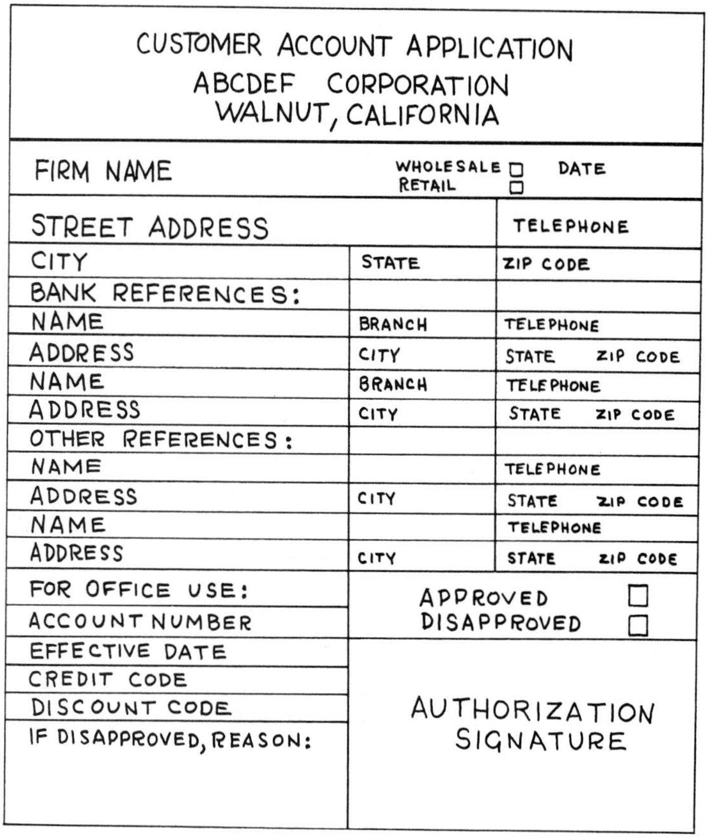

CUSTOMER ACCOUNT APPLICATION ABCDEF CORPORATION WALNUT, CALIFORNIA			
FIRM NAME	WHOLESALE ☐ RETAIL ☐		DATE
STREET ADDRESS		TELEPHONE	
CITY	STATE	ZIP CODE	
BANK REFERENCES:			
NAME	BRANCH	TELEPHONE	
ADDRESS	CITY	STATE ZIP CODE	
NAME	BRANCH	TELEPHONE	
ADDRESS	CITY	STATE ZIP CODE	
OTHER REFERENCES:			
NAME		TELEPHONE	
ADDRESS	CITY	STATE ZIP CODE	
NAME		TELEPHONE	
ADDRESS	CITY	STATE ZIP CODE	
FOR OFFICE USE:	APPROVED ☐		
ACCOUNT NUMBER	DISAPPROVED ☐		
EFFECTIVE DATE			
CREDIT CODE	AUTHORIZATION SIGNATURE		
DISCOUNT CODE			
IF DISAPPROVED, REASON:			

NOTE: The customer account application is shown to
illustrate input. The other MARS inputs, the billing
notice and the payment/credit memo, would remain
essentially unchanged from the current system. Since
these were presented in this text previously, they
are not repeated. They appear in Figure 12-9, "Inputs
to manual A/R system."

FIGURE E1-5. MARS high-level system flowchart and narrative

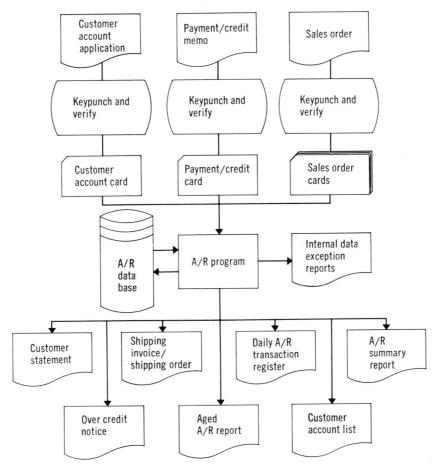

SYSTEM FLOWCHART
MODIFIED A/R SYSTEM (MARS)

SYSTEM FLOWCHART NARRATIVE

1. Customer account applications, payment/credit memos, and sales orders are the three major system inputs.

2. Each source document is keypunched and verified.

3. The A/R program inputs the transaction data cards and reads/updates the master file on magnetic disk. Program edit routines produce exception reports whenever invalid input data is detected.

4. The seven major outputs of the system are the customer statements, invoice/shipping order, A/R transaction register, A/R summary report, overcredit notice, aged A/R report, and a customer account list.

FIGURE E1-6. Project plan and status report—MARS Study Phase

	PROJECT PLAN AND STATUS REPORT	

PROJECT TITLE: MARS - STUDY PHASE

PROJECT STATUS SYMBOLS
O Satisfactory
□ Caution
△ Critical

J. Herring
PROGRAMMER/ANALYST

PLANNING/PROGRESS SYMBOLS
□ Scheduled Progress   ∨ Scheduled Completion
■ Actual Progress   ▼ Actual Completion

COMMITTED DATE 12/19/xx
COMPLETED DATE
STATUS DATE 12/12/xx

ACTIVITY/DOCUMENT	PERCENT COMPLETE	STATUS	PERIOD ENDING (week)
			1 2 3 4 5 6
STUDY PHASE	95	O	
Initial Investigation	100	O	
Project Directive	100	O	
Performance Definition	100	O	
Feasibility Analysis	100	O	
Performance Spec.	100	O	
Study Phase Report	100	O	
Study Phase Review	0	O	

FIGURE E1-7. Project cost report—MARS Study Phase

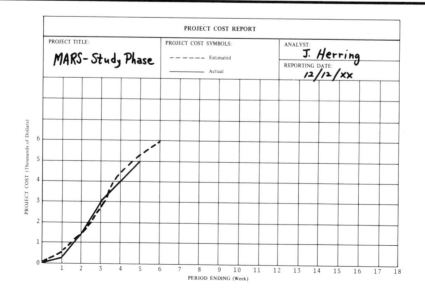

PROJECT COST REPORT

PROJECT TITLE: MARS- Study Phase

PROJECT COST SYMBOLS:
- - - - - Estimated
———— Actual

ANALYST: J. Herring
REPORTING DATE: 12/12/xx

FIGURE E1-8. Project plan and status report—major milestones

PROJECT PLAN AND STATUS REPORT																			
PROJECT TITLE MARS - MAJOR MILESTONES	PROJECT STATUS SYMBOLS O Satisfactory □ Caution △ Critical PLANNING/PROGRESS SYMBOLS □ Scheduled Progress ∨ Scheduled Completion ■ Actual Progress ▼ Actual Completion						J. Herring PROGRAMMER/ANALYST												
							COMMITTED DATE 6/19/xy			COMPLETED DATE			STATUS DATE 12/12/xx						
							PERIOD ENDING (week)												
ACTIVITY/DOCUMENT	PERCENT COMPLETE	STATUS	1	2	3	4	5	6	7	8	9	10	11	12	13	14		
STUDY PHASE	95	0																
Initial Investigation	100	0																
Performance Spec.	100	0																
Study Phase Report	100	0																
Study Phase Review	0	0																
DESIGN PHASE	0	0																
Allocation of Functions	0	0																
Computer Prog. Functions	0	0																
Test Requirements	0	0																
Design Spec.	0	0																
Design Phase Report	0	0																
Design Phase Review	0	0																

PROJECT PLAN AND STATUS REPORT																			
PROJECT TITLE MARS - MAJOR MILESTONES (cont.)	PROJECT STATUS SYMBOLS O Satisfactory □ Caution △ Critical PLANNING/PROGRESS SYMBOLS □ Scheduled Progress ∨ Scheduled Completion ■ Actual Progress ▼ Actual Completion						J. Herring PROGRAMMER/ANALYST												
							COMMITTED DATE 6/19/xy			COMPLETED DATE			STATUS DATE 12/12/xx						
							PERIOD ENDING (week)												
ACTIVITY/DOCUMENT	PERCENT COMPLETE	STATUS	15	16	17	18	19	20	21	22	23	24	25	26	27	28	29	30	31	32
DEVELOPMENT PHASE	0	0																		
Implementation Plan	0	0																		
Equipment Acquisition	0	0																		
Computer Program Dev.	0	0																		
Personnel Training	0	0																		
System Tests	0	0																		
Changeover Plan	0	0																		
System Spec.	0	0																		
Dev. Phase Report	0	0																		
Dev. Phase Review	0	0																		

FIGURE E1-9. Project cost report—total project

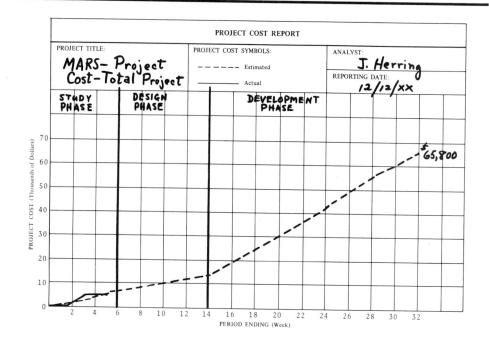

FIGURE E1-10. Project plan and status report—Design Phase

PROJECT PLAN AND STATUS REPORT																			
PROJECT TITLE MARS - DESIGN PHASE	**PROJECT STATUS SYMBOLS** O Satisfactory □ Caution △ Critical							J. Herring PROGRAMMER/ANALYST											

PLANNING/PROGRESS SYMBOLS
□ Scheduled Progress V Scheduled Completion
■ Actual Progress ▼ Actual Completion

| | | COMMITTED DATE 2/13/xy | COMPLETED DATE | STATUS DATE 12/12/xx |

PERIOD ENDING (week)

ACTIVITY/DOCUMENT	PERCENT COMPLETE	STATUS	1	2	3	4	5	6	7	8
DESIGN PHASE	0	0								
Allocation of Functions	0	0								
Manual Functions	0	0								
Task Definition	0	0								
Ref. Manual Iden.	0	0								
Equipment Functions	0	0								
Function Def.	0	0								
Equipment Spec.	0	0								
Computer Prog. Functions	0	0								
Data Base Design	0	0								
Data Edit CPC	0	0								
Invoice CPC	0	0								
A/R Tran. Reg. CPC	0	0								
Cust. Stmt. CPC	0	0								

PROJECT PLAN AND STATUS REPORT																			
PROJECT TITLE MARS - DESIGN PHASE (cont.)	**PROJECT STATUS SYMBOLS** O Satisfactory □ Caution △ Critical							J. Herring PROGRAMMER/ANALYST											

PLANNING/PROGRESS SYMBOLS
□ Scheduled Progress V Scheduled Completion
■ Actual Progress ▼ Actual Completion

| | | COMMITTED DATE 2/13/xy | COMPLETED DATE | STATUS DATE 12/12/xx |

PERIOD ENDING (week)

ACTIVITY/DOCUMENT	PERCENT COMPLETE	STATUS	1	2	3	4	5	6	7	8
DESIGN PHASE (cont.)	0	0								
Comp.Prog.Functions(cont.)	0	0								
A/R Summary CPC	0	0								
Utility CPC	0	0								
Test Requirements	0	0								
System Test Req.	0	0								
Comp. Prog. Test Req.	0	0								
Design Spec.	0	0								
Design Phase Report	0	0								
Design Phase Review	0	0								

FIGURE E1-11. Project cost report—Design Phase

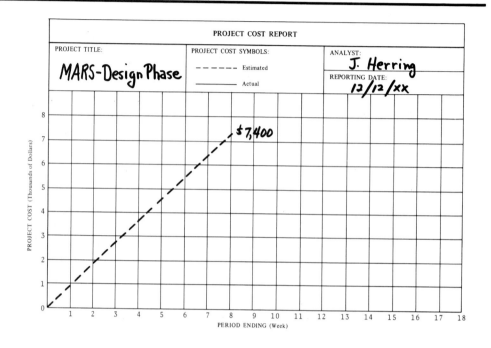

UNIT FOUR

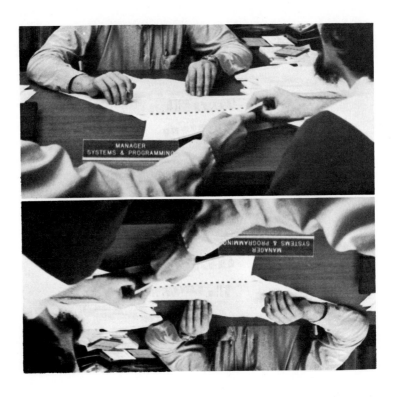

THE
DESIGN
PHASE

15

Design Phase Overview

In the Design Phase, the system selected in the Study Phase is designed, and a user-oriented Performance Specification is converted into a technical Design Specification. The goal of this chapter is to identify the major Design Phase activities and show the relationships between them. You will gain an overview and perspective of the design phase that will provide you with a reference and guide as you study the specific topics in this unit.

DESIGN PHASE ORGANIZATION

In the course of the Design Phase, the Performance Specification is expanded into the Design Specification. The user-oriented baseline document prepared in the Study Phase becomes a baseline document oriented to the needs of the programmers and other professional personnel who will actually develop the system. A smooth transition from the Study Phase to the Design Phase is necessary because the Design Phase continues the activities begun in the earlier phase. However, the project becomes enlarged in scope, and personnel are added. As examples:

1. The user organization assigns additional personnel to participate in the project as intermediaries between the project and the user organization. These persons are particularly concerned with defining user requirements and developing the resources (e.g., training manuals, procedures, and personnel) required by the user organization to insure successful operation of the system.

2. The information service organization assigns additional technical personnel, such as analyst/programmers and equipment specialists, to the project. These persons develop the technical requirements for computer programming and operations support. They are particularly concerned with the effective translation of system performance requirements into computer program design requirements. They aid in the selection of the best techniques for utilizing existing computer hardware and software. They also aid in the development of specifications on which to base the selection of new computer systems or components.

242

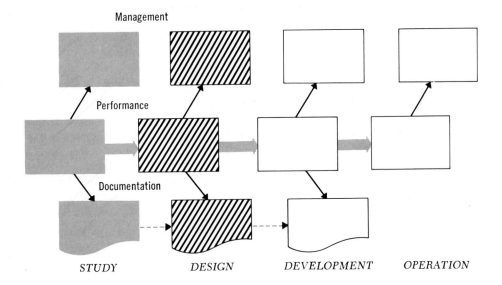

Management

Performance

Documentation

STUDY   *DESIGN*   *DEVELOPMENT*   *OPERATION*

DESIGN PHASE ACTIVITIES

The flowchart of Figure 15-1, *Design Phase activities for the computer-based business system,* is a pictorial overview of the Design Phase. Each of the activities shown in this flowchart is described briefly as follows:

1. *Allocation of functions:* The information-oriented and high-level system flowcharts prepared during the Study Phase are reviewed and expanded in order to allocate functions between manual tasks, equipment functions, and computer program functions. The alternatives are analyzed until all functions have been allocated. With respect to the computer program in particular, the expanded flowcharts identify the inputs, outputs, and files that are accessed by the set of subprograms. These subprograms are called computer program components because they are the building blocks of the computer program. The expanded flowcharts also identify the controls required to ensure valid system performance.

Interfaces between the computer system under development and other computer systems and equipment are defined by specifying the data that must be made available to or accessed from other systems.

2. *Manual task definition:* Requirements resulting from human interfaces with the computer system are described. Human interfaces include preparation of source documents, operation of equipment (e.g., machine operation, display console operation, keypunching), and other input- and output-related activities.

3. *Reference manual identification:* Reference manuals required by user personnel, programmers, and equipment operators are identified.

**FIGURE 15-1. Design Phase activities for
the computer-based business system**

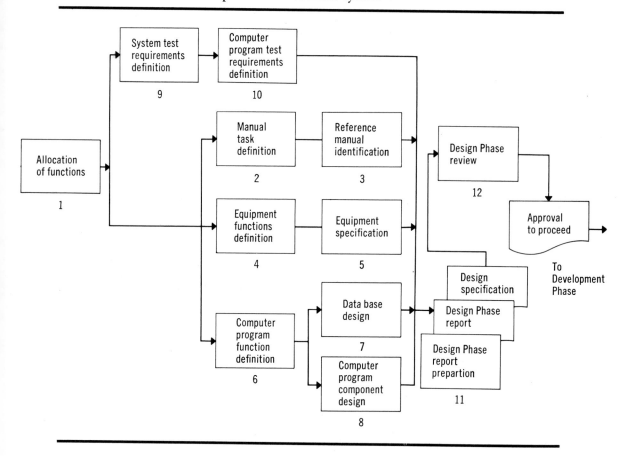

4. *Equipment functions definition:* The functions to be performed by hardware (rather than by computer programs or manual operations) are defined. Special functions unique to the application (e.g., console displays) are described in detail.

5. *Equipment specification:* The hardware configuration used to convert input data to meaningful output information is described. If existing hardware is not adequate, alternatives, which may range from adding special equipment to procuring an entire computer system, must be considered. Since computer hardware may be a long lead-time item, it may be necessary to initiate procurement of critical equipment during the Design Phase.

6. *Computer program function definition:* The specific functions of the overall computer program are defined, and design requirements for external system inputs are established. For example, when a punched card is to be prepared from an input source document, a punched card layout is made. In addition, input

frequency, quantity, and source are specified. Similarly, the design requirements for system outputs are established. Thus, if a printed report is an output, a printer output layout is prepared. Report frequency, size, quantity, and number of copies are stated. Control requirements are specified. These requirements include input preparation, input acceptance, and processing controls.

The above activities lead to establishing requirements for the data base and for each computer program component.

7. *Data base design:* Relationships between data elements, functions to be performed, and techniques for file organization are studied in detail so that the most appropriate storage device(s) can be selected and an efficient data base design can be achieved.

The storage requirements for all the data elements on which the computer program operates are calculated, taking into account the size and volume of the records to be stored and the methods of file organization and access.

The interfaces between the system data base and other data bases are identified by specifying the data that must flow between them.

8. *Computer program component design:* The computer program components share the system data base. However, they have their own output, input, and processing requirements, which must be specified for each one. Special hardware and supporting software requirements also are identified. As necessary, additional expanded system flowcharts are prepared at the computer program component level. Narratives, equations, algorithms, and decision tables may be developed as aides in defining the functions of computer program components. Control requirements are extended to the computer program components.

9. *System test requirements definition:* Requirements are established for the tests necessary to verify the performance of the entire computer-based system. This is accomplished in parallel with the activities associated with system design.

10. *Computer program test requirements definition:* Requirements also are determined for the tests necessary to verify the performance of the major computer program components. This is done after the definition of the system test requirements. (However, these tests are performed prior to the system tests.)

11. *Design Phase report preparation:* A Design Phase report is prepared at the conclusion of the Design Phase. This report is the outgrowth of the data acquired and added to the project file during the Design Phase. An extension of the Study Phase report, it contains a summary of the results of all significant activities undertaken during the Design Phase. An important element of the Design Phase report is a recommendation relative to proceeding with the Development Phase. If the recommendation is to proceed, a detailed project plan is provided for the remainder of the project.

Included in the Design Phase report is the Design Specification—the second major baseline document. It represents an expansion of the Performance Specification into a "blueprint" for the development of the computer-based business system.

12. *Design Phase review:* The system design is reviewed at the conclusion of the Design Phase by the management of the user organization and by representa-

tives of the information systems organization. The principal documents upon which the review is based are the Study Phase report, including the Performance Specification; and the Design Phase report, including the Design Specification. Any changes to the Performance Specification as a result of the Design Phase activities are identified and discussed. The detailed progress plan and the cost schedule for the Development Phase are reviewed, as are the estimates of operational costs.

After the conclusion of a successful Design Phase review, manpower and other resources are committed. Written approval to proceed with the Development Phase is provided by the user organization.

16   System Design

At this point in the life cycle, the Design Phase begins. The problem has been identified, solutions have been studied, and a management review has ended with an authorization to proceed with a recommended solution. The goal of this chapter is to introduce the processes of allocating system functions and defining test requirements. You will learn how system functions are allocated among humans, equipment, and computer programs. In addition, you will learn how to identify test requirements and how to use the structured walk-through technique.

ALLOCATION OF FUNCTIONS

Expanded system flowcharts

The first major activity of the Design Phase is the allocation of functions to manual operations, to equipment, or to computer programs. This is accomplished by expanding the results of the Study Phase activities to greater levels of detail. The information and system flowcharts of the earlier phase are reviewed and expanded until all the functions the system must perform are evident. Because of the importance of identifying system functions, the analyst may draw HIPO charts instead of or in addition to the process-oriented flowcharts.

FIGURE 16-1, *Expanded accounts receivable system flowchart*, is an intermediate level flowchart, with an accompanying narrative, prepared for the example MARS system. It displays all the major data processing functions that must be performed by individual computer program components (CPCs). In addition, the major processing control functions are shown.

FIGURE 16-2, *MARS HIPO charts*, is an example of a hierarchy chart and an IPO chart used to show system functions. A HIPO chart set should

Figure 16-1. Expanded accounts receivable system flowchart

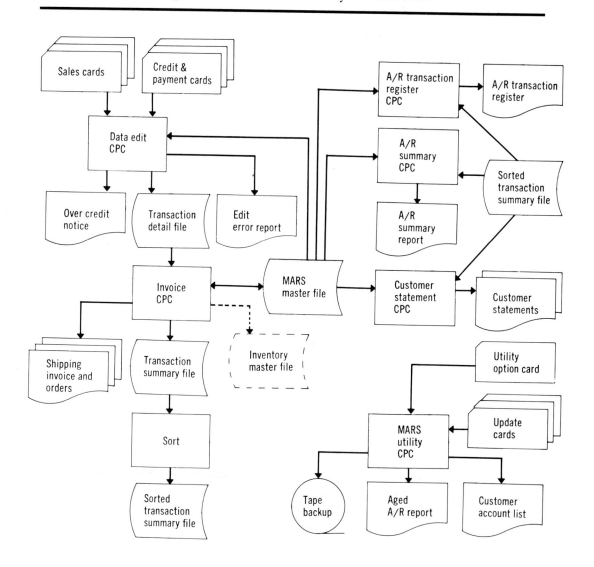

MARS Expanded Flowchart Narrative

Data Edit CPC:
    The data for sales and credit is keypunched and selectively
verified. The resulting cards are read and all data fields are
checked for validity. Any invalid field will cause an error message to be printed on an Edit Error Report. All valid records will
be written on magnetic disk. In addition, the amount of the sale
is calculated and added to the customer's balance. If the calculated new balance exceeds the customer's credit limit, an over-

credit notice is produced and the data is not recorded on the disk.
The Data Edit CPC does not update the master file record.

Invoice CPC:
    The Invoice CPC reads the transaction records and produces a
shipping invoice and shipping orders. As the shipping invoice is
produced, the Invoice CPC verifies the availability of stock via
the master file of the inventory system. The inventory master file
is reduced by the quantity to be shipped. Short orders or out-of-
stock conditions are so noted on the shipping invoice. The MARS
master file is updated in the month-to-date purchases and credit
fields and in the aged accounts receivable fields. The summary
data, i.e., total purchase and total credits, for each customer
are recorded in the transaction summary file.

Accounts Receivable Transaction Register CPC:
    Sorted transaction summary data and MARS master data are used
to produce a daily accounts receivable transaction register.

Customer Statement CPC:
    Sorted transaction summary records and MARS master records are
inputs to the Customer Statement CPC, which generates customer monthly
statements. One third of the customers are billed on the first of
each month; a second third on the 10th of each month; the last third
on the 20th of each month. The region number of the customer account
number determines which billing date is used. The MARS master file is
updated with new current balances, and month-to-date fields are reset
to zero.

Accounts Receivable Summary CPC:
    Sorted transaction summary and MARS master file data is used to
generate a weekly accounts receivable summary report.

MARS Utility CPC:
    The Utility CPC has five functions:
    1. Updating MARS master file, e.g., adding new customers, delet-
       ing customers, and changing customer data.
    2. Creating a magnetic tape back-up for the master file.
    3. Restoring the master file from tape in case of disaster or
       periodic reorganization of the master file.
    4. Printing customer account lists on an on-demand schedule.
    5. Producing the aged accounts receivable report.
The option or options to be executed are selected through a utility
option card.

include an IPO chart for each block of the hierarchy chart, but in this
example, only the IPO for the data edit function is shown. Note that the
HIPO charts show the same CPCs as the expanded process-oriented flowchart. The major differences in the HIPO charts are the chart structure
and the emphasis on system functions.

Identification of controls

The purpose of controls is to minimize incorrect data, and so they are an indis-
pensable part of any information system. To ensure that the appropriate controls
are built into the system, the analyst should plan for them early in the Design
Phase. Later in the Development Phase, there will be pressures from programming schedules, test schedules, and storage limitations that will tend to distract
from the importance of controls.

Although controls help to prevent or detect theft and fraud, the vast majority
of problems detected through controls arise from honest mistakes. The principal

FIGURE 16-2. MARS HIPO charts

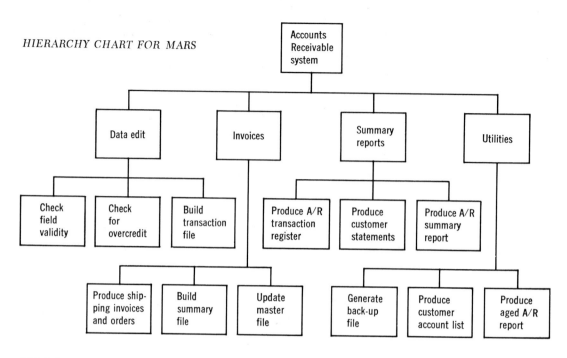

HIERARCHY CHART FOR MARS

IPO DETAIL CHART: DATA EDIT MODULE

INPUTS	PROCESSING	OUTPUTS
1. Sales cards	1. Check validity of account number	1. Transactions detail file (disk)
2. Credit and payment cards	2. Check validity of all numeric fields	2. Edit error report
3. Master file	3. Check for overcredit status	3. Overcredit notices

controls used relate to input, processing, and output. FIGURE 16-2, *Example control techniques*, identifies some commonly encountered controls with which the systems analyst should be familiar. Some of the controls are simply standards to be established and used; some involve manual operations; and others are accomplished through computer program components.

The example expanded A/R system flowchart in Figure 16-1 and the HIPO charts in Figure 16-2 illustrate two control techniques. First, the MARS Utility CPC is used to protect the master file with magnetic tape backups for recovery of the master file data. It also provides the only general access to the master file. All updates involving new customers added to the file, address changes, or credit limit changes must be a part of a processing run separate from the daily transaction runs. Accessibility of the file can be limited through controlling the use of the Utility CPC. A second control, the Data Edit CPC, utilizes software checks for data validity, e.g., valid inventory codes, customer account numbers, and numeric fields. It also prevents customers from exceeding their credit limit without specific authorization.

Allocation process

Key project personnel, as a team, determine the most effective means of performing each function. This determination is made by studying and evaluating alternatives. The process follows steps similar to those of the feasibility analysis, but alternatives are studied at a level of greater detail. For example, during the Study Phase it might have been found that a remote terminal was the most cost-effective means of entering data into the system. Now, in the Design Phase, a particular terminal must be selected from the many models or types available to perform the input function. As another example, it might be decided that certain

FIGURE 16-3. Example control techniques

CONTROL TECHNIQUES

INPUT CONTROLS:
1. Define responsibility for input preparation and delivery.
2. Verify keypunched data for significant numeric fields.
3. Utilize self-checking numbers and codes where practical.
4. Sequence number input data.
5. Number and take hash totals for each batch. Keep a transmittal tape for each batch.

PROCESSING CONTROLS:
1. Establish a comprehensive program of computer program and system testing.
2. Centralize the authority for all computer program changes or modifications.
3. Protect files with backups and limited accessibility.
4. Provide standards for utilizing hardware checks.
5. Provide standards for the development and use of software checks.
6. Log all machine time usage.

OUTPUT CONTROLS:
1. Assign responsibility for output handling and distribution.
2. Insist upon an auditable trail from outputs back to inputs.
3. Inspect all outputs for reasonableness.

data could be evaluated more effectively by manual techniques than by a computer. This could be the case if human judgment or particularly rapid handling of an exceptional situation were required.

MANUAL TASKS

Manual task definition

Typically humans interface with computer-based systems in at least six principal ways:

1. Humans prepare source documents.
2. Humans keypunch data from source documents into a machine-readable format.
3. Humans prepare and use control documents.
4. Humans write computer programs.
5. Humans operate equipment.
6. Humans use computer-produced outputs.

All the humans who are involved with a computer-based system must know certain aspects of the system. This information is provided by reference manuals.

Reference manual identification

All the reference manuals to be used by programmers, users, and operators are identified in the Design Phase. Their principal content may be outlined. There may be a large number of these manuals because of the varying needs of many different types of users. The manuals are prepared during the Development Phase, and they are an essential part of personnel training. Training plans and programs, including reference manuals, are discussed in Chapter 22: Preparing for Implementation.

EQUIPMENT FUNCTIONS

Equipment functions definition

The process of allocating functions between manual tasks, equipment, and the computer program took into account the computer equipment resources currently available and additional resources that might be required. The range of equipment options includes:

1. Acquire a computer system.
2. Current computer equipment is adequate.
3. Add some components to the current equipment.
4. Greatly modify the current equipment.
5. Replace the current equipment by a new computer system.

Within each of the above options, there may be many equipment choices. The process for evaluating specific equipment model choices is similar to that used during the feasibility analysis activities of the Study Phase.

As an example, consider a situation in which it has been found necessary to replace the current equipment with a computer system in order to handle an anticipated increase in workload. The equipment selection process would involve the following steps:

1. Define the functions to be performed by the computer system.
2. Identify the required capabilities of the computer system.
3. Evaluate the candidate computer systems.
4. Select the computer system to be acquired on the basis of its performance and cost.

The definition of the functions to be performed by the system begins with an analysis of the workload that the system is expected to process. This includes the continuing current workload plus the estimated additional future workload. The purpose of analyzing workload is to develop representative samples that can be used to test the performance of various computer configurations. These samples are commonly drawn from either actual programs currently in use, a composite made up to represent the planned workload, or simulation of the workload and computer.

Whichever technique is used, the sample workload should be representative of the tasks the computer must perform. This is called "benchmark" testing because identical series of tasks can be used to compare two or more computers. Typical tasks are compilations, updates, sorts, edits, report generation, and input and output handling. If it is cumbersome to assemble an adequate and representative sample from problems currently being processed, then a composite can be made of tasks currently being performed and expected to be performed. This composite is not an actual production program. It is a series of tasks of the types described above. It can, however, be used as a benchmark for measuring the relative performance of proposed hardware and software.

Another alternative is the use of a simulation program, which makes one computer appear to perform like another computer. The inputs to the simulation program are the input, processing, and output tasks desired, and the frequency of their occurrence. The result of the simulation is data on timing, price, and performance.

Equipment specification

After the functions to be performed have been converted to a representative workload sample, the additional requirements for the computer equipment can be stated, and the candidate systems can be evaluated. FIGURE 16-4, *Vendor evaluation matrix*, depicts performance and cost factors that typically are considered.

Workload analysis and measurement were discussed in the preceding section on the definition of equipment functions.

Growth is the ability of the equipment to meet not only the current workload but also future workloads. Three common ways of providing for growth are (1) equipment with reserve power, (2) equipment with add-on capability, and (3) equipment that is compatible for upward conversion.

Reserve power usually is the least economical way of providing for growth, because it involves paying for capability not being used. Add-on capability is

FIGURE 16-4. Vendor evaluation matrix

VENDOR / FACTOR	Vendor A	Vendor B	Vendor C
PERFORMANCE:			
Workload			
Growth			
Hardware			
Software			
Support Services			
COSTS:			
Rental			
Third-Party Lease			
Purchase			

attractive because it offers an increase in capability when needed. Compatibility for upward conversion gives the potential for replacing the equipment by a more powerful system on which all of the existing programs will run without modification. Since most vendors provide upward-compatible equipment, this, too, often is a feasible route to follow. However, possible pitfalls, such as subtle differences between operating systems, should be evaluated carefully.

Hardware performance is measured by factors such as memory size, internal speed of the central processor, and idle time waiting for input or output. Software performance depends on the efficiency of the operating system, the quality and quantity of utility programs, the programming languages provided, and the applications packages which the vendor may supply. Support services include field engineering, e.g., maintenance, back up, and response to problems; systems (i.e., software) support; and education and training of customer employees.

The three most common ways of acquiring computer equipment are rental, lease, and purchase. If the equipment is to be used for an extended period of time, both purchase and lease plans are less expensive than rental. Many lease plans provide an option to purchase. The lease of equipment from someone other than the vendor is called a third-party lease. There are many leasing companies, and a variety of lease plans are available. Third-party leasing can result in cost savings because the leasing company, anticipating a continuing market, often can spread the cost of the equipment over a longer period of time. If the equipment is to be retained for a long period of time, usually in excess of four years, then outright purchase may be the most economical means of acquisition. Among the most important factors that affect cost decisions are changes in technology (which still appear to be producing more performance for less cost), confidence in workload projections, interest rates, flexibility, and lead times for equipment delivery.

The equipment acquisition process has not been described in detail. Rather, by identifying the factors that must be considered, we have emphasized the need for evaluation procedures. The systems analyst must realize that he cannot rely entirely upon vendors. He must know his own needs, be able to determine his own performance requirements, and to evaluate vendor responses to those requirements.

COMPUTER PROGRAM FUNCTIONS

Computer program functions definition

Computer programs can be broken down into their computer program components (CPCs). Each component performs one or more functions. These are typical functions provided by CPCs:

1. Master file load or creation
2. Master file update
3. Master file back-up
4. Master file maintenance
5. Input data editing
6. Report generation

While systems are unique in their overall functions, the above six functions of CPCs are common to most computer programs.

Interface management

An important Design Phase task is the review of interfaces between the new system and existing or proposed future systems. This is particularly important because the success of the integrated data base system concept depends on the planning of each system so that it is capable of accepting data from, and providing data for, related data-base-oriented systems.

An interface with another system is a concern in the example MARS system. The Invoice CPC of MARS produces a shipping invoice and shipping orders containing a detailed listing of all items ordered and shipped. In order to avoid printing shipping invoices and then discovering that some items are out of stock during the distribution process, the MARS is to interface with an inventory system. The Invoice CPC is to determine the availability of merchandise prior to printing the invoice. If the merchandise is short or out of stock, that condition should be noted on the shipping invoice, and the customer charges should represent goods actually shipped. If the merchandise is not out of stock, the Invoice CPC is to reduce the inventory by the amount to be shipped.

The inventory system already exists. The MARS project must interface with it in a manner that will not require extensive redesign or modification of the inventory system.

TEST REQUIREMENTS

Identification of test requirements

The requirements for tests are established after the allocation of functions is completed. They are established in the following sequence:

1. System test requirements
2. Subsystem test requirements
3. Component test requirements

The requirements for overall system performance are established first because they will determine the requirements for each subsystem. The requirements for testing the components of each subsystem are defined last.

A computer-based business system has manual, equipment, and computer program subsystems. Typically, the most important subsystem is the computer program subsystem. Its components are computer program components (**CPCs**).

In the Design Phase, the tests that must be performed are identified in the sequence indicated above, progressing from the system level to the component level. In the Development Phase, test plans are prepared to correspond to the test requirements. In this phase, also, actual testing takes place. The tests are performed in a planned sequence, progressing from the component level to the system level. Development Phase testing activities are discussed in Chapter 22: Preparing for Implementation.

Structured walk-throughs

Structured reviews are a technique used in developing efficient and reliable systems. A *structured walk-through* is a technical review to assist the technical people working on a project. It is a "structured" review because it is one of a series of reviews that are a planned part of the system design and development activities. It is referred to as a "walk-through" because the project is reviewed in a step-by-step sequence. Structured walk-throughs can be a valuable tool in the design and development of any system component. They are especially valuable in the design and development of computer programs.

The purpose of a structured walk-through is to discover errors in logic of a computer program or other system component. The underlying philosophy is that others often can see errors that are not obvious to the programmer or analyst.

The review team consists of selected peers of the project developer. For example, if the project is a computer program, the review group consists of other programmers. The project developer "walks" the review group through the logic of the project. If any errors, omissions, or discrepancies are uncovered, they are recorded by one of the group members. The structured walk-through allows problems to be discovered early when it is easier and less costly to correct them. If the structured walk-through technique is used consistently, fewer errors will be found during system testing, and less debugging time required. It should be noted that successful structured walk-throughs must be positive and nonthreatening experiences for the project developer; therefore, management does not attend, and the review must not be a basis for employee evaluation.

The structured walk-through technique is consistent with the entire life-cycle approach to the design and development of systems. The Study, Design, and Development Phase reviews are structured reviews. Structured walk-throughs are meaningful supplements to those reviews for the purpose of examining the technical logic of system components. Structured walk-throughs are particularly valuable in the Development Phase, which usually is much longer and costlier than the Study and Design phases. Therefore, it is essential that periodic structured management and technical reviews be held as work progresses.

KEY TERMS

computer program component (CPC)   *computer program functions*
manual tasks   *interface management*
equipment functions   *structured walk-through*

FOR DISCUSSION

1. How do the expanded system flowchart and HIPO charts aid in the allocation of functions?

2. Why is it important to plan controls as early as possible in system design?

3. What is a CPC? How does it relate to the computer program depicted in the high-level flowchart drawn during the Study Phase activities?

4. Who determines the most effective means of performing each system function?

5. Name and discuss some ways in which humans interface with computer-based systems.

6. What alternatives may be required in the equipment functions definition activities?

7. What is a "workload sample"? How is it obtained?

8. What are some typical computer program functions?

9. What is interface management?

10. What test requirements must be identified?

11. What is a structured walk-through? What is its purpose?

17   Input
         Design

The most common source of data processing errors is
inaccurate input data. If poor input design allows
bad data to enter a computer system, the outputs
produced are of little value. The goal of this chapter
is to describe techniques for effective input design. You
will learn the design principles for punched cards
and other common input media.

THE INPUT DESIGN PROCESS

Input design is the process of converting a user-oriented description of the inputs
to a computer-based business system into a programmer-oriented specification.
The input design process was initiated in the Study Phase where, as a part of the
feasibility study:

1. Input data were found to be available for establishing and maintaining
master and transaction files and for creating output records.

2. The most suitable types of input media, for either off-line or on-line devices,
were selected after a study of alternative data capture techniques.

In the Design Phase, as discussed earlier in this unit, the input design process
was continued. Specifically:

1. The expanded system flowchart identified master files (the data base), transaction files, and the computer program components.

2. The input media selected in the Study Phase were reviewed. Additional
studies of alternatives were performed as required, and tasks were allocated
among equipment, manual operations, and computer programs.

In this chapter we will describe the rest of the input design process. Although
punched cards still are an important input media, other techniques that speed up
the entry of error-free input data are finding widespread acceptance. We will
examine punched card design, and then extend the discussion to other output
media, including key-to-tape and key-to-disk devices, cathode ray tube (CRT)
display stations, and optical readers.

PUNCHED CARD DESIGN

Types of punched cards

A *punched card* is a card that contains data or instructions coded in machine-readable format. This data is not read directly by the computer. A device, such as a card reader, converts the data coded on the card into electrical impulses that are transmitted to the computer. The data is recoded and recorded in main memory. Many different types of cards and card readers are available. Among the more commonly encountered punched cards are transcript cards, dual cards, mark-sense cards, Port-A-Punch cards, and combination cards.

The *transcript card* is a card that is punched from information previously recorded on another document. It is the most frequently encountered type of punched card. FIGURE 17-1, *Stock IBM 5081 card,* displays the punched card equivalent of a cut form. Specialty transcript cards are available from card manufacturers. As is shown in FIGURE 17-2, *Typical specialty transcript card,* specialty cards contain preprinted information, such as card name, column headings, and column dividing lines.

The *dual card* is punched from information previously written on the card itself. The dual card serves both as a source document and as a punched card. For this reason, it sometimes is called a "turnaround" card. The dual card is a specialty card obtained from a card manufacturer. Particular care must be taken in its design because the fields in which the data are recorded must be offset from those in which the data is punched. As shown in FIGURE 17-3, *Visibility in a keypunching station,* this offset is necessary because the punching station obscures several card columns. FIGURE 17-4, *Typical dual card,* clearly displays the offset between the student name and the social security number recording and punching fields.

The *mark-sense card* is punched from electrographic pencil marks that are recorded in mark-sensing positions on the face of the card and are read by an

FIGURE 17-1. Stock IBM 5081 card

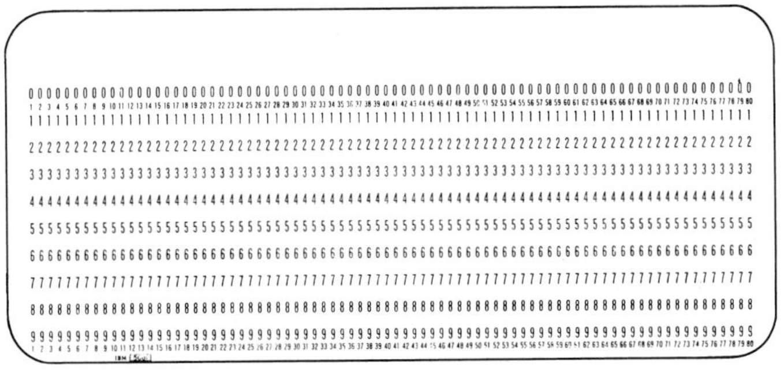

Courtesy of IBM Corporation

FIGURE 17-2. **Typical specialty transcript card**

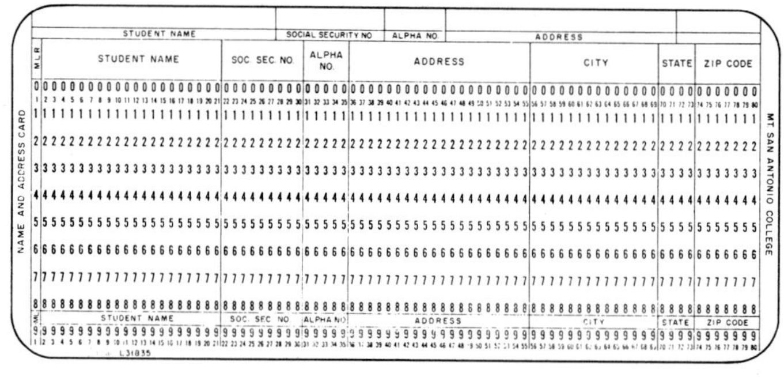

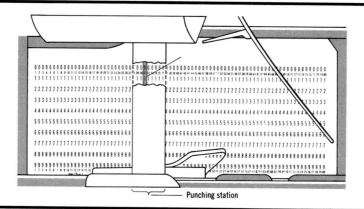

Courtesy of Mt. San Antonio College

FIGURE 17-3. **Visibility in a keypunching station**

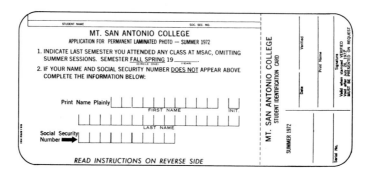

FIGURE 17-4. **Typical dual card**

Courtesy of Mt. San Antonio College

FIGURE 17-5. Typical mark-sense card

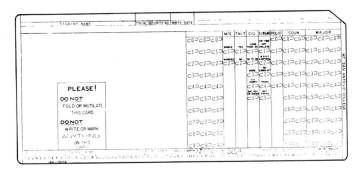

FIGURE 17-6. Typical Port-A-Punch card

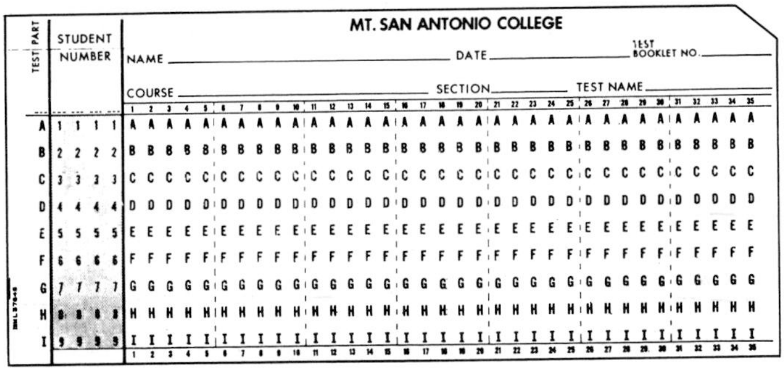

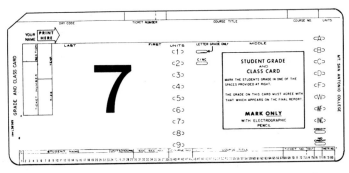

FIGURE 17-7. Typical combination card

optical mark-reader machine. They are punched into the same card or into a different card for subsequent processing. Figure 17-5, *Typical mark-sense card,* displays mark-sense positions on a punched card. The mark-sense card is a specialty card.

The *Port-A-Punch card* is a card made up of "prescored" rectangular chips which can be removed by pressure from a stylus or other pointed instrument. This type of specialty card is punched manually; hence, the rectangles are over-sized. It contains only forty card columns because only the even numbered card columns are used. The Port-A-Punch card is used for on-the-spot data punching. Figure 17-6, *Typical Port-A-Punch card,* shows a card used to administer examinations.

The *combination card* combines the data recording characteristics of more than one type of specialty punched card. Figure 17-7, *Typical combination card,* shows a combination card with mark-sense positions on a dual card.

There are no invariable rules for card design. However, some useful guidelines which have emerged from trial-and-error experience can provide a "ballpark" preliminary design. Thereafter, the card, the source document, or both can usually be modified easily if necessary. The result is a card that can be punched rapidly with minimum errors caused by the form. The design of the layout for a transcript card is explained in detail in the following section. The same process underlies the manufacture of specialty cards.

Transcript card layout design

The Card Design Aid. Two valuable tools for implementing the card design guidelines are the card design aid and the multiple-card layout form. Figure 17-8, *Card design aid,* is a worksheet that is valuable in the trial-and-error card design process. This process is most easily described by explaining the meaning of the entries on the card design aid, as shown in Figure 17-8:

1. *Card name:* The name of the card being designed.
2. *Source document:* The document from which the data to be punched into the card is obtained.
3. *Designer:* The name of the individual designing the card.
4. *Date:* The date of the card design.
5. *Card type:* Transcript, dual, etc.
6. *Data elements required:* The list of all the data elements, or fields, that must be punched into the card. This list includes only source document fields required to perform logical or arithmetic operations within the computer, to create or maintain files, or to produce reports.
7. *Columns in other cards:* The data elements that appear in previously designed cards. The first priority in card design is to use the same field locations for data that is common to two or more cards. This procedure is important because repeated fields frequently are, or may become, key fields, i.e., fields by which records are to be sorted, filed, or retrieved. In addition, this scheme tends to standardize keypunching procedures and to simplify visual comparisons between related data records.

FIGURE 17-8. Card design aid

CARD DESIGN AID

CARD NAME _____   SOURCE DOCUMENT _____

DESIGNER _____ DATE _____ CARD TYPE _____

DATA ELEMENTS REQUIRED	Columns in other cards	Sequence on source document	FIELD FORMAT	CARD FIELD SIZE			FINAL DESIGN		REMARKS
				Trial	Trial	Final	Card Columns	Sequence	
		TOTALS →							

8. *Sequence on source document:* The sequence in which data elements appear on the source document. This factor has second priority. Source documents should be designed for ease of reading, i.e., readable from left to right and from top to bottom. Otherwise, both keypunching speed and error rate will be adversely affected.

9. *Field format:* The format (alphabetic, alphanumeric, or numeric) in which the data is to be processed. The format designation is particularly important for numeric fields that are to be used in calculations or edited as report items because the position of the decimal point must be indicated. One acceptable convention is to indicate the size of a numeric field as follows: $XXX_\wedge XX$. The caret indicates the decimal point, but is not punched in the card and does not count as part of the field size. The indication of field format is also a means of carrying forward information from the system designer to the programmer.

10. *Card field size:* The columns in which the trial and final card field sizes are determined. The trial field size is the estimated number of card columns required for each data element. The final field size is the number of card columns finally assigned to each data element. The card design aid provides for two trials before the final field size is selected. If possible, no more than one card should be used for a single transaction or record. As "rules of thumb":

    a. If the total of the trial field sizes is less than 80 columns, the trial fields become the final fields.

b. If the total of the trial field sizes exceeds 100, it probably is not possible to avoid using more than one card.

c. If the total of the trial field sizes falls between 80 and 100, the decision to use another card should be made only after considering ways to reduce the size of some fields so that the total will be 80 or less.

Techniques that can be considered in reducing total field size include recoding to reduce the size of fields, such as reference numbers and dates; eliminating redundant information; and using one column for recording several one-digit codes.

If two or more cards are required, the data should be separated on a meaningful basis. Examples are repetitive and nonrepetitive data, a logical division of a source document, or one card per source document.

It is necessary to repeat the key field if more than one card is required to complete a logical record. For example, when business reports are produced, a key field, such as customer number, may be used to identify separate accounts. Also, in referring to multiple input records with a common key, such as customer number, an additional key field is needed to distinguish between input cards.

11. *Final design:* The recording of the specific card columns and the sequence in which they are to appear on the punched card. Card fields should be assigned in accordance with the priorities discussed above (i.e., columns on other cards and sequence on source documents). Special considerations, such as unique machine or manual operations, should be taken into account. After the final field assignment is made, the sequence in which these fields are to appear on the punched card is entered into the card design aid. This sequence should be compared with the sequence of the data elements on the source document to determine if an additional design cycle is required. This design cycle would allow modification of the source document, the punched card layout, or both, so as to improve the speed and accuracy of source document preparation and of keypunching.

The Multiple-card Layout Form. A multiple-card layout form is a repeated enlargement of the nines-row of a punched card. As shown in FIGURE 17-9, *Multiple-card layout form,* this form is approximately twice the scale of a punched card and made up of a reproduction of the nines-rows and column numbers for six punched cards. Space is provided for lettering in the card name and field titles. The form is an intermediate design tool that is particularly useful when several related cards are designed. It presents clearly the results of the trial-and-error design process for final review or revision.

The multiple-card layout form also is an effective means of communication between the systems analyst and the programmer because it describes the input data records and their specific relationships in detail.

The Keypunch Instruction Form. A single-card layout form may be used to communicate with the keypunch operator. It may be supplemented or replaced by a special keypunch instruction form, like the one shown in FIGURE 17-10,

FIGURE 17-9. Multiple-card layout form

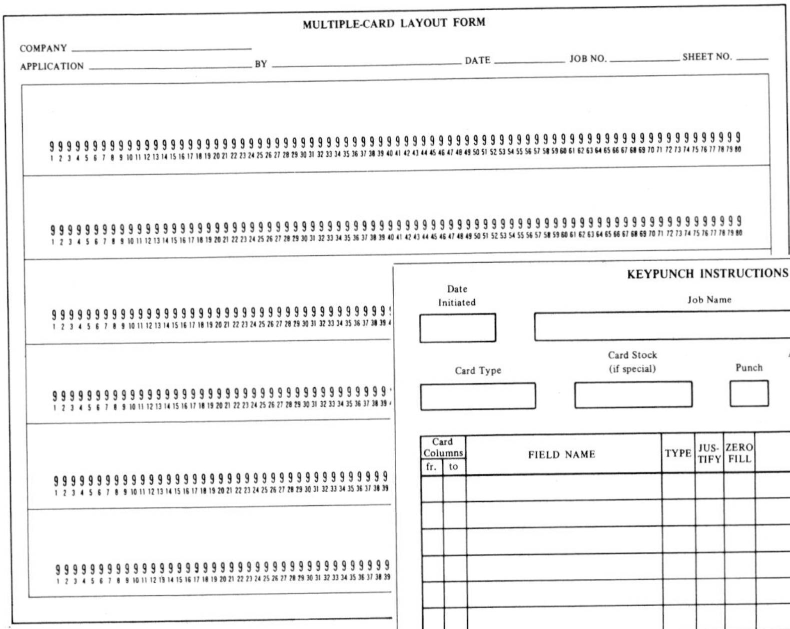
MULTIPLE-CARD LAYOUT FORM

COMPANY ____

APPLICATION ____ BY ____ DATE ____ JOB NO. ____ SHEET NO. ____

Courtesy of IBM Corporation

FIGURE 17-10. Keypunch instructions

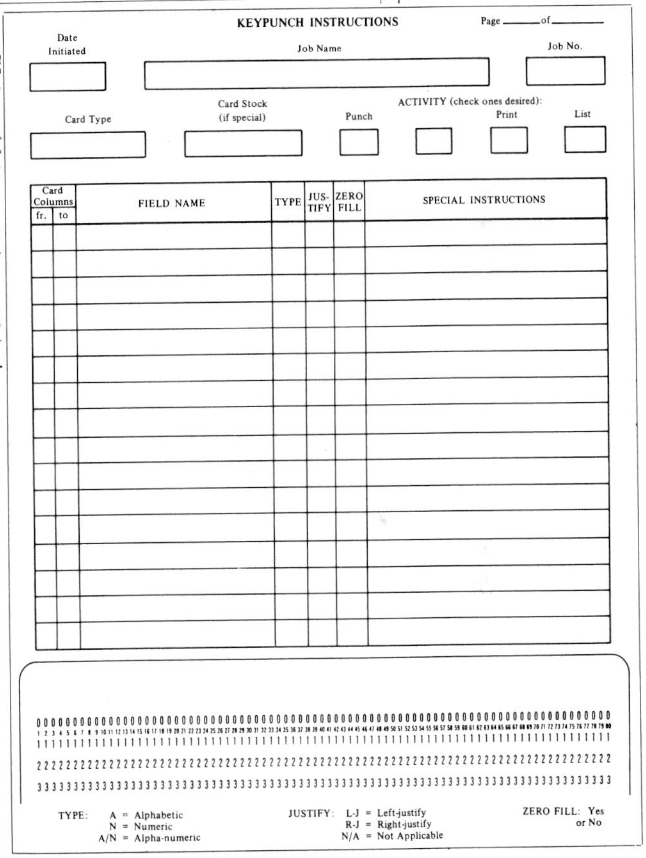
KEYPUNCH INSTRUCTIONS Page ____ of ____

Date Initiated | Job Name | Job No.

Card Type | Card Stock (if special) | ACTIVITY (check ones desired): Punch | Print | List

Card Columns fr.	to	FIELD NAME	TYPE	JUS-TIFY	ZERO FILL	SPECIAL INSTRUCTIONS

TYPE: A = Alphabetic, N = Numeric, A/N = Alpha-numeric

JUSTIFY: L-J = Left-justify, R-J = Right-justify, N/A = Not Applicable

ZERO FILL: Yes or No

Keypunch instructions. As this form shows, the analyst or programmer can indicate card columns, name, type, justification, zero fill, and special instructions to the keypunch operator for every field to be punched. Figure 17-10 also provides for a sketch of the actual card layout.

The use of these techniques is illustrated in the following example of a transcript card design.

Figure 17-11. Sketch of customer account application

```
┌─────────────────────────────────────────────────┐
│         CUSTOMER ACCOUNT APPLICATION             │
│            ABCDEF  CORPORATION                   │
│             WALNUT, CALIFORNIA                   │
├─────────────────────┬───────────────────────────┤
│ FIRM NAME           │ WHOLESALE ☐    DATE        │
│                     │ RETAIL    ☐               │
├─────────────────────┴────────┬──────────────────┤
│ STREET ADDRESS               │ TELEPHONE        │
├──────────────┬───────────────┼──────────────────┤
│ CITY         │ STATE         │ ZIP CODE         │
├──────────────┴───────────────┴──────────────────┤
│ BANK REFERENCES:                                 │
├──────────────┬───────────────┬──────────────────┤
│ NAME         │ BRANCH        │ TELEPHONE        │
├──────────────┼───────┬───────┴──────────────────┤
│ ADDRESS      │ CITY  │ STATE    ZIP CODE        │
├──────────────┼───────┼──────────────────────────┤
│ NAME         │ BRANCH│ TELEPHONE                │
├──────────────┼───────┼──────────────────────────┤
│ ADDRESS      │ CITY  │ STATE   ZIP CODE         │
├──────────────┴───────┴──────────────────────────┤
│ OTHER REFERENCES:                                │
├──────────────┬───────────────────────────────── │
│ NAME         │ TELEPHONE                        │
├──────────────┼───────┬──────────────────────────┤
│ ADDRESS      │ CITY  │ STATE   ZIP CODE         │
├──────────────┼───────┴──────────────────────────┤
│ NAME         │ TELEPHONE                        │
├──────────────┼───────┬──────────────────────────┤
│ ADDRESS      │ CITY  │ STATE   ZIP CODE         │
├──────────────┴───────┴──────────────────────────┤
│ FOR OFFICE USE:      │ APPROVED        ☐        │
│ ACCOUNT NUMBER       │ DISAPPROVED     ☐        │
│ EFFECTIVE DATE       │                          │
│ CREDIT CODE          │   AUTHORIZATION          │
│ DISCOUNT CODE        │    SIGNATURE             │
│ IF DISAPPROVED, REASON:                         │
└─────────────────────────────────────────────────┘
```

Example transcript card design

One MARS source document is shown in Figure 17-11, *Sketch of customer account application.* The application is submitted to the Credit department, which performs a credit check and approves or disapproves the credit application. If the application is approved, an account number, a credit code, and a trade discount code are assigned as follows:

1. *Account number:* an assigned number identifying an account by region and by sequence within region. Its format is XX—XXXXXXX

Region—sequence number

2. *Credit code:* a two-digit number indicating the customer credit limit:

$$01 = \$ \ \ 500 \qquad 04 = \$25,000$$
$$02 = \$ \ 2,500 \qquad 05 = \text{Special}$$
$$03 = \$10,000$$

3. *Trade discount code:* a single alphabetic character identifying the customer as a wholesale or retail firm:

$$W = \text{wholesale}$$
$$R = \text{retail}$$

Not all the data on the customer account application need to be key-punched for computer processing. For example, the wholesale or retail information, when verified, is reflected in the discount code. Also, the application date and credit references are not stored as part of the data base after the application has been approved. However, the fields required as inputs for accounts receivable processing or data storage must be punched into a customer account card. The fields to be punched are shown in their source document sequence in FIGURE 17-12, *Card design aid for customer account card I.*

Inspection of the trial field size column of Figure 17-12 reveals that all the data cannot be made to fit on one card. The account number is a key field that must appear on all cards. Hence, it is assigned to columns 1 through 10 on the punched card. Since all the address information (street, city, state, and ZIP code) will not fit along with firm name, the decision was made to enter this information on the second card. These decisions are reflected in the remarks column of Figure 17-12. In addition, a card code field is assigned to distinguish between the two cards. Although it is not to be shown on the application form, the necessary directions are to be supplied to the keypunch operator. In this case the second trial field size column becomes the final field size column. No columns in other cards are indicated because, for illustrative purposes, this card is assumed to be the first card designed for the accounts receivable system.

FIGURE 17-12. **Card design aid for customer account card I**

CARD DESIGN AID

CARD NAME **Customer Account Card I**   SOURCE DOCUMENT **Customer Account Application**
DESIGNER **J. Herring**   DATE **2/17/xx**   CARD TYPE **Transcript**

DATA ELEMENTS REQUIRED	Columns in other cards	Sequence on source document	FIELD FORMAT	CARD FIELD SIZE Trial	CARD FIELD SIZE Trial	CARD FIELD SIZE Final	FINAL DESIGN Card Columns	FINAL DESIGN Sequence	REMARKS
Firm Name		1	Alpha	26	26	26	11-36	2	Card 1
Street Address		2	Al-Num	30	—	—			Card 2
Telephone		3	Num	10	10	10	43-52	4	Card 1
City		4	Alpha	20	—	—			Card 2
State		5	Alpha	2	—	—			Card 2
Zip Code		6	Num	5	—	—			Card 2
Effective Date		7	Num	6	6	6	37-42	3	Card 1
Account Number		8	Num	10	10	10	1-10	1	All Cards
Credit Code		9	Alpha	1	1	1	53	5	Card 1
Discount Code		10	Num	1	1	1	54	6	Card 1
Card Code			Num		1	1	80	7	All Cards; not on source document
			TOTALS →	111	55	55			

Figure 17-13. Card design aid for customer account card II

CARD DESIGN AID

CARD NAME __Customer Account Card II__   SOURCE DOCUMENT __Customer Account Application__
DESIGNER __J. Herring__   DATE __2/17/xx__   CARD TYPE __Transcript__

| DATA ELEMENTS REQUIRED | Columns in other cards | Sequence on source document | FIELD FORMAT | CARD FIELD SIZE | | | FINAL DESIGN | | REMARKS |
				Trial	Trial	Final	Card Columns	Sequence	
Account Number	1-10	8	Num	10		10	1-10	1	All Cards
Street Address		2	Al-Num	30		30	11-40	2	
City		4	Alpha	20		20	41-60	3	
State		5	Alpha	2		2	61-62	4	
Zip Code		6	Num	5		5	63-67	5	
Card Code	80		Num	1		1	80	6	All Cards; not on source document
			TOTALS →	68		68			

Figure 17-13, *Card design aid for customer account card II*, illustrates the design of the card into which the address portion of the input data is to be punched. The fields previously assigned columns on the first card design aid are entered under the heading "Columns on other cards." In this case the first trial field size column becomes the final field size column.

Figure 17-14, *A/R multiple-card layout form*, is prepared in part from the data on the card design aids for the customer account card. The customer account card layouts are shown in the upper two nine-rows. The next two rows display the card layout for the other two inputs to the A/R system.

Before considering the card design process complete, we must consider the final design of the source documents—the customer account application sketched in Figure 17-11. Its design should be based on both ease of customer use and keypunching efficiency. Figure 17-15, *Final design of customer account application*, reflects these considerations. Note that the data to be keypunched is identified by "boxes." The placement of the data elements on the form corresponds to the sequence shown on the multiple-card layout form of Figure 17-14. It was decided not to include the card codes on the application form itself but to convey this information to the keypunch operator on the keypunch instruction sheet.

FIGURE 17-14. A/R multiple-card layout form

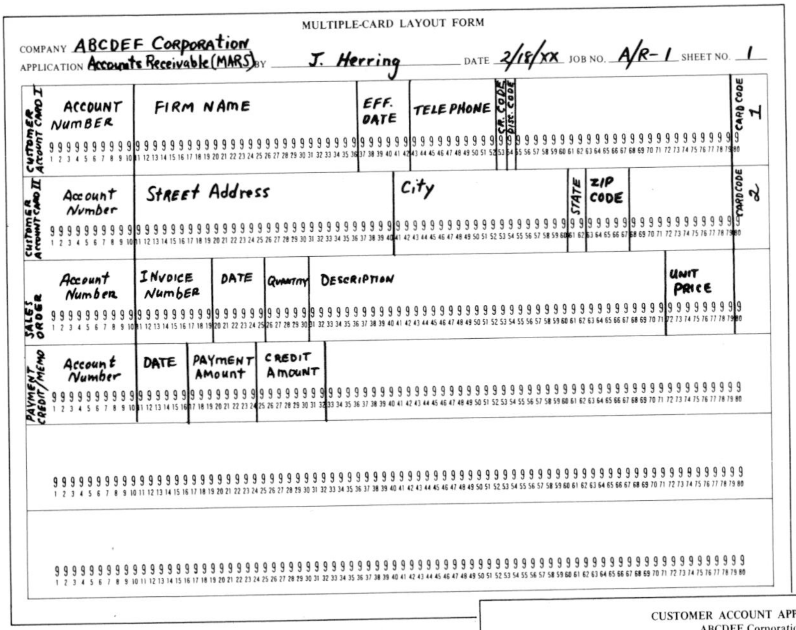

FIGURE 17-15. Final design of customer account application

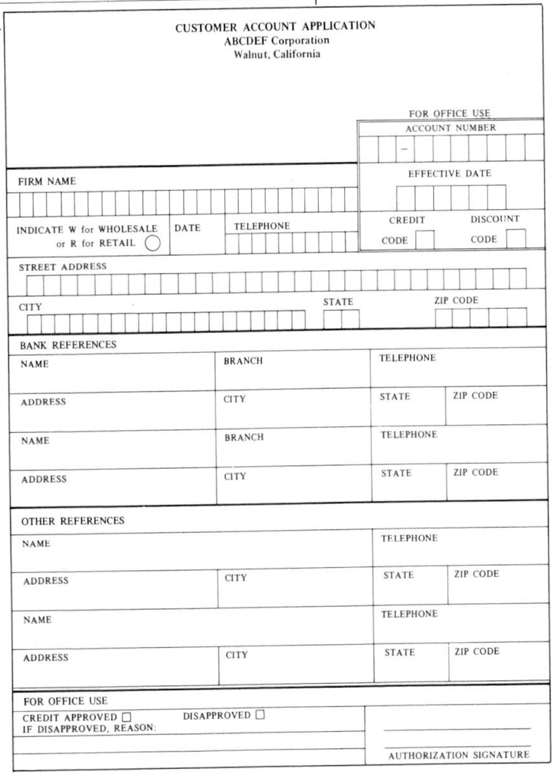

FIGURE 17-16. Keypunch instructions for customer account card I

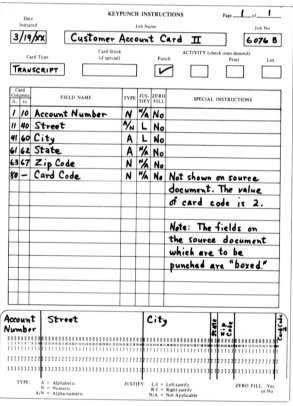

FIGURE 17-17. Keypunch instructions for customer account card II

FIGURES 17-16 and 17-17, *Keypunch instructions for customer account cards I and II*, respectively, illustrate the specific instructions given to the keypunch operator.

If it is desirable to use a manufactured card rather than a stock card, the layout of a specialty card would continue the design process. The most commonly used card layout forms are discussed in the next section.

FIGURE 17-18. Typical card layout forms

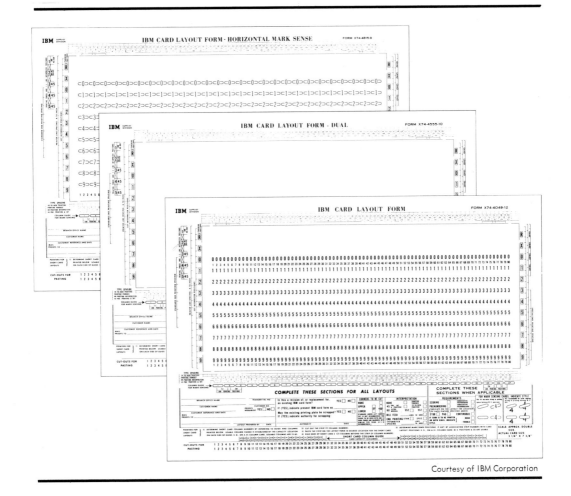

Courtesy of IBM Corporation

Specialty card design

Several types of card layout forms are available to assist the card designer in communicating with the card manufacturer. The card manufacturers themselves provide manuals to assist in preparing such layouts.[1] FIGURE 17-18, *Typical card layout forms*, displays the transcript, mark-sense, and dual card layout forms, which use a standard set of scales and instructions. Combination forms can be prepared using the dual card layout form, which is blank in the design working area. Working with the card layout form and using photographic reducing techniques, the forms manufacturer can make printing plates.

---

1. *Data Processing Techniques: Form and Card Design* (C20-8078) (White Plains: IBM Technical Publications Department, 1961).

FIGURE 17-19. IBM 96-column card

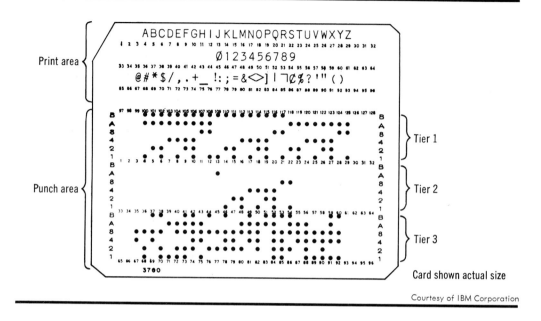

Card shown actual size

Courtesy of IBM Corporation

In general, before undertaking the expense of specialty forms, it is desirable to test the card design. This usually involves a trial operation using stock cards, such as the 5081 transcript card. Specialty forms are seldom developed for the convenience of the keypunch operator alone. If many individuals are involved in card handling or if there is a significant amount of data to be entered into cards, it is often justifiable to consider specialty cards.

The 96-column card

Design considerations for input media other than the 80-column card are not discussed in detail in this text. However, there are other important input media, such as the 96-column card, key-to-tape and key-to-disk devices, and terminals. FIGURE 17-19, *IBM 96-column card,* displays the type of card used with IBM System/3 installations.[2] There are three tiers for punching data and four lines for printing. Data punched in tier one is printed on print line one. Similarly, data punched in tiers two and three is printed on print lines two and three. Print line four does not have a corresponding tier, but may be used for printing.

The card design aid used with the 80-column card can also be used with the 96-column card. A special multiple-card layout form is available for use with the

---

2. *IBM System/3: Card System Introduction* (GC21-7505-0) (Rochester: IBM Corporation, Programming Publications, Department 425, 1969).

FIGURE 17-20. 96-column multiple-card layout form

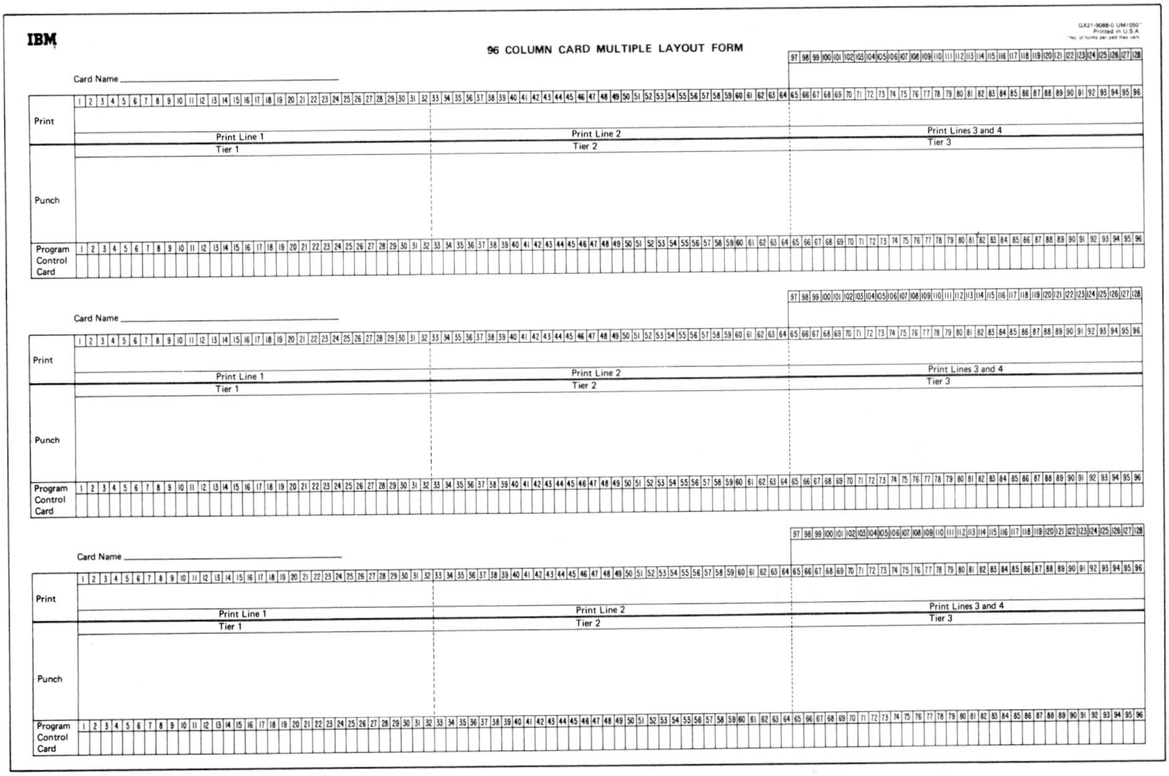

Courtesy of IBM Corporation

96-column card. As FIGURE 17-20, *96-column multiple-card layout form*, illustrates, this form provides for the layout of three 96-column cards. The program control card area is used to identify characters as alphabetic or numeric.

OTHER INPUT MEDIA

Key-to-tape and key-to-disk devices

Punched cards are limited in data capacity and are cumbersome to prepare and to handle. In addition, punched card readers are a relatively slow means of making input data available to a computer. The data rates (i.e., the rate at which data can be transferred to the computer memory) of punch card machines are much slower than those of magnetic tape and magnetic disk devices. For these reasons, keyboard equipment that can transfer operator keystrokes directly to magnetic tape or magnetic disk has been introduced.

Key-to-tape devices record data magnetically on reels of tape, cassettes, or cartridges. The data is then entered into the computer at relatively rapid (compared with card readers) data rates.

Key-to-disk devices are often used as input stations on multiterminal, shared processor systems. Typically, eight or more stations are linked to a minicomputer that provides magnetic disk storage for each station. This computer, in turn, can act as an "intelligent" terminal for a larger, central-site machine. It is able to perform local editing, validation, and correction of data, greatly speeding up the entry of error-free data. Some input data stations are equipped with a cathode ray tube (CRT) screen, on which the data that has been "keyed in" can be inspected visually and verified before it is recorded magnetically.

Although key-to-tape and key-to-disk devices provide a means of entering data into a computer without using punched cards, operators of these devices work with source documents in much the same way as key punch operators do. As with the punched card, there is an interface with a human, so source documents still must be designed to take into account readability and rapid, accurate keying of data.

Typewriter terminals and display stations

Terminals are becoming increasingly important as input devices. Some terminals provide input to processing systems without requiring that a human operator be involved, except perhaps to monitor the system or be alerted to exceptional conditions. Examples are process control and military warning systems. In these systems, the terminal design often is integrated with that of the central processing system. This integration usually is performed at a highly technical level. Most terminals, however, are operated by or receive their inputs from humans.

Typewriter-like terminals are increasingly being used for the on-line entry of source transactions. Many of these direct data entry stations include CRT's, which provide both a visual verification of input data and a means of prompting the user. As data is entered, it is displayed on the screen, and the user can modify or delete any data display before sending it to the computer system for storage and processing. Display stations often are equipped with printers that can provide "hard-copy" records of input messages. (The use of display stations as output devices is discussed in Chapter 18: Output Design.)

Each display station has its own memory, called a *buffer*, for storing data. In FIGURE 17-21, *Display station and buffer*, the size of the buffer is 480 characters (12 rows of 40 characters each). As the message indicates, a typical larger size display is 1,920 characters (24 rows of 80 characters each).

If the operator uses the display screen in a free-form manner, the mode of operation is said to be *unformatted*. If prompting information or other entries are supplied by a computer program, the display is said to be *formatted*. FIGURE 17-22, *Formatted display*, is an example of such a display. The dotted squares, called control characters, are defined by the program and are not visible to the operator. The control characters define the start of the data fields; define the type of data to be entered in the fields (e.g., numeric, alphanumeric, or symbols);

Figure 17-21. Display station and buffer

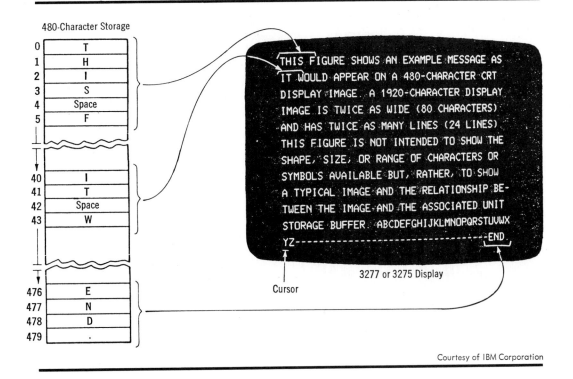

Courtesy of IBM Corporation

Figure 17-22. Formatted display

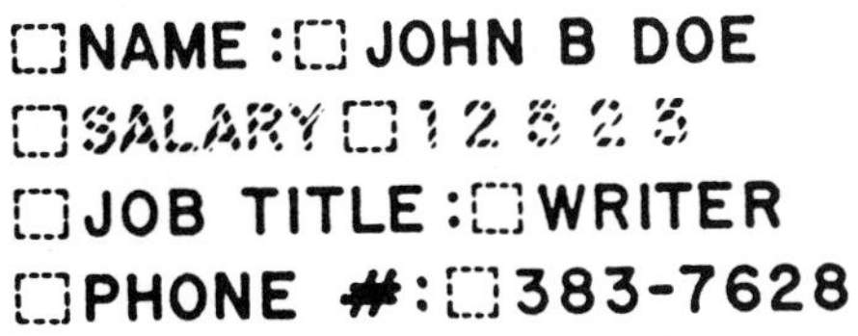

☐NAME :☐ JOHN B DOE
☐SALARY☐ 1 2 5 2 5
☐JOB TITLE :☐WRITER
☐PHONE #:☐383-7628

Courtesy of IBM Corporation

and perform other display management functions.[3] In the example shown, name, salary, job title, and phone are protected entries (i.e., entries that cannot be modified) that prompt the operator to enter the requested data.

3. *IBM-3270 Information Display System* (GA27-249-1) and *Operator's Guide for IBM-3270 Information Display System* (GA27-2742-1).

Figure 17-23. Bar codes

Optical readers

Optical readers are examples of input devices that can capture data directly. Three important types of optical devices are mark readers, bar-code readers, and character readers. Optical mark readers are able to accept data in the form of pencil marks on paper. Figure 17-5, earlier in this chapter, is an example of optical mark-reader design.

Optical bar-code readers detect combinations of marks by which data is coded. These systems usually are complex to design; the most widely known is the Universal Product Code (UPC), which appears on most retail packages. Figure 17-23, *Bar codes,* shows several of the variety of sizes and shapes in which bar codes can be printed.[4] The human-readable characters are printed alongside.

Optical character reader (OCR) devices have been designed for applications that can make use of special, optically readable symbols. A typical design application is embossed credit cards, which produce an imprint that can be read by optical scanners. Documents that use special type fonts are in common use; a typical application is in customer billing.

---

4. Yasaki, Edward K., *Bar Codes for Data Entry,* Datamation, May 1975, pp 63-68.

Optical readers are good examples of the expanding trend toward using technology to minimize the role of error-prone humans in creating large volumes of input transaction data. To the extent that human operations can be replaced by machine operations, the integrity of input data, and therefore of system output, can be improved.

KEY TERMS

punched card	*multiple-card layout form*	*cathode ray tube* (CRT)
transcript card	*keypunch instruction form*	*optical reader*
dual card	*96-column card*	*optical mark reader*
mark-sense card	*key-to-tape*	*optical bar code*
Port-A-Punch card	*key-to-disk*	*optical character reader* (OCR)
card design aid	*display station*	

FOR DISCUSSION

1. Describe the input design process.
2. What are punched cards? How common is their use?
3. Distinguish between the following:
   a. transcript card
   b. dual card
   c. mark-sense card
   d. Port-A-Punch card
   e. combination card
4. What is a card design aid? How is it used?
5. Describe a multiple-card layout form. How is it used as an intermediate card design tool? Why is it of value to the analyst in communicating with programmers?
6. What type of information must be provided to a keypunch operator? How can it be provided?
7. Under what conditions would the design of a specialty punched card be considered?
8. Discuss the differences and similarities between the designs of 80- and 96-column cards.
9. What input design principles carry over to other input media? Give some examples related to: a) key-to-disk media; b) typewriter terminals and display stations.

18

Output
Design

Output design has been an ongoing activity almost from the beginning of the project. In the Study Phase, outputs were identified and described generally in the project directive. Then a tentative output medium was selected and sketches made of each output. In the feasibility analysis, a "best" new system was selected; its description identified the input and output media. In the Design Phase, the system design process has included an evaluation of specific equipment for the system. The goal of this chapter is to show how Study Phase output sketches are converted into output descriptions detailed enough for a programmer to use. You will learn how to read and draw computer print charts.

COMPUTER OUTPUT

With few exceptions, output designs describe "lines of characters." The most common output medium is the line printer. However, data often is displayed on other devices, such as cathode ray tubes (CRT) and typewriter-like terminals. In all cases, the format descriptions are similar. Chapter 17: Input Design discussed the design considerations of the cathode ray tube and typewriter terminals. In this chapter, we shall limit our design discussion to the line printer.

COMPUTER PRINTER OUTPUT

Computer print charts

The detailed description of outputs includes the identification of the print positions to be used for the title, column headings, detail data, and totals. Figure 18-1, *Print chart*, depicts a typical form used to make this detailed description. The example print chart allows for 144 possible printing positions. Computer

FIGURE 18-1. Print chart

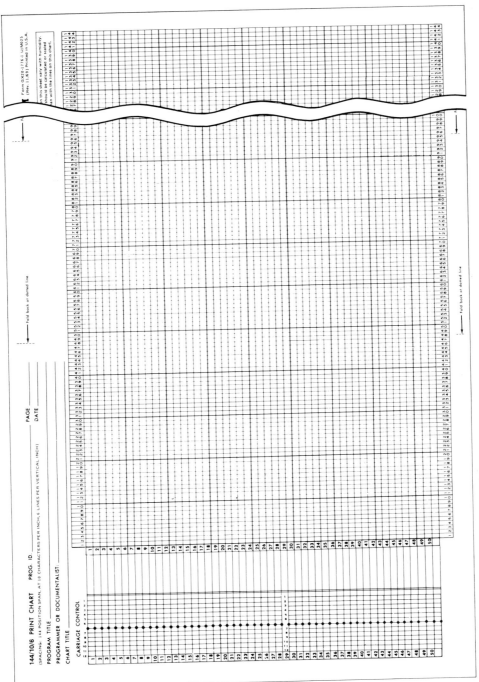

printers typically have a maximum of either 120 or 132 print positions, and may use forms of much narrower width. A vertical line should be drawn to indicate the desired width of the form. Form length also varies with the needs of users. Common form lengths are 3⅓, 3½, 3⅔, 5½, 6, 7, 7½, 8½, and 11 inches.

On the left end of the print chart is an area to describe a carriage control tape. Carriage control tapes are most often used to identify the first and last line of printing on a form for the computer. The control tape is a closed loop mounted on a reading device within the printer. The loop moves through the reader as the forms are moved through the printer; that is, the tape reader reads "line 1" of the tape as line 1 of the form is printed, reads "line 2" as line 2 of the form is printed, etc. The carriage control tape is divided into read areas called channels. Two standard uses of channels are channel 1, which indicates the position of the first line to be printed on a page, and channel 12, which indicates the position of the last line of print on a page. Channels 2 through 11 are used at the discretion of the programmer.

When printer forms are moved one line at a time, the carriage control tape unit is used only to detect the channel 12 punch—the bottom of the form. This process is called spacing. Skipping is the process of releasing the form, or moving it rapidly through the printer carriage, until a designated channel punch is detected by the carriage control tape reader. The skipping technique is useful because most printers skip faster than they space when the form is to be moved four lines or more.

As examples, let us consider some of the seven MARS printer outputs.

The two parts of Figure 18-2, *Sample overcredit notice*, depict the sketch and the data element list of the overcredit notice developed in the MARS system performance definition. This information is the basis for preparing the output design of Figure 18-3, *MARS overcredit notice*. The field sizes and formats come from the data element list, and the layout comes from the sketch. The width and length of the form are outlined on the print chart. The location of the channel 1 punch in the carriage control tape is on the same line as the first line of printing, the title line. A channel 12 punch to indicate the last line of printing is not required because each line on this form is different from all others. Thus, the computer program logically can determine when the bottom of the form is reached.

Figure 18-4, *MARS transaction register*, is an example of a form with several detail lines. When several detail lines of the same format are to be printed, it is not necessary to show all the lines on the print chart. The first two detail lines should be shown to illustrate the spacing of the body. If the report has totals, the last detail line also is required, to show the spacing between detail lines and total lines. The wavy lines between the second and last detail lines indicate that the format is repeated without change.

Edit characters, e.g., dollar signs, commas, and decimal points, should be included in field descriptions. For example, if a numeric field could have a value of

FIGURE 18-2. Sample overcredit notice

REPORT SPECIFICATION

TITLE: **Overcredit Notice**

LAYOUT:

Overcredit Notice

Sales Order No. _____
Sales Order Date _____
Account Number _____
Name and Address _____
_____
_____

Current Balance _____
Sales Order Amount _____
Total _____
Credit Limit _____
Amount Overcredit [_____]

☐ Overcredit Approved
☐ Return Sales Order

_____
AUTHORIZATION

FREQUENCY: Daily
SIZE: 1 page
QUANTITY: 40 max.
COPIES: 2

DISTRIBUTION: 1. Credit Dept. (2)

SPECIAL CONSIDERATIONS:

DATA ELEMENT LIST

TITLE: **Overcredit Notice**

DESCRIPTION	FORMAT	SIZE
Sales Order Number	XXXXXXXX	8 characters
Sales Order Date	xx/xx/xx	8 "
Account No. Region No.–Sequence No.	XX-XXXXXXX	10 "
Name		26 "
Address		
Street		20 "
City		18 "
State		2 "
Zip Code		5 "
Current Balance	XXX,XXX.XX	10 "
Sales Order Amount	XXX,XXX.XX	10 "
Total	XXX,XXX.XX	10 "
Credit Limit	XX,XXX.XX	9 "
Amount Overcredit	XX,XXX.XX	9 "

FIGURE 18-3. MARS overcredit notice

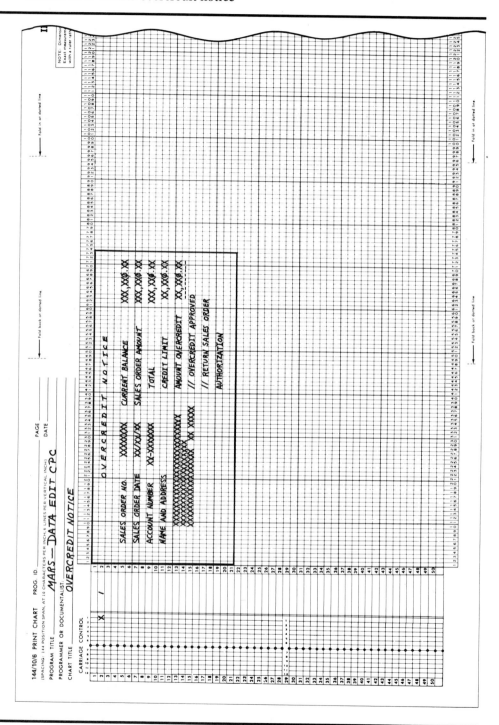

Figure 18-4. MARS transaction register

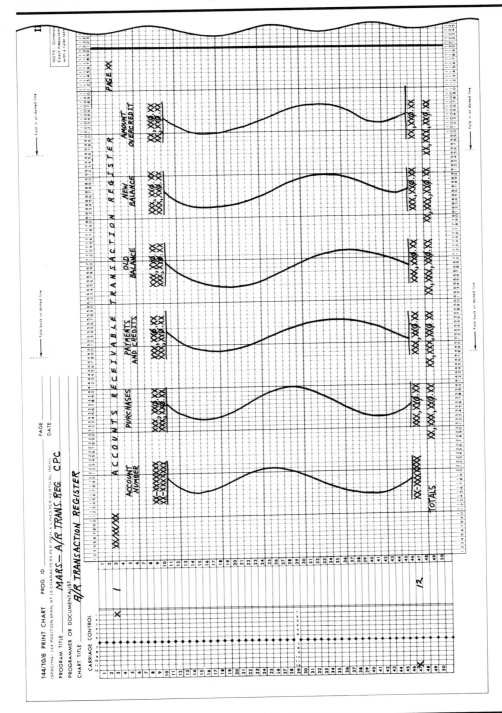

FIGURE 18-5. Preprinted form

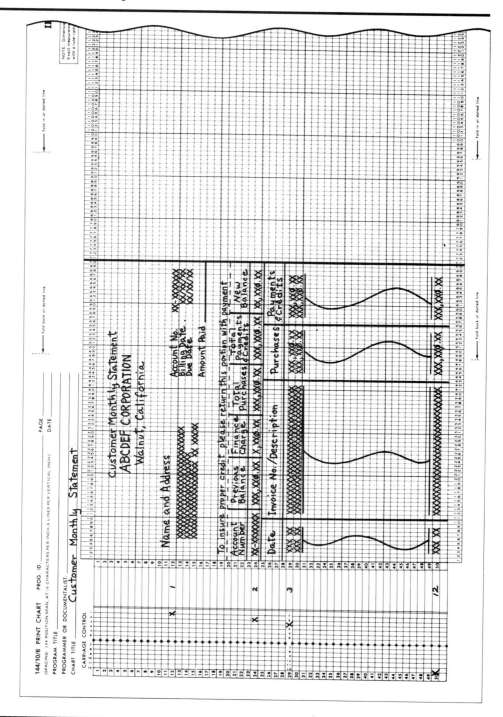

zero, the number of zeros to be printed should be depicted on the print chart. The placement of a zero in a data field indicates the first significant digit to print. The format XXX,XXO.XX indicates to the programmer that 0.00 should be printed if the field value is zero, 0.99 if the field value is 99 cents.

Specialty forms

Forms manufacturers can provide a wide variety of specialty forms on a custom-designed basis. FIGURE 18-5, *Preprinted form*, depicts the MARS customer monthly statement. These are the advantages of this type of form:

1. Column headings can be much more flexible with different sizes and styles of type.

2. Numeric fields may be edited by the form itself, e.g., dashed vertical lines to separate dollars and cents.

3. Fewer lines need to be printed by the computer, saving computer time.

The obvious disadvantages are higher cost and the need to maintain a larger forms inventory.

Specialty printer forms include continuous forms with built-in carbon copies (called multi-part forms); envelopes; mailing labels; and forms presealed into envelopes, which are printed through the envelope by carbon copy techniques.

KEY TERMS

print chart	*channel 12*	*edit characters*
carriage control tape	*spacing*	
channel 1	*skipping*	

FOR DISCUSSION

1. What is the most common output medium?

2. What is the purpose of a print chart?

3. What is the difference between spacing and skipping?

4. What are the "standardized" uses of channels on a carriage control tape?

5. Why should at least two detail lines of a report be shown on a print chart?

6. Under what conditions should an analyst consider the use of a preprinted specialty form?

19   File Design

So far in the Design Phase the analyst has (1) developed
expanded system flowcharts identifying each task
to be accomplished by the system; (2) allocated each
task as a manual, equipment, or computer program
function; (3) designed inputs to the system; and (4)
prepared layouts for all outputs. The goal of this
chapter is to introduce the concepts of file design.
You will learn about data formats, record formats,
file access methods, file organizations, and data base
management systems (DBMS).

OBJECTIVES OF FILE DESIGN

In the design of a system's files, two types of files must be designed—master files
and transaction files. Master files contain relatively permanent data, such as
customer names, addresses, balances, and year- or month-to-date information.
Transaction files contain data with a limited useful life, typically one processing
cycle. Transaction information on sales or payments, for example, is of value
only during the current billing cycle.

The objectives of file design are to provide effective auxiliary storage and to
contribute to the overall efficiency of the computer program. The auxiliary storage medium must provide efficient access to the data. The data, in turn, must be
in a form that minimizes the need for computer program instructions to change
data formats.

FILE DESIGN CONCEPTS

The following concepts are presented as a review of principles that are important
in file design, but not as a detailed presentation on data management concepts.
The discussion assumes the use of a computer utilizing an eight-bit byte and the
Extended Binary Coded Decimal Interchange Code (EBCDIC) as the internal
storage code.

Data formats

There are four basic data formats: (1) EBCDIC characters; (2) packed decimal; (3) fixed point; and (4) floating point. The fixed point and floating point formats are used mainly in scientific applications. EBCDIC character and packed decimal formats are, then, the primary concern of the analyst developing a business-oriented system.

EBCDIC characters include all letters, numbers, and special symbols that can be punched into a card or can be printed. Each character has a four-bit zone and a four-bit digit indication and occupies one byte of storage. FIGURE 19-1, *EBCDIC graphic characters*, depicts the zone-digit combinations used to record each character. Note that many of the zone-digit combinations are used for control purposes or are unused. The unused combinations are available for further expansion of the number of characters.

EBCDIC characters 0 through 9 are also referred to as zoned decimal. The number 123 would be represented as F1F2F3. Each decimal digit is associated with an F zone; hence, the term of zoned decimal. (Note: Internally the number 123 would be stored in three bytes as 11110001 11110010 11110011. However, the hexa-

FIGURE 19-1. EBCDIC graphic characters

ZONE \ DIGIT	0	1	2	3	4	5	6	7	8	9	A	B	C	D	E	F
0																
1																
2																
3																
4												¢	.	<	(	+	ǀ
5	&											!	$	*	)	;	¬
6	-	/										¦	,	%	—	>	?
7									`	:	#	@	'	=	"
8		a	b	c	d	e	f	g	h	i						
9		j	k	l	m	n	o	p	q	r						
A		~	s	t	u	v	w	x	y	z						
B																
C	{	A	B	C	D	E	F	G	H	I			ʃ		⊔	
D	}	J	K	L	M	N	O	P	Q	R						
E	\		S	T	U	V	W	X	Y	Z			⊓			
F	0	1	2	3	4	5	6	7	8	9	ǀ					

FIGURE 19-2. Zoned and packed decimal

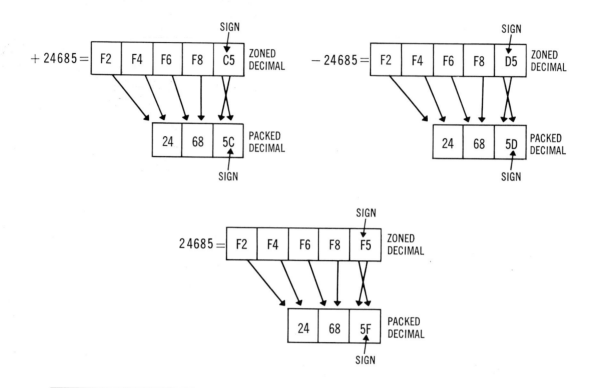

decimal digits 0 through F are used as a shorthand notation for binary 0000 through 1111. Hence, 123 can be referred to as F1F2F3.) One problem with zoned decimal is that most computers do not use zoned decimal numbers in arithmetic operations. They require another format such as packed decimal. FIGURE 19-2, *Zoned and packed decimal*, shows the relationship of packed decimal to zoned decimal and the conversion process used. All zone indications are dropped with the exception of the zone in the low-order byte, i.e., the byte occupying the position of lowest place value. The zone of the low-order byte is retained as the sign of the number. A hexadecimal C is a standard plus sign, hexadecimal D is a standard minus sign, and hexadecimal F indicates an unsigned number.

The packed decimal format is important in file design for its contribution to efficiency. First, note that the packed decimal format in Figure 19-2 requires fewer bytes of storage than does zoned decimal. This allows more data to be stored in a given amount of space. In addition, input and output operations are more efficient because data records can be read or written in a shorter time. The rule for calculating the number of bytes of storage required for a number in packed decimal is: Add 1 (for the sign) to the number of digits in the number and divide by 2. Always round upward if the division has a remainder.

Second, since numbers in packed decimal are ready to be handled arithmetically, instructions in the computer program to convert from zoned decimal to packed decimal can be eliminated. This contributes to smaller, faster-running computer programs.

Numeric data that is not to be involved in arithmetic operations, e.g., dates, is usually left in zoned decimal format unless the space saved by packing is significant.

Record formats

There are two "records" involved with auxiliary storage—logical records and physical records. A *logical record* is defined as the unit of data that is operated upon by a computer program. It is a collection of logically related fields, e.g., one customer's accounts receivable data. A *physical record* is the unit of data transferred by one input or output operation. It is made up of one or more logical records. When a physical record contains one logical record, the record is said to be unblocked. If the physical record contains more than one logical record, the records are said to be blocked. The number of logical records in each physical record is called the *blocking factor*. FIGURE 19-3, *Blocked and unblocked records*, illustrates both format choices and identifies the logical and physical records.

FIGURE 19-3. Blocked and unblocked records

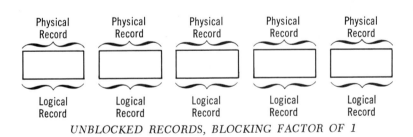

UNBLOCKED RECORDS, BLOCKING FACTOR OF 1

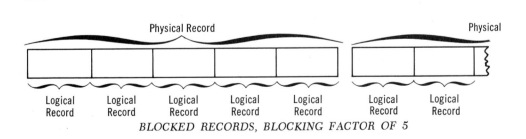

BLOCKED RECORDS, BLOCKING FACTOR OF 5

The spaces between physical records depicted in Figure 19-3 are an important consideration in file design. If the storage medium is magnetic tape, the space is needed as room to start and stop the tape between each physical record that is read or written. This space, called an interrecord gap, is approximately ¾ inch long. If the blocking factor were increased from one to five, four interrecord gaps totaling three inches of tape ($4 \times ¾''$) would be eliminated. The file length in inches of tape would be reduced three inches for each five logical records in the file, greatly increasing the capacity of the reel of tape. In general, the larger the blocking factor, the more efficiently the magnetic tape is used. Reducing the length of tape to be passed reduces the time required for input or output operations. Unfortunately, the larger the blocking factor, the larger the physical record. Since the entire physical record must be read or written at one time, adequate main storage must be available to hold it. Magnetic tape blocking factors are selected as a compromise between tape efficiency and the amount of main storage available for input or output areas.

Direct access storage devices, such as magnetic disk, have additional limitations. A physical record must be wholly contained on one *track*, the magnetic surface covered by one read-write head with the access arms in one position. Also, address, key length, and data length information are recorded, in addition to gaps, for each physical record. As with magnetic tape, the blocking factor used with magnetic disk is a compromise between disk efficiency and main storage usage. One difference between tape and disk storage is that the disk's efficiency varies as the blocking factor is increased. This variation is due to wasted space at the end of a track, which occurs when the space is too small to hold a physical record. FIGURE 19-4, *Efficiency of blocking factors*, illustrates the typical change in disk efficiency with changes in blocking factor. The most efficient blocking factors correspond to the charted peaks. The blocking factor to use is the "peak" for which the physical record size does not exceed the available input/output areas.

A common installation standard is the specification of a blocking factor for which the physical record does not exceed approximately 3,000 bytes. The examples presented in this chapter assume the use of an IBM 3340 disk drive. The largest physical record that does not exceed 3,000 bytes is a record of 2,678 bytes. Three records of this size will fit on each track. This blocking factor would therefore result in third-track blocking. The MARS example has a logical record size of 133 bytes. A blocking factor of 20 ($2,678 \div 133 = 20.13$) would result in physical records of 2,660 bytes (20 x 133 = 2,660) for third-track blocking.

Calculations relating to blocking factor, track capacity, and physical record size are made by the use of reference data for the particular device. The use of reference data is illustrated in the file design example in this chapter.

File access methods

Access methods pertain to the sequence in which records will be written or read. The two choices are sequential and random. The sequential access method is simply to start reading or writing at the beginning of the file, and then continue through the file one record after another, in sequence. If a transaction file is be-

FIGURE 19-4. Efficiency of blocking factors

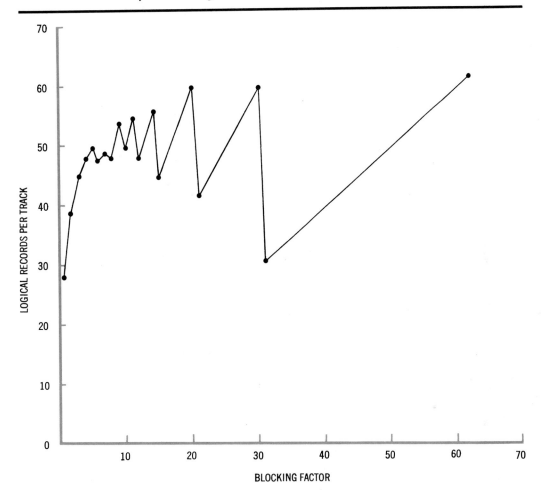

Note: This data is for a 133-byte logical record, without keys, on an IBM 3340 disk storage system.

ing processed against a master file sequentially, both files must have their records in the same sequence. The random access method provides for the reading or writing of unsequenced records, i.e., in random order. The advantage of this method is the ability to go directly to the desired record without handling any other records ahead of it. To locate the desired record, its address must be supplied to the operating system before an attempt is made to read the record. The address may be determined either by calculating it with a mathematical algorithm, or formula, or by looking up the address in a table or index generated at the time the file was created. In either case, the address consists of the cylinder number, the track number, and optionally a record number. A *cylinder* is defined as the

FIGURE 19-5. Magnetic disk unit schematic

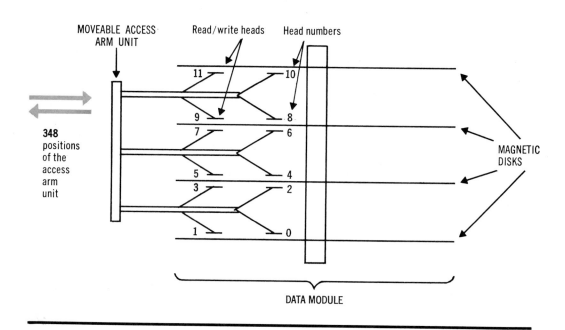

DATA MODULE

surface area covered by all read-write heads in one position of the access mechanism. FIGURE 19-5, *Magnetic disk unit schematic,* depicts a typical magnetic disk drive.

File organizations

There are many file organizations in use, but we will discuss only three of the most popular: sequential, direct, and indexed sequential.

Sequential files are created by writing records on the storage medium in sequence according to a control field within each logical record; for example, employee records to be recorded alphabetically would be sorted by the name field (control field). The addresses of the records are not recorded as the file is created. Without these addresses, it is not possible to use random access methods. Therefore, the sequential file must always be accessed by starting at the beginning of the file and processing each record in sequence—the order it occurs on the medium. For this reason, transactions should be batched to accumulate a reasonable number of updates for efficient processing. This organization is the only choice for magnetic tape files.

Direct files are created by calculating the address (cylinder, track, and record number, or cylinder and track number) of the record from its control or key field. Direct files are always accessed randomly by recalculating the record address each time the record is required; they cannot be accessed sequentially because the records are not physically recorded in any particular sequence. Also, there are probably many addresses throughout the file that are not used, leaving "holes" in the file. In addition, different record keys sometimes produce the same file address. When this occurs, the second record is called a synonym. The synonym record is recorded at the next available location and "chained to" (i.e., referred to) the original calculated address by a field indicating the address of the synonym. The only way to reorganize a direct file to eliminate synonyms is to change the algorithm used to calculate the addresses.

Indexed sequential files are created in sequential order just as sequential files are. However, in addition to the file itself, a set of address indexes is created. These indexes may be used to look up the address of any desired record and to access it randomly. If sequential processing is desired, the file may also be accessed sequentially. Thus, the indexed sequential organization is a compromise between a sequential file and a direct file. FIGURE 19-6, *File organization advantages and disadvantages,* summarizes the advantages and disadvantages of the three file organizations.

FIGURE 19-6. **File organization advantages and disadvantages**

SEQUENTIAL FILES

ADVANTAGES:
1. Efficient use of storage.
2. Programming to access records is straightforward.

DISADVANTAGES:
1. Transactions must be batched and in file sequence.
2. Additions and deletions require rewriting the file.

DIRECT FILES

ADVANTAGES:
1. Can efficiently handle large numbers of unsequenced transactions against a volatile file.

DISADVANTAGES:
1. Storage efficiency is reduced by gaps.
2. Processing efficiency is reduced by synonyms.
3. File may be difficult to reorganize.

INDEXED SEQUENTIAL FILES

ADVANTAGES:
1. Either sequenced or unsequenced transactions may be routinely processed.
2. Programming is relatively straightforward.
3. File may be reorganized easily.

DISADVANTAGES:
1. Unsequenced transactions tend to reduce processing efficiency.
2. A volatile file may have to be re-created frequently.

FILE DESIGN EXAMPLES

Indexed sequential file organization

The following example file design is for the ABCDEF Corporation's modified accounts receivable system (MARS).

Logical record layout. The first step in file design is to determine the record layout for the file. FIGURE 19-7, *Record layout worksheet*, depicts a typical worksheet for documenting this record layout. The worksheet has enough room for two records, each with a maximum length of 256 bytes. Each byte of the record is pictured and numbered, and its data format (i.e., characteristic) is identified.

The data format of each field must be selected before the field size in bytes can be determined. FIGURE 19-8, *Output data element source analysis*, depicts the same worksheets that were used to make a gross storage estimate during the feasibility analysis. They identify the master file record fields and indicate the number of characters in each field (excluding edit symbols in numeric fields). The worksheets are updated to reflect any changes made since the feasibility analysis. They describe the master file record. The analyst indicates on the worksheets the numeric fields to be in packed decimal format and the number of bytes required. In Figure 19-8, all fields to be packed are circled, and the packed field sizes are indicated. FIGURE 19-9, *MARS record layout worksheet*, depicts the master file record layout for the MARS project. Each field is identified. Alphabetic or alphanumeric fields have a character (C) characteristic. Numeric fields have either a zoned (Z) or a packed (P) characteristic. Note that the byte count is numbered relative to zero; hence, the record length is 133 bytes even though the last byte in the example record is number 132.

File organization selection. The advantages and disadvantages of sequential, direct, and indexed sequential organizations were listed in Figure 19-6. The analyst must evaluate the processing requirements of the systems computer program components identified in the system design activities. High activity files—those with a high percentage of their records processed each run—are very efficient as sequential files. Files that are processed against large numbers of unsequenced transactions or that are volatile (that is, with a large number of records added or deleted) are most efficient as direct files. If the file has both sequential and random processing requirements, an indexed sequential file often is the best choice.

Since magnetic tape can only support sequential files, magnetic disk was the storage medium chosen. The MARS master file organization selection was indexed sequential. The requirements of low activity processing of sales orders and payments combined with the very high activity of customer statement processing, plus the rapid growth projected for the customer accounts, made this the best choice.

FIGURE 19-7. Record layout worksheet

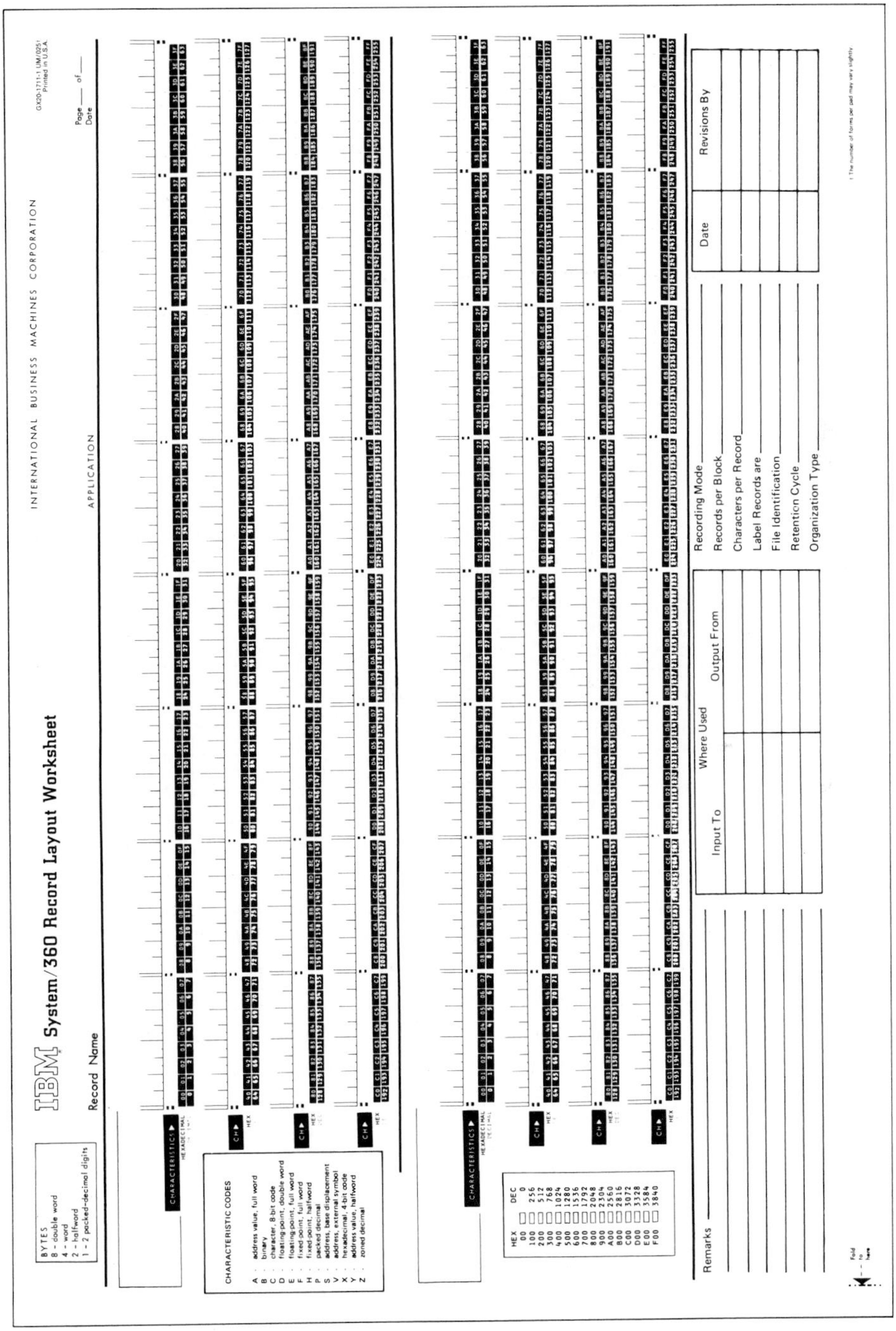

Courtesy of IBM Corporation

FIGURE 19-8. Output data element source analysis

OUTPUT DATA ELEMENT SOURCE ANALYSIS — Page 1 of 3

COMPUTER PROGRAM: Modified A/R System (MARS)

OUTPUT DATA ELEMENT	Cust. Mo. Statement	A/R Trans. Register	A/R Summary Report	Aged A/R Report	Cust. Account List	Overcredit Notice	Shipping Invoice	MASTER FILE	TRANS. FILE 1	TRANS. FILE 2	TRANS. FILE 3	CALCULATED RESULT
Name	✓		✓	✓	✓	✓	✓	26	26			
Address	✓				✓	✓	✓	45	46			
Account Number	✓	✓	✓	✓	✓	✓	✓	9*6	9			
Billing Cycle Date	✓			✓						8		
Due Date	✓									8		
Amount Paid	✓							8*5				8
Previous Balance	✓	✓	✓	✓		✓		8*5				8
Finance Charge	✓											6
Total Purchases	✓							8*5				8
Total Payments & Credits	✓							8*5				8
New Balance	✓	✓	✓			✓						8
Purchase Date (Cur.)	✓	✓			✓	✓	✓					6
Invoice No./Desc.	✓					✓	✓					30
Purchases	✓	✓	✓			✓	✓					8
Payments & Credits	✓	✓	✓									8
Amount Overcredit		✓				✓						7
Total Daily Purchases		✓										10
Total Daily Pay. & Credits		✓										10
TOTALS								112	80	68		73

OUTPUT DATA ELEMENT SOURCE ANALYSIS — Page 2 of 3

Modified A/R System (MARS)

OUTPUT DATA ELEMENT	Cust. Mo. Statement	A/R Trans. Register	A/R Summary Report	Aged A/R Report	Cust. Account List	Overcredit Notice	Shipping Invoice	MASTER FILE	TRANS. FILE 1	TRANS. FILE 2	TRANS. FILE 3	CALCULATED RESULT
Total Daily ...e. Bal.	✓											10
Total Daily New Bal.	✓											10
Total Daily Overcredit	✓											10
Date— Week Ending		✓									8	
Purchases— Month-to-Date		✓						8*5				8
Credits— Month-to-Date		✓						8*5				8
Balance Change		✓										8
Weekly Cust. Purchases		✓										10
Cust. Purchases— MTD		✓										10
Weekly Cust. Credits		✓										10
Cust. Credits— MTD		✓										10
Cust. Bal. Net Change		✓										10
Cust. Bal.- 30 Days			✓					8*5				8
Cust. Bal.- 60 Days			✓					8*5				8
Cust. Bal.- 90 Days			✓					8*5				8
Cust. Bal.- Over 90 Days			✓					8*5				8
Total A/R Balance			✓									10
Total Cur. A/R Bal.			✓									10
TOTALS								160	80	76		229

OUTPUT DATA ELEMENT SOURCE ANALYSIS — Page 3 of 3

Modified A/R System (MARS)

OUTPUT DATA ELEMENT	Cust. Mo. Statement	A/R Trans. Register	A/R Summary Report	Aged A/R Report	Cust. Account List	Overcredit Notice	Shipping Invoice	MASTER FILE	TRANS. FILE 1	TRANS. FILE 2	TRANS. FILE 3	CALCULATED RESULT
...Days Old				✓				160	80	76		10
Total A/R- 60 Days Old				✓								10
Total A/R- 90 Days Old				✓								10
Total A/R- Over 90 Days				✓								10
Cust. Credit Code					✓	✓		2	2			
Trade Discount							✓	5	5			
Order Quantity							✓				4	
Order Description							✓				23	
Unit Price							✓				6	
List Price							✓				8	
Discount							✓					7
Net Price							✓					8
Total List Price							✓					8
Total Discount							✓					7
TOTALS								167	87	76	41	299

FIGURE 19-9. MARS record layout worksheet

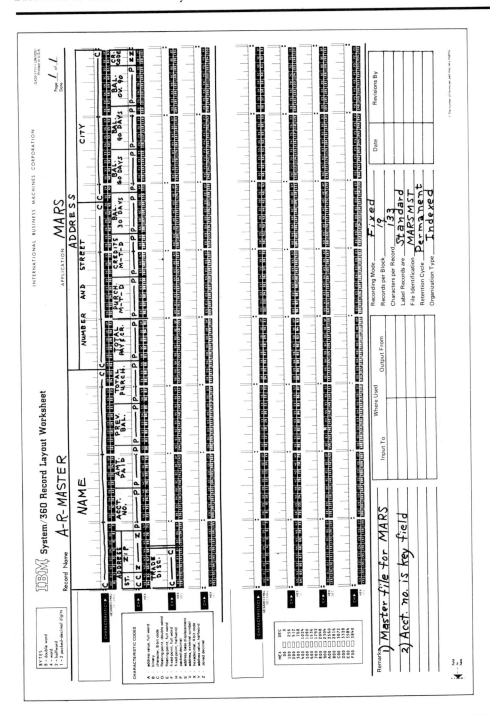

Blocking factor selection and file size calculation. The ABCDEF Corporation adopted the standard of third-track blocking for all disk files; in other words, no physical record will be larger than one-third a disk track. This standard was adopted because it was felt that approximately 2,600 bytes (one-third track) per input/output area should be the maximum main storage to be used for this purpose, considering the total main storage available.

There are two sets of reference data, one "with keys" and one "without keys." Recording a copy of the key or control field with the physical record helps to locate records when random access methods are being used. Reference data "without keys" is used for sequential files. "With keys" reference data is used with direct files and indexed sequential files. Since the MARS master file organization is indexed sequential, "with keys" reference data is used.

FIGURE 19-10, *IBM 3340 reference data: with keys*, gives the DASD reference data used to select blocking factors and calculate file size for the MARS. Since each physical record can take up to one-third track, there will be three physical records per track. Using Figure 19-10, we locate 3 in the records-per-track column. The corresponding entry in the maximum bytes-per-record column indicates a maximum *physical record* size of 2,603 bytes. FIGURE 19-11, MARS *file calculations*, illustrates the remaining calculations required to determine the master file size. The blocking factor is equal to the maximum physical record size (from the reference data table) divided by the logical record size (from the record layout worksheet). Since physical records must be multiples of logical records, disregard any fraction as remainder. The physical record size is equal to the blocking factor times the logical record size plus the key field length. The key field for the MARS is the customer account number, which is 5 bytes in length. (Note: If the physical record size exceeds the maximum third-track physical record size after the key field length is added, either the blocking factor or the logical record must be reduced in size, and the calculations repeated.)

The number of logical records per track is determined by multiplying the blocking factor by the number of physical records per track (3 for third-track blocking).

The next step is to determine a load factor for the file. The load factor is the percentage of the maximum capacity of the file to be utilized. A load factor of 90 percent was selected for the MARS. This gives a 10 percent margin if the projected size of the file is underestimated. The file size, in tracks, is equal to the projected number of logical records divided by the load factor and by the number of logical records per track. Fractional file sizes are rounded upward.

On the IBM 3340 disk drive, each cylinder of storage has 12 tracks. With an indexed sequential file, however, all 12 tracks are not available for data (prime data area). The track covered by head 0 is used as an

FIGURE 19-10. IBM 3340 reference data: with keys

IBM 3340 REFERENCE DATA: WITH KEYS

BYTES PER RECORD		RECORDS PER	
MINIMUM	MAXIMUM	TRACK	CYLINDER
4026	8293	1	12
2604	4025	2	24
1892	2603	3	36
1466	1891	4	48
1181	1465	5	60
978	1180	6	72
825	977	7	84
707	824	8	96
612	706	9	108
534	611	10	120
470	533	11	132
415	469	12	144
368	414	13	156
328	367	14	168
292	327	15	180
261	291	16	192
233	260	17	204
208	232	18	216
185	207	19	228
165	184	20	240
146	164	21	252
130	145	22	264
114	129	23	
100	113	24	
87	99	25	
75	86	26	
63	74	27	
53	62	28	
43	52	29	
34	42	30	
25	33	31	
17	24	32	
10	16	33	
2	9	34	

**FIGURE 19-11.
MARS file calculations**

IBM 3340 Disk Storage: With Keys

Third-Track Blocking = 2,603 bytes maximum

Logical Record Size = 133 bytes

Blocking Factor = maximum physical record size/logical record size
                 = 2,603/133
                 = 19.57
                 = 19

Physical Record Size = (blocking factor x logical record size) +
                         key field length
                      = (19 x 133) + 5
                      = 2,527 + 5
                      = 2,532 bytes

Logical Records per Track = blocking factor x physical records
                              per track
                           = 19 x 3
                           = 57

File Size in Tracks = (logical records/load factor)/logical records
                        per track
                     = (10,000/.90)/57
                     = 11,111/57
                     = 194.92
                     = 194

File Size in Cylinders = file size in tracks/data tracks
                           per cylinder
                        = 194/9
                        = 21.55
                        = 22

index (track index), and the last tracks of each cylinder are used as a cylinder overflow area. An overflow area is usually required whenever records are added to the file. Typically the last two tracks (heads 10-11) are used as the cylinder overflow area. Thus, out of the 12 tracks per cylinder, only 9 are available as the prime data area.

The file size in cylinders is the file size in tracks divided by the number of data tracks per cylinder (9 in this case). Indexed sequential files are required to be multiples of whole cylinders. Thus, the calculated file size in cylinders is always rounded upward. The MARS master file size will be 22 cylinders. There are other indexes (one required, one optional) used with indexed sequential files, but the index sizes are small and do not significantly alter the calculated file size.

Sequential file organization

If a sequential file organization had been selected for the MARS, the only difference, as illustrated in the following figures, would be in the file size calculations. FIGURE 19-12, *IBM 3340 reference data: without keys,* was used to perform the calculations summarized in FIGURE 19-13, *Sequential file calculations.*

There are four differences in calculations with a sequential file as compared with an indexed sequential file. For the sequential file:

1. The maximum physical record size for third-track blocking is larger.
2. There is no key field length to add to the calculated physical record size.
3. All 12 tracks of each cylinder are available for data.
4. The file size in cylinders need not be rounded up to a whole number of cylinders.

DATA BASE MANAGEMENT SYSTEMS

As the number of computer-based systems within a company increases, larger amounts of data must be stored in support of them. The maintenance and control of a large, complex set of files is a costly and difficult task. Often data elements are recorded in several different files. For instance, employee name and employee number may be recorded in the personnel file, the payroll file, and other employee-related files. These redundant or duplicated data items cause two major problems: (1) they increase the total amount of file storage space needed; and (2) they necessitate multiple updates whenever a change occurs.

A solution for the problem of redundant data is to combine files with common elements into larger, shared files. To eliminate all redundant data, all files could be combined into one large file. However, the creation of large files that are shared by multiple systems introduces two additional problems. First, each program using the file must input and hold all the data in the record, not just the data elements used in its processing. This increases the time required to input or output data and causes a greater amount of main storage to be used for input/output areas. Second, data elements that do not apply to a system may become available to system users. This is especially true for on-line inquiry

FIGURE 19-12. IBM 3340 reference data: without keys

IBM 3340 REFERENCE DATA: WITHOUT KEYS

BYTES PER RECORD		RECORDS PER	
MINIMUM	MAXIMUM	TRACK	CYLINDER
4101	8368	1	12
2679	4100	2	24
1967	2678	3	36
1541	1966	4	48
1256	1540	5	60
1053	1255	6	72
900	1052	7	84
782	899	8	96
687	781	9	108
609	686	10	120
545	608	11	132
490	544	12	144
443	489	13	156·
403	442	14	168
367	402	15	180
336	366	16	192
308	335	17	204
283	307	18	216
260	282	19	228
240	259	20	240
221	239	21	252
205	220	22	264
189	204	23	276
175	188	24	288
162	174	25	300
150	161	26	312
138	149	27	
128	137	28	
118	127	29	
109	117	30	
100	108	31	
92	99	32	
85	91	33	
77	84	34	
71	76	35	
64	70	36	
58	63	37	
52	57	38	
47	51	39	
42	46	40	
37	41	41	
32	36	42	
27	31	43	
23	26	44	
19	22	45	
15	18	46	
11	14	47	
8	10	48	
4	7	49	
1	3	50	

FIGURE 19-13. Sequential file calculations

```
              IBM 3340 Disk Storage:  Without Keys


Third-Track Blocking =  2,678 bytes

Logical Record Size  =  133 bytes

Blocking Factor  =  maximum physical record size/logical record size
                 =  2,678/133
                 =  20.13
                 =  20

Physical Record Size  =  blocking factor  x  logical record size
                      =  20  x  133
                      =  2,660 bytes

Logical Records per Track  =  blocking factor  x  physical records
                              per track
                           =  20  x  3
                           =  60

File Size in Tracks  =  (logical records/load factor)/logical records
                        per track
                     =  (10,000/.90)/60
                     =  11,111/60
                     =  185.18
                     =  186 tracks

File Size in Cylinders  =  file size in tracks/data tracks
                           per cylinder
                        =  186/10
                        =  18.6 cylinders
```

system (i.e., terminals in user locations), where users might see confidential data they are not authorized to use. Considering the public's right to privacy and the several laws that require privacy of confidential data, this must be a major concern for the corporation.

For many companies, the solution to the problems of maintaining and controlling the data base has been the use of a data base management system. A *data base management system (DBMS)* is a software system used to maintain and control large, shared files.

DBMS functions

Data base management systems have two major functions: (1) to maintain the data base independently from the application programs that use the data; and (2) to provide a measure of data security so that unauthorized users will not have access to the data.

In traditional application programs, all files, records, and data elements used by the program must be described within the program. If the size of the record or any data element changes, all the application programs using the file must be modified to reflect the change. In a shared file, changes may have been made in only one system, but data description changes are required in all programs that use the file.

Data base management systems avoid this problem by removing the data descriptions from the application programs and putting them in the DBMS. This allows the data to be described once, within the DBMS, instead of within every application program. If any changes are made to the data base, only the DBMS description must be altered. Application programs are not affected. The DBMS description of the data elements and the relationships between the data elements in the data base is called the *schema*.

Since the application program no longer contains data descriptions, it cannot directly access the data base. When an input or output dealing with the data base is required, the application program will "call" for the data from the DBMS. The DBMS will then access the data base and transfer the data to or from the application program. It should be noted that the application program cannot be written in all languages. Each data base management system is designed to interface with one or more host languages. All data base management systems support COBOL as a host language; many support FORTRAN, and a few support RPG and other languages.

Although the application program does not contain data descriptions, it does use a list of data elements that make up the program's logical record. The description of the data elements available to the program is called the *subschema*. The data elements of the logical record described in the subschema may actually come from several different records in several different files. The DBMS "manufactures" a logical record for the application program to match the subschema. If the contents of the subschema are controlled, control can be exercised also over the data that the user can see. Data elements that do not apply to the user's program or data that the user is not authorized to see will not be provided to the application program. If different subschema are provided to different users, what the user sees is controlled. Users can be limited in what they do with the data. They may be limited to inquiry only, allowed to update data elements, add records to the file, delete records from the file, or any combination of these functions.

An additional security function in most data base management systems is provided by a system of privacy locks or a password system. Before users can access data through a terminal, for example, they are required to enter personal passwords. The password communicates to the DBMS the level of authority the user has in dealing with the data.

DBMS components

Four major components are common to most data base management systems. The first two are a data description component and a data manipulation component. The use of these components is illustrated in FIGURE 19-14, *Data base management systems* (DBMS) modules. Application programs call for data through the data description component, which communicates the data requirements to the data manipulation component. All data retrievals, updates, additions, and deletions are accomplished through the data manipulation component. This component then transmits the requested data to the application program, which processes the data and can output the results to the user. These two components are the heart of the DBMS.

A third component is a query language. This is a simplified programming language that allows users to specify the data wanted and the format that will

FIGURE 19-14. **Data base management system (DBMS) modules**

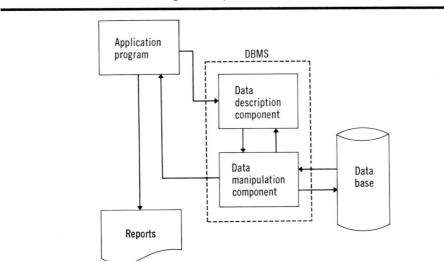

meet user information needs. The query language is easy to use and typically requires only a few key words to create a user output. It is especially valuable in on-line systems where a user can specify the data through the terminal and see the resulting output almost immediately.

The last component is a DBMS utility. It is a series of programs used to create, back up, and restore the data base. The utility programs allow the data processing center to protect itself against possible loss of the data base.

The data base administrator (DBA)

The data base management system separates data descriptions from the application programs and provides a measure of data security. The data base administrator is the authority that controls the DBMS by controlling the data base schema and subschema. The DBA also authorizes the use of passwords by users. The job of data base administrator may range from a part-time position in smaller companies to full-time administration with a staff of several assistants in larger companies. The data base administrator's job is to provide services to both data processing personnel and users; this person must be able to work with both groups. The administrator has the ultimate responsibility for the organization and control of the data base.

KEY TERMS

EBCDIC	*direct files*	*indexed sequential files*
zoned decimal	*logical record*	*data base management system* (DBMS)
packed decimal	*physical record*	*data base administrator* (DBA)
cylinder	*blocking factor*	
sequential files	*track*	

FOR DISCUSSION

1. What are the objectives of file design?

2. In what ways is packed decimal more efficient than zoned decimal?

3. Explain the relationship between a logical record and a physical record.

4. How are record addresses supplied to the computer system to locate records randomly?

5. Which file organization is the simplest? The fastest with unsequenced transactions? Capable of both sequential and random access?

6. What is a DBMS?

7. What are the major functions of a DBMS?

8. What are the functions of the data base administrator (DBA)?

20 Design Phase Report and Review

At the conclusion of the Design Phase, the analyst prepares a report and reviews it with the user of the system. The goal of this chapter is to describe the structure and content of the Design Phase report and the purpose and importance of the Design Phase review. You will learn how to organize a Design Phase report.

DESIGN SPECIFICATION

The Design Phase activities are concluded by three major events. These are (1) completion of the Design Specification; (2) preparation of the Design Phase report; and (3) conduct of the Design Phase review.

The Design Specification is the technical core of the Design Phase report. This second major baseline document is the "blueprint" for constructing the computer-based business system. It is the communication link between the analyst and the programmers who will be assigned to the project.

FIGURE 20-1, *Design Specification outline,* displays the content of a typical Design Specification. The Design Specification is an extension of the Performance Specification prepared at the conclusion of the Study Phase. It also is divided into two parts. The first part is an external design requirement that relates to the interaction between the system and its operating environment. The second part of the Design Specification is an internal design requirement. This part establishes design requirements for the computer program and for its subprograms, the computer program components, which are the building blocks of the computer program. The requirements for the computer program and computer program components result from the Design Phase activities which were described in Chapters 16, 17, 18, and 19. The continuing documentation of these activities resulted in the expansion of the Performance Specification into the Design Specification. This expansion is displayed in FIGURE 20-2, *Performance Specification– Design Specification gozinto chart.* This chart is called a "gozinto" chart because it shows how each element of the Performance Specification goes into ("gozinto")

FIGURE 20-1. Design Specification outline

DESIGN SPECIFICATION

A. EXTERNAL DESIGN REQUIREMENT:
1. Information-oriented flowchart
2. System output requirements
3. System input requirements
4. System interface requirements
5. System test requirements
6. Equipment specifications
7. Personnel and training requirements

B. INTERNAL DESIGN REQUIREMENT:
1. Computer Program Design Requirement

   a. System flowchart
   b. Expanded system flowcharts (process and/or HIPO)
   c. Data base requirements
   d. Computer program control requirements
   e. Computer program test requirements

2. Computer Program Component (CPC) Design Requirements (for each CPC as required)

   a. Detailed system flowcharts
   b. Transaction file requirements
   c. Control requirements
   d. Interface requirements
   e. Test requirements
   f. Special requirements

---

the Design Specification. The gozinto chart is an excellent illustration of "cumulative documentation." Note that the Performance Specification "descriptions" become Design Phase "requirements." Not surprisingly, the greatest expansion during the Design Phase is internal to the computer program.

DESIGN PHASE REPORT

Structure and content

The structure and content of the Design Phase report are shown in FIGURE 20-3, *Design Phase report outline.* As shown in this figure, the Design Phase report has the same five major parts as the Study Phase report.

Elements of the Study Phase report, appropriately expanded or modified, are carried forward into the Design Phase report. For instance, the system scope section is brought forward to refamiliarize reviewers with the project. Of course, the system scope section in the Design Phase report should identify and explain any changes that occurred during this phase. As mentioned earlier, the Performance Specification "gozinto" the Design Specification.

The life-cycle project plan and the cost schedule, which were prepared at the conclusion of the Study Phase, are updated to show progress in reaching the Design Phase milestones. Of course, significant departures from or changes in the

FIGURE 20-2. Performance Specification—Design
              Specification gozinto chart

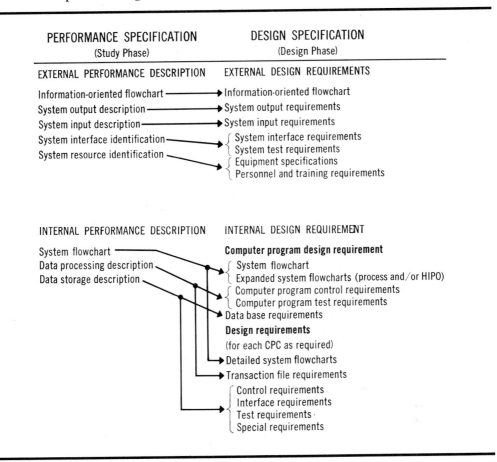

PERFORMANCE SPECIFICATION
(Study Phase)

DESIGN SPECIFICATION
(Design Phase)

EXTERNAL PERFORMANCE DESCRIPTION

EXTERNAL DESIGN REQUIREMENTS

Information-oriented flowchart ⟶ Information-oriented flowchart
System output description ⟶ System output requirements
System input description ⟶ System input requirements
System interface identification ⟶ { System interface requirements
                                    { System test requirements
System resource identification ⟶ { Equipment specifications
                                  { Personnel and training requirements

INTERNAL PERFORMANCE DESCRIPTION

INTERNAL DESIGN REQUIREMENT

System flowchart
Data processing description
Data storage description

Computer program design requirement
{ System flowchart
{ Expanded system flowcharts (process and/or HIPO)
{ Computer program control requirements
{ Computer program test requirements
Data base requirements
Design requirements
(for each CPC as required)
Detailed system flowcharts
Transaction file requirements
{ Control requirements
{ Interface requirements
{ Test requirements
{ Special requirements

plan should be noted and explained. A detailed milestone plan and cost schedules now are prepared and presented for the Development Phase, for which authorization to proceed is now being requested. FIGURE 20-4, *Detailed milestones for the Development Phase,* lists appropriate milestones. These are described in Chapter 21: Development Phase Overview.

Appendices should be included in the Design Phase report as required. It usually is a good idea to place complicated analyses in appendices. These analyses can be referred to, and the significant results can be presented in the body of the report without diverting the reader from the "mainstream" message. Other materials, such as tables and charts that support the conclusions and recommendations of the Design Phase report, should be placed in an appendix unless it is appropriate to present them in the body of the report.

FIGURE 20-3. Design Phase report outline

DESIGN PHASE REPORT

I. SYSTEM SCOPE:	A. System title
	B. Problem statement and purpose
	C. Constraints
	D. Specific objectives
	E. Method of evaluation
II. CONCLUSIONS AND RECOMMENDATIONS:	A. Conclusions
	B. Recommendations
III. DESIGN SPECIFICATIONS:	A. External design requirement
	B. Internal design requirement
IV. PLANS AND COST SCHEDULES:	A. Detailed milestones—Design Phase
	B. Major milestones—all phases
	C. Detailed milestones—Development Phase
V. APPENDICES:	As appropriate

FIGURE 20-4. Detailed milestones for the Development Phase

DEVELOPMENT PHASE—DETAILED MILESTONES

IMPLEMENTATION PLAN:	Test plan
	Training plan
	Conversion plan
EQUIPMENT ACQUISITION AND INSTALLATION	
COMPUTER PROGRAM DEVELOPMENT:	Computer program design
	Coding and debugging
	Computer program tests
REFERENCE MANUAL PREPARATION:	Programmer's reference manual
	Operator's reference manual
	User's reference manual
PERSONNEL TRAINING	
SYSTEM TESTS	
CHANGEOVER PLAN	
SYSTEM SPECIFICATION	
DEVELOPMENT PHASE REPORT	
DEVELOPMENT PHASE REVIEW	

Example Design Phase report

An example of a Design Phase report based on the ABCDEF Corporation's modified accounts receivable system (MARS) appears on the following pages as Exhibit 2.

DESIGN PHASE REVIEW

The Design Phase review is a particularly critical review. It is a true test of sponsor confidence. Up to this point, the computer-based business system activities were "visible" to the user-sponsor. He was able to follow the Study Phase efforts which resulted in the preparation of the Performance Specification and the Study Phase report. He can comprehend most of the design tasks that are summarized in the Design Specification. Now the system is on the verge of moving into the Development Phase. The user must make a decision about future activities that he cannot visualize clearly or expect to follow in detail. He is being asked to make the most significant cost commitment to date. Usually, this commitment is for a greatly enlarged project scope, involving many complex development activities over an extended time. For example, programmers will be added to the project, and the results of their activities will not be visible to the user until shortly before the system is scheduled to become operational.

The analyst must plan the Design Phase review with great care. The user should be provided with a well-written Design Phase report in advance of the review and given the Study Phase report as a reference document. At the review, an effective presentation is necessary so that the user will retain his faith in the analyst's ability to continue with the detailed development of the system.

KEY TERMS

external design requirement   *internal design requirement*

FOR DISCUSSION

1. What is the purpose of the Design Phase report?

2. What is the content of the Design Phase report?

3. Discuss the importance of the Design Specification, including its relationship to the Performance Specification.

4. What project plans and schedules are presented at the Design Phase review?

5. What is the purpose of the Design Phase review?

EXHIBIT 2

MARS DESIGN PHASE REPORT

I. SYSTEM SCOPE

A. System Title
Modified Accounts Receivable System (MARS)

B. Problem Statement and Purpose
The ABCDEF Corporation's manual accounts receivable system currently handles 1,000 accounts each month. This number is expected to double within one year and to reach 10,000 in five years. The manual system is not able to meet this projected growth. Serious problems have already been encountered in processing the current volume of accounts. Specific problems that have been identified are:

1. A significant increase in late customer billings.
2. An accompanying increase in billing errors.
3. An increase in delinquent accounts.
4. Inadequate control of credit limits.
5. An inability to access current accounts receivable information.

Therefore, the purpose of the MARS project is to replace the present accounts receivable system with one that can eliminate the problems enumerated above and meet the company's growth requirements. The use of a computer-based system is to be considered.

C. Constraints
The MARS constraints are:

1. Design and development of the system are to be completed within six months.
2. MARS is to have a growth potential to handle 10,000 customer accounts.
3. The use of the current in-house IBM System/3 computer will be considered.
4. MARS is to interface with an existing perpetual inventory system.

D. Specific Objectives
The specific objectives of MARS are:

1. To establish three billing cycles per month--one for each region.
2. To mail customer statements no later than 2 days after the close of each billing cycle.
3. To provide a daily list of A/R transactions.
4. To provide weekly and monthly A/R summary reports.
5. To initiate a finance charge of 1% per month on accounts more than 30 days overdue.
6. To identify accounts that have exceeded their credit limit prior to order processing.

7. To introduce controls to reduce the customer monthly statement error rate by 90%--a reduction in errors from 1% to 1/10 of 1%.
8. To provide a capability for listing customer accounts by region.

E. Method of Evaluation
   After MARS has been operational from 60 to 90 days:

   1. A statistical analysis will be made of customer billings in order to verify elapsed time between the close of the billing cycle and the mailing of customer statements.
   2. Errors in monthly statements will be recorded for a 30-day period, and the percentage of errors will be calculated.
   3. The processing of any overcredit accounts without authorization will be determined by an audit of one month's transactions.
   4. The timeliness and accuracy of the daily and weekly accounts receivable reports will be verified by an audit of one week's transactions.
   5. A random sample of the customer account lists for each region will be audited for validity.
   6. Personal evaluations of the effectiveness of the system will be obtained from its principal users.

II. CONCLUSIONS AND RECOMMENDATIONS

A. Conclusions
   The Design Phase activities have led to the conclusion that no major changes are required in the MARS. On the basis of the vendor/equipment evaluation, the IBM System/370, Model 138 computer was selected. The lowest cost for the computer was through a 5-year lease from Compulease, Inc., a third-party leasing company. A letter of intent was written to Compulease to establish a delivery date (pending our final approval).
   No special problems have been encountered, and the MARS is on schedule and within budget.

B. Recommendations
   It is therefore recommended that the MARS project be approved for the Development Phase.

III. DESIGN SPECIFICATION

A. External Design Requirement

   1. Information-oriented flowchart. Figure E2-1, "MARS information-oriented flowchart," displays the flow of data in the MARS. The accompanying narrative appears as Figure E2-2, "MARS information-oriented flowchart narrative."

2. System output requirements. The seven MARS outputs are:
   a. Customer monthly statement
   b. Accounts receivable transaction register
   c. Accounts receivable summary report
   d. Aged accounts receivable report
   e. Customer account list
   f. Shipping invoice
   g. Overcredit notice
   A print chart and a data element list for an output are
   presented as Figure E2-3.

3. System input requirements. The three MARS inputs are:
   a. Customer account application
   b. Billing notice
   c. Payment/credit memo
   An example of the system inputs is included as
   Figure E2-4.

4. System interface requirements. The MARS must interface
   with (i.e., transfer data to and from) the existing inventory system. Inventory must be on hand for shipment
   prior to billing the customer, and inventory quantities
   should be reduced as merchandise is committed for shipment.

5. System test requirements. The system tests will be
   conducted in two stages. The first stage of testing
   will be run as in an actual operating system but using
   test input and files.
      The second stage will involve the use of live
   data and a copy of a live file. Initial tests will
   be with low volume, with the volume gradually increasing as successful tests are completed.
      All tests will utilize user personnel under the
   supervision of the test team.

6. Equipment specifications. An IBM System/370, Model
   138 computing system was selected. The configuration
   is as follows:
   a. Central Processing Unit (CPU) model FE (144 K bytes)
   b. Integrated file adapter
   c. 3340-A1 disk storage (2 drives 70 MB each)
   d. 3411 Model-1 magnetic tape subsystem
   e. 2540 card read punch
   f. 2821 control unit
   g. 1403 printer model-2 (600 l.p.m.)
   h. 3210 console printer-keyboard

7. Personnel and training requirements. Three additional
   programmers are the only new personnel required.
   Training sessions will be required for personnel of
   the Shipping, Accounts Receivable/Credit, and Data
   Processing departments. The personnel of these departments will be acquainted with the new forms and
   procedures required for the operation of MARS.

B. Internal Design Requirement

1. <u>Computer program design requirements.</u>
   a. System flowchart, shown in Figure E2-5.
   b. Expanded system flowcharts. Figure E2-6 depicts the MARS expanded system flowchart and HIPO charts.
   c. Data base requirements. The MARS master file will be an indexed sequential file. Each logical record will be 133 bytes in length. Figure E2-7 depicts the disk record layout. The blocking factor is to be 19. The file size is initially to be 4 cylinders. This file size is adequate for 2,052 logical records; it will grow to 22 cylinders to accommodate 10,000 accounts.
   d. Computer program control requirements. The MARS computer program will provide controls in the following ways:
      (1) Edit all input data for validity.
      (2) Detect overcredit conditions prior to processing invoices.
      (3) Detect short or out-of-stock conditions prior to processing invoices.
      (4) Provide a tape backup for the MARS master file.
   e. Computer program test requirements. The computer program is to be tested by the test team. The tests will be "string" tests beginning with the first CPC and adding an additional CPC after each successful test. This "string" will continue to grow until the complete program is tested. The test data will contain both valid and invalid data.

2. <u>Computer program component design requirements--Data Edit CPC</u>
   a. Detailed system flowchart, presented as Figure E2-8.
   b. Transaction file requirements. The transaction file requirements for MARS are shown in Figure E2-9. The figure depicts the card layouts for all three system inputs; however, only the sales order and payment/credit memo cards are input to the Data Edit CPC.
   c. Control requirements. The Data Edit CPC must edit all input data for validity and detect overcredit conditions. If an overcredit condition exists, an overcredit notice is to be produced. Records containing invalid data are to be noted on an edit error report.
   d. Interface requirements. The Data Edit CPC output on disk must interface with the Invoice CPC.
   e. Test requirements. The CPC programmer is responsible for testing the CPC. The programmer will generate his own test data, consisting of both valid and invalid data; the test plan must be approved by his supervisor. All test data and test results are to be turned over to the test team when the programmer is satisfied that his CPC is functioning according to specifications.

NOTE: This example Design Specification is not complete. The Data Edit CPC is shown as one example of the CPC Design Requirements. A complete specification would contain a description of all CPCs.

IV. PLANS AND COST SCHEDULES

A. Detailed Milestones--Design Phase
Figure E2-10 depicts the detailed schedule for the nearly completed MARS Design Phase. The Design Phase is on schedule.
The Design Phase costs ran higher than was estimated by approximately $4,000. Figure E2-11 shows the Design Phase costs.

B. Major Milestones--All Phases
Figure E2-12 is a schedule for the entire MARS project. The project is on schedule. The 18-week Development Phase is scheduled for completion on 6/19/xy.
The estimated cumulative cost for the entire project is graphed in Figure E2-13. The total cost is estimated to be $65,800.

C. Detailed Milestones--Development Phase
Figure E2-14 presents the detailed projections for the Development Phase over the 18-week period.
Figure E2-15 is the accompanying cumulative cost estimate for the Development Phase. The total Development Phase cost is estimated to be $52,400.

V. APPENDICES

NOTE: The appendices include all supporting data for the report. For the purpose of this exhibit, such detail is not included. The following is a list of typical appendices.

Project directive

Study of alternatives for computer and computer source selection

Details of Development Phase costs and schedules

FIGURE E2-1. MARS information-oriented flowchart

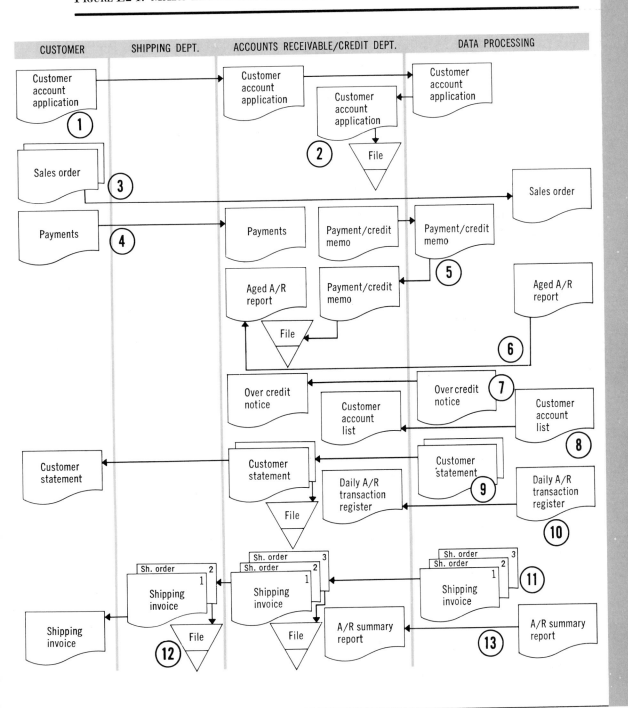

FIGURE E2-2. MARS information-oriented flowchart narrative

INFORMATION-ORIENTED FLOWCHART NARRATIVE

1. Customers submit account applications which are processed by the Accounts Receivable/Credit department.

2. If an application is accepted, it is sent to Data Processing for entry into the system. Data Processing returns the application for filing.

3. Sales orders are sent directly to Data Processing for order processing. The customer retains the carbon copy.

4. Payments are sent to the Accounts Receivable/Credit department.

5. A payment/credit memo is generated and sent to Data Processing. Data Processing returns the memo for filing.

6. An aged A/R report is sent to the Accounts Receivable/ Credit department from Data Processing each month.

7. Data Processing sends overcredit notices to a credit clerk whenever a new order would exceed the customer's credit limit. If the additional credit is approved, the notice is returned to Data Processing with an authorization to process the order. If the additional credit is disapproved, the order and the notice are returned to the customer.

8. Customer account lists are produced on demand and sent to the Accounts Receivable/Credit department for distribution.

9. Customer statements are sent to Accounts Receivable/Credit in duplicate. The original copy is sent to the customer; the duplicate is filed. One-third of the statements are produced each ten days of the month, i.e., on the 1st, 10th, and 20th.

10. A daily A/R transaction register is sent to the Accounts Receivable/Credit department.

11. Three copies of the shipping invoice/shipping order are sent to the Accounts Receivable/Credit department. The original copy is entitled shipping invoice; the two carbon copies are entitled shipping order. The third copy is filed by A/R.

12. The shipping invoice and the first copy of the shipping order are sent to the Shipping department. The shipping order is used to "pick" inventory items for shipment and is then filed. The shipping invoice is packed with the merchandise and is sent to the customer.

13. The accounts receivable summary report is prepared weekly and sent to the Accounts Receivable/Credit department for distribution.

FIGURE E2-3. MARS output requirements: overcredit notice

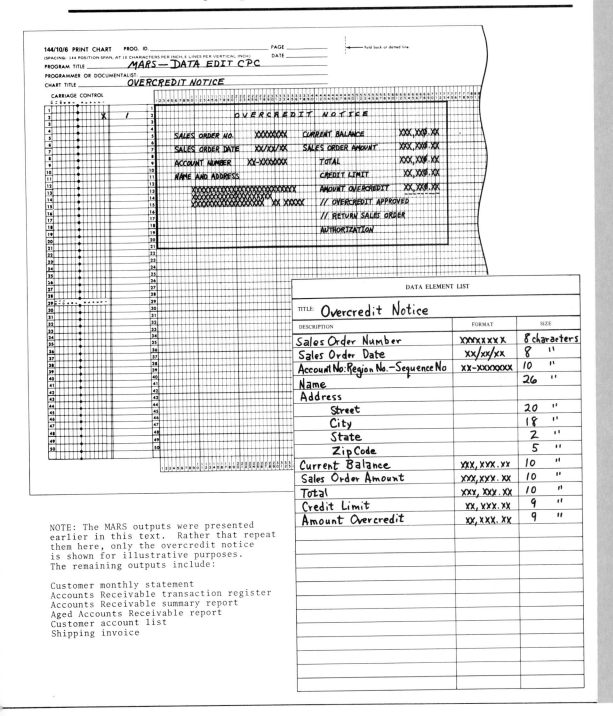

NOTE: The MARS outputs were presented earlier in this text. Rather that repeat them here, only the overcredit notice is shown for illustrative purposes. The remaining outputs include:

Customer monthly statement
Accounts Receivable transaction register
Accounts Receivable summary report
Aged Accounts Receivable report
Customer account list
Shipping invoice

FIGURE E2-4. MARS input requirement: customer account application

CUSTOMER ACCOUNT APPLICATION
ABCDEF Corporation
Walnut, California

FOR OFFICE USE
ACCOUNT NUMBER

FIRM NAME

EFFECTIVE DATE

INDICATE W for WHOLESALE
or R for RETAIL

DATE   TELEPHONE

CREDIT CODE   DISCOUNT CODE

STREET ADDRESS

CITY   STATE   ZIP CODE

BANK REFERENCES

NAME	BRANCH	TELEPHONE	
ADDRESS	CITY	STATE	ZIP CODE
NAME	BRANCH	TELEPHONE	
ADDRESS	CITY	STATE	ZIP CODE

OTHER REFERENCES

NAME		TELEPHONE	
ADDRESS	CITY	STATE	ZIP CODE
NAME		TELEPHONE	
ADDRESS	CITY	STATE	ZIP CODE

FOR OFFICE USE
CREDIT APPROVED ☐   DISAPPROVED ☐
IF DISAPPROVED, REASON:

AUTHORIZATION SIGNATURE

NOTE: The customer account application is shown to
illustrate input. The other MARS inputs, the billing
notice and the payment/credit memo, would remain
essentially unchanged from the current system. Since
these were presented in this text previously, they
are not repeated. They appear in Figure 12-9, "Inputs
to manual A/R system."

FIGURE E2-5. MARS high-level system flowchart and narrative

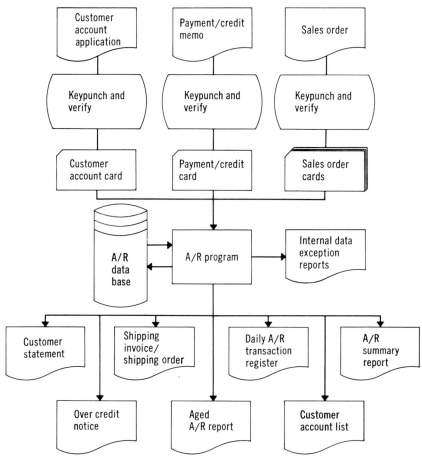

SYSTEM FLOWCHART
MODIFIED A/R SYSTEM (MARS)

SYSTEM FLOWCHART NARRATIVE

1. Customer account applications, payment/credit memos, and sales orders are the three major system inputs.

2. Each source document is keypunched and verified.

3. The A/R program inputs the transaction data cards and reads/updates the master file on magnetic disk. Program edit routines produce exception reports whenever invalid input data is detected.

4. The seven major outputs of the system are the customer statements, invoice/shipping order, A/R transaction register, A/R summary report, overcredit notice, aged A/R report, and a customer account list.

FIGURE E2-6. **MARS expanded system flowchart and HIPO charts**

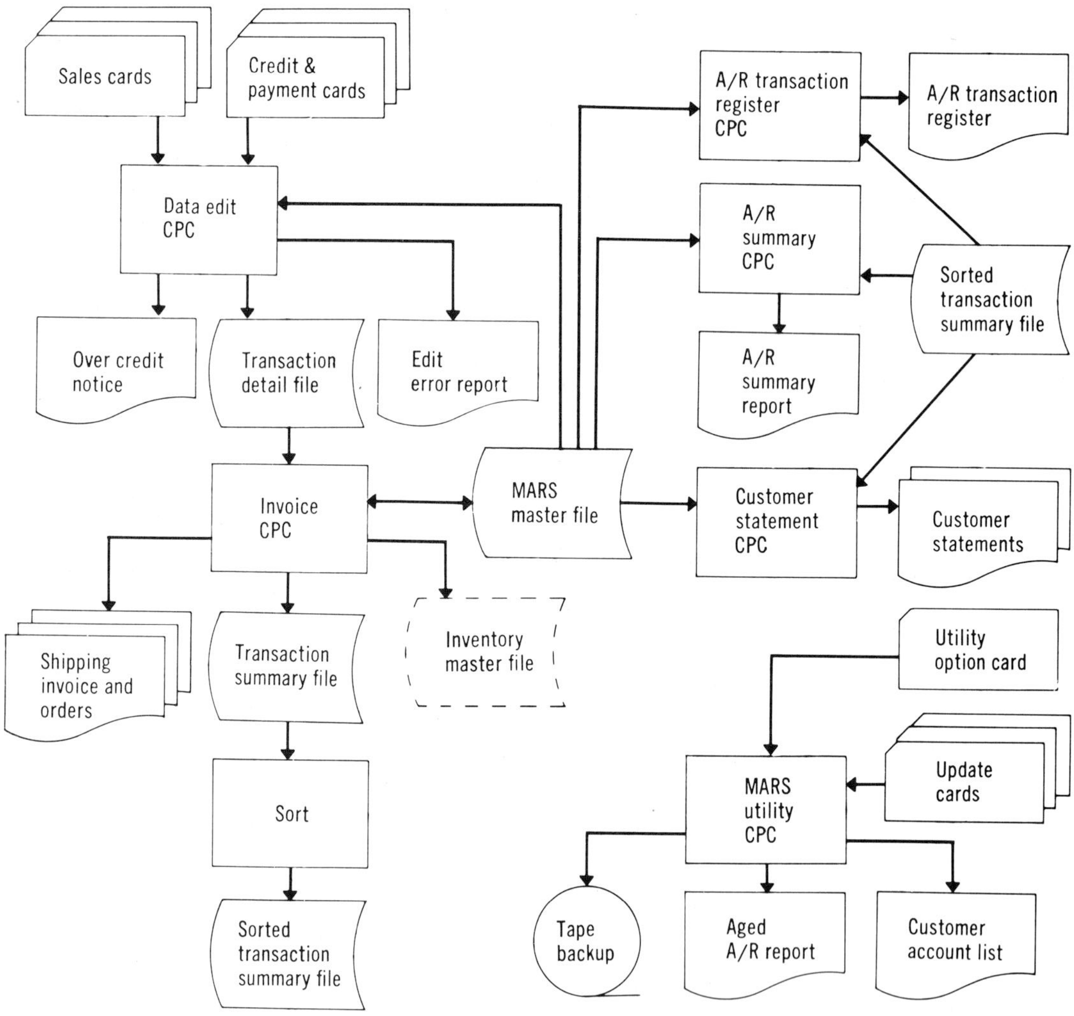

NOTE: The narrative is not included here,
but may be found on pages 248-249.

FIGURE E2-6 continued

HIERARCHY CHART FOR MARS

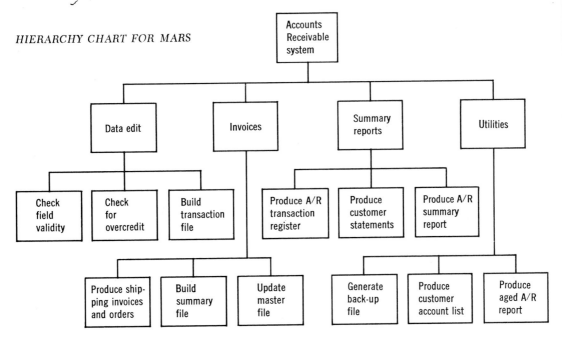

IPO DETAIL CHART: DATA EDIT MODULE

INPUTS	PROCESSING	OUTPUTS
1. Sales cards	1. Check validity of account number	1. Transactions detail file (disk)
2. Credit and payment cards	2. Check validity of all numeric fields	2. Edit error report
3. Master file	3. Check for overcredit status	3. Overcredit notices

FIGURE E2-7. Disk record layout worksheet

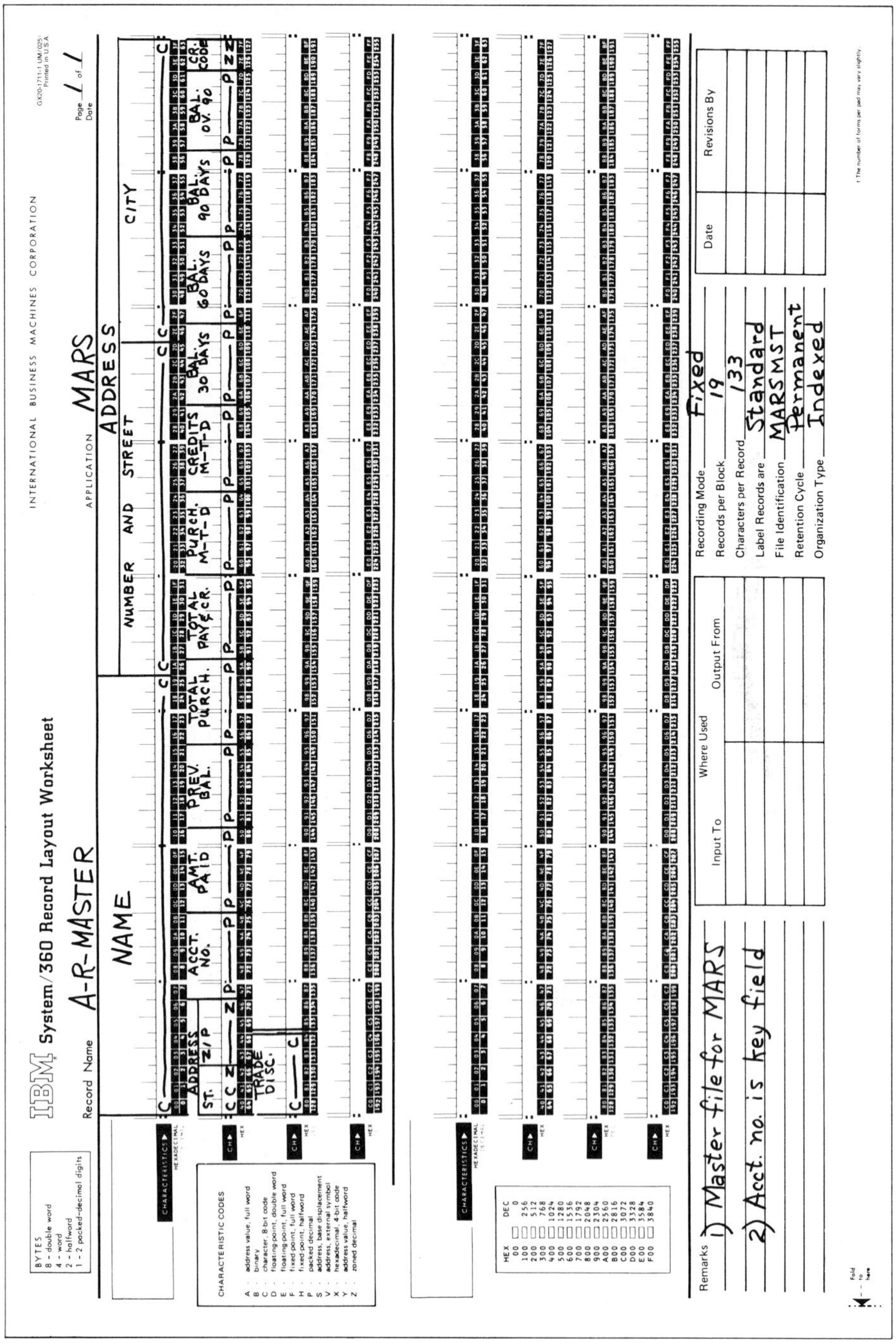

FIGURE E2-8. MARS system flowchart—Data Edit CPC

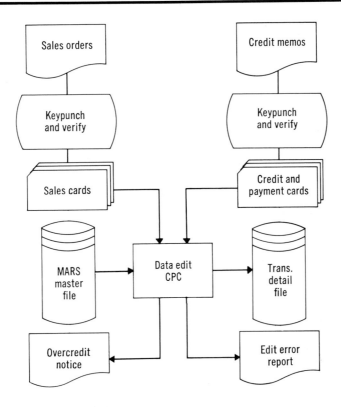

Data Edit CPC--MARS

1. Sales order and credit memo data are keypunched. Batches will be verified at random.

2. Sales and credit cards are batched for input to the Data Edit CPC.

3. Input cards are sorted into ascending order by account number. All fields are checked for validity. The amounts of the order less credits are added to customer balance. If the new balance exceeds the credit limit (stored in the master file), special approval is required or the order is rejected. A rejected order results in the creation of an overcredit notice. All transaction details not causing an overcredit condition are written into the transaction detail file.

FIGURE E2-9. Multiple-card layout formats

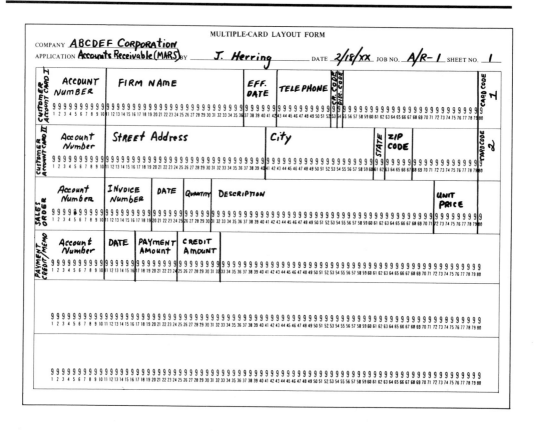

Figure E2-10. Detailed milestones—Design Phase

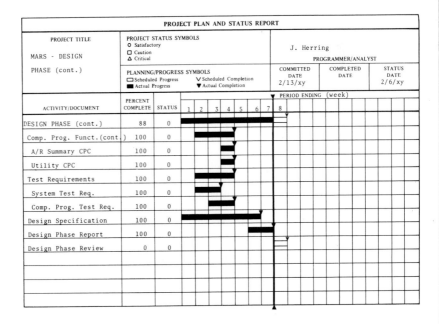

PROJECT PLAN AND STATUS REPORT

PROJECT TITLE
MARS - DESIGN PHASE

PROJECT STATUS SYMBOLS
O Satisfactory
☐ Caution
△ Critical

PLANNING/PROGRESS SYMBOLS
☐ Scheduled Progress   V Scheduled Completion
■ Actual Progress   ▼ Actual Completion

J. Herring
PROGRAMMER/ANALYST

COMMITTED DATE 2/13/xy
COMPLETED DATE
STATUS DATE 2/6/xy

PERIOD ENDING (week)

ACTIVITY/DOCUMENT	PERCENT COMPLETE	STATUS
DESIGN PHASE	88	0
Allocation of Functions	100	0
Manual Functions	100	0
Task Definition	100	0
Ref. Man. Ident.	100	0
Equipment Functions	100	0
Function Definition	100	0
Equip. Specifications	100	0
Computer Prog. Functions	100	0
Data Base Design	100	0
Data Edit CPC	100	0
Invoice Edit CPC	100	0
A/R Tran. Reg. CPC	100	0
Cust. Stmt. CPC	100	0

PROJECT PLAN AND STATUS REPORT

PROJECT TITLE
MARS - DESIGN
PHASE (cont.)

PROJECT STATUS SYMBOLS
O Satisfactory
☐ Caution
△ Critical

PLANNING/PROGRESS SYMBOLS
☐ Scheduled Progress   V Scheduled Completion
■ Actual Progress   ▼ Actual Completion

J. Herring
PROGRAMMER/ANALYST

COMMITTED DATE 2/13/xy
COMPLETED DATE
STATUS DATE 2/6/xy

PERIOD ENDING (week)

ACTIVITY/DOCUMENT	PERCENT COMPLETE	STATUS
DESIGN PHASE (cont.)	88	0
Comp. Prog. Funct.(cont.)	100	0
A/R Summary CPC	100	0
Utility CPC	100	0
Test Requirements	100	0
System Test Req.	100	0
Comp. Prog. Test Req.	100	0
Design Specification	100	0
Design Phase Report	100	0
Design Phase Review	0	0

FIGURE E2-11. Design Phase costs

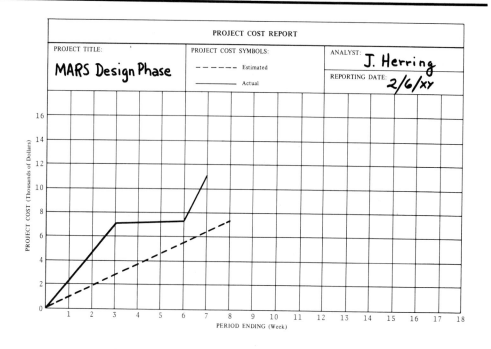

FIGURE E2-12. Major milestones—total project

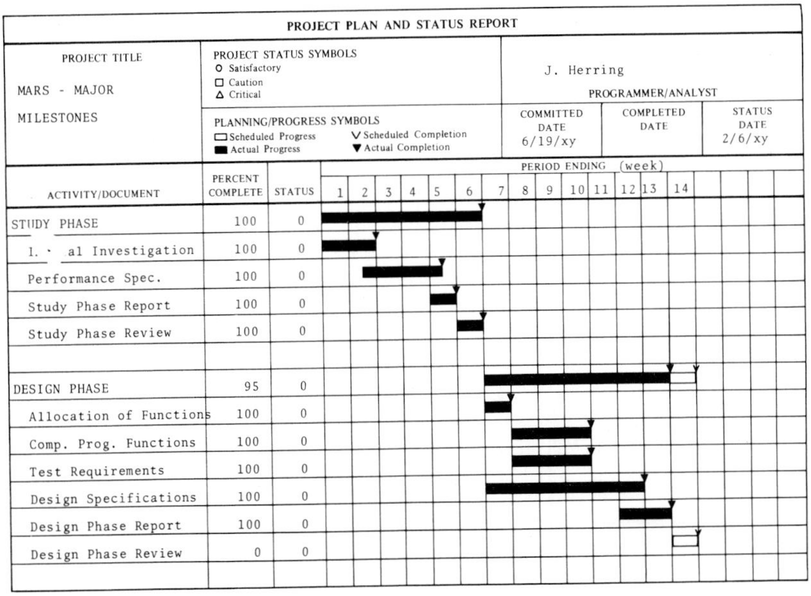

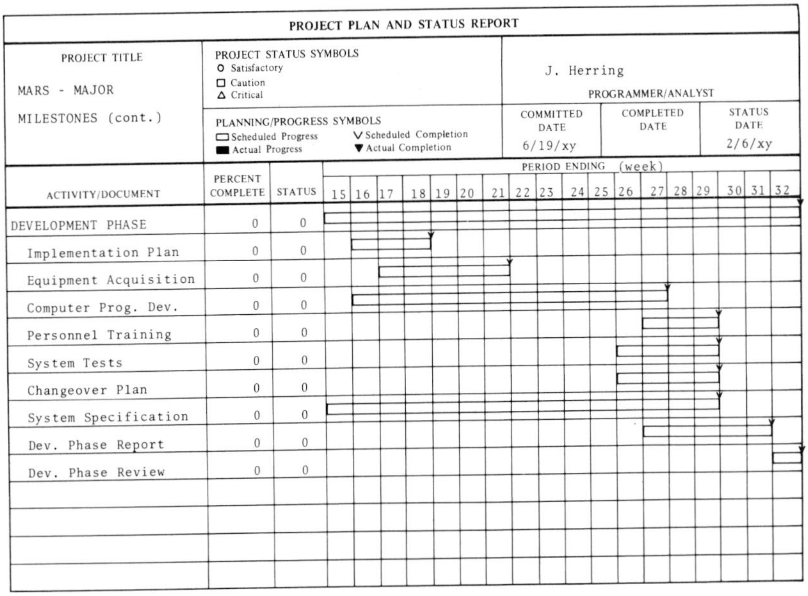

PROJECT PLAN AND STATUS REPORT

PROJECT TITLE	PROJECT STATUS SYMBOLS			
MARS - MAJOR MILESTONES	O Satisfactory □ Caution △ Critical	J. Herring PROGRAMMER/ANALYST		

PLANNING/PROGRESS SYMBOLS
□ Scheduled Progress　∨ Scheduled Completion
■ Actual Progress　▼ Actual Completion

	COMMITTED DATE 6/19/xy	COMPLETED DATE	STATUS DATE 2/6/xy

PERIOD ENDING (week)

ACTIVITY/DOCUMENT	PERCENT COMPLETE	STATUS	1 2 3 4 5 6 7	8 9 10 11 12 13 14
STUDY PHASE	100	O		
I. ·al Investigation	100	O		
Performance Spec.	100	O		
Study Phase Report	100	O		
Study Phase Review	100	O		
DESIGN PHASE	95	O		
Allocation of Functions	100	O		
Comp. Prog. Functions	100	O		
Test Requirements	100	O		
Design Specifications	100	O		
Design Phase Report	100	O		
Design Phase Review	0	O		

PROJECT PLAN AND STATUS REPORT

PROJECT TITLE	PROJECT STATUS SYMBOLS			
MARS - MAJOR MILESTONES (cont.)	O Satisfactory □ Caution △ Critical	J. Herring PROGRAMMER/ANALYST		

PLANNING/PROGRESS SYMBOLS
□ Scheduled Progress　∨ Scheduled Completion
■ Actual Progress　▼ Actual Completion

	COMMITTED DATE 6/19/xy	COMPLETED DATE	STATUS DATE 2/6/xy

PERIOD ENDING (week)

ACTIVITY/DOCUMENT	PERCENT COMPLETE	STATUS	15 16 17 18 19 20 21 22 23 24 25 26 27 28 29 30 31 32
DEVELOPMENT PHASE	0	O	
Implementation Plan	0	O	
Equipment Acquisition	0	O	
Computer Prog. Dev.	0	O	
Personnel Training	0	O	
System Tests	0	O	
Changeover Plan	0	O	
System Specification	0	O	
Dev. Phase Report	0	O	
Dev. Phase Review	0	O	

FIGURE E2-13. Project cost report—total project

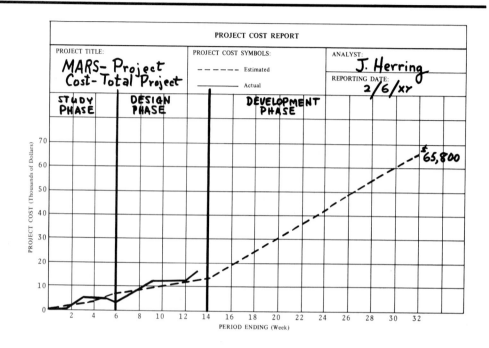

FIGURE E2-14. Detailed milestones—Development Phase

PROJECT PLAN AND STATUS REPORT

PROJECT TITLE: **MARS — DEVELOPMENT PHASE**

PROJECT STATUS SYMBOLS:
O Satisfactory
□ Caution
△ Critical

J. Herring — PROGRAMMER/ANALYST

PLANNING/PROGRESS SYMBOLS:
□ Scheduled Progress ■ Actual Progress
V Scheduled Completion ▼ Actual Completion

	COMMITTED DATE	COMPLETED DATE	STATUS DATE
	6/19/xy		2/6/xy

PERIOD ENDING (week)

ACTIVITY/DOCUMENT	PERCENT COMPLETE	STATUS	1	2	3	4	5	6	7	8	9	10	11	12	13	14	15	16	17	18
DEVELOPMENT PHASE	0	0																		
Implementation Plan	0	0																		
Test Plan	0	0																		
Training Plan	0	0																		
Conversion Plan	0	0																		
Equip.Acquisition&Instal.	0	0																		
Computer Prog. Dev.	0	0																		
Comp. Prog. Design	0	0																		
Coding & Debugging	0	0																		
Comp. Prog. Tests	0	0																		
Reference Manual Prep.	0	0																		
Programmer's Man.	0	0																		
Operator's Man.	0	0																		
User's Manual	0	0																		

PROJECT PLAN AND STATUS REPORT

PROJECT TITLE: **MARS — DEVELOPMENT PHASE (cont.)**

PROJECT STATUS SYMBOLS:
O Satisfactory
□ Caution
△ Critical

J. Herring — PROGRAMMER/ANALYST

PLANNING/PROGRESS SYMBOLS:
□ Scheduled Progress ■ Actual Progress
V Scheduled Completion ▼ Actual Completion

	COMMITTED DATE	COMPLETED DATE	STATUS DATE
	6/19/xy		2/6/xy

PERIOD ENDING (week)

ACTIVITY/DOCUMENT	PERCENT COMPLETE	STATUS	1	2	3	4	5	6	7	8	9	10	11	12	13	14	15	16	17	18
Personnel Training	0	0																		
System Tests	0	0																		
Changeover Plan	0	0																		
System Specification	0	0																		
Dev. Phase Report	0	0																		
Dev. Phase Review	0	0																		

FIGURE E2-15. Cost estimate—Development Phase

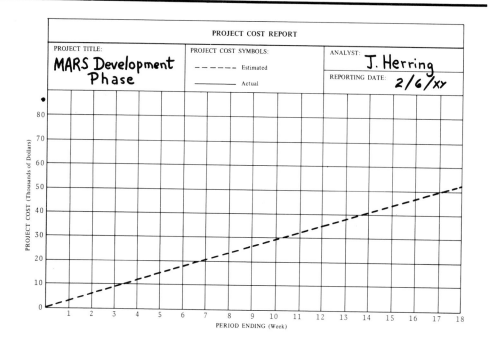

UNIT FIVE

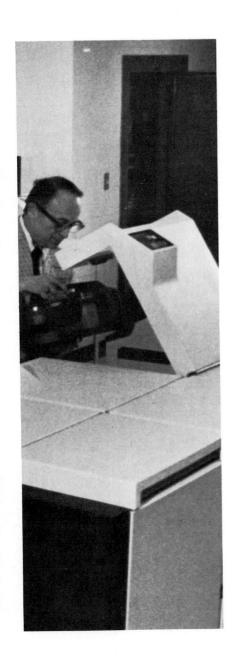

THE
DEVELOPMENT
PHASE

21   Development Phase Overview

In the Development Phase, the actual system is constructed from the specification prepared in the Design Phase. The goal of this chapter is to identify the major activities of this phase and to show the relationships between them. You will obtain an overview and perspective of the Development Phase that will provide a reference and a guide as you study the specific topics in this unit.

DEVELOPMENT PHASE ORGANIZATION

In the Development Phase, the computer-based business system is developed to conform to the Design Specification prepared in the preceding phase. The Design Specification, a "build to" specification, evolves into the System Specification, an "as built" specification. The largest project expenditures occur during this third phase. Additional personnel, such as analyst/programmers, programmers, and technical writers, are assigned to the project. Additional dollars are committed for the use of computer facilities. The increased expenditure rate usually continues for a relatively long period. It is not uncommon for the Development Phase to be two or three times as long as the combined Study and Design Phases. Hence, the project management techniques introduced during the Study and Design Phases should be expanded to correspond to the enlarged project scope. Project plan, status report, and project cost report schedules should be prepared for the principal Development Phase activities. The level of detail should correspond to the complexity and scope of the work to be done.

The principal activities performed during the Development Phase can be divided into two major related sequences. These are (1) external (to the computer program) system development; and (2) internal (to the computer program) system development. The primary external system development activities are implementation planning; preparation of manuals and personnel training; and equipment acquisition and installation. The principal internal system development

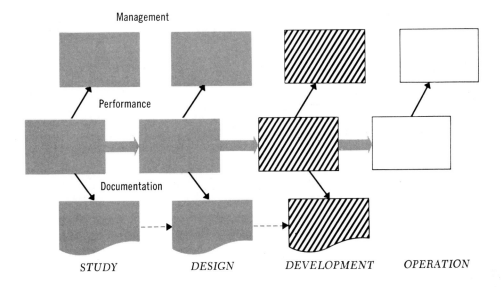

Management

Performance

Documentation

STUDY   DESIGN   DEVELOPMENT   OPERATION

activities are computer program development and performance testing. An overview of the major Development Phase activities is provided in the section which follows.

DEVELOPMENT PHASE ACTIVITIES

FIGURE 21-1, *Development Phase activities for the computer-based business system,* displays the relationship between the principal Development Phase activities. Each of the activities shown in Figure 21-1 is discussed briefly:

1. *Implementation planning:* After the initiation of the Development Phase is approved, implementation planning begins. Essential parts of the implementation plan are:

    a. A plan for testing the computer program, both as the integrated assembly of its components and as an element of the overall business system.

    b. A plan for training the personnel who are to be associated with the new system. This includes persons who will provide inputs to, receive outputs from, and operate or maintain the new system.

    c. A conversion plan. This plan provides for the conversion of procedures, programs, and files preparatory to actual changeover from the old system to the new one. The conversion plan also includes a preliminary plan for the changeover.

2. *Computer program design:* Computer program design is begun parallel with the implementation planning effort. As necessary, system flowcharts are ex-

FIGURE 21-1. Development Phase activities
for the computer-based business system

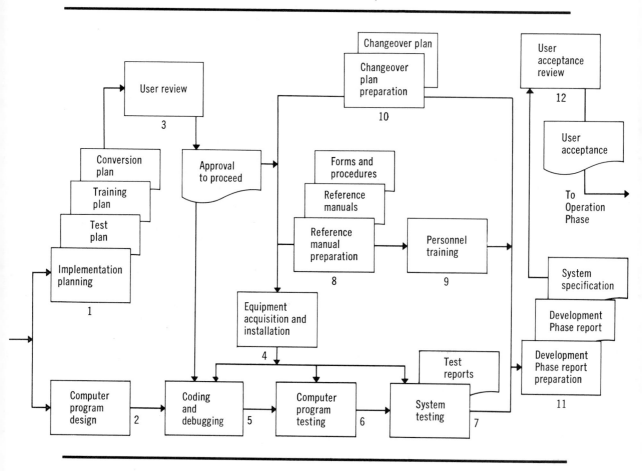

panded to show additional detail for the computer program components. The complete data base is developed. Input and output files are identified and computer program logic flowcharts prepared for each computer program component.

3. *User review:* Reviews are held with the user throughout the Development Phase. The first review block shown in Figure 21-1 is indicative of an interim Development Phase review. This type of review normally is not held to reevaluate the decision that initiated the Development Phase, but rather to keep the user informed of general project progress and to secure his cooperation in areas in which he can be of assistance to the project. As illustrated, a review of test plans, training plans, and conversion plans is essential because user personnel are directly involved in the implementation activities. The user's concurrence with the implementation plan reaffirms his support, which is documented by a written

"approval to proceed." As shown in Figure 21-1, the "approval to proceed" also applies to the ongoing computer program design and development activities.

4. *Equipment acquisition and installation:* In the Design Phase, special hardware required to support the system may have been identified. If not ordered during the Design Phase, this equipment is ordered now, and delivered, installed, and tested. Often all hardware components need not arrive at the same time because needs vary as the computer program develops from coding through testing. Therefore, an appropriate schedule is established and maintained for the acquisition of hardware items.

5. *Coding and debugging:* Each computer program component is coded and debugged. This means that each component is compiled without error and that it successfully executes its program logic, using data supplied by the programmer.

6. *Computer program testing:* The computer program components are tested in a planned sequence. The testing continues until the components can be assembled as a computer program that can be tested as a unit. The analyst supplies data for testing the program.

7. *System testing:* System tests are performed to verify that the computer-based business system has met its design objectives. The system includes the computer program as one of its major elements. The user is responsible for supplying the input data and for participating in the evaluation of the system test results. System test reports are prepared to verify system performance.

8. *Reference manual preparation:* Appropriate reference manuals for the various individuals who will work with the new computer-based information system must be prepared. These reference documents are based upon the System Specification. The three principal manuals are for programmers, operators, and users.

Forms and procedures are important elements of the reference manuals. Procedures are written, and appropriate forms are designed. The forms are prepared in-house or ordered from a manufacturer of forms.

9. *Personnel training:* Operating, programming, and user personnel are trained, using the reference manuals, forms, and procedures as training aids. The training schedule is closely coordinated with the schedule for completing the Development Phase. All essential training must be completed prior to the user acceptance review, which occurs at the end of the Development Phase.

10. *Changeover plan preparation:* The preliminary changeover plan, which was an element of the conversion plan, is updated. Changeover from the old to the new system takes place at the beginning of the Operation Phase. The changeover plan specifies the method of changeover, giving a detailed schedule of activities to be performed and identifying the responsibilities of all personnel involved in these activities.

11. *Development Phase report preparation:* At the conclusion of the Development Phase, the Development Phase report is prepared, documenting the development of the system in accordance with requirements specified in the Design Phase report. It contains a summary of all of the pertinent activities undertaken during the Development Phase. The Development Phase report includes a System Specification—the third major baseline document—which evolves from the

Performance and the Design Specifications. The System Specification contains the complete technical specification for the computer program and its components. It contains, for instance, detailed flowcharts, data base specifications, and computer program component listings. The System Specification is the baseline reference for the preparation of manuals and training aids.

12. *User acceptance review:* At the conclusion of the Development Phase, the computer-based business system is reviewed by the management of the user organization. Representatives of the information service organization and other affected organizations participate in this review. The principal documents upon which the acceptance review is based are the Design Phase report, the Development Phase report, test reports, and the changeover plan.

After the conclusion of a successful acceptance review, the user organization issues a written memorandum of acceptance, and the system enters the Operation Phase of its life cycle.

22

Preparing for Implementation

Preparation for implementing a developed system is a continuing activity throughout the Development Phase. The goal of this chapter is to identify and to explain the major implementation activities. You will learn the purpose and importance of plans for testing, for training, for installing equipment, and for converting to the new system.

IMPLEMENTATION PLANNING

The implementation process

Implementation is the process of bringing a developed system into operational use and turning it over to the user. Implementation activities extend from planning through conversion from the old system to the new. At the beginning of the Development Phase, a preliminary implementation plan is created to schedule and manage the many different activities that must be integrated into the plan. The implementation plan is updated throughout the Development Phase, culminating in a changeover plan for the Operation Phase.

The implementation plan

A common implementation management technique is to assign the responsibility for each element of the implementation plan to a team. The head of each team is selected from the organization best qualified to perform the specific implementation task. For example, a user-manager would head the conversion team, and the data processing manager would head the equipment installation team.

The major elements of the implementation plan are test plans, training plans, an equipment installation plan, and a conversion plan. We will discuss each of these elements in later sections of this chapter. In a final section, we will describe a critical path network technique that can be used to manage the diverse implementation activities.

TEST PLANS

The implementation of a computer-based system requires that test data be prepared and that the system and its elements be tested in a planned, structured manner. The computer program is a major subsystem of the computer-based system, and particular attention should be given to structuring the testing of this system element as it is developed.

There are two methods of planning for the development and testing of computer programs. These are the traditional "bottom-up" method and the contemporary "top-down" method.

Bottom-up computer program development

The traditional method for scheduling and managing the tests of computer program components is to develop a hierarchical structure within which the lowest level components are tested individually and then are combined into higher-level modules, which are tested next. This process, which sometimes is called "string testing," is illustrated in Figure 22-1, *Traditional bottom-up computer program development*.

A typical development and testing sequence (from 1 to 11) is shown in this figure. Modules that have been coded from the bottom-up and those that are not yet coded are shown. Eventually, all the modules will be strung together at successively higher levels to form the complete computer program.

There have been many difficulties with this traditional method of developing computer programs. Often "driver" programs have to be written to test the higher-level modules as they are created. For example, in Figure 22-1, modules 3, 4, and 8, which are the highest-level coded modules at the stage of development depicted, must be tested with driver programs that supply calling and control instructions not yet available from other modules in the computer program development hierarchy.

In addition, interfaces between modules must be developed, and the modules must be integrated successfully to create a complete and functional computer program. Failure of all the components to mesh at the end of the project has caused serious errors. Changes made then, high in the level of the system hierarchy, could cause much of the lower-level development and testing to be redone, causing overruns in cost and failures to meet schedules. Because of these problems, a contemporary, top-down method for developing computer programs is finding increasing use and acceptance.

Top-down computer program development

The top-down computer program development and testing approach is a structured technology compatible with the life-cycle methodology, which starts with a general description of the system and expands it into successively greater levels of detail.

The top-down approach to computer program development and testing is shown in Figure 22-2, *Contemporary top-down computer program development*.

FIGURE 22-1. Traditional bottom-up computer program development

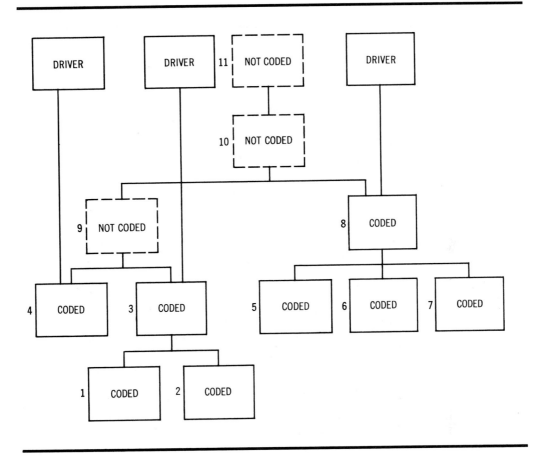

This structured technique for computer program development is a logical extension of the top-down, hierarchical approach to system design characteristic of HIPO charts (Chapter 16).

As the typical development sequence (from 1 to 11) in Figure 22-2 shows, modules are developed downward from nucleus at the top of the computer program hierarchy. Driver programs are not necessary. Instead, modules that display a message acknowledging receipt of higher-level program control are used. These modules are called stubs; their use is illustrated in Figure 22-2.

A major advantage of top-down structured testing and development is that the computer program continues to operate as stubs are removed and modules added. Managers thus have continuous control over the computer program development process, and the problems that can arise from an overall integration effort are minimized. An important aspect of this advantage is illustrated in FIGURE 22-3, *Comparative machine usage in top-down and bottom-up computer*

FIGURE 22-2. Contemporary top-down computer program development

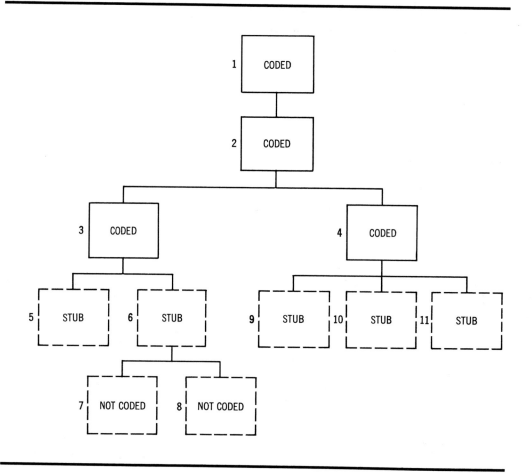

development. An end-of-project integration effort is eliminated, and total machine usage for testing is reduced.[1] Early testing can verify the correctness of the higher-level computer program routines that are responsible for the major logic and for overall program control, and it can increase the reliability of the final product.

Formal test planning

Plans must be made for the formal evaluation of the computer program as it is developed as well as for internal technical reviews, such as structured walk-throughs. The results of these tests should become part of the cumulative Development Phase documentation.

---

1. Joan C. Hughes and Jay I. Michtom, *A Structured Approach to Programming* (Englewood Cliffs: Prentice-Hall, Inc., 1977).

**FIGURE 22-3. Comparative machine usage for top-down
and bottom-up computer program development**

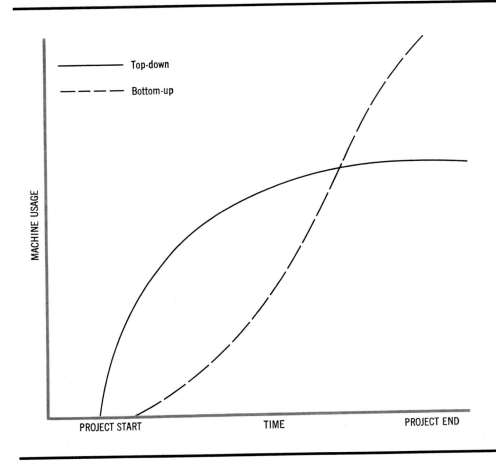

A standardized test plan document is useful, such as the general format shown in FIGURE 22-4, *Annotated test plan format.* The comments relate to the questions of "why, where, when, who, what, and how" that a test plan should answer. The format illustrated is suitable for both computer subsystem and overall system tests. An entry identifying the type of test is inserted at the top of the test plan document.

At the conclusion of each test, a written report is prepared to record the results; a standardized test report document relating to the test document can be used. FIGURE 22-5, *Annotated test report format,* outlines a general test report format and describes the entries to be made on the document.

Final system tests are performed after the subsystem tests have been completed. Their purpose is to exercise the entire system, including the computer program subsystem, under "live" environmental conditions. The main objective

FIGURE 22-4. Annotated test plan format

(SUBSYSTEM/SYSTEM) TEST PLAN

Scope

1. NAME:	A name or number which identifies the test.
2. PURPOSE:	**Why:** the specific objectives of the test, including identification of the computer program components involved in the test.
3. LOCATION:	**Where** the test is to be performed.
4. SCHEDULE:	**When** the test is to be performed.
5. RESPONSIBILITIES:	**Who:** the individuals involved in the test and their specific duties.
6. GENERAL PROCEDURES:	**What:** a general overview of the test inputs, events, and anticipated results.

Data Collection and Evaluation

1. DATA TO BE USED:	**What:** a detailed description of live or simulated input data to be used in the test.
2. DATA TO BE COLLECTED:	**What:** a detailed description of the data to be obtained as test results.
3. METHOD OF DATA RECORDING:	**How** the data is to be recorded, e.g., listings, punched cards, etc.
4. METHOD OF DATA EVALUATION:	**How** the test results are to be analyzed.

Special Procedures

What procedures are unique to this test, e.g., equipment
operating procedures, operator intervention procedures,
abnormal condition procedures.

---

of system tests is to subject the computer-based business system to all foreseeable operating conditions. The user should specify and conduct these tests; system test responsibility should not be delegated to programmers or even to systems analysts.

Systems tests become progressively more complex. Initial tests may involve selected samples of input data and a small test file; later, pilot tests (called "history processing") can be performed using complete files and a large number of past data transactions.

Figure 22-5. Annotated test report format

(SUBSYSTEM/SYSTEM) TEST REPORT

Scope

1. NAME: The name shown on the corresponding test plan.

2. PURPOSE: The purpose stated on the corresponding test plan.

3. REFERENCES: Indentification of the corresponding test plan and other pertinent documents, such as previous test results.

Description of Results

1. TEST METHODS: How the test was performed.

2. OBJECTIVES MET: Identification of specific test accomplishments.

3. PROBLEM AREAS: Discussion of problems encountered.

4. RECOMMENDATIONS: Specific actions to be taken, e.g., accept test results, perform additional tests, revise coding.

The persons who will be involved in the "live" operation of the system should prepare the system test data for computer processing. If the user is involved appropriately in the system level tests, progress can be made toward two supplementary goals: user training and user acceptance. User training is vital to the successful conversion to the new system. User participation in earlier top-down tests of the computer program subsystem and in structured walk-throughs is a powerful training technique. The final system tests, if sufficiently thorough, can serve as acceptance tests, which can assure the user that the system is ready for operation.

TRAINING

Training: An overview

Training plans are an important element of the implementation plan. Their purpose is to ensure that all the personnel who are to be associated with the computer-based business system possess the necessary knowledge and skills. Operating, programming, and user personnel are trained using reference manuals as training aids. The training schedule is coordinated with the schedule for completing the Development Phase, for all essential training must be completed prior to the user acceptance review at the end of this phase. However, training should not be completed too far in advance of need, or the personnel are liable to lose interest or forget their training.

Training programs begin with the selection of appropriate participants and the preparation of different types of training programs for programmers, operators, and user personnel. User personnel are the persons who will prepare inputs, follow procedures, and use outputs. Additional training programs must be conducted for management level personnel, not only to familiarize managers with the new system, but also to obtain their active support and cooperation during implementation.

Before training programs can be initiated, materials must be prepared. The basic training resources are reference manuals appropriate to the needs and interests of each type of trainee—programmer, operator, or user. These reference manuals are based largely upon the System Specification. This baseline document usually is not in a final format before the end of the Development Phase, at which time it is included in the Development Phase report. However, because the Design Specification is added to continuously throughout the Development Phase, an interim System Specification exists. Drafts of the reference manuals can be prepared for the initial training programs from the interim specification. The reference manuals are prepared in their final formats at the end of the Development Phase, and they are available for training purposes throughout the life of the system.

In the next section we will describe the training programs established to meet the needs of programmers, operators, and users, outlining the general content of the training manuals.

Programmer training

Programmers are assigned to the computer-based business system project at the beginning of the Development Phase. These programmers, who will develop the computer program components, are indoctrinated by the analysts and programmer/analysts who prepared the Design Specification. They help to create the programmer's reference manual, used to train other programmers assigned to the system throughout its operational life.

The programmer's reference manual is the most comprehensive of the reference manuals. It informs an experienced programmer, unfamiliar with the system, about all of the aspects of the computer program. The manual should enable him to (1) understand existing program components; (2) modify existing program components; and (3) write new program components. Figure 22-6, *Programmer's reference manual,* is a guide to typical contents of such a manual. The external specification relates to elements of the system external to the computer program subsystem; the internal specification relates to elements internal to the computer program subsystem.

Operator training

If new equipment is to be installed, operator training is completed in conjunction with its installation and checkout. If new equipment is not required for the com-

Figure 22-6. Programmer's reference manual

GUIDE TO PROGRAMMER'S REFERENCE MANUAL

1. TITLE: Name of computer-based system

2. PURPOSE: General description of system and its major objectives

3. EXTERNAL SPECIFICATION:
   a. Information-oriented flowchart
   b. Output, input, and interface descriptions
   c. System level test input-output samples
   d. Equipment specification

4. INTERNAL SPECIFICATION:
   a. Computer program:
      1) System flowcharts
      2) Expanded system flowcharts and HIPO charts
      3) Data base specification
      4) Control specifications
      5) Test input-output samples

   b. Computer program components:
      1) Detailed system flowcharts
      2) Logic flowcharts
      3) Transaction file specifications
      4) Control specifications
      5) Interface specifications
      6) Listings
      7) Test input-output samples

---

puter-based system, operators still must become familiar with the operational requirements of the new system. Different kinds of operational personnel may be involved in the operation of the system, such as computer operators, console operators, and keypunch operators. Therefore, more than one type of manual may be required. Each manual should acquaint the operators with the system and its purpose and provide a ready reference to specific duties and step-by-step operating instructions. These instructions should cover both normal and abnormal situations. They should be written in a style that is easily understood by the intended users of the manual; detailed discussions of complex and lengthy system descriptions should not be included. A guide to the typical contents is shown in Figure 22-7, *Operator's reference manual*.

Training programs for operators are scheduled to coincide with the needs of the computer-based business system as it is developed, tested, and approaches operational status. Users, analysts, and programmers may participate in the training of operators.

User training

For the system to begin operation, a sufficient number of users must be trained before the end of the Development Phase. Thereafter, additional personnel are

FIGURE 22-7. Operator's reference manual

GUIDE TO OPERATOR'S REFERENCE MANUAL

1. TITLE: Name of computer-based system

2. PURPOSE: General description of system

3. OPERATING PROCEDURES,   as appropriate to specific operational duties:

    a.   Operator inputs: A complete description of all inputs, including:

        1) Purpose and use   4) Limitations
        2) Title of input   5) Format and content
        3) Input and media

    b.   Operator outputs: A complete description of all outputs, including:

        1) Purpose and use   3) Output media
        2) Title of output   4) Format and content

    c.   File summary: A complete description of all files, including:

        1) File identification
        2) Medium
        3) Type: Master, transaction, etc.

    d.   Error and exception handling: Procedures for handling
        hardware and software error conditions

---

trained, and training continues throughout the operational life of the system. As with operator's reference manuals, usually more than one type of user's reference manual is required. Each one should be self-contained and should explain the system in terms of the user's specific needs. The text should be factual, concise, specific, and clearly worded and illustrated. Sentences should be simple and direct; discussions of theory and detailed technical matters should be avoided. The manual should provide users with a general overview of the system. However, primary emphasis is on the specific steps to be followed, the results to be expected, and the corrective actions to be taken when such results are not obtained. FIGURE 22-8, *User's reference manual,* lists the typical contents.

Training sessions for user personnel usually involve larger numbers of people than do operator or programmer training programs. These sessions should be planned to meet the needs of each type of user. Normally several sessions should be scheduled for all trainees, so that they fully understand the new system and have an opportunity to familiarize themselves with the handling of documents and equipment.

The training team should be certain that sufficient user personnel are thoroughly trained and prepared to support the new system at the time of its implementation. Individuals who are not willing to cooperate or who cannot follow procedures can cause great difficulties at the time of changeover from the old system to the new.

FIGURE 22-8. User's reference manual

GUIDE TO USER'S REFERENCE MANUAL

1. TITLE: Name of computer-based system

2. PURPOSE: General description of system and its major objectives, including an information-oriented flowchart

3. USER PROCEDURES, as appropriate to each user:

    a. Instructions for input preparation:

1) Title	5) Limitations
2) Description	6) Format and content
3) Purpose and use	7) Relation to outputs
4) Media	

    b. Instructions for output use:

1) Title	5) Limitations
2) Description	6) Format and content
3) Purpose and use	7) Relation to inputs
4) Media	

    c. Operating instructions: Procedures for operating equipment with which the user must be familiar

---

Management orientation

The life-cycle process for the development of computer-based business systems automatically includes numerous reviews to keep user management informed about and committed to the support of the project. However, before changeover to a new system, it is important to augment the scheduled reviews with a series of management presentations. The purpose of these presentations is to inform all managers affected by the new system and to solicit their support during its implementation. These presentations, which should be made by the senior personnel involved in the development of the system, should include these subjects:

1. Review of system objectives, costs, and benefits.

2. Organizational and procedural changes associated with the new system.

3. Responsibilities of the organizations which report to the management attendees.

It is important that the implementation team's responsibilities be understood and that each organization involved in the implementation be assigned a constructive role during the critical changeover period.

EQUIPMENT INSTALLATION

Earlier in the life cycle of a computer-based system, fundamental equipment decisions were made. During the Study Phase, for example, alternative configurations were evaluated and decisions made about using available in-house equipment and obtaining new computer components or systems. Early in the Design Phase, when functions were allocated between manual, hardware, and software tasks, a final process of equipment evaluation and vendor selection took place. If new equipment was needed, it was placed on order. The Development Phase implementation plan must include all activities related to the installation and check-out of equipment scheduled to be delivered at various times throughout the Development Phase.

The principal equipment-related activities which must be implemented are (1) site preparation, (2) equipment installation, and (3) hardware and software check-out.

Equipment vendors can provide the specifications for equipment installation. They usually work with the project's equipment installation team in planning for adequate space, power, and light, and a suitable environment (e.g., temperature, humidity, dust control, and safety measures). After a suitable site has been completed, the computer equipment can be installed. Although equipment normally is installed by the manufacturer, the implementation team should advise and assist. Participation enables the team to aid in the installation and, more importantly, to become familiar with the equipment.

Usually manufacturers will check out the hardware and the software they supply. The implementation team also should perform its own check-out tests, using application-oriented test programs.

CONVERSION

Conversion: An overview

Conversion is the process of initiating and performing all the physical operations that result directly in the turnover of the new system to the user. It has two parts:

1. The creation of a conversion plan at the start of the Development Phase and the implementation of this plan throughout the Development Phase.

2. The creation of a system changeover plan at the end of the Development Phase and the implementation of the plan at the beginning of the Operation Phase.

We shall discuss the conversion plan and its implementation in this chapter. We shall also discuss the changeover plan, whose implementation is described in Chapter 26: Changeover and Routine Operation.

Conversion activities (Development Phase)

A conversion plan is prepared at the start of the Development Phase. Its principal elements concern procedures, program, and file conversion.

Procedures Conversion. Often a new system will incorporate many of the old system's forms and procedures, but some of these may require modification to fit into the new system. Also, the new system may interface with a network of other systems; this, too, may cause some modification of procedures. The procedures that require change must be identified, and the changes explained during training of personnel.

Program Conversion. The new computer-based system may include some computer program components that are part of an existing system. A conversion problem may arise if new equipment is installed, if the inputs and outputs of existing programs change, or if the existing programs are not efficient in their new environment. Even if new equipment is not involved, all the existing programs must be reevaluated. Reprogramming should be considered when programs are poorly documented, heavily patched, or not efficient enough. For instance, many small programs might be replaced by a single program that performs a repetitive function more effectively.

System interfaces with other computer programs also must be examined. Programming modifications may be required to enable the new system to supply or receive data through these interfaces.

File Conversion. File conversion can be the most time-consuming and expensive step in the entire project. The magnitude of this task often is underestimated. For example, if many thousands of customer account records are to be stored on a magnetic disk instead of kept in filing cabinets—possibly located in different parts of the company—the conversion effort could be extensive. Existing files must be converted into a format acceptable to the computer program and equipment. Duplicate files must be consolidated and errors corrected before changeover to the new system starts. Otherwise a series of data errors may plague users of the new system for a long time after its implementation.

File conversion activities include many basic systems analysis activities, such as fact finding and analysis, forms design, procedure writing, and computer program design. We can divide file conversion into a sequence of three major activities. These are (1) collection of file conversion data, (2) conversion of files, and (3) testing of converted files.

In many circumstances file conversion data must be collected from a variety of sources. Some data may already be in machine-readable form; however, it often is necessary to create new data to supplement that which is already filed in some form. Forms may have to be designed and procedures written to transfer data from an existing file to a new file. Often intermediate files are created. For example, the data to be transferred may be entered into specially designed input documents and then punched into cards for verification before being written onto a disk or tape.

Verifying data going into the new files is an important and often laborious task. All too often a high percentage of "current" data is incomplete or in error. Discrepancies are common, for instance, between data stored in two redundant files that are to be consolidated into a shared data base. Before consolidation can take place, it must be determined which (if either) file is correct. Verification usually requires the extensive assistance of user personnel. The analyst must remember that the new file manager is to be a computer, which will not be as flexible as the human file manager it may replace. Humans often can detect and ignore "garbage." The computer cannot.

Computer programs are required to perform the actual file conversion. These programs must be written and checked out before they are needed. They must sort data, validate data, and create the file in the new format. After the files have been converted, the conversion team must check their accuracy. Even if the original files have been "purified" before the data stored on them is entered into the new system, errors may be introduced during conversion. All file data should be printed out and verified. This, again, requires the assistance of user personnel. Special file correction forms may have to be designed, and several conversion runs may be required if a large data base is being assembled. Involving the user in file conversion activities is healthy because it tends to build user confidence in the new data base and in the computer-based system.

Changeover plan (Operation Phase)

The activities described in the preceding sections were the elements of a conversion plan that is implemented throughout the Development Phase. By the time of the acceptance review at the end of the Development Phase, forms and procedures have been prepared and used, computer programs have been written and tested, and old files have been converted to new files. The next step in the conversion process is the actual changeover from the old system to the new, which takes place at the beginning of the Operation Phase.

A changeover plan that identifies and schedules all changeover activities should be available at the acceptance review. It should specify the method of changeover and identify the roles and responsibilities of all personnel. The three general methods of changeover from the old system to the new system are parallel operation, immediate replacement, or phased changeover.

In parallel operation, data is processed by both the old and new systems. In theory, this method offers many advantages. The user has maximum flexibility because he does not have to begin using the new system until he is certain that it is producing acceptable outputs. He knows that he can always revert to the old system in the event of disaster. In practice, unfortunately, there are several reasons why a "pure" parallel operation method of changeover seldom is possible:

1. The new system is "different" from the old system. It probably has been designed to perform functions and produce outputs that were not available with the old system.

2. Parallel processing may be too time-consuming or expensive, particularly if personnel are not available to operate both systems. This is particularly true if the volume of work is large.

3. Determining which system is in error can be difficult. People tend to be biased toward the familiar, in this case toward the old system.

4. Parallel processing tends to delay adoption of the new system. People tend to cling to a "security blanket," thus prolonging the problems the new system was designed to solve.

Immediate replacement—requiring immediate use of the new system—is a risky alternative. The outputs of the new system may be compared with the "last" outputs of the old system to identify errors. Correcting errors usually creates crisis situations during the early stages of immediate replacement. The circumstances under which immediate replacement usually occurs are those in which:

1. A high percentage of outputs are new.
2. The system is not so critical that failure is a disaster.
3. No type of parallel processing is possible.
4. The user exerts "pressure" for use of the system outputs.
5. An alternate, or fallback, system is available.

Phased changeover is a compromise between parallel operation and immediate replacement; it is recommended over the other two methods. In this method, users process some percentage, perhaps 10 percent, of their normal volume of transactions through the new system and the remainder through the old system. Thus, users can become familiar with the operation of the new system, and the task of correcting errors is manageable with existing resources. After the user is assured that normal transactions are being processed correctly, more complex transactions can be introduced. The volume of data handled by the new system can then be increased until the old system is phased out. The success of phased changeover is enhanced if the changeover plan is properly scheduled for sequence and timing, for introducing elements of the new system, and for terminating corresponding parts of the old system.

Whatever changeover method is selected, problems will arise. We will discuss the actual changeover in Chapter 26: Changeover and Routine Operation.

An initial operating schedule also should be prepared. Its purpose is to demonstrate how the new computer program can perform its functions in a timely fashion in the "real world." The schedule should identify groups of computer program components that must be run without interruption on a regular basis. These groups are called run modules. Such a schedule is prepared in conjunction with the operations staff of the Data Processing department.

IMPLEMENTATION MANAGEMENT

The implementation committee

We have discussed the four major elements of the implementation plan: test plans, training plans, an equipment installation plan, and a conversion plan. Each of these elements may be complex, involving the combined efforts of a large number of people, many of whom are unfamiliar with the new system. At the beginning of this chapter, we suggested that one technique for managing the entire implementation task was to establish implementation teams, each one to be responsible for a major element of the implementation plan. However, for the team approach to be effective, there must be a central reporting point. Often the implementation teams will report to a coordination committee. The membership of such a committee should include the heads of the implementation team, the primary users of the system, and representatives from the computer service organization. The senior systems analyst is responsible for forming this committee and for selecting its members. In doing so, he should consult with the principal user of the new system.

The responsibility of heading the implementation committee belongs to the principal user, not the systems analyst. This user already has a major financial commitment to the success of the system. As head of the implementation committee, he will increase his emotional commitment and his readiness to accept the system as it approaches operational status. There are also other advantages:

1. User leadership will demonstrate that the system is "real" and not just an "exercise."

2. The user, as a "line" manager, can bring additional authority to the project. He can take direct action to resolve and to prevent problems.

3. Because of his involvement in implementation management, the user will be prepared to conduct a knowledgeable acceptance review at the end of the Development Phase. He will be predisposed to accept a system that he feels is ready for operational status.

4. The user's involvement in and commitment to the success of the system will carry over into the Operation Phase. This will help the analyst during the critical changeover period.

Although the systems analyst does not head the implementation committee, he is an important member. Often he functions as the committee secretary. He provides the planning and scheduling skills needed to manage the many implementation tasks. Because these tasks can be defined and are similar for almost all computer-based systems, it is appropriate to consider using critical path networks, such as were mentioned in Chapter 7: Charting Techniques. The use of these graphic techniques to manage the implementation tasks is discussed in the following section.

Network techniques: PERT

Fundamentals of PERT. As introduced in Chapter 7, critical path networks are project management charting techniques that use a graphical format to depict the relationships between tasks and schedules. As an example, we shall consider the application of one of these techniques, PERT (Program Evaluation Review Technique), to managing the implementation of a computer-based business system.

PERT is a management planning and analysis tool that uses a graphical display, called a network, to show relationships between tasks that must be performed to accomplish an objective. PERT is a means of creating a "master plan" for the control of complex projects. Developed in the 1960s by the United States Navy, Lockheed Aircraft Corporation, and the consulting firm of Booz, Allen, and Hamilton for use on the Polaris submarine program, PERT has been applied widely to both civil and military projects.

PERT is a management tool. It provides a manager with an orderly approach to planning. By forcing him to construct a network, PERT points out relationships

FIGURE 22-9. **Elementary PERT network**

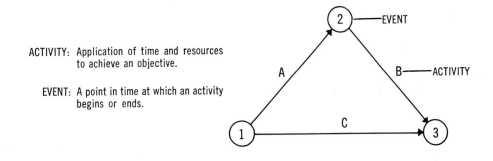

between tasks that he might otherwise overlook. It also brings about coordination of effort since it requires that participants in a project communicate with each other in order to establish and review the network. In short, PERT is a technique that helps managers answer questions such as these:

1. What work is to be done?
2. How will the work be done?
3. When is the work to be done?
4. What management actions can be taken?

We will develop the basic knowledge required to use PERT as we show how it can help provide answers to the above questions.

To answer the question "What is to be done?" we must specify objectives and develop a plan identifying the tasks to be completed to achieve these objectives. In PERT the plan is represented by a "network" like that in FIGURE 22-9, *Elementary PERT network,* which displays related activities and events. A *network* is a graphical representation of related activities and events. An *activity* is the application of time and resources to achieve an objective. It is measured in units of time, usually weeks, and is represented on the PERT network by an arrow. The arrows labeled *A, B,* and *C* in Figure 22-9, represent activities. These activities are similar to horizontal bars on a Gantt chart; however, they differ in that elapsed time is not necessarily proportional to the length of the arrow.

An *event* is a point in time at which an activity begins or ends. It is represented on a PERT by a circle network. Thus, in Figure 22-9, Event 2 represents the end of Activity *A* and the start of Activity *B*. That is, each internal activity has a predecessor and a successor event. Events are similar to milestones on a Gantt chart, but the relationships between events are expressed much more explicitly than are those between milestones. Typically, events are identified by phrases such as "training manuals prepared," "training completed," and "equipment installed."

The PERT network helps to answer the question "How will the work be done?" by displaying the sequences in which activities must occur if specified events are to be reached. For example, the network of Figure 22·9 tells us that three separate jobs, *A*, *B*, and *C*, must be performed in order to achieve the end objective denoted by Event 3. Further, it identifies two independent paths along which activities must be completed. Along one path, Activities *A* and *B* must be performed in sequence. Along the other path, Activity *C* must be performed concurrently with Activities *A* and *B*.

PERT networks also help to answer the question "When is the work to be done?" This is accomplished by estimating an expected time for each activity. The expected activity time is based upon three estimates: optimistic, pessimistic, and most likely. It is calculated according to the following formula:

$$t_e = \frac{O + 4M + P}{6}$$

where

t_e = Expected activity time (in weeks)
O = Optimistic estimate (how long the activity would take if everything went well)
M = Most likely estimate (the normal time the activity should take)
P = Pessimistic estimate (how long the activity could take under adverse conditions)

The above formula is the essential difference between CPM (Critical Path Method) and PERT. CPM uses only one estimate to obtain a value for t_e. The time to reach any event along a network path can be calculated as the sum of the activity times along the path. However, since more than one path may lead to an event, it is necessary to select the largest sum of activity times, i.e., the longest path, as the determining time. This time is defined as the expected event time, T_E. Thus:

$$T_E = \text{sum of all expected activity times } (t_e\text{'s}) \text{ along} \\ \text{the longest path leading to an event.}$$

The longest T_E is the time needed to proceed by the longest path from the first to the last event in the network. This is the minimum amount of time which must be scheduled for the project represented by the PERT network. The path along which the longest T_E is measured is called the *critical path*. Slippage along the critical path can cause the scheduled completion date, which usually corresponds to the longest T_E, to be missed.

There is time to spare along all other paths in the network leading from the first event to the last event (unless there are multiple critical paths). This time to spare is called slack (*s*). Slack is calculated for each event by subtracting the T_E for that event from the latest allowable time, T_L, which is the latest time that an event can be reached without causing any path on which the event lies to exceed the critical path.

Thus:

$$s = T_L - T_E$$

Figure 22-10. Example of PERT calculations

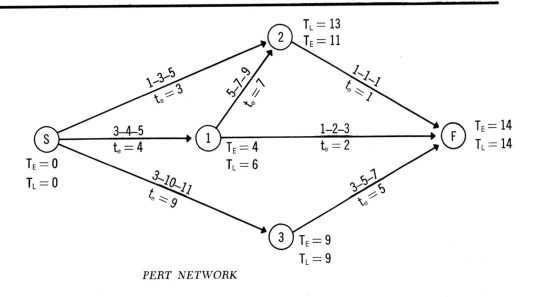

PERT NETWORK

Event	Predecessor Events	Expected Event Time T_E	Latest Allowable Time T_L	Slack $s = (T_L - T_E)$
S	—	0	0	0
1	S	4	6	2
2	S, 1	11	13	2
3	S	9	9	0
F	1, 2, 3	14	14	0

TABLE OF PERT CALCULATIONS

We will use the network previously presented as Figure 7-17 in Chapter 7 to illustrate the basic calculations performed to obtain values for t_e, T_E, T_L, and s. This network is redrawn as the first part of Figure 22-10, *Example of PERT calculations*. The values of the optimistic, most likely, and pessimistic expected activity times are shown above each activity line. For example, for the activity extending from Event S (start) to Event 2:

$$t_e = \frac{1 + 4\,(3) + 5}{6} = \frac{18}{6} = 3 \text{ weeks}$$

The second part of Figure 22-10 is a useful format for a table for calculations. We will illustrate its use as we proceed with our example. The procedure for the use of the table is as follows:

1. All events are entered in the Event column in sequence, from first to last.

2. The numbers of all events that immediately precede each event are entered in the Predecessor Events column. Note that an event may have more than one predecessor.

3. The values of the expected event time, T_E, are calculated and entered in the Expected Event Time column. All T_E's are calculated by starting with the first event and continuing until the last event is reached. The successive values are cumulative and are calculated from the following relationship:

$$T_E = T_E \text{ (predecessor)} + t_e \text{ (activity)}.$$

Thus:

T_E (Event S) $= 0$
T_E (Event 1) $= 4$
T_E (Event 2) $= 4 + 7 = 11$, or 3
Event 2 has two predecessor events. Hence, there are two possible values for T_E. We use the larger, in this case, 11.
T_E (Event 3) $= 9$
T_E (Event F) $= 4 + 2 = 6$, or $11 + 1 = 12$, or $9 + 5 = 14$
We use the largest, which is 14. To illustrate the results, we have entered the values for all T_E's on the PERT network.

4. The values for the latest allowable time, T_L, are calculated by subtracting t_e from the T_L for its successor event. T_L is calculated by working from the last event toward the first event. The relationship for calculating T_L is:

$$T_L = T_L \text{ (successor)} - t_e \text{ (activity)}.$$

Whenever there are multiple paths leading back to an event, there is more than one possible value for T_L. The smallest value is used. Thus:

T_L (Event F) $= T_E$ (Event F) $= 14$
T_L (Event 3) $= 14 - 5 = 9$
T_L (Event 2) $= 14 - 1 = 13$
T_L (Event 1) $= 13 - 7 = 6$, or $14 - 2 = 12$, and we use 6.
T_L (Event S) $= 13 - 3 = 10, 6 - 4 = 2$, or $9 - 9 = 0$, and we use 0.

Again, for illustrative purposes, we also have entered the values of T_L on the PERT network. The reason why there is no slack along paths that contain Events S, 3, and F is that each of these events appears on the critical path, which is S-3-F.

It is important to note that slack applies to an entire path and not to each event on the path. Also, the value of slack is not always obvious. For example, it would be incorrect to assume that there is a slack of 10 weeks along path S-2-F by observing that the expected times from Event S to Event 2 and from Event 2 to Event F are 3 weeks and 1 week, respectively. Subtracting 4 weeks from the critical path time of 14 weeks would, in this case, result in an erroneous result. Event 2 cannot be completed in 3 weeks. It requires the prior completion of Event 1. The path S-1-2 (which is the T_E for Event 2) is 11 weeks long. The identification of slack time by inspection is very difficult for complex networks. In such cases, the use of a computer is warranted.

We now can consider the question: "What management actions can be taken?" The PERT network lends itself to "exception" reporting. This means that the manager need focus his attention only on those activities and events that are not proceeding according to schedule. The PERT network can be expanded to provide more detailed coverage in areas requiring management attention. Also, conventional Gantt-type charts may be prepared from the PERT networks.

PERT provides the manager with an early warning of possible difficulties. He has many ways of reacting to problems if he is made aware of them with sufficient time for action. For example:

1. He may add new resources along a path with zero or negative slack. (Negative slack occurs when the slippage is such that the path length exceeds that of the critical path.)

2. He may trade off resources by shifting them from less critical to more critical activities.

3. He may extend the scheduled completion time.

The manager may utilize PERT networks to answer "What if?" questions. This is an effective technique for exploring the implications of alternative actions when complex PERT networks are maintained on a computer. The PERT network becomes a model he can use to simulate the effect of changes of allocations of time and other resources.

To further illustrate the value of PERT, we will consider, as an example, a PERT network for implementing a computer-based system.

> *PERT network for system implementation.* FIGURE 22-11, *Implementation network,* is a PERT network that displays the major implementation activities we have discussed in this chapter. We will use this network to illustrate some of the management options made possible by PERT. The events are numbered, and they are described in the table accompanying the network. The expected activity times (t_e) have been calculated, and they appear beneath each activity line. The second part of Figure 22-11, the table of PERT calculations for this network, presents the results of the significant calculations. Examination of this table leads to the following observations.
>
> 1. The critical path is the path along which the computer program development takes place (S-4-5-6-10-11-12-F). The length of this path is 43 weeks. The next longest path is that along which the interim and final System Specifications are prepared (S-2-10-11-12-F). This path has a slack of 4 weeks. The manager may be able to reduce the longest path by several weeks if he diverts resources from other paths and applies them to computer program development and testing.

FIGURE 22-11. **Implementation network**

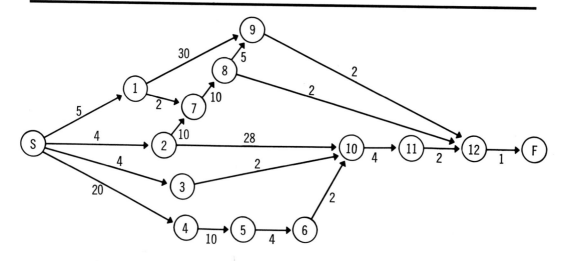

Event	Description
S	Start of Development Phase
1	Implementation plan prepared
2	Interim system specification prepared
3	Equipment installed
4	Computer programming and testing completed
5	System tests completed
6	Test reports prepared

Event	Description
7	Training manuals prepared
8	Completion of training
9	Changeover plan prepared
10	Final system specification completed
11	Development Phase report completed
12	Acceptance review completed
13	Approval to proceed received

Event	Predecessor Events	T_E	T_L	S
S	—	0	0	0
1	S	5	10	5
2	S	4	8	4
3	S	4	18	14
4	S,3	20	20	0
5	4	30	30	0
6	5	34	34	0

Event	Predecessor Events	T_E	T_L	S
7	1,2	14	25	11
8	7	24	35	11
9	1,8	35	40	5
10	2,3,6	36	36	0
11	10	40	40	0
12	8,9,11	42	42	0
F	12	43	43	0

Critical Path   S-4-5-6-10-11-12-F

TABLE OF PERT CALCULATIONS FOR IMPLEMENTATION NETWORK

2. The path along which training occurs (S-2-7-8-12-F) has a slack of 11 weeks. This may present both a problem and an opportunity. The problem is that the expected event time, T_E, for Event 8, Complete Training, is 24 weeks. Personnel training will be completed too soon, and people may forget their training. The opportunity is the possibility of rescheduling the training program and using the available resources to accelerate progress along the critical path and along other paths with little slack.

3. Along the critical path (S-4-5-6-10-11-12-F) the longest T_E is associated with Event 4, Complete System Tests. The manager may wish to review all program development and test plans. They may already be represented by subordinate PERT networks. If they are not, he may request that such networks be constructed to aid him in his review.

The above network example illustrates some of the possible uses of PERT as a management tool. For actual management control of a project of moderate size, the network would be expanded to at least one additional level of detail. In this event, the manager would probably want to use a computer to maintain and to analyze the detailed PERT network. PERT computer programs and other software tools are available to aid in the design, construction, and implementation of computer-based systems.

KEY TERMS

implementation	*conversion*
bottom-up program development	*changeover*
top-down program development	*Program Evaluation Review Technique* (PERT)

FOR DISCUSSION

1. Distinguish between implementation, conversion, and changeover.

2. Define and describe bottom-up and top-down development and testing of computer programs.

3. What are the advantages of top-down development and testing of computer programs?

4. Discuss the importance of testing prior to changeover.

5. What are the principal reference manuals? Describe the content of each.

6. What are the values of including management orientation sessions in a training program?

7. Describe and distinguish between the three general changeover methods.

8. What is an implementation team? What is the implementation committee? What roles should the principal user and the systems analyst play?

9. Describe PERT and discuss its value as a management tool.

23

Computer Program Development

In the Design Phase, the functions to be performed by the computer were identified, the input records were described, print charts for the printed outputs were drawn, and the files were designed. The goal of this chapter is to describe the development of the computer program. You will learn the steps involved in computer program component (CPC) development.

STEPS IN COMPUTER PROGRAM COMPONENT DEVELOPMENT

The steps in the development of computer program components (CPCs) are (1) define the function of the CPC; (2) plan the CPC; (3) code the CPC; and (4) test and debug the CPC.

The function of each CPC was defined for the programmer when functions were allocated during system design. A detailed system flowchart is prepared for each CPC from the expanded system flowchart created during the Design Phase. This flowchart and its narrative define the function of each CPC.

In program planning, the logic to be used to solve the problem is developed. Algorithms and computer program flowcharts are useful tools for program planning. *Algorithms* are sets of rules or instructions used to accomplish tasks. They may be stated as formulas, decision tables, or narratives. The program flowchart and algorithms that result from program planning are retained and become part of the program documentation.

The next step, writing, or coding, a program, is the actual writing of computer instructions. These instructions can be translated to machine code and followed by the computer; they should follow the logical steps of the program plan or flowchart.

Several programming languages, particularly Assembly, COBOL, and RPG, are commonly used to solve business-oriented problems. Each language has its advantages and disadvantages. Most computer installations have a "standard" language used by their programmers. Programmers usually are not given a choice of languages unless some special circumstances exist.

Testing and debugging a program involve (1) translating the coded program into machines language, a process called *compilation;* and (2) testing the translated or compiled program with example data and checking the result. If the results of testing are not correct, the program is said to have "bugs." "Debugging" is the process of correcting computer code to obtain correct results.

As described in Chapter 22, testing must be planned and structured to reduce the chance that errors will be overlooked.

CPC CODING AND DEBUGGING EXAMPLE

The Data Edit CPC of the MARS (modified accounts receivable system) provides an example of computer program development.

The problem definition is provided for the programmer in the form of a detailed system flowchart and narrative.

FIGURE 23-1, *System flowchart—MARS Data Edit CPC*, illustrates the required detail. The system flowchart is derived from the MARS expanded flowchart, Figure 16-1 (Chapter 16).

Before the programmer can prepare the computer program, additional details of the CPC input, storage, and output must be provided.

Card layouts were developed during input design (Chapter 17), print charts during output design (Chapter 18), and file descriptions during file design (Chapter 19). FIGURE 23-2, *Overcredit notice print chart*, is the print chart from output design.

To aid the programmer, algorithms to express the rules or logic of solving the problem may be provided. The programmer then develops a program flowchart.

FIGURE 23-3, *Example decision table*, depicts the logic used to determine the requirement for an overcredit notice. FIGURE 23-4, *MARS computer program flowchart segment*, shows one page of a flowchart.

After completing the flowchart, the programmer can code the program logic.

FIGURE 23-5, *MARS Data Edit coding sample*, depicts the coding of the flowchart segment in Figure 23-4. It uses COBOL (COmmon Business Oriented Language) coding.

Each CPC should be tested by the programmer until all errors are found and corrected. Each output must match the planned output in the print charts.

FIGURE 23-6, *Data Edit sample output*, illustrates the overcredit notice produced by the Data Edit CPC. Note that the output corresponds to the print chart of Figure 23-2.

FIGURE 23-1. System flowchart—MARS Data Edit CPC

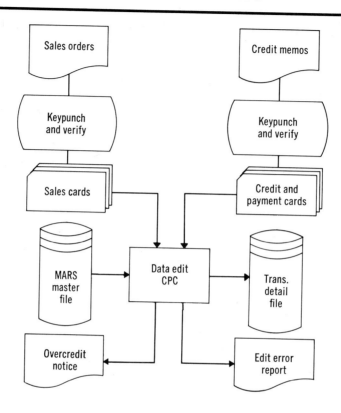

Data Edit CPC--MARS

1. Sales order and credit memo data are keypunched. Batches
   will be verified at random.

2. Sales and credit cards are batched for input to the Data
   Edit CPC.

3. Input cards are sorted into ascending order by account
   number. All fields are checked for validity. The amounts
   of the order less credits are added to customer balance.
   If the new balance exceeds the credit limit (stored in
   the master file), special approval is required or the
   order is rejected. A rejected order results in the
   creation of an overcredit notice. All transaction
   details not causing an overcredit condition are written
   into the transaction detail file.

FIGURE 23-2. Overcredit notice print chart

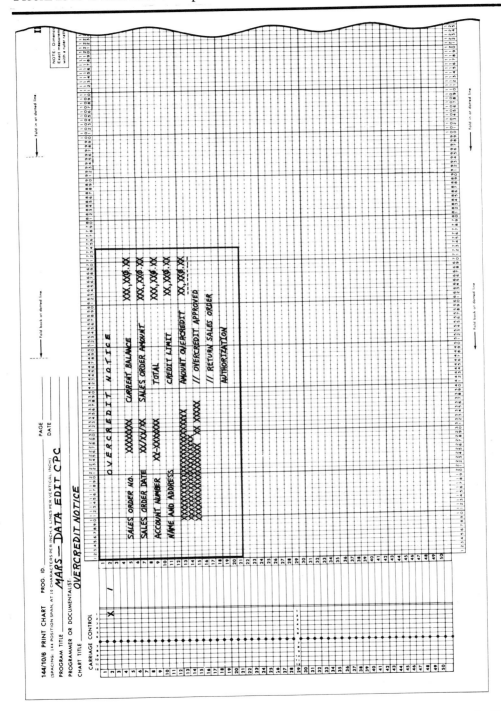

Figure 23-3. Example decision table

Overcredit Policy		1	2	3
CONDITIONS	Is new balance > credit limit?	N	Y	Y
	Has special approval been given?		N	Y
ACTIONS	Process the order	X		X
	Reject the order (overcredit notice)		X	

Figure 23-4. MARS computer program flowchart segment

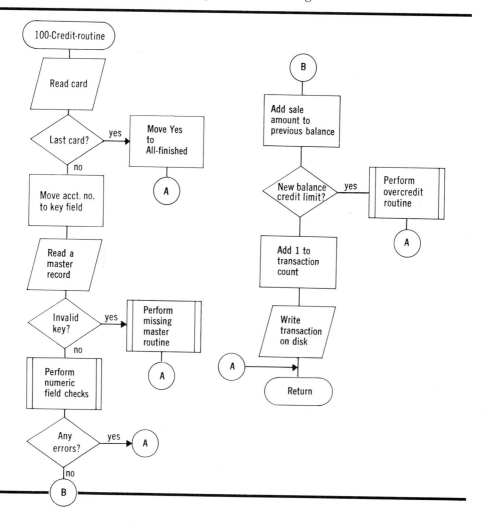

FIGURE 23-5. MARS Data Edit coding sample

```
080010    100-NOTE.
080020        NOTE*********************************************************
080030        *    THIS ROUTINE IS PERFORMED FOR CREDIT CARDS.           *
080040        *    IT CHECKS FOR INVALID NUMERIC FIELDS AND SALE AMOUNT  *
080050        *    OVER CREDIT LIMIT.                                     *
080060        **********************************************************.
080070
080080
080090    100-CREDIT-ROUTINE.
080100
080110        READ CARD-FILE
080120          AT END
080130             MOVE 'YES' TO ALL-FINISHED
080140             GO TO 100-CREDIT-ROUTINE-EXIT.
080150        MOVE ACCOUNT-NUMBER TO RECORD-KEY.
080160        READ MASTER-FILE
080170          INVALID KEY
080180             PERFORM 1001-MISSING-MASTER
080190             GO TO 100-CREDIT-ROUTINE-EXIT.
080200        PERFORM 1002-NUMBER-FIELD-CHECK.
090010        IF ANY-ERRORS
090020             PERFORM 1003-WRITE-EXCEPTION-RECORD,
090030             GO TO 100-CREDIT-ROUTINE-EXIT.
090040        ADD SALE-AMOUNT, PREVIOUS-BALANCE GIVING NEW-BALANCE.
090050        IF NEW-BALANCE IS GREATER THAN CREDIT-LIMIT (CREDIT-CODE),
090060             PERFORM 1004-WRITE-OVERCREDIT-NOTICE,
090070             GO TO 100-CREDIT-ROUTINE-EXIT.
090080        ADD 1 TO TRANS-COUNTER.
090090        WRITE TRANS-RECORD.
090100
090110    100-CREDIT-ROUTINE-EXIT.
090120        EXIT.
```

FIGURE 23-6. MARS Data Edit sample output

```
                    O V E R C R E D I T   N O T I C E


SALES ORDER NO.    00069721    CURRENT BALANCE        2,320.50

SALES ORDER DATE   10/15/74    SALES ORDER AMOUNT       516.02

ACCOUNT NUMBER   02-0000367    TOTAL                  2,836.52

NAME AND ADDRESS               CREDIT LIMIT           2,500.00

    ABC CORPORATION            AMOUNT OVERCREDIT        336.52
    2234 WASHINGTON BLVD.                              -------
    BIG CITY          CA 91789 // OVERCREDIT APPROVED

                               // RETURN SALES ORDER

                               AUTHORIZATION
```

After testing and debugging each CPC, the programmer turns over all documentation to the analyst so that the CPC can replace its "stub" in the overall system top-down testing.

KEY TERMS

computer program component (CPC)	*coding*
algorithm	*debugging*

FOR DISCUSSION

1. What are the steps in computer program component development?

2. What is program planning?

3. What is an algorithm? Give an example.

4. Who is responsible for testing a computer program component? For subsystem testing?

24 Development Phase Report and Review

At the conclusion of the Development Phase, the analyst prepares a report and reviews it with the user of the system. The goal of this chapter is to describe the structure and content of the Development Phase report and the purpose and importance of the Development Phase review. You will learn how to organize a Development Phase report.

SYSTEM SPECIFICATION

The Development Phase is concluded by the completion of three major milestone activities. These are:

1. Preparation of the System Specification
2. Preparation of the Development Phase report
3. Conduct of the Development Phase review

The Development Phase report is built around the System Specification—the third, and final, major baseline document. It evolves from the Design Specification just as that baseline specification evolved from the Performance Specification. Whereas the Design Specification is a "build to" specification, the System Specification is an "as built" specification. It is the major reference document for all personnel who will use, maintain, or operate the computer-based business system.

FIGURE 24-1, *System Specification outline*, illustrates the content of a typical System Specification. Like the Performance and Design Specifications, the System Specification is divided into two parts. The first part is an external specification relating to the interaction of the system with its environment; the second part is an internal specification. The System Specification is the result of documenting the Development Phase activities previously described in Chapters 22 and 23.

FIGURE 24-2, *Performance Specification—Design Specification—System Specification gozinto chart*, is an extension of Figure 20-2. It traces the growth of the baseline documentation all the way from the Performance Specification to the System Specification.

FIGURE 24-1. System Specification outline

SYSTEM SPECIFICATION

A. EXTERNAL SYSTEM SPECIFICATION:
1. Information-oriented flowchart
2. System output specification
3. System input specification
4. System interface specification
5. System test specification
   a. Test data
   b. Test results-samples
6. Equipment specification
7. Personnel specification and training procedures
   a. User's reference manual
   b. Programmer's reference manual
   c. Operator's reference manual

B. INTERNAL SYSTEM SPECIFICATION:
1. Computer program specification
   a. System flowchart
   b. Expanded system flowcharts and HIPO charts
   c. Data base specification
   d. Computer program control specification
   e. Computer program test specification
      (1) Test data
      (2) Test results-samples
2. Computer program component (CPC) specification (for ech CPC, as required)
   a. Detailed system flowcharts
   b. Computer program (CPC) logic flowchart
   c. Transaction file specifications
   d. Control specifications
   e. Interface specifications
   f. Computer program (CPC) listings
   g. Test specifications
      (1) Test data
      (2) Input-output samples
   h. Special specifications

DEVELOPMENT PHASE REPORT

Structure and content

FIGURE 24-3, *Development Phase report*, displays the structure and content of this report, which is similar to that of the Study Phase and Design Phase reports. It has the same five major divisions. When completed, the Development Phase report completely documents the internal system design.

Unless changes to the Performance Specification, the Design Specification, or both, occur during the Development Phase, the system scope section is not altered. If there have been any changes in scope, these should be discussed fully.

The conclusions and recommendations relate to the next life-cycle phase, the Operation Phase, and focus on the next major decision. This is the decision to

FIGURE 24-2. Performance Specification—Design Specification—
System Specification gozinto chart

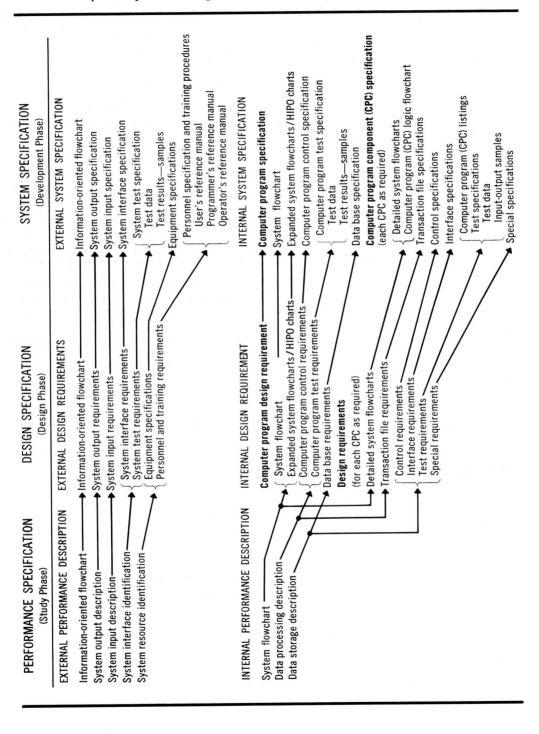

FIGURE 24-3. **Development Phase report**

DEVELOPMENT PHASE REPORT

I. SYSTEM SCOPE:
- A. System title
- B. Problem statement and purpose
- C. Constraints
- D. Specific objectives
- E. Method of evaluation

II. CONCLUSIONS AND RECOMMENDATIONS:
- A. Conclusions
- B. Recommendations

III. SYSTEM SPECIFICATION:
- A. External system specification
- B. Internal system specification

IV. PLANS AND COST SCHEDULES:
- A. Progress plans
  1. Detailed milestones—Development Phase
  2. Major milestones—all Phases
  3. Changeover plan
  4. Operational plan
- B. Cost schedules
  1. Project cost—Development Phase
  2. Project cost—major milestones
  3. Operation Phase—recurring costs

V. APPENDICES

---

change over from the existing system to the new system. Important inputs to the changeover decision are (1) the completed System Specification, (2) satisfactory system test reports, (3) the availability of trained personnel, and (4) a changeover plan.

In preparing his conclusions and recommendations, the analyst must take into consideration the environment in which the computer-based system will be maintained and operated after complete conversion. Preliminary operational schedules, prepared as part of the changeover plan, should be used to demonstrate that the new system will mesh with the schedules for ongoing data processing jobs.

The System Specification follows the conclusions and recommendations in the Development Phase report. Its major elements were outlined in Figure 24-1. Referring to the figure, we note that the reference manuals for programmers, operators, and users appear as part of the external system specification. These manuals were discussed previously (Chapter 22) as important training tools. Because much of the content of these documents is based on other parts of the System Specification and because they are stand-alone manuals that are used for training, the entries shown under the external specification may refer the reader to appendices in which these manuals are contained. FIGURE 24-4, *Relationship between Development Phase report elements and reference manuals,* identifies the elements of the report on which the content of each reference manual is based.

FIGURE 24-4. Relationship between Development Phase report elements and reference manuals

DEVELOPMENT PHASE REPORT ELEMENT	PROGRAMMER'S REFERENCE MANUAL	OPERATOR'S REFERENCE MANUAL	USER'S REFERENCE MANUAL
SYSTEM SCOPE			
Title	✓	✓	✓
Problem Statement and General Objective	✓	✓	✓
SYSTEM SPECIFICATION—EXTERNAL			
Information-Oriented Flowchart	✓	✓	✓
System Output Specification	✓	✓	✓
System Input Specification	✓	✓	✓
System Interface Specification	✓	✓	✓
System Test Specification	✓	✓	
Equipment Specification	✓	✓	
SYSTEM SPECIFICATION—INTERNAL			
Computer Program			
System Flowcharts	✓	✓	✓
Expanded System Flowcharts	✓	✓	
Data Base Specification	✓		
Control Specifications	✓	✓	
Test Specifications	✓	✓	
Computer Program Components			
Detailed System Flowchart	✓	✓	
Logic Flowchart	✓		
Transaction File Specification	✓	✓	
Control Specifications	✓	✓	
Interface Specifications	✓	✓	
Listings	✓		
Test Specifications	✓	✓	
Special Specifications	✓	✓	

The analyst updates the major milestones project plan and the cost schedules to display the completion of the Development Phase. He identifies and describes significant changes that have occurred since the Design Phase review, and also prepares cost estimates for operating and maintaining the new system elements.

The appendices that appeared in the Design Phase report are reviewed, modified, and incremented as necessary.

Example Development Phase report

An example of a Development Phase report appears on the following pages as Exhibit 3, MARS Development Phase report.

DEVELOPMENT PHASE REVIEW

A successful Development Phase review marks the beginning of the transition from a "project" to an "operational" system. The immediate consequence of an approval to proceed is the initiation of the changeover activity. Therefore, it is critically important that all the factors that will ensure an effective transition from the old system to the new system be considered. All organizations involved in or significantly affected by the pending conversion should be alerted and be invited to participate in the review; the Development Phase report should be distributed to them beforehand; the Study Phase and Design Phase reports, prepared at the conclusion of earlier phases, are provided as reference documents. In addition, the review group should have had an opportunity to read the changeover plan and the test reports. A commitment to the changeover activities should be obtained from each major participant before a decision is made to embark on the Operation Phase.

KEY TERMS

external development specification   *internal development specification*

FOR DISCUSSION

1. What is the purpose of the Development Phase report?

2. What is the content of the Development Phase report?

3. Discuss the importance of the System Specification, including its relationship to the Performance and Design Specifications.

4. What project plans and schedules are presented at the Development Phase review?

5. What is the purpose of the Development Phase review?

EXHIBIT 3.

MARS DEVELOPMENT PHASE REPORT

I. SYSTEM SCOPE

A. System Title
   Modified Accounts Receivable System (MARS)

B. Problem Statement and Purpose
   The ABCDEF Corporation's manual accounts receivable system
   currently handles 1,000 accounts each month. This number is expected to double within one year and to reach 10,000 in five
   years. The manual system is not able to meet this projected
   growth. Serious problems have already been encountered in processing the current volume of accounts. Specific problems that
   have been identified are:

   1. A significant increase in late customer billings.
   2. An accompanying increase in billing errors.
   3. An increase in delinquent accounts.
   4. Inadequate control of credit limits.
   5. An inability to access current accounts receivable
      information.

   Therefore, the purpose of the MARS project is to replace
   the present accounts receivable system with one that can eliminate the problems enumerated above and meet the company's growth
   requirements. The use of a computer-based system is to be considered.

C. Constraints
   The MARS constraints are:

   1. Design and development of the system are to be completed
      within six months.
   2. MARS is to have a growth potential to handle 10,000
      customer accounts.
   3. The use of the current in-house IBM System/3 computer
      will be considered.
   4. MARS is to interface with an existing perpetual inven-
      tory system.

D. Specific Objectives
   The specific objectives of MARS are:

   1. To establish three billing cycles per month--one for
      each region.
   2. To mail customer statements no later than 2 days after
      the close of each billing cycle.
   3. To provide a daily list of A/R transactions.
   4. To provide weekly and monthly A/R summary reports.
   5. To initiate a finance charge of 1% per month on
      accounts more than 30 days overdue.
   6. To identify accounts that have exceeded their credit
      limit prior to order processing.
   7. To introduce controls to reduce the customer monthly

statement error rate by 90%--a reduction in errors
from 1% to 1/10 of 1%.
8. To provide a capability for listing customer accounts
by region.

E. Method of Evaluation
After MARS has been operational from 60 to 90 days:

1. A statistical analysis will be made of customer billings in order to verify elapsed time between the close
of the billing cycle and the mailing of customer statements.
2. Errors in monthly statements will be recorded for a
30-day period, and the percentage of errors will be
calculated.
3. The processing of any overcredit accounts without
authorization will be determined by an audit of one
month's transactions.
4. The timeliness and accuracy of the daily and weekly
accounts receivable reports will be verified by an
audit of one week's transactions.
5. A random sample of the customer account lists for
each region will be audited for validity.
6. Personal evaluations of the effectiveness of the
system will be obtained from its principal users.

II. CONCLUSIONS AND RECOMMENDATIONS

A. Conclusions
The Modified Accounts Receivable System (MARS) is ready
for operation. The system tests have been successfully
completed, all required personnel have completed training,
and the changeover plan has been reviewed and approved.
All phases were completed on schedule and within budget.

B. Recommendations
It is therefore recommended that the MARS project be
accepted for changeover.

III. SYSTEM SPECIFICATION

A. External System Specification

1. Information-oriented flowchart. Figure E3-1, "MARS
information-oriented flowchart," displays the flow
of data in the MARS. The accompanying narrative
appears as Figure E3-2, "MARS information-oriented
flowchart narrative."

2. System output specification. The seven MARS outputs are:
a. Customer monthly statement
b. Accounts receivable transaction register
c. Accounts receivable summary report
d. Aged accounts receivable report

 e. Customer account list
 f. Shipping invoice
 g. Overcredit notice
 Print charts and data element lists for each output are
 presented as Figure E3-3.

3. <u>System input specification</u>. The three MARS inputs are:
 a. Customer account application
 b. Billing notice
 c. Payment/credit memo
 An example of the system inputs is included as
 Figure E3-4.

4. <u>System interface specification</u>. The MARS must interface
 with (i.e., transfer data to and from) the existing
 inventory system. Inventory must be on hand for shipment prior to billing the customer, and the inventory
 quantities should be reduced as merchandise is committed
 for shipment.

5. <u>System test specification</u>. The system was tested
 according to the MARS test plan. No major problems
 were detected. A copy of the test plan, test data,
 and test results can be found in the appendix.

6. <u>Equipment specification</u>. An IBM System/370, Model 138
 computing system was selected. The configuration is
 as follows:
 a. Central Processing Unit (CPU) model FE (144 K bytes)
 b. Integrated file adapter
 c. 3340-A1 disk storage (2 drives 70 MB each)
 d. 3411 model-1 magnetic tape subsystem
 e. 2540 card read punch
 f. 2821 control unit
 g. 1403 printer model-2 (600 l.p.m.)
 h. 3210 console printer-keyboard

7. <u>Personnel specification and training procedures</u>. The
 user's reference manual, programmer's reference manual,
 and the operator's reference manual are attached to
 this system specification in the appendix.

B. Internal System Specification

 1. <u>Computer program specification</u>.
 a. System flowchart, shown in Figure E3-5.
 b. Expanded system flowcharts. Figure E3-6 depicts
 the MARS expanded system flowchart and HIPO charts.
 c. Data base specification. The MARS master file
 will be an indexed sequential file. Each logical
 record will be 133 bytes in length. Figure E3-7
 depicts the disk record layout. The blocking
 factor is to be 19. The file size is initially
 to be 4 cylinders. This file size is adequate for
 2,052 logical records; it will grow to 22 cylinders
 to accommodate 10,000 accounts.
 d. Computer program control specification. The MARS

computer program will provide controls in the
following ways:
(1) Edit all input data for validity.
(2) Detect overcredit conditions prior to
    processing invoices.
(3) Detect short or out-of-stock conditions
    prior to processing invoices.
(4) Provide a tape backup for the MARS master file.
  e. Computer program test specification. The MARS test
     plan, test data, and test results are included in
     the report appendix. All tests were in accordance
     with the test plan.

2. Computer program component (CPC) specification--Data Edit.
   a. Detailed system flowchart, presented as Figure E3-8.
   b. Computer program component (CPC) logic flowchart.
      Figure E3-9 illustrates the computer logic flowchart
      for the Data Edit CPC.
   c. Transaction file specifications. The transaction file
      requirements for MARS are shown in Figure E3-10. The
      figure depicts the card layouts for all three system
      inputs; however, only the sales order and payment/
      credit memo cards are input to the Data Edit CPC.
   d. Control specifications. The Data Edit CPC must edit
      all input data for validity and detect overcredit
      conditions. If an overcredit condition exists, an
      overcredit notice is to be produced. Records contain-
      ing invalid data are to be noted on an edit error report.
   e. Interface specifications. The Data Edit CPC output
      on disk must interface with the Invoice CPC.
   f. Computer program component (CPC) listings. The Data
      Edit CPC source listing is included as Figure E3-11.
   g. Test specification. The test plan, test data, and
      the test input-output samples are included in the
      report appendix.

IV. PLANS AND COST SCHEDULES

   A. Detailed Milestones--Development Phase
      The project progress for the MARS Development Phase is
   depicted in Figure E3-12. The Development Phase was completed on schedule with the acceptance review scheduled
   for 6/19/xy. The costs for the Development Phase are
   shown in Figure E3-13.

   B. Major Milestones--All Phases
      The progress plan and status report for the MARS project
   is included as Figure E3-14. Figure E3-15 depicts the total
   MARS project costs.

   C. Changeover
      The approved changeover plan appears in the report
   appendix.

   D. Operational--Recurring
      The weekly recurring costs per account for MARS are
   depicted in Figure E3-16.

V. APPENDICES

NOTE: The appendices include all supporting data for the report. For the purpose of this exhibit, such detail is not included. The following is a list of typical appendices.

Project directive

System test plan

System test data and results

User, programmer, and operator manuals

Computer program test plan

Computer program test data and results

CPC test plans

CPC test data and results

System changeover plan

System operational plan

FIGURE E3-1. MARS information-oriented flowchart

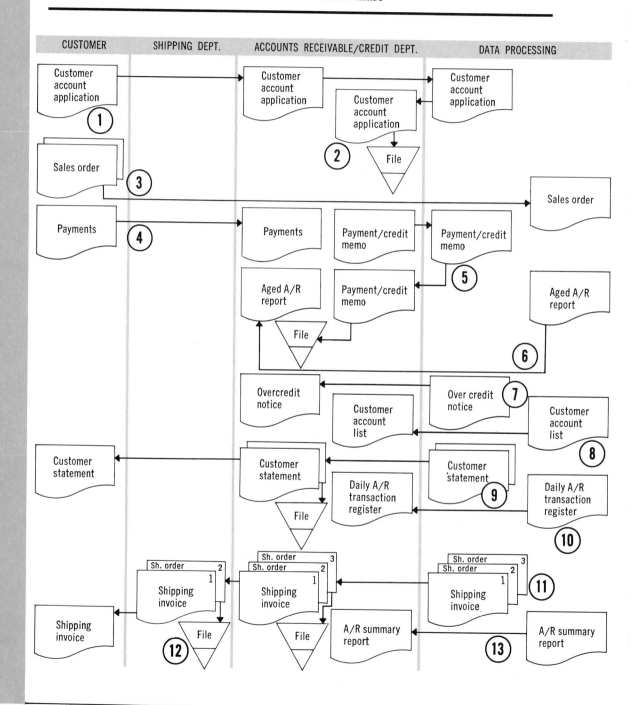

FIGURE E3-2. MARS information-oriented flowchart narrative

INFORMATION-ORIENTED FLOWCHART NARRATIVE

1. Customers submit account applications which are processed by the Accounts Receivable/Credit department.

2. If an application is accepted, it is sent to Data Processing for entry into the system. Data Processing returns the application for filing.

3. Sales orders are sent directly to Data Processing for order processing. The customer retains the carbon copy.

4. Payments are sent to the Accounts Receivable/Credit department.

5. A payment/credit memo is generated and sent to Data Processing. Data Processing returns the memo for filing.

6. An aged A/R report is sent to the Accounts Receivable/Credit department from Data Processing each month.

7. Data Processing sends overcredit notices to a credit clerk whenever a new order would exceed the customer's credit limit. If the additional credit is approved, the notice is returned to Data Processing with an authorization to process the order. If the additional credit is disapproved, the order and the notice are returned to the customer.

8. Customer account lists are produced on demand and sent to the Accounts Receivable/Credit department for distribution.

9. Customer statements are sent to Accounts Receivable/Credit in duplicate. The original copy is sent to the customer; the duplicate is filed. One-third of the statements are produced each ten days of the month, i.e., on the 1st, 10th, and 20th.

10. A daily A/R transaction register is sent to the Accounts Receivable/Credit department.

11. Three copies of the shipping invoice/shipping order are sent to the Accounts Receivable/Credit department. The original copy is entitled shipping invoice; the two carbon copies are entitled shipping order. The third copy is filed by A/R.

12. The shipping invoice and the first copy of the shipping order are sent to the Shipping department. The shipping order is used to "pick" inventory items for shipment and is then filed. The shipping invoice is packed with the merchandise and is sent to the customer.

13. The accounts receivable summary report is prepared weekly and sent to the Accounts Receivable/Credit department for distribution.

FIGURE E3-3. MARS output specifications: overcredit notice

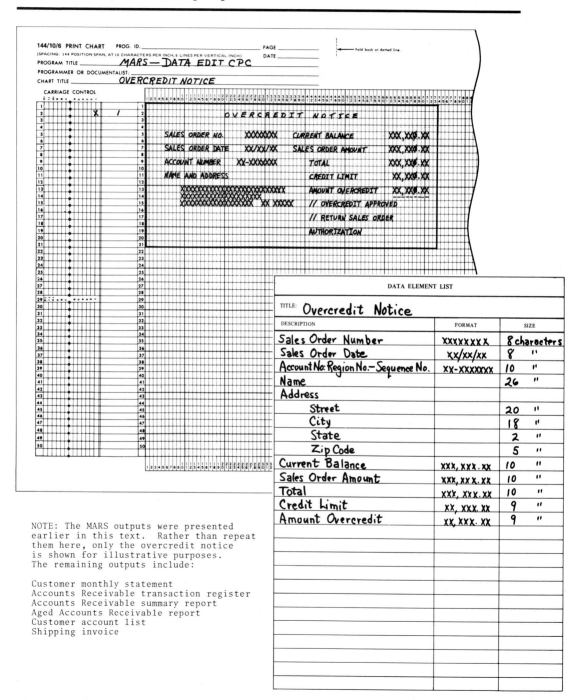

NOTE: The MARS outputs were presented
earlier in this text. Rather than repeat
them here, only the overcredit notice
is shown for illustrative purposes.
The remaining outputs include:

Customer monthly statement
Accounts Receivable transaction register
Accounts Receivable summary report
Aged Accounts Receivable report
Customer account list
Shipping invoice

FIGURE E3-4. MARS input specification: customer account application

CUSTOMER ACCOUNT APPLICATION
ABCDEF Corporation
Walnut, California

FOR OFFICE USE
ACCOUNT NUMBER
–
EFFECTIVE DATE

FIRM NAME

INDICATE W for WHOLESALE or R for RETAIL ○ | DATE | TELEPHONE | CREDIT CODE | DISCOUNT CODE

STREET ADDRESS

CITY | STATE | ZIP CODE

BANK REFERENCES

NAME	BRANCH	TELEPHONE	
ADDRESS	CITY	STATE	ZIP CODE
NAME	BRANCH	TELEPHONE	
ADDRESS	CITY	STATE	ZIP CODE

OTHER REFERENCES

NAME		TELEPHONE	
ADDRESS	CITY	STATE	ZIP CODE
NAME		TELEPHONE	
ADDRESS	CITY	STATE	ZIP CODE

FOR OFFICE USE
CREDIT APPROVED ☐ DISAPPROVED ☐
IF DISAPPROVED, REASON:

AUTHORIZATION SIGNATURE

NOTE: The customer account application is shown to illustrate input. The other MARS inputs, the billing notice and the payment/credit memo, would remain essentially unchanged from the current system. Since these were presented in this text previously, they are not repeated. They appear in Figure 12-9, "Inputs to manual A/R system."

Figure E3-5. MARS high-level system flowchart

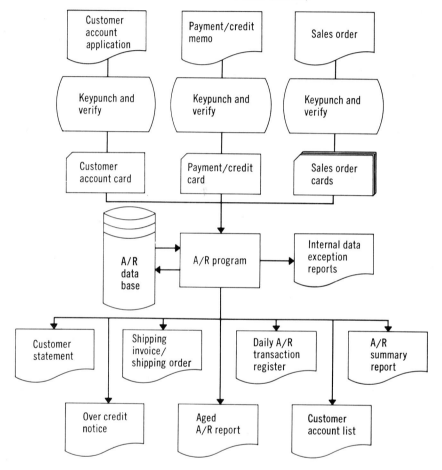

SYSTEM FLOWCHART
MODIFIED A/R SYSTEM (MARS)

SYSTEM FLOWCHART NARRATIVE

1. Customer account applications, payment/credit memos, and sales orders are the three major system inputs.

2. Each source document is keypunched and verified.

3. The A/R program inputs the transaction data cards and reads/updates the master file on magnetic disk. Program edit routines produce exception reports whenever invalid input data is detected.

4. The seven major outputs of the system are the customer statements, invoice/shipping order, A/R transaction register, A/R summary report, overcredit notice, aged A/R report, and a customer account list.

FIGURE E3-6. MARS expanded system flowchart and HIPO charts

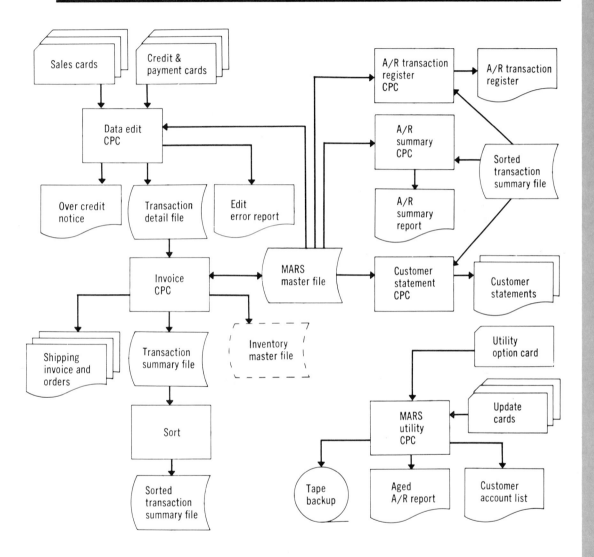

NOTE: The narrative is not included here, but may be found on pages 248-249.

FIGURE E3-6 continued

HIERARCHY CHART FOR MARS

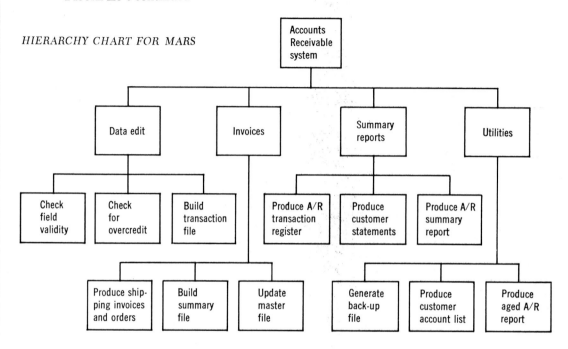

IPO DETAIL CHART: DATA EDIT MODULE

INPUTS	PROCESSING	OUTPUTS
1. Sales cards	1. Check validity of account number	1. Transactions detail file (disk)
2. Credit and payment cards	2. Check validity of all numeric fields	2. Edit error report
3. Master file	3. Check for overcredit status	3. Overcredit notices

FIGURE E3-7. Disk record layout worksheet

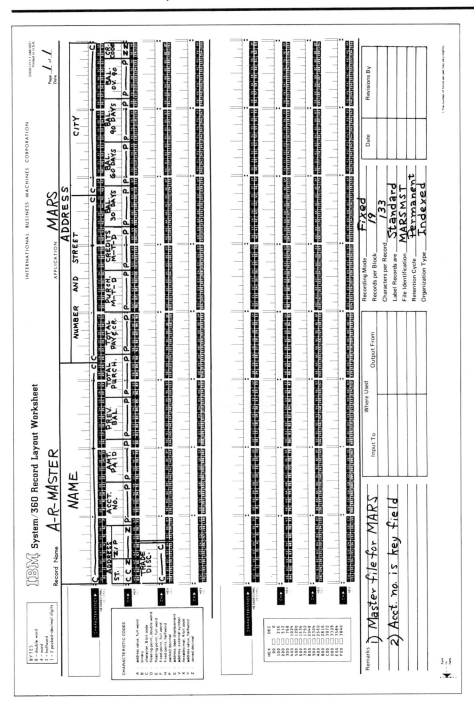

FIGURE E3-8. MARS system flowchart—Data Edit CPC

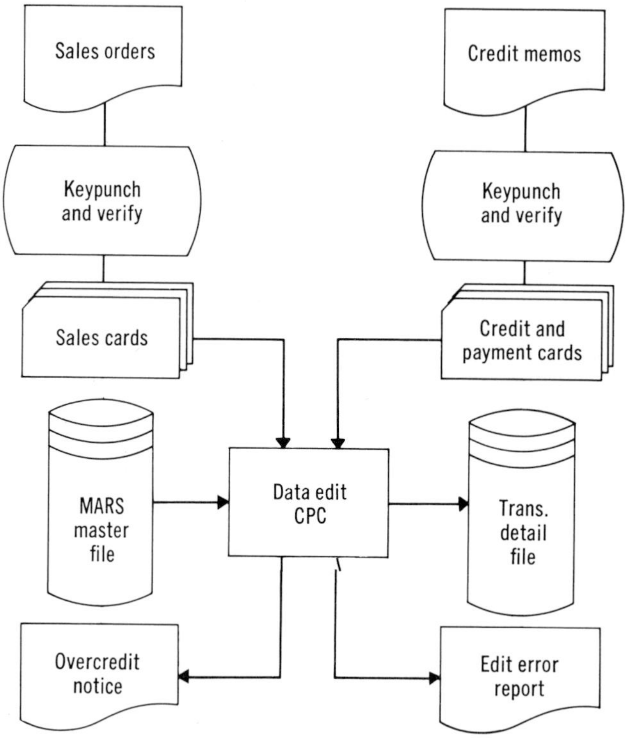

Data Edit CPC--MARS

1. Sales order and credit memo data are keypunched. Batches will be verified at random.

2. Sales and credit cards are batched for input to the Data Edit CPC.

3. Input cards are sorted into ascending order by account number. All fields are checked for validity. The amounts of the order less credits are added to customer balance. If the new balance exceeds the credit limit (stored in the master file), special approval is required or the order is rejected. A rejected order results in the creation of an overcredit notice. All transaction details not causing an overcredit condition are written into the transaction detail file.

Figure E3-9. Computer program flowchart—Data Edit CPC

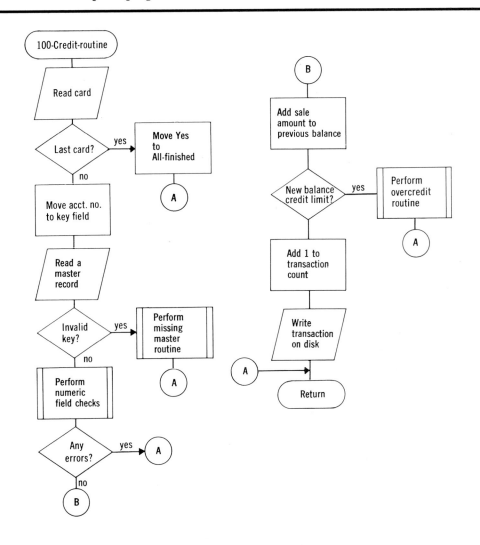

FIGURE E3-10. Multiple-card layout formats

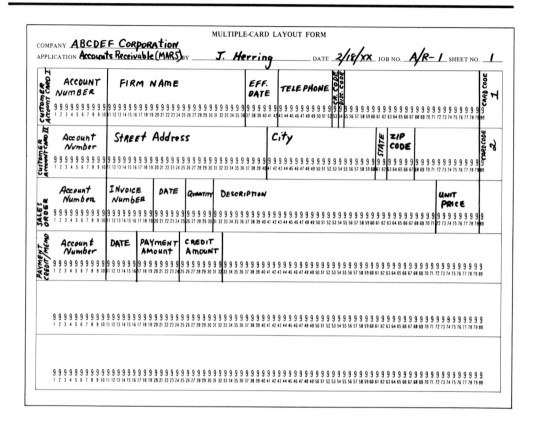

FIGURE **E3-11.** Data Edit coding sample

```
080010    100-NOTE.
080020        NOTE********************************************************
080030        *     THIS ROUTINE IS PERFORMED FOR CREDIT CARDS.            *
080040        *     IT CHECKS FOR INVALID NUMERIC FIELDS AND SALE AMOUNT   *
080050        *     OVER CREDIT LIMIT.                                     *
080060        *********************************************************** .
080070
080080
080090    100-CREDIT-ROUTINE.
080100
080110        READ CARD-FILE
080120            AT END
080130                MOVE 'YES' TO ALL-FINISHED
080140                GO TO 100-CREDIT-ROUTINE-EXIT.
080150        MOVE ACCOUNT-NUMBER TO RECORD-KEY.
080160        READ MASTER-FILE
080170            INVALID KEY
080180                PERFORM 1001-MISSING-MASTER
080190                GO TO 100-CREDIT-ROUTINE-EXIT.
080200        PERFORM 1002-NUMBER-FIELD-CHECK.
090010        IF ANY-ERRORS
090020            PERFORM 1003-WRITE-EXCEPTION-RECORD,
090030            GO TO 100-CREDIT-ROUTINE-EXIT.
090040        ADD SALE-AMOUNT, PREVIOUS-BALANCE GIVING NEW-BALANCE.
090050        IF NEW-BALANCE IS GREATER THAN CREDIT-LIMIT (CREDIT-CODE),
090060            PERFORM 1004-WRITE-OVERCREDIT-NOTICE,
090070            GO TO 100-CREDIT-ROUTINE-EXIT.
090080        ADD 1 TO TRANS-COUNTER.
090090        WRITE TRANS-RECORD.
090100
090110    100-CREDIT-ROUTINE-EXIT.
090120        EXIT.
```

Figure E3-12. Detailed milestones—Development Phase

PROJECT PLAN AND STATUS REPORT		
PROJECT TITLE	PROJECT STATUS SYMBOLS O Satisfactory	
MARS	□ Caution △ Critical	J. Herring
DEVELOPMENT		PROGRAMMER/ANALYST
PHASE	PLANNING/PROGRESS SYMBOLS □ Scheduled Progress V Scheduled Completion ■ Actual Progress ▼ Actual Completion	COMMITTED DATE 6/19/xy COMPLETED DATE STATUS DATE 6/12/xy

ACTIVITY/DOCUMENT	PERCENT COMPLETE	STATUS	PERIOD ENDING (week) 1–18
DEVELOPMENT PHASE	95	O	
Implementation Plan	100	O	
Test Plan	100	O	
Training Plan	100	O	
Conversion Plan	100	O	
Equip.Acquisition&Install.	100	O	
Computer Prog. Dev.	100	O	
Comp. Prog. Design	100	O	
Coding & Debugging	100	O	
Computer Prog. Tests	100	O	
Reference Manual Prep.	100	O	
Programmer's Man.	100	O	
Operator's Man.	100	O	
User's Manual	100	O	

PROJECT PLAN AND STATUS REPORT		
PROJECT TITLE	PROJECT STATUS SYMBOLS O Satisfactory	
MARS	□ Caution △ Critical	J. Herring
DEVELOPMENT		PROGRAMMER/ANALYST
PHASE (cont.)	PLANNING/PROGRESS SYMBOLS □ Scheduled Progress V Scheduled Completion ■ Actual Progress ▼ Actual Completion	COMMITTED DATE 6/19/xy COMPLETED DATE STATUS DATE 6/12/xy

ACTIVITY/DOCUMENT	PERCENT COMPLETE	STATUS	PERIOD ENDING (week) 1–18
Personnel Training	100	O	
System Tests	100	O	
Changeover Plan	100	O	
System Specification	100	O	
Dev. Phase Report	100	O	
Dev. Phase Review	0	O	

FIGURE E3-13. Development Phase costs

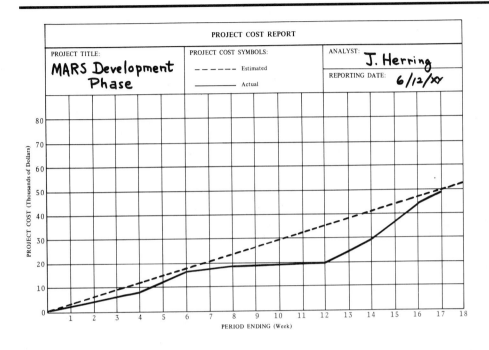

FIGURE E3-14. Major milestones—total project

PROJECT PLAN AND STATUS REPORT																			

PROJECT TITLE: MARS - MAJOR MILESTONES

PROJECT STATUS SYMBOLS
O Satisfactory
□ Caution
△ Critical

J. Herring
J. Herring
PROGRAMMER/ANALYST

PLANNING/PROGRESS SYMBOLS
□ Scheduled Progress   ∨ Scheduled Completion
■ Actual Progress   ▼ Actual Completion

COMMITTED DATE 6/19/xy   COMPLETED DATE   STATUS DATE 6/12/xy

ACTIVITY/DOCUMENT	PERCENT COMPLETE	STATUS	PERIOD ENDING (week) 1–14
STUDY PHASE	100	0	
Initial Investigation	100	0	
Performance Spec.	100	0	
Study Phase Report	100	0	
Study Phase Review	100	0	
DESIGN PHASE	100	0	
Allocation of Functions	100	0	
Comp. Prog. Functions	100	0	
Test Requirements	100	0	
Design Specifications	100	0	
Design Phase Report	100	0	
Design Phase Review	100	0	

PROJECT PLAN AND STATUS REPORT

PROJECT TITLE: MARS - MAJOR MILESTONES (cont.)

PROJECT STATUS SYMBOLS
O Satisfactory
□ Caution
△ Critical

J. Herring
PROGRAMMER/ANALYST

PLANNING/PROGRESS SYMBOLS
□ Scheduled Progress   ∨ Scheduled Completion
■ Actual Progress   ▼ Actual Completion

COMMITTED DATE 6/19/xy   COMPLETED DATE   STATUS DATE 6/12/xy

ACTIVITY/DOCUMENT	PERCENT COMPLETE	STATUS	PERIOD ENDING (week) 15–32
DEVELOPMENT PHASE	95	0	
Implementation Plan	100	0	
Equipment Acquisition	100	0	
Computer Prog. Dev.	100	0	
Personnel Training	100	0	
System Tests	100	0	
Changeover Plan	100	0	
System Specification	100	0	
Dev. Phase Report	100	0	
Dev. Phase Review	0	0	

FIGURE E3-15. Project cost report—total project

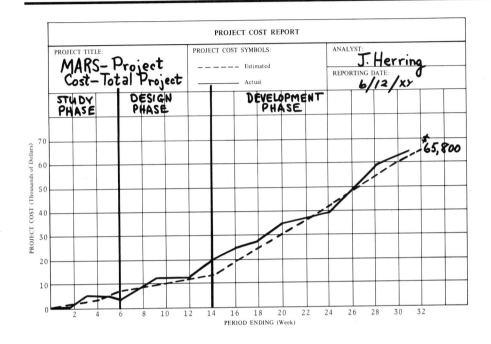

FIGURE E3-16. Weekly operating cost per account

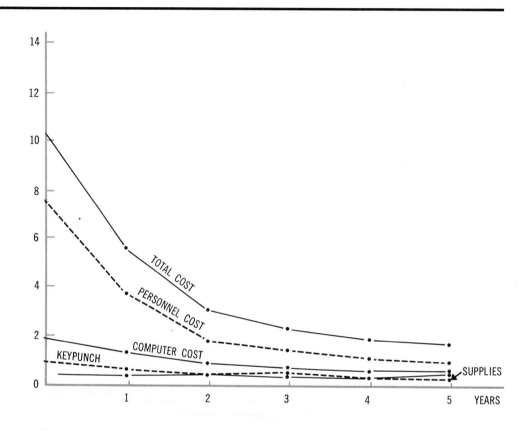

UNIT SIX

THE
OPERATION
PHASE

25   Operation Phase Overview

In the Operation Phase, the system designed and developed in the preceding phases enters operational use and is maintained as an on-going system. The goal of this chapter is to identify the major Operation Phase activities and show the relationships between them. You will obtain an overview and perspective of this phase that will provide a reference and a guide as you study the specific topics in this unit.

OPERATION PHASE STAGES

The Operation Phase follows the Development Phase. Usually it is the longest of the life-cycle phases and is characterized by several distinct stages. Initially, the new system must be introduced into the business activity mainstream. This stage is called changeover. The changeover transition period may take weeks or even months. After it is completed, the system enters the operation and routine maintenance stage. Early in this stage an evaluation of system performance should be made, based on measurements of performance to determine whether the specific benefits claimed for the system have been achieved. Finally, the new system, like all operational systems, must be able to accommodate change. Change is perhaps the most important stage in the life of a computer-based business system. Whether or not change can be managed is the final measure of the success or failure of the entire system effort.

The principal activities and documents that characterize the stages of the Operation Phase are described briefly in the following section.

OPERATION PHASE ACTIVITIES

The major activities of this phase are shown pictorially in the flowchart of FIGURE 25-1, *Operation Phase activities for the computer-based business system.* Each of these activities is summarized as follows:

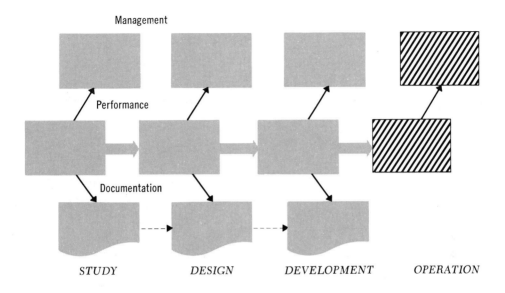

Management

Performance

Documentation

STUDY   DESIGN   DEVELOPMENT   OPERATION

1. *System Changeover.* Normally a period of transition is required to change from an old system to a new one. If all the Development Phase implementation activities have been performed adequately, the necessary manuals and documentation for the new system are available. There is a nucleus of trained personnel (user, programming, and operations) to assume responsibility for the new system. However, it is critically important for the project team to remain heavily involved and in control during changeover. Changeover usually is a one-way process; it must result in a system that is operationally acceptable. No matter how completely changeover activities are planned, numerous unforeseen incidents and problems will arise. This period is the most critical one in the entire life cycle of the computer-based system. Positive support by all user organizations is essential.

2. *Routine Operation.* At the conclusion of the changeover process, the system is considered to be operational. The user organization and other operating personnel assume their respective responsibilities, and procedures are established for change control. Except for routine surveillance and participation in subsequent change activities, the systems analysts' responsibilities to the project are reduced. They and other members of the project team become available to assume other assignments.

3. *System Performance Evaluation.* After the computer-based business system has been operational for a reasonable period, its performance is formally evaluated. The results of the evaluation are documented in an evaluation report, which

**FIGURE 25-1. Operation Phase activities for
the computer-based business system**

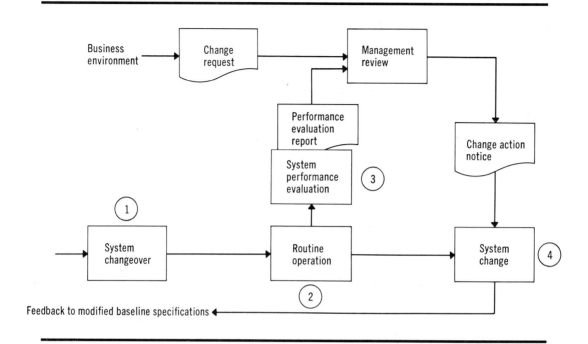

should be presented to a management review board, usually called a performance review board. Although the information service organization should be represented on the performance review board, it should be mainly user-oriented. The board should be headed by the principal user of the system.

4. *System Change.* The modern business system environment is dynamic. It is subject to many internal and external influences. As shown in Figure 25-1, the business environment may trigger a change request, which then is reviewed by management. This process may range from a brief analysis of the requested change to an extensive investigation. This investigation may cause a return to an early point in the life cycle. How far back in the life cycle the investigation might reach would depend upon the original baseline specification affected by the change. The investigation could cause a return to the Study Phase, in which case the resulting new design and development activities might yield a greatly modified system.

At the conclusion of the review and analysis of the requested change, the responsible management organization issues a change action notice. The actual change action is then taken. The potential impact of the change action is shown in Figure 25-1 by the arrow which indicates feedback to the modified baseline specifications.

26 Changeover and Routine Operation

Changeover, which is the period of transition from an old system to a new one, is followed by routine operation. The goal of this chapter is to explain the changeover process and to describe the operation of a data processing organization. You will acquire an understanding of the difficulties of changeover; of how data processing departments are organized; and of the importance of standards, timeliness, and good customer relations.

CHANGEOVER

The changeover "crisis"

The acceptance review, held at the conclusion of the Development Phase, assured the user that the new computer-based business system was ready for operation. At that review, the user was presented with evidence that system-level tests had verified the performance of the system; with assurances that personnel had been trained; and with a detailed plan for changeover. He then decided to proceed to the first stage of the Operation Phase, changeover from the old system to the new one. It might seem, then, that there are no further obstacles to prevent successful implementation and that the project team can be released for new assignments. Nothing could be farther from the truth. Changeover is the most critical and problem-beset period in the life of most computer-based systems. It is the period that tends to prove the truth of the so-called "Murphy's Law": "Anything that can go wrong will go wrong."

The reasons for the "crisis-like" nature of changeover are these:

1. Implementation planning, however complete, cannot possibly take into account all the "real-life" situations that can occur.

2. The more complete the implementation planning, the fewer the unforeseen problems. However, no matter how complete rehearsals have been, it is unrealistic to expect perfect harmony during the initial system performance. For this to occur, all the computer program components must function without error;

Figure 26-1. Changeover crisis frequency

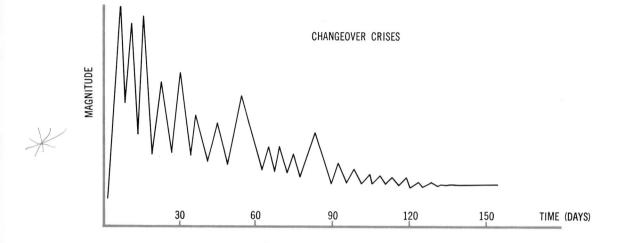

people must not make mistakes; equipment must not malfunction; files must not contain residual elements of contaminated data; and, above all, everyone should be pulling for the success of the system. It is unlikely that the orchestration will be this perfect when the system goes "on stage" for the first time.

3. All changeover methods contain risks. In Chapter 22: Preparing for Implementation, we discussed three changeover methods: parallel operation, immediate replacement, and phased changeover. All introduce new tasks into an actual operational environment. Therefore, mistakes and crises are to be expected.

4. Changeover is an emotional activity. Change suddenly becomes a reality. Things will be different. This realization is sufficient to create tensions which cause and amplify mistakes.

If we were to prepare a graph to illustrate the frequency of the occurrence of crises during a typical changeover, it might look like Figure 26-1, *Changeover crisis frequency.* Initially, everything appears to go wrong at once. Then, after a period of time, the crisis environment begins to improve. The frequency and the magnitude of the crises tend to become less. Finally, a relatively tranquil state is reached. This usually occurs from 60 to 90 days after changeover is initiated.

Changeover activities

The project team must remain intact during changeover. The team contains members of user organizations who must be available on a full-time basis. Here are some practical guidelines for the team's activities during turnover.

1. Compare new outputs with old outputs as much as possible. If outputs differ only in format, it usually is possible to verify content.

2. Check inputs and outputs to be certain that they conform to specifications.

FIGURE 26-2. Changeover action log

CHANGEOVER ACTION LOG				
ACTION NUMBER	ACTION DESCRIPTION	RESPONSIBILITY	DATE ASSIGNED	DATE COMPLETED

3. Follow up immediately on all errors. Correct the manual or machine processes causing the errors.

4. Keep a log. Use this log to record actions, responsibilities, assignments, and completion dates. FIGURE 26-2, *Changeover action log,* is an example.

5. Solve all problems promptly. Seek the cooperation of the user groups in resolving problems and in deciding on immediate corrective measures.

6. Defer any refinements or changes in the system until changeover has been completed.

7. Never expect problems that have not been solved before changeover begins to be solved during changeover. Unsolved problems only tend to multiply.

Changeover is the time at which the project leader must make every effort to keep team spirits high. The project must maintain its momentum. The situation is similar to that of a football team which has the ball on the two-yard line. The entire team must be "charged up" to carry the ball over the goal line. At this time, the earned support and confidence of user groups will pay off. Even a poor system can be made to work with user support. Without it, a good system will fail. Systems are never more vulnerable to attack than during changeover.

If allowed to stay on the sidelines, some users (who are perhaps a bit fearful of the system anyway) will derive satisfaction from the "failures of the computer." It appears to be human nature to mock the failure of a machine, even if the machine is only performing as instructed. To keep them involved, the systems analyst should assign specific responsibilities to all users. They should be made responsible for the prompt solution of systems problems that arise in their areas of operation.

The project leader should strive to sell "success." He must keep the team success-oriented by emphasizing the obstacles overcome rather than those yet to be encountered. Success will breed more success. The crisis environment will begin to abate, and the system will approach a level of performance that justifies its turnover to the user.

User turnover

As we noted when discussing Figure 26-1, crises tend to be reduced to manageable proportions by about 60 to 90 days after the initiation of changeover. The analyst can then consider turning over the system to its users. At this time, all the error conditions noted during changeover will have been corrected, and the system will have gone through several cycles of successful operation. It then becomes the responsibility of the user to operate the system. The project team can be disbanded, and its members can return to their own organizations. Although the information services organization will retain some responsibilities for the system, these will be of a maintenance nature. An analyst will be assigned as a liaison with the user, to participate in resolving system problems. The manner in which maintenance and changes to the system are handled is discussed in Chapter 27: Performance Evaluation and Change Management.

The Data Processing department assumes full responsibility for data processing activities. Turnover to the user initiates a new stage in the Operation Phase. This stage is called routine operation.

ROUTINE OPERATION

Organizing for data processing

We concluded our discussion of changeover by stating that after the system had been turned over to the user, its routine operation became the responsibility of the Data Processing department. In a large Data Processing department, "routine" day-to-day processing is anything but "routine." The operations environment itself, is crisis-laden. The typical environment is one in which a large number of jobs some scheduled and some unscheduled, must be processed amid changing priorities and daily emergencies.

Before discussing "routine" operations in greater detail, let us review the organizational location of the Data Processing department within the company, as well as its internal organization. As we have discussed in earlier chapters, the location of the systems and data processing functions has been changing. FIGURE 26-3, *Trend in location of data processing organization,* illustrates three of the possible locations for the data processing function:

1. *DP-1:* The Data Processing department reports to the financial function. It provides programming and machine operation support. The systems developed are largely financial, and few services are provided to other organizations.

FIGURE 26-3. Trend in location of data processing organization

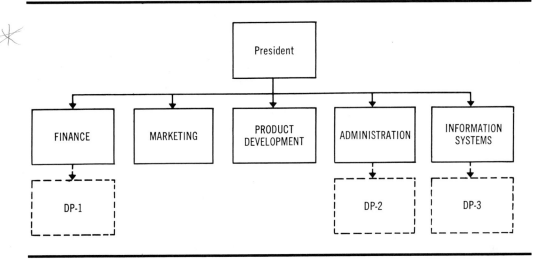

2. *DP-2:* The Data Processing department reports to a general administrator who also has other functional responsibilities. Support services, essentially programming and machine operation, are provided to all functional groups, e.g., finance, marketing, and product development. Systems analysis responsibility is fragmented among users. Applications are limited in scope. The data processing manager usually does not have sufficient authority to initiate or to implement systems that extend beyond organizational boundaries.

3. *DP-3:* The Data Processing department reports to a top executive whose principal responsibility is the development of information systems. These systems often are corporate-wide. A strong systems analysis capability exists in the information systems organization. Innovation is encouraged and is made possible by the status of the organization.

The observable trend in the location of the data processing organization is from DP-1 toward DP-3. We shall limit our discussion to a DP-3-type organization.

Even in an environment in which the data processing and systems analysis functions report to a senior information systems executive, there are many organizational possibilities. For example:

1. Programming and systems analysis may be separate or combined.

2. System analysis may be organized by functions or by projects.

Again, the observable trend is toward an information system organization in which programming is integrated with systems analysis and in which the overall organization is mixed. That is, some activities are organized by function, and others are organized by project. Most commonly, new systems applications are handled on a project basis, and other operations are performed according to function.

FIGURE 26-4. Contemporary information systems organization

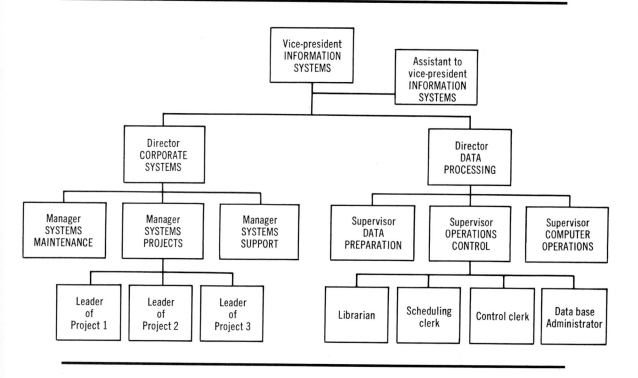

FIGURE 26-4, *Contemporary information systems organization,* illustrates a contemporary organization structure. The director of Corporate Systems and the director of Data Processing report to the vice-president of Information Systems. The corporate systems activity includes both systems analysis and programming. The organization structure is mixed. Systems projects are set up for each new application and, as such, are carried through to turnover to the user. Thereafter, the operational systems become the responsibility of a systems maintenance group. In the event of significant changes, a particular application can revert from maintenance status to project status. System support activities are functional because they are not oriented toward specific applications.

In addition to conventional systems functions such as forms design, records management, and work measurement, the support activities may include the development of techniques such as critical path methods, simulation, and data base management.

As also shown in Figure 26-4, the data processing organization usually is functional rather than project-oriented. An exception would be the dedication of a computer system to a single large project. The principal functional operations are data preparation, computer operations, and operations control. FIGURE 26-5, *Typical data processing job descriptions,* is a brief summary of the operational

FIGURE 26-5. Typical data processing job descriptions

JOB TITLE	DESCRIPTION
Supervisor of Data Preparation	Supervises keypunch and verifier operators in the preparation of data for computer processing. Schedules workloads and distributes work assignments.
Supervisor of Operations Control	Supervises library activities, preparation of schedules, production control procedures, and data base maintenance.
Librarian	Stores and issues program documentation and data files kept on cards, disk, or tape.
Scheduling Clerk	Prepares and maintains daily, weekly, and monthly schedules for all schedulable jobs.
Control Clerk	Checks receipt and acceptability of input data. Establishes batch controls. Checks output. Maintains error records. Dispatches acceptable output to users.
Data Base Administrator	Maintains the integrity of a data base. Organizes, reorganizes, and controls data base definitions and changes. Controls access to the data base.
Supervisor of Computer Operations	Supervises the operation of all computing equipment. Maintains records of equipment performance. Develops techniques to improve performance.

duties associated with the organization chart shown in Figure 26-4. More comprehensive and detailed discussions of job descriptions are available.[1] A relatively new job is that of data base administrator, which has come into existence because of the increasing number and complexity of the data bases being created to support integrated systems. The data base administrator is responsible for the integrity of the data base. He monitors the data base, controls changes to it, maintains its structure, and reorganizes it as required. A data base administrator is essential to the successful implementation and maintenance of the data base management systems (DBMS) discussed in Chapter 19.

It is not our purpose in this chapter to examine data processing operations in detail. Rather, it is to develop for the users of these services (including analysts

1. M. R. Gore and J. W. Stubbe, *Computers and Data Processing* (New York: McGraw-Hill Book Company, 1979).

and programmers) an appreciation of the nonroutine nature of so-called "routine" data processing operations. We will, therefore, discuss data processing operations as they affect a user's evaluation of service.

A data processing operation is evaluated by the service it provides to its users. Good service means that the output is correct and that it gets to the users on time. Accuracy and timeliness are related. We will describe this relationship by referring to two factors by which the performance of a data processing center can be measured: performance standards and timeliness.

Data processing performance standards

The Standards Manual. The rules under which analysts, programmers, operators, and other personnel in an information service organization work are its *standards*. They are the reference against which performance can be measured. Standards vary from organization to organization. While it is not essential that standards be the same in all organizations, it is essential that complete and current *written* standards exist and be understood. Some reasons for the importance of standards are these:

1. The work of analysts and programmers must be understood by other analysts and programmers. This provides back-up.

2. The field of systems analysis, particularly where computers are involved, is changing rapidly. Techniques can be kept current.

3. Communications within a department and between departments are improved.

4. New employees can be trained and can become effective sooner if they learn standard procedures.

5. Changes can be implemented more easily when existing standards can be used as references.

Because they affect all members and functions of the information system organization, standards should be established at an appropriate management level. For example, in the information system organization shown in Figure 26-4, the establishment and maintenance of standards could be a responsibility of a group that reports to the assistant to the vice-president of Information Systems. An information systems organization that lacks standards is not "organized," and therefore is poorly equipped to provide lasting user satisfaction.

Standards are kept in a manual. FIGURE 26-6, *Contents of a standards manual,* lists typical topics. The standards policy is a statement to the effect that all work performed in an organization will be in accordance with the content of the manual. Administrative standards relate to organization charts, job descriptions, training of personnel, and administrative information. Systems analysis standards govern the analysts' activities throughout the life cycle of a business system. For example, standards for coding, forms design, charting, and documentation would appear in a manual for information system development.

Programming standards are rules for activities such as computer program flowcharting, language selection, programming techniques, and program documentation. Operating standards relate to computer and peripheral equipment

FIGURE 26-6. Contents of a standards manual

STANDARDS MANUAL FOR THE
DEVELOPMENT OF INFORMATION SYSTEMS

TABLE OF CONTENTS

I.   STANDARDS POLICY

II. ADMINISTRATIVE STANDARDS

III. SYSTEMS ANALYSIS STANDARDS

IV. PROGRAMMING STANDARDS

V.   OPERATING STANDARDS

operations. The need to pause to comply with standards sometimes appears to conflict with a need for timeliness. Actually, standards contribute to accuracy and so lead to faster service because there are fewer errors and fewer complaints.

Timeliness: Response time, throughput time, and turnaround time

Response Time. The time that elapses between the release of input data by a user and his receipt of computer output is the *response time*. It is the yardstick by which a user measures the timeliness of the output he receives from a computing center. It is a "door-to-door" measurement. Response time includes some elements that are under the control of the data processing manager and some that are not. We can illustrate this by defining two other important "times," throughput time and turnaround time. The relationship between the three times is illustrated in FIGURE 26-7, *Data processing performance times.*

Throughput time is the time required for work to flow through the machine room. *Turnaround time* is the time that elapses between data arrival at the computing center and the availability of output for pickup. Clearly, the time required to deliver the data to the computer center and that required to deliver the output to a user may be beyond the control of the data processing manager. Yet, these times also contribute to response time.

However, throughput time and turnaround time are very much the responsibility of the data processing manager. An effective manager can do much to keep these times to a minimum. We shall discuss throughput time and turnaround time briefly as they relate to the effectiveness of the data processing manager and his supervisor of computer operations.

Throughput Time. Throughput time depends on the efficiency of the computer programs, of the computing equipment, of the operating system, and of the operators. The efficiency of the programs is fixed during the Development Phase,

FIGURE 26-7. Data processing performance times

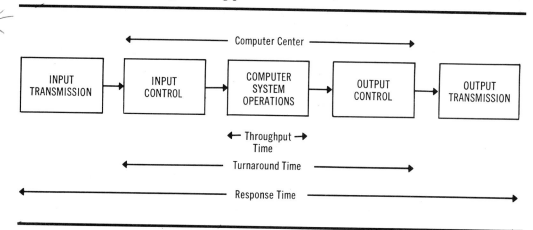

The efficiency of the equipment and of the operating system is of prime concern to the manager of the Data Processing department. By measuring productive machine time (e.g., production processing and program checkout and test), nonproductive machine time (e.g., reruns and set-up time), and maintenance (scheduled and unscheduled), the data processing manager can develop performance standards for equipment. In a multi-programming environment (i.e., when available machine resources can be utilized to process more than one job concurrently), he should determine the best relationship between job mix and computer configuration. As necessary, changes in equipment can be identified and justified. Examples are changes in main storage capacity; selection of peripheral devices, such as card readers and printers; and requirements for tape or disk storage.

Similarly, general installation standards increase the efficiency of operators and thus reduce throughput time. Examples of general installation standards are (1) rules for machine room safety and security; and (2) rules for computer startup and shutdown and for console operation.

Standards for the preparation of operator's reference manuals also are important. We described the general content of the operator's reference manual in Figure 22-5 (Chapter 22). FIGURE 26-8, *Operator's reference manual*, is the same figure. Our purpose in presenting this figure again is to emphasize the fact that specific operating procedures must be developed for each set of related operational duties. Often the entire computer program is not run at once. The sequence and number of computer runs required by an application must be specified in the manual, and the operator must be instructed in a set of duties for each "run." (For this reason, the operator's reference manual is sometimes called a "run manual.") The number of runs required depends on both the installation and the application. Typical factors related to the installation include computer main storage capacity, available direct access storage, and number of tape drives. Examples

FIGURE 26-8. Operator's reference manual

GUIDE TO OPERATOR'S REFERENCE MANUAL

    1. TITLE: Name of computer-based system

    2. PURPOSE: General description of system

  3. OPERATING PROCEDURES,   as appropriate to specific operational duties:

      a.   Operator inputs: A complete description of all inputs, including:

          1) Purpose and use   4) Limitations
          2) Title of input   5) Format and content
          3) Input and media

      b.   Operator outputs: A complete description of all outputs, including:

          1) Purpose and use   3) Output media
          2) Title of output   4) Format and content

      c.   File summary: A complete description of all files, including:

          1) File identification
          2) Medium
          3) Type: Master, transaction, etc.

      d.   Error and exception handling: Procedures for handling
         hardware and software error conditions

---

of factors that depend on the application are file maintenance runs and time taken to detect and correct input data errors before proceeding with mainline processing. FIGURE 26-9, *Computer run sheet,* is an example of the detailed input, output, file, and exception-handling information that must be provided in the operator's reference manual for every run required to process a complete computer program. Meaningful flowcharts also are an aid to the operator. FIGURE 26-10, *File assignment and disposition chart,* is an example of a form for preparing a "picture" that might be contained in a manual as part of run documentation.

A major purpose of standards is to assure that meaningful and accurate outputs are produced. This means that steps taken to ensure valid output may sometimes increase the throughput time. This is one reason why timeliness and accuracy must be considered as related factors which, taken together, determine a user's evaluation of computer center service.

Turnaround Time. Turnaround time is made up of throughput time plus the time required for jobs to pass through input and output control operations. FIGURE 26-11, *Data processing work flow,* is drawn to illustrate the input and output control functions that contribute to turnaround time. This figure is drawn for a typical data processing center that receives work from several plants. The work may be scheduled or unscheduled. The plants may be local or remote. The figure is

FIGURE 26-9. Computer run sheet

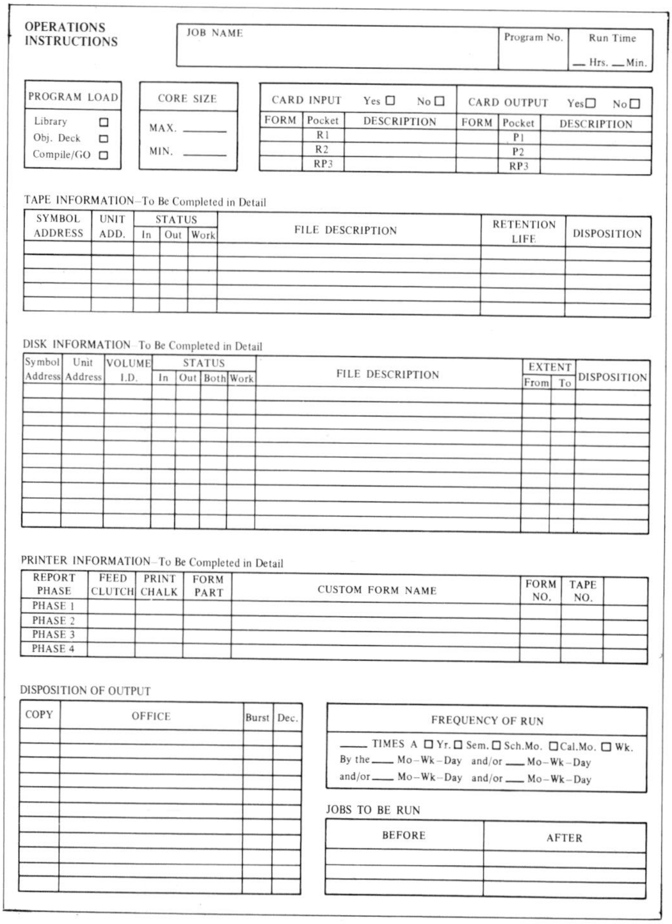

OPERATIONS INSTRUCTIONS

JOB NAME	Program No.	Run Time
		__ Hrs. __ Min.

PROGRAM LOAD	CORE SIZE
Library ☐	MAX. ____
Obj. Deck ☐	MIN. ____
Compile/GO ☐	

CARD INPUT Yes ☐ No ☐		
FORM	Pocket	DESCRIPTION
	R1	
	R2	
	RP3	

CARD OUTPUT Yes☐ No☐		
FORM	Pocket	DESCRIPTION
	P1	
	P2	
	RP3	

TAPE INFORMATION–To Be Completed in Detail

SYMBOL ADDRESS	UNIT ADD.	STATUS In	Out	Work	FILE DESCRIPTION	RETENTION LIFE	DISPOSITION

DISK INFORMATION–To Be Completed in Detail

Symbol Address	Unit Address	VOLUME I.D.	STATUS In	Out	Both	Work	FILE DESCRIPTION	EXTENT From	To	DISPOSITION

PRINTER INFORMATION–To Be Completed in Detail

REPORT PHASE	FEED CLUTCH	PRINT CHALK	FORM PART	CUSTOM FORM NAME	FORM NO.	TAPE NO.	
PHASE 1							
PHASE 2							
PHASE 3							
PHASE 4							

DISPOSITION OF OUTPUT

COPY	OFFICE	Burst	Dec.

FREQUENCY OF RUN

___ TIMES A ☐ Yr. ☐ Sem. ☐ Sch.Mo. ☐ Cal.Mo. ☐ Wk.
By the ___ Mo–Wk–Day and/or ___ Mo–Wk–Day
and/or ___ Mo–Wk–Day and/or ___ Mo–Wk–Day

JOBS TO BE RUN

BEFORE	AFTER

drawn to emphasize the work flow responsibilities of the supervisor of operations control. The only operations shown that relate directly to throughput time are computer processing and printing. Also, as Figure 26-11 indicates, the operations control group is a principal point of contact with the users. It is the point at which inputs are received and outputs are distributed. Often it handles complaints. Therefore, this group must maintain the good user (customer) relations that are essential to the success of the information systems organization.

Customer relations

Good customer relations are important because there will be times when the constructive support and understanding of users are essential to the success of "routine" operations. Fast response, coupled with standards to ensure a quality prod-

FIGURE 26-10. File assignment and disposition chart

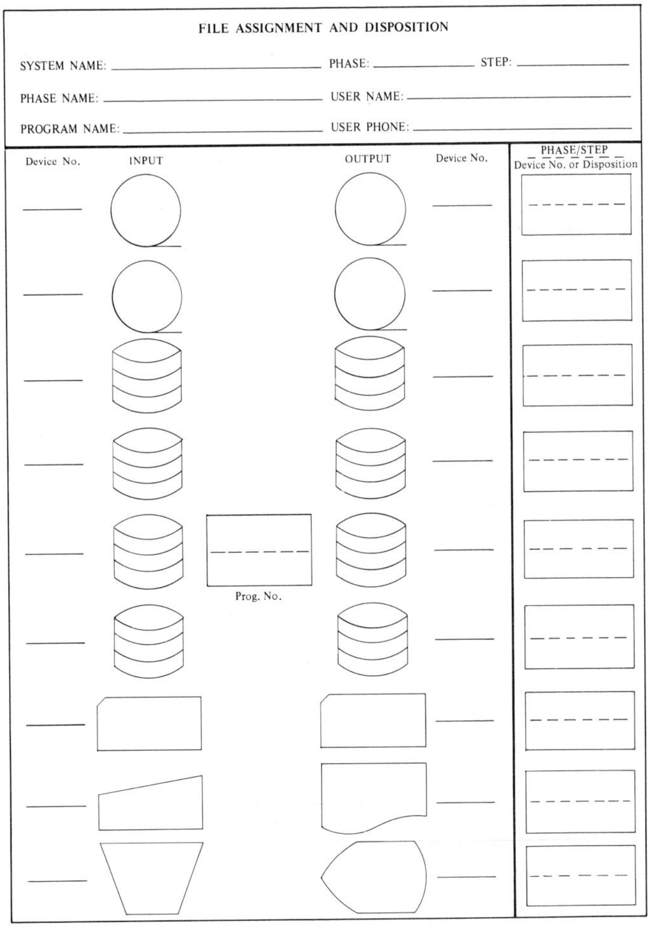

uct, is not always possible. Most computer installations are not "sized" to handle peak loads, such as occur at month end and year end. Priority tasks will arise without warning. At these times performance may slip. Also there always will be unplanned unproductive periods which will cause schedules to slip. Typical causes are machine malfunction and human error. Without customer understanding and support, these periods can be demoralizing and can impair the effectiveness of the entire information services operation.

Security

Management concern about the security of computers often is inflamed by highly publicized incidents of computer-related fraud. The data processing center is

FIGURE 26-11. Data processing work flow

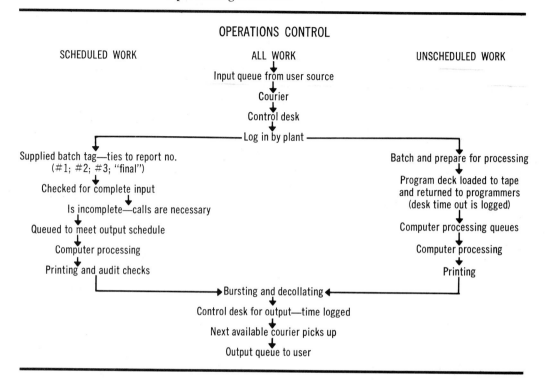

OPERATIONS CONTROL

SCHEDULED WORK   ALL WORK   UNSCHEDULED WORK

Input queue from user source

Courier

Control desk

Log in by plant

Supplied batch tag—ties to report no.
(#1; #2; #3; "final")

Checked for complete input

Is incomplete—calls are necessary

Queued to meet output schedule

Computer processing

Printing and audit checks

Batch and prepare for processing

Program deck loaded to tape
and returned to programmers
(desk time out is logged)

Computer processing queues

Computer processing

Printing

Bursting and decollating

Control desk for output—time logged

Next available courier picks up

Output queue to user

expected to provide not only adequate input, processing, and output controls, but also protection against fraud and disaster. This protection should be a shared responsibility. It is the responsibility not only of the data processing manager, but also of top management, insurance companies, security specialists, and users of data processing service. To provide protection against disasters, certain steps should be taken:[2]

1. *Physical location:* Select a computer site away from natural hazards. Take steps to reduce known risks. For example, water risk can be reduced by storing data in high locations and by providing drains, pumps, and plastic covers for equipment.

2. *Physical access control:* Use badges and controlled entry points. However, the key factor is an alert computer staff who will challenge all strangers.

3. *Fire protection:* Locate the computer center away from fire hazards. Construct the computer area of flame retardant materials. Minimize combustible materials in the computer area. Provide early warning devices, fire detectors, portable extinguishers, and emergency procedures.

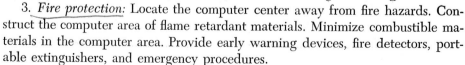

4. *Media protection:* Store vital files in a separate room or vault.

2. Harold Weiss, "Computer Security: An Overview" *Datamation* (January 1974), pp. 42–47.

5. *Back-up and "fall back" capabilities:* If possible, make arrangements with similarly equipped data processing centers.

6. *Risk insurance:* Evaluate insurance policies to cover data processing losses.

In spite of publicity to the contrary, natural disasters are more frequent causes of catastrophe than is fraud. Nonetheless, steps can, and should, be taken to minimize people-induced security problems. These steps include:

1. Division of duties in data processing.
2. Built-in system controls.
3. File and program change controls.
4. Use of a security specialist.
5. •Frequent audits by external auditors.
6. Thorough personnel investigations before hiring.
7. Bonding of staff.
8. Prompt removal of discharged personnel.
9. Protect against voluntary termination by good documentation and cross-training of personnel.

Thus, a well-organized, well-managed, and secure Data Processing department that uses standards effectively can provide the response time and quality of output that will cause a user to evaluate "routine" operations as effective. This attitude is conducive to user tolerance and support during exceptional "non-routine" situations.

KEY TERMS

changeover "crisis"	standards manual	response time
changeover action log	throughput time	computer run sheet
	turnaround time	

FOR DISCUSSION

1. What is the "changeover crisis"?

2. Describe actions which can be taken to manage changeover.

3. What occurs at user turnover time?

4. Why are so-called routine data processing operations not routine?

5. Discuss the organization of a contemporary Data Processing department.

6. What standards are contained in a data processing standards manual? Distinguish between them.

7. Discuss the interaction between standards, timeliness, and user satisfaction.

8. Distinguish between throughput time, turnaround time, and response time.

9. What is the purpose of a run sheet? What is its general content?

10. Discuss steps that may be taken to protect the computer center against natural disasters and against fraud.

ypes of Changeover : parallel, immediate, phased

27

Performance Evaluation and Management of Change

The performance of operational computer-based systems must be evaluated, and they must be modified to meet changes in their environments. The goal of this chapter is to extend the life-cycle management process to the operational life of the system. You will learn a method, involving a performance review board, for evaluating operational systems; and you will learn how to apply the life-cycle methodology to the management of change.

PERFORMANCE EVALUATION

Performance review board

A system cannot be forgotten after it has been accepted for routine operation. The dynamic nature of information systems is an essential aspect of the life-cycle concept. Internal and external factors will cause changes to the operating environment of the system. Typical internal factors that can affect system performance are changes in equipment, in work load, in programming languages, and in personnel. Among the external factors are new or revised reporting needs, increases in required output, and changes in schedules.

Thus, the life-cycle management process continues throughout the operational life of the system. Computer-based business systems tend to fall apart rapidly if formal management control is removed, principally because the validity of system documentation is destroyed. One way in which this occurs is the introduction of many small and inadequately documented changes by programmers who deal informally with members of user groups. Although an informal relationship can be healthy, it should not be permitted to destroy the integrity of the system. If laxity in documentation is tolerated, sooner or later a disaster will occur, and the good relationship with the user will disappear. Another type of change, which usually is poorly documented, is the system patch. A patch is a "quick fix" programming change that is made under the pressure of an immediate operational need. Most often the patch changes one or more of the computer program components. At the time the change is made, the intent is to remove the patch and to rewrite the affected routines in the future—but this particular future never arrives, unless the intent is supported by an approved management plan. In an environment in which managed actions continually are secondary to "crisis responses," the original system quickly becomes completely hidden by patches.

One technique for ensuring system integrity is the establishment of a performance review board (PRB). Both the user and information systems are represented on the PRB. It is, however, a user-oriented board, which should be headed by the principal user. The PRB is continuously aware of the computer-based system through user organization involvement in the routine operation of the system and through a designated member of the systems maintenance staff. The PRB should not be involved continuously in operational problems, but should respond only to exceptional conditions of a nonroutine nature. In addition, periodic reviews (perhaps quarterly) should be scheduled. The first of these scheduled reviews should take place two to three months after the new system has been installed, to compare actual results with planned results. This review is called the post-installation review. Other PRB actions are triggered by requests for changes to the system. The functions of the PRB related to post-installation and periodic reviews are illustrated in FIGURE 27-1, *Performance evaluation.*

Post-installation review

System performance evaluation begins with the post-installation review, which is intended to determine how well actual performance compares with promised

FIGURE 27-1. Performance evaluation

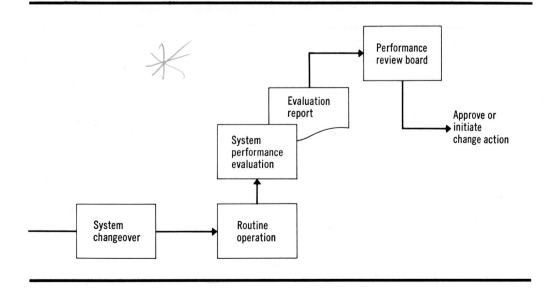

performance. The "promises" were documented as the specific performance objectives, which were in turn derived from the general objectives and anticipated benefits stated in the project directive. This process was described in detail in Chapter 12: System Performance Definition.

The post-installation review should not be scheduled until the changeover crisis is over. Usually this is two to three months after the system has been declared operational. The review should be performed by persons who are not directly responsible for system implementation and operation. They can be selected from the user and system staffs or can be outside auditors or consultants. The first review activity is to gather information related to current system operation. Information-gathering techniques, such as those discussed in Chapter 11: Initial Investigation, can be employed. For example, as a member of the review team, you should:

1. Examine the actual system outputs. Compare them with the outputs in the System Specification.

2. Use the distribution list to send correspondence inquiring about the operating status of the system and its effectiveness. Ask about any problems that have been encountered or that still exist. Solicit suggestions for improvements.

3. Follow up correspondence by interviews with appropriate users of the system outputs, with operating personnel, and with user management.

After completing its information gathering, the team should compare observed current performance with the specific performance objectives. Some specific objectives with which actual performance can be compared are:

1. Elimination of duplicated files.
2. Reduction or reassignment of personnel.
3. Cost savings achieved.
4. Cost avoidance accomplished.
5. Comparison of past and present error rates.

The team then prepares a system performance evaluation report for submission to the PRB. A typical format is shown in FIGURE 27-2, *System performance*

FIGURE 27-2. System performance evaluation report

```
                    SYSTEM PERFORMANCE EVALUATION REPORT


        1. Name of System:


        2. Specific Performance Objectives:


        3. Method of Evaluation:


        4. Results of Evaluation:


        5. Recommendations:
```

Figure 27-3. Specific objectives of MARS

<u>SPECIFIC OBJECTIVES OF MODIFIED</u>
<u>ACCOUNTS RECEIVABLE SYSTEM (MARS)</u>

1. To establish three billing cycles per month—one for each region.

2. To mail customer statements no later than 2 days after the close of each billing cycle.

3. To provide a daily list of A/R transactions.

4. To provide weekly and monthly A/R summary reports.

5. To initiate a finance charge of 1% per month on accounts which are overdue more than 30 days.

6. To identify accounts which have exceeded their credit limit prior to order processing.

7. To introduce controls to reduce the customer monthly statement error rate by 90%—a reduction in errors from 1% to 1/10 of 1%.

8. To provide a capability for listing customer accounts by region.

---

evaluation report. The main elements of the performance evaluation report are these:

1. *Name of system:* Identifies the computer-based business system being evaluated.

2. *Specific performance objectives:* States the specific performance objectives of the computer-based system.

3. *Method of evaluation:* Describes how the system performance was reviewed and evaluated.

4. *Results of evaluation:*

   a. Compares measured performance with the specific performance objectives.

   b. Summarizes other factors, such as user and operator satisfaction, intangible benefits, and pertinent observations of the review team.

5. *Recommendations:* Recommends actions to the PRB. The range of possible recommendations includes (a) accept the system "as is"; (b) recommend minor modification; (c) recommend major revision; and (d) reject and start over.

For examples of some specific performance objectives that might be evaluated after implementations, let us again consider the ABCDEF Corporation's modified accounts receivable system (MARS).

Figure 27-3, *Specific objectives of MARS*, lists the objectives presented in Chapter 12: System Performance Definition. Each of these objectives is "measurable." Each can be evaluated by examining system outputs over several billing cycles and by interviewing users of the system. Thus, actual performance measurement coupled with an assessment of users' satisfaction and suggestions results in a meaningful performance evaluation report. This example, by contrast, clearly illustrates the dilemma that management all too often faces in evaluating systems for which specific performance objectives have not been established.

Periodic review

The post-installation review is followed by periodic reviews, which are intended to ensure that the integrity of the system is maintained and to identify special areas requiring management attention. Two major requirements for system integrity are valid documentation and valid outputs. Management can help to keep documentation valid by supporting performance standards that do not accept undocumented changes. Systems and programming staffs often are under pressure to "perform" and not "write," but continual pressure of this kind usually is due to management's lack of understanding of the true cost of poor documentation. The PRB can rectify this situation, in most cases, by allocating the resources necessary to keep the system intact.

Management also can help to maintain the validity of system output. Errors may remain undetected long after changeover has been completed, or they may creep in as a result of changes made to the system. The PRB should request a periodic audit of the accuracy of system outputs.

Audits may be performed "around" or "through" the system. Those performed "around" the system are external, not an integral part of the system data processing operations. Audits performed "through" the system are designed into the system; they are computer program components that operate upon system data as it is being processed. This type of audit is becoming more common. Statistical sampling techniques also are coming into use as auditing tools. The results of periodic audits should be reported to the performance review board.

Special areas for management attention may come to light only after the system has operated for an extended period. An example is the performance of the system under unplanned conditions, such as an overload due to unanticipated volumes of data to be processed. Some manifestations of problems are subtle. For example, an increasing circumvention of procedures may be the result of system deficiencies that need to be corrected. As another example, absenteeism can disclose much about the effectiveness of the system. If personnel are misplaced or are subjected to continuing high levels of pressure, they will take time off in order to get relief. Reassigning people and rescheduling some of the processing from peak to slack periods may correct this problem.

Throughout all of its reviews, the PRB should be particularly sensitive to users' evaluations of the system. In the final analysis, a system is effective only as long as it continues to be accepted by its users.

MANAGEMENT OF CHANGE

Guidelines for system modification

Computer-based business systems are dynamic. They must be able to accommodate changes in information needs resulting from changes in the business environment. These changes occur not only during the Study, Design, and Development Phases of the life cycle of the system, but also throughout its operational life. Provision must be made for modifying an operational system, for if it cannot be modified without destroying the integrity of its data base and its outputs, it is a failure. Change can be managed by continuing the life-cycle management process by which the system was created. Inherent in this process are two elements that are essential to the management of change. They are (1) the performance review board, which can make management-level decisions about system modifications; and (2) baseline documentation, which can be referred to, to determine the extent and impact of proposed modifications.

In addition to the conduct of post-installation and periodic reviews, the PRB also must evaluate requests for modification of the operational system. Some requests will be planned; others will be unplanned. Some will be extremely significant, others much less so. Obviously, the PRB should not be involved on a continuing daily basis, but only when requirements for system modification rise above a certain threshold of importance. We can identify this threshold by dividing system modifications into two categories and relating each one to the type of baseline specification it affects, as has been done in Figure 27-4, *Modification categories for computer-based business systems*. The categories shown in this figure are *change* and *maintenance*. *Change* is defined as a system modification that requires performance review board action. *Maintenance* is defined as a system modification that does not require performance review board action.

The need for PRB action depends upon the "impact" of a proposed modification, a concept that can be illustrated by again referring to Figure 27-4. Let us first consider the two extremes. We recall that a user-oriented Performance Specification was created at the end of the Study Phase. In the figure, the first entry in the "baseline specification affected" column refers to the user-oriented Performance Specification (as this baseline specification was carried forward into the final System Specification). This type of modification always involves the users of the system. Therefore, the PRB always should be involved. For example, a

FIGURE 27-4. Modification categories for
                    computer-based business systems

MODIFICATION CATEGORY	BASELINE SPECIFICATION AFFECTED
Change (PRB action)	Performance Specification
	Design Specification
Maintenance (no PRB action)	System Specification

change in company credit policy could change the method of billing customers. As another example, a new tax law requiring state withholding tax payroll deductions could affect all of the employees of a company.

At the other extreme, it is not likely that the PRB would be concerned with modifications to the content of the System Specification that are not derived from the original Performance Specification or the original Design Specification. Examples are the development of a more efficient computer program component and minor changes in hardware and software. We can define this type of modification as technical maintenance rather than as change.

However, we must be careful not to include major programming, hardware, and operating system changes in this definition of technical maintenance. These are changes that should be brought to the attention of the performance review boards for all the ongoing computer-based business systems. The reason is that data processing changes of large magnitude probably cannot be made without errors. Some of these errors will cause strange and sometimes catastrophic things to happen to user outputs. Therefore, it is imperative to have the concurrence and support of all principal users throughout the process of planning and implementing major changes to the computer-based business system environment.

To make sure that the potential impact of technical maintenance modifications is not underestimated because of errors of judgment by programmers or the data processing operations staff, the maintenance analyst should approve *all* modifications made to an operational system. Together with the supervisor of programming, the analyst should make certain that specification and documentation standards are observed regardless of the pressure of work load. Following standards is as necessary for a change in a single instruction as it is for the rewriting of large and complicated parts of the overall computer program.

In between the extremes shown in Figure 27-4 are modifications to the System Specification which are derived from the Design Specification written at the conclusion of the Design Phase. The maintenance analyst must judge whether or not the PRB should be involved. Typical situations are those resulting from modifications to the internal system design. Examples are changes in file structure, changes in internal data flow, and minor output revisions. For example, if a report were to be modified slightly by changing the relative position of two output items and by adding a subtotal, the maintenance analyst probably could handle this situation as routine maintenance, and he would deal directly with the users of the report (who probably requested the modification in the first place). However, for any proposed design changes that could have a significant impact on persons supplying input to the system, maintaining the data base, or using the outputs, the maintenance analyst should request the concurrence of the PRB.

We can summarize the foregoing discussion of change and maintenance with the following guidelines for the person designated as the systems analyst responsible for systems maintenance:

1. Evaluate *all* system modifications.
2. Determine whether the modification is maintenance or change.
3. If it is change, bring the modification to the PRB for a decision.

4. Present a written summary of all maintenance modifications at the next periodic meeting of the PRB.

The importance of establishing guidelines and standards for system modification is underscored when we consider the size of the company investment that the maintenance analyst must safeguard. It is estimated that 25 to 50 percent of all systems and programming effort is spent on maintenance. The continuing annual cost to support a newly operational system is approximately 15 percent of the cost to develop it. Because companies have such a large stake in maintaining computer-based systems, a major value of the life-cycle management process is to provide a framework within which modifications can be accomplished, documented, and approved by management. We call this framework change control.

Change control

Change control is the means by which major modifications (changes) to a computer-based business system are managed. By extension, change control also includes the activities and documentation required to preserve the integrity of a system throughout minor modifications (maintenance). Change control is a management process centered on the PRB, which acts as the change control agency. It also relies upon the completeness of the documentation of the computer-based business system. FIGURE 27-5, *Change management process*, is a flowchart that

FIGURE 27-5. Change management process

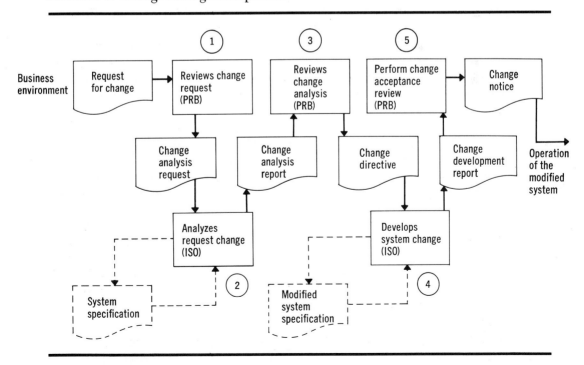

FIGURE 27-6. **Change analysis request format**

CHANGE ANALYSIS REQUEST

1. Name of Computer-based System:

2. Description of Change:

3. Reason for Change:

4. Date of Need:

5. Special Considerations:

---

illustrates this process. The process symbols identified by (PRB) refer to action of the performance review board; those identified by (ISO) refer to actions by the information service organization. With reference to Figure 27-5:

1. The PRB receives all change requests. These may be internal or external in origin. The major internal sources of requests for change are the systems analyst who is responsible for maintaining the system and the operational users of the system. They usually are the persons who can best decide whether a modification is minor and can be handled as maintenance or whether it is major and must be handled as a change. There are many possible external sources of change, e.g., a change in the tax laws. Usually external changes must be implemented, but the process is not much different than the process for implementing changes.

The PRB reviews all requests for change. Those the board does not reject are transmitted to the information services organization by means of a change analysis request. FIGURE 27-6, *Change analysis request format,* outlines its general content. This request initiates a new systems analysis activity. If appropriate, the change analysis request should be accompanied by an Information Service Request (ISR) of the type discussed in Chapter 11: Initial Investigation.

2. Upon receipt of the change analysis request, the information services organization assigns a responsible systems analyst, who will determine the effect of the change on the operational system. The effect depends on the nature of the change and on its impact on the System Specification. Hence, change analysis is an important area in which the necessity for good baseline documentation is evident. As a result of his investigation, the analyst determines how far back in its life cycle the system is affected by the change. For example, a need for new and different user outputs (i.e., an external performance change) would relate to the part of the System Specification that was derived from the original Performance Specification. In this case many Performance, Design, and Development Phase activities might have to be repeated. This process of analyzing the System Specification to determine the effect of the change is shown by the first dashed-line feedback loop of Figure 27-5.

FIGURE 27-7. Change analysis report format

CHANGE ANALYSIS REPORT

1. Name of Computer-based System:

2. Description of Change:

3. Reason for Change:

4. System Modifications:
   a. External Specification:
   b. Internal Specification:

5. Date of Availability:

6. Special Considerations:

After he completes his analysis of the proposed change, the responsible analyst prepares a change analysis report. FIGURE 27-7, *Change analysis report format,* outlines its general content. If the change is feasible, the analyst prepares a draft of an Information Service Request (ISR) to accompany the change analysis report.

3. The PRB receives the change analysis report and reviews it with the systems analyst and with other persons who know the system well. If the board decides to implement the change, a directive to that effect is prepared and sent to the information systems organization. The ISR form is appropriate for this change directive, as is shown in FIGURE 27-8, *Change directive.*

4. Upon receipt of the change directive, the information service organization transfers the computer-based system from maintenance to project status. A project leader is assigned, and modification of the system is started. The steps followed are identical to the life-cycle process for developing a new system. The figure showing this process was originally presented in Chapter 2; it is repeated as FIGURE 27-9, *The life cycle of a computer-based business system.* As previously discussed, the point of reentry into the life cycle depends on which baseline specification is modified. On some occasions it is necessary to start at the beginning and to develop new Performance, Design, and System Specifications. The effort to change the ongoing system sometimes is greater than the effort to develop it in the first place. The requirement for reentering the life-cycle process to modify the system is shown by the second dashed-line feedback loop in Figure 27-5.

The documented result of these activities is a change development report, which is analogous to the Development Phase report prepared when the original system was developed. The change activities correspond to those previously derived from the life-cycle process of Figure 27-9—including the preparation of a change study report and a change design report, if required.

FIGURE 27-8. Change directive

INFORMATION SERVICE REQUEST			Page 1 of 1	

JOB TITLE: Change of Modified Accounts Receivable System	NEW ☒ REV. ☐	REQUESTED DATE: 6/15/xx	REQUIRED DATE: 7/15/xx	

		AUTHORIZATION			
OBJECTIVE: To provide a monthly listing of overcredit accounts		LABOR		OTHER	
		HOURS	AMOUNT	HOURS	AMOUNT
		20	$2,000		

ANTICIPATED BENEFITS:
1. Detection of chronic overdue accounts
2. Revision of credit limits

OUTPUT DESCRIPTION	INPUT DESCRIPTION
TITLE: Overcredit Summary Report	TITLE:
FREQUENCY: Monthly QUANTITY: 1	FREQUENCY:
PAGES: 3 max. COPIES: 4	QUANTITY:
DESCRIPTION: Copies to Regional Sales Managers (3) and Credit Manager (1).	DESCRIPTION:
TITLE:	TITLE:
FREQUENCY: QUANTITY:	FREQUENCY:
PAGES: COPIES:	QUANTITY:
DESCRIPTION:	DESCRIPTION:

TO BE FILLED OUT BY REQUESTOR				
REQUESTED BY: *S. Davis*	DEPARTMENT: 310	TITLE: Head A/R Dept.	TELEPHONE: X3250	
APPROVED BY: *Ben Franklin*	DEPARTMENT: 300	TITLE: Manager Account. Div.	TELEPHONE: X3208	

TO BE FILLED OUT BY INFORMATION SERVICES				
FILE NO: ISR-310-1C	ACCEPTED ☒ NOT ACCEPTED ☐			
SIGNATURE: *C. Hampton*	DEPARTMENT: 200	TITLE: Manager Info. Ser. Div.	TELEPHONE: X2670	
REMARKS: This ISR is accepted as a Change Directive. J. Herring is assigned responsibility for its implementation.				

FORM NO: C-6-1	ADDITIONAL INFORMATION: USE REVERSE SIDE OR EXTRA PAGES

---

5. The change development report is presented to the PRB for a change acceptance review. This review is similar to the original acceptance review. Again, the PRB requires inputs to prove that personnel are trained, the changed system has been tested, and a changeover plan exists.

After a successful acceptance review, the PRB issues a change notice. This notice informs all personnel of the changes to the system and their effective date. The change notice also acts as a cover sheet to which the replacement pages for all affected specifications and other system documentation are attached. FIGURE 27-10, *System change notice format,* shows the typical format.

We have described the formal change process for significant system modifications. As we have previously noted, modifications that have taken place as part of system maintenance activities should be presented at the next scheduled periodic PRB meeting. A formal change notice can then be issued to ensure that these modifications are included as a part of current system documentation.

FIGURE 27-9. The life cycle of a computer-based business system

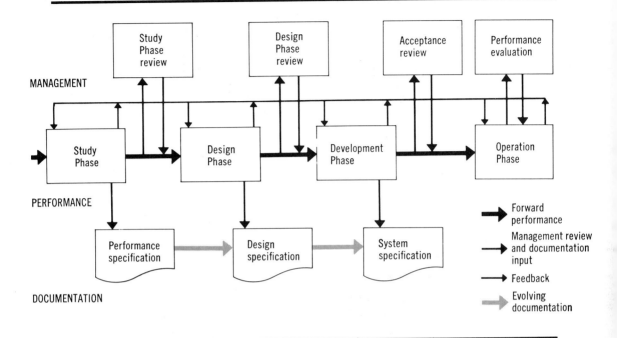

FIGURE 27-10. System change notice format

<u>SYSTEM CHANGE NOTICE</u>

1. Name of Computer-based System:

2. Summary of Change:

3. Effective Date of Change:

4. Log of Specification/Documentation Changes:

    Specification/Documentation   Change pages

In sum: Documentation is the computer-based system

In this final chapter, we have again returned to the concept of a dynamic life cycle and again have stressed the importance of maintaining current system documentation. FIGURE 27-11, *Expanded life-cycle flowchart,* summarizes the theme

FIGURE 27-11. Expanded life-cycle flowchart

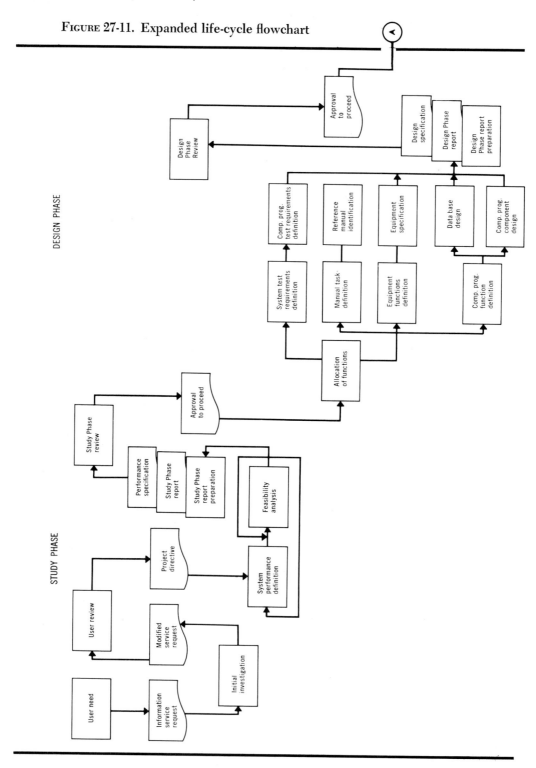

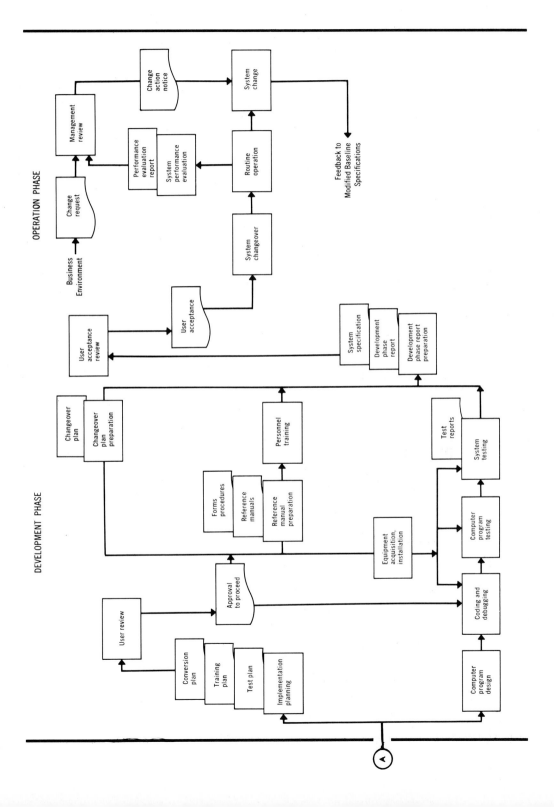

FIGURE 27-12. Documentation structure for
computer-based business systems

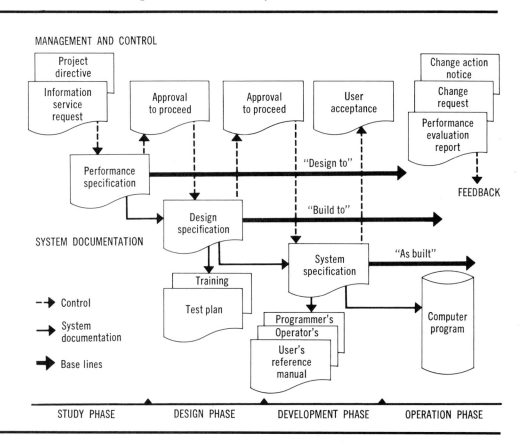

MANAGEMENT AND CONTROL

Project directive

Information service request

Approval to proceed

Approval to proceed

User acceptance

Change action notice

Change request

Performance evaluation report

Performance specification

"Design to"

FEEDBACK

"Build to"

Design specification

SYSTEM DOCUMENTATION

System specification

"As built"

Training

Test plan

Programmer's
Operator's
User's reference manual

Computer program

-→ Control

→ System documentation

▶ Base lines

STUDY PHASE   DESIGN PHASE   DEVELOPMENT PHASE   OPERATION PHASE

of this text. It illustrates the performance, management, and documentation activities that occur throughout all four phases of the life cycle of a computer-based business system. Key documents, extracted from this figure, are shown in FIGURE 27-12, *Documentation structure for computer-based business systems*. This figure is a final summary of the relationship between documentation and effective life-cycle management. The three baseline documents are indicated by lines and arrows extending forward in time. Other important documents are also shown. This figure should remind us that, for a computer-based system, *documentation* is the system.

KEY TERMS

performance review board (PRB)   *periodic review*   *maintenance*
post-installation review   *change*   *change control*

FOR DISCUSSION

1. What is the purpose of a performance review board? Who should be on this board?

2. Under what circumstances are undocumented changes acceptable?

3. What is the purpose of the post-installation review? When should it be scheduled?

4. Why are periodic reviews held?

5. Distinguish between modification, change, and maintenance.

6. Describe the change management process.

7. Discuss the statement: "Documentation is the computer-based system."

GLOSSARY

Achievement Index—Actual achievement divided by planned achievement.

Activity—The application of time and resources to achieve an objective.

Algorithm—A set of rules or instructions used to accomplish tasks.

Alphabetic code—A code that describes an item by the use of letter and number combinations.

Alphabetic derivation code—A code that uses characters taken from the name or description of the coded item according to a set of rules.

Analysis—The process of breaking something down into its parts so that the whole may be understood.

Baseline specification—A document that is a reference for change. The three baseline documents for a computer-based business system are the Performance Specification, the Design Specification, and the System Specification.

Block sequence code—A series of consecutive numbers divided into blocks. Each block is reserved for identifying a group of items with a common characteristic.

Blocking factor—The number of logical records in each physical record.

Box style—A forms design style that allocates space to each data item. Each box is clearly identified by name or by a brief description.

Buffer—A memory area used to store data temporarily. A typical use is as a component of an intelligent terminal.

Business—A combination of personnel, material, facilities, and equipment into an enterprise to accomplish specific objectives and to achieve defined goals. A business is made up of integrated elements called systems. See *System.*

Business system—See *System.*

Carriage control tape—A loop of paper containing coded holes used to identify positions on continuous forms being run on line printers.

Cathode ray tube (CRT) display—A television-like input or output station that displays information.

Change—A system modification that requires performance review board action.

Change control—The means by which major modifications (changes) to a computer-based business system are managed.

Changeover—The period of transition from the old system to the new system.

Chart—A graphical or pictorial method of expressing relationships or movement.

COBOL—*CO*mmon *B*usiness *O*riented *L*anguage. A business data processing language.

Code—A group of characters used to identify an item of data and to show its relationship to other items of a similar nature.

Code plan—A plan identifying the particular characteristics of an item to be contained in a code.

Coding—The writing of program instructions in a programming language such as COBOL, FORTRAN, or RPG.

Communication—The process of transferring information from one point to another.

Computer-based business system—A business system that uses a computer for storing and processing data essential to the performance of the system.

Computer-oriented system—A system in which the capabilities of humans and computer have been blended to take advantage of the unique capabilities of each.

Computer output microfilm (COM)—Computer output that is photographed onto small areas of film called microfilm.

Computer program—A major subsystem of a computer-based business system; it is the collection of all components or modules which share a data base. See *Computer program component.*

Computer program component (CPC)—A module consisting of a set of instructions for inputting data, processing data, and producing output. A computer program component is a major subdivision of a computer program and shares a data base with other computer program components.

Constraint—A condition, such as time or money, that limits the solutions a systems analyst may consider.

Control—The actions taken to bring the difference between an actual output and the desired output within an acceptable range.

Conversion—The process of initiating and performing all the physical operations that result directly in the turnover of the new system to the user.

Cost Index—Actual costs divided by planned costs.

CPC—See *Computer program component.*

Critical path network—A planning and management tool that uses a graphical format to depict the relationship between tasks and schedules.

Cut forms—Single-page forms designed by a user and printed in-house or by a local printer.

Data—Any set of related characters organized in a manner that facilitates identification, storage, or processing. Data may be in the form of fields, records, or files. It usually is considered as an input to computer processing.

Data base—One or more linked master files containing non-redundant data that is shared by related computer applications.

Data base administrator—The administrator with authority to control the data base management system (DBMS).

Data base management system (DBMS)—Software that allows data base descriptions to be independent from computer program components. It provides the capability of describing the logical relationships between files, records, or fields to facilitate efficient maintenance and access of the data base.

Data element—See *Field.*

Debugging—The process of correcting computer code to obtain correct results.

Decision table—A tabular technique for describing logical rules.

Design Phase—The phase during which the problem solution that was selected in the Study Phase is designed. The design includes the allocation of system functions; the design of inputs, outputs, and files; and the identification of system and component test requirements.

Design Specification—A baseline specification that defines how to construct a computer-based business system.

Detail file—See *Transaction file*.

Development Phase—The phase in which the computer-based system is constructed from the "blueprint" prepared in the Design Phase. Equipment is acquired and installed. All necessary procedures, manuals, and other documentation are completed. Personnel are trained, and the complete system is tested for operational readiness.

Edit characters—Symbols used to punctuate numeric data fields to increase readability. Common examples are dollar signs, commas, and decimal points.

Environment—The assembly of external factors that affect a business or a system. These factors are constraints on the study leading to the creation of a computer-based business system.

Era—A significant interval in the development of computers. The eras are Early Era (1940–1955), the Growing Era (1955–1964), the Refining Era (1964–1979), and the Maturing Era (1979–?).

Event—The point in time at which an activity begins or ends.

Feasibility analysis—The feasibility of designing the system is determined by evaluating alternate methods of converting available input data into the required outputs in order to achieve the system objectives.

Feedback—The process of comparing an actual output with a desired output for the purpose of improving system performance.

Field—A meaningful collection of characters; a data element.

File—A meaningful collection of records. See *Master file* and *transaction file*.

Flowchart—A pictorial representation using predefined symbols to represent data flow in a business system or the decision logic of a computer program. See *System flowchart* and *Program flowchart*.

FORTRAN—*FOR*mula *TRAN*slation. A mathematically oriented data processing language.

Goal—A broadly stated purpose of a business. See *Objective*.

Group classification code—A code that designates major, intermediate, and minor data classifications by successively lower orders of digits.

Hardware—A physical end-product that is described primarily in terms related to characteristics that can be readily observed and measured as it moves from concept to end-product.

Hierarchy chart—A planning chart that shows the hierarchy of functions. It is one chart of the HIPO charting technique.

HIPO (Hierarchy plus Input, Process, Output)—A graphic design method for describing the functions that a system must perform. HIPO design proceeds from the most general level to the most detailed. The method uses two charts: a hierarchy chart and an IPO chart.

Human-oriented systems—Business systems designed around a pattern of manual operations.

Implementation—The process of bringing a developed system into operational use and turning it over to the user.

Information—Meaningful data upon which action can be based. It is usually the result of processing, which transforms raw data into useful outputs, such as reports.

Information flow—The network of administrative and operational documentation necessary for product flow. See *Product flow*.

Information-oriented flowchart—Flowcharts that show information (document) flow through an organization.

Information Service Request (ISR)—Formal request for systems analysis support.

Initial investigation—An investigation directed toward clarifying the problem assignment and strengthening the analyst's background in the problem area.

Input design—The process of converting a user-oriented description of computer-based business system inputs into a programmer-oriented specification.

Integrated information system—An information system that uses multiple linked data bases, each designed to meet a limited corporate information need.

Intelligent terminal—A computer system input or output station that can be used for local processing of data, e.g., data editing, validation, and correction.

Interface—A shared boundary, e.g., the linkage between two data bases provided by common data element descriptions.

IPO (Input, Process, Output)—A detail-level chart listing the inputs, processing steps, and outputs of each functional module of a hierarchy chart. One of two charts used for the HIPO charting technique.

Key-to-disk—A data recording unit that records data on a magnetic disk.

Key-to-tape—A data recording unit that records data on a magnetic tape, cassette, or cartridge.

Life cycle—The cycle of a computer-based business system which has four time-dependent phases: Study, Design, Development, and Operation. It includes the concept of feedback. See *Feedback*.

Linear programming—A management science technique, which often makes use of the computer. It involves the use of a mathematical model to find the best combination of available resources to achieve a desired result.

Logical record—The unit of data that is operated on by a computer program.

Maintenance—A system modification that does not require performance review board action.

Management Information System (MIS) An information system that provides decision information needed by managers. An MIS is characterized by at least one level of vertical integration and by feedback and control.

Manual—Printed and assembled pages of instructional material.

Manual systems—See *Human-oriented systems*.

Matrix—A table used to formalize the process of selecting and evaluating alternatives.

Master file—A file that contains relatively permanent (i.e., slowly changing) data.

Mnemonic codes—Letter and number combinations obtained from descriptions of the coded item which serve as a memory aid.

Modification—Action taken to maintain or to change an operating system.

Narrative—Informal technical writing in a "story" style.

Network—A graphical representation of related activities and events.

Objective—A concrete and specific accomplishment necessary to the achievement of a goal. See *Goal.*

Open style—A form consisting of headings and open areas in which data can be entered. No specific data item is called for, nor is any specific space allocated.

Operation Phase—The phase in which changeover from the old system to the new system occurs. The system is then operated and maintained. System performance is audited, and change to the system is managed.

Optical character reader (OCR)—A computer system input unit that can recognize special, written character symbols.

Organization function list—A document prepared for each organization shown on an organization chart to describe the specific major activities performed by that organization.

Payback analysis—The determination of the length of time necessary to recover system development costs.

Performance review board—A user oriented board responsible for monitoring and evaluating the performance of a computer-based system and for maintaining the system's integrity.

Performance Specification—A baseline specification that describes what a computer-based business system is to do. It is completed at the conclusion of the Study Phase.

PERT—Program Evaluation Review Technique. It is a management planning and analysis tool that uses a graphical display (network) to show relationships between tasks that must be performed to accomplish an objective.

Phase—One of the four major stages (Study, Design, Development, and Operation) making up the life cycle of a system.

Physical record—The unit of data transferred by one input or output operation.

Policy—Broad written guidelines for conduct or action. See *Procedure.*

Principal user—The person who, in practice, will accept or reject the computer-based business system.

Print chart—A form used in the design of printer outputs. It allows for a description of titles, column headings, detailed data, and totals. It also shows print positions and vertical spacing.

Procedure—Specific statements that tell how policies are to be carried out. See *Policy.*

Procedure-analysis flowchart—A flowchart which records the details of manual operations in pictorial form.

Process—An operation that converts, or transforms, inputs into outputs.

Process-oriented flowchart—Identifies the sequence of operations performed upon data. Commonly referred to as "system flowchart."

Product flow—The flow of raw materials into subassemblies, then into assemblies, and finally into finished goods. See *Information flow.*

Program flowchart—A pictorial representation, using predefined symbols, of the operations and decision logic required to prepare a computer program.

Project directive—The formal, mutual commitment that binds the user and the analyst throughout an information system project (as distinguished from less comprehensive or intermediate Information Service Requests).

Punched card—A card that contains data or instructions coded in a machine-readable format.

Record—A meaningful collection of fields, or data elements.

Report—A formal communication of results and conclusions from a particular set of actions.

Response time—The time that elapses between the user's release of input data and his receipt of computer output.

Self-checking code—A code using a check digit to check the validity of the code.

Sequence codes—Coding systems in which codes are assigned in sequence. See *Simple sequence codes* and *block sequence codes.*

Significant digit code—A numeric code in which the numbers describe a measurable physical characteristic of the item.

Simple sequence code—The assignment of consecutive numbers (e.g., 1, 2, 3, . . .) to a list of items as they occur.

Simulation—One of the techniques for the design of business systems.

Software—A collection of programs and routines that facilitate the use of the computer. Software includes compilers, assemblers, utility routines, and application programs. The latter is normally the end-product associated with computer-based business systems. Unlike hardware, software does not have physical characteristics that can be readily observed and measured as it moves from concept to end-product.

Specialty forms—Forms that are complex enough in their construction to require special equipment for their manufacture or use. Examples are multiple-copy forms, forms with special binding, and forms designed to be completed with the use of a machine.

Specification—Documents that contain basic detailed data.

Standards—The rules under which analysts, programmers, operators, and other personnel in an information service organization work.

Status Index—Achievement Index divided by the Cost Index.

Structured walk-through—A technical review performed to assist the technical people working on a project. It is one of a series of reviews that should be a planned part of system design and development activities.

Study Phase—The phase during which a problem is identified, possible solutions are studied, and recommendations are made with regard to committing the resources required to design a system.

Subsystem—A subdivision of a system, which produces an intermediate or final system output. See *System.*

Symbolic language—Languages that permit the programmer to write his program using symbols more meaningful to him than machine language.

Synthesis—The process of putting parts together to form a new whole.

System—A combination of personnel, material, facilities, and equipment working together to convert inputs into outputs. A system includes its methods and procedures. A system may be made up of subsystems. It is, in turn, a major element of a business.

System flowchart—A pictorial representation, using predefined symbols, of operations performed by or of information flow between the elements of a business system.

System Specification—A baseline specification containing all the essential computer-based business system documentation. It is completed at the end of the Development Phase.

System team—A group of involved, interested people who can represent their respective areas to help define system problems and develop methods of solution. Typically, user organizations, management, and data processing should be represented on the team.

Systems analysis—The performance, management, and documentation of the four phases of the life cycle of a business system.

Systems analyst—An individual who is responsible for the performance of systems analysis for all or part of the business system during any, or all, of the phases of its life cycle.

Systems and procedures—The predecessor organization to systems analysis, which dealt primarily with manual systems.

Terminal—An input or output device located apart from a computer.

Throughput time—The time required for work to flow through the machine room. See *Response time* and *Turnaround time*.

Top-down—A procedure by which a system is developed first as major modules, which are then expanded into levels of more detailed modules.

Total information system—An information system that attempts to satisfy all the information needs of a corporation from a single large data base.

Transaction file—A file that contains relatively transient (i.e., rapidly changing) data. It is also called a detail file.

Turnaround time—The time that elapses between data arrival at the computing center and the availability of output for pickup. See *Response time* and *Throughput time*.

Usability—The worth of data processing systems to the end-users, as users perceive the systems' quality and contribution to productivity.

User—An individual who, in the course of the performance of his job, must provide input data to, or use information generated by, a computer-based business system. A user also is an individual who, to a significant degree, is affected by a computer-based business system.

BIBLIOGRAPHY

The ABC's of Effective Charts. Skokie, Ill.: International Minerals and Chemical Corporation.

This publication describes the four basic types of charts and provides guidelines for their construction and use. Many examples are included.

Awad, Elias M. *Business Data Processing.* Englewood Cliffs: Prentice-Hall, 1971 (pp. 52-66).

Chapter 3 describes the key business operations within an information flow framework. This description is valuable in distinguishing between product flow and information flow in a business organization.

Business Systems. Cleveland: Systems and Procedures Association, 1966 (pp. 9-1 to 9-22).

The referenced chapter, entitled Formalizing, is a good introduction to the preparation of policies, procedures, and manuals.

Carnegie, Dale. *How to Win Friends and Influence People,* New York: Simon and Schuster, 1936.

This book is a classic and highly successful salesmanship primer. It is highly recommended reading for all systems analysts.

Chapin, Ned. *Computers: A Systems Approach.* New York: Van Nostrand-Reinhold, 1971 (pp. 150-426).

Section III, Computer Hardware, and Section IV, Computer Software, provide a complete, not highly technical, overview of these two important areas.

Chapin, Ned. *Flowcharts.* Princeton: Auerbach Publishers, 1971.

This brief, comprehensive book covers system flowcharts, computer program flowcharts, and the use of templates. It describes the history of flowcharts, their interpretation, and their use. It includes many examples of flowcharts and is recommended reading for all programmers, analysts, and users of computer-based systems.

Data Processing Techniques: Form and Card Design (C20-8078) White Plains: IBM Technical Publications Department, 1961.

This publication is a summary description of card design techniques, including discussions of field size, data sequence, card types, and card layout. Detailed instructions are presented for preparing specialty card layout forms.

Feingold, Carl. *Introduction to Data Processing.* Dubuque: Wm. C. Brown Company Publishers, 1971 (pp. 1-29).

Part I, Introduction to Data Processing, reviews the history of computers and includes some speculations about their future.

Forrester, Jay. *Industrial Dynamics.* New York: John Wiley and Sons, 1961.

This book is a classic. It is an analytic approach to the design of business information systems. The author's approach is based on feedback and control theory, decision-making theory, and the use of the digital computer as a simulation tool. Forrester has in subsequent books extended this approach to include urban and world dynamics.

Huff, Darrel, *How to Lie with Statistics.* New York: W. W. Norton, 1954.

This excellent small book is a humorous and informal primer on the misuses that may be made of statistics. For example, Chapter 5, entitled the Gee-Whiz Graph, exposes the trickery in unscrupulous manipulation of the scales between the ordinate and abscissa on charts. It is similarly enlightening in other areas of numerical and graphical communications.

Hughes, Joan K., and Jay I. Michtom. *A Structured Approach to Programming.* Englewood Cliffs: Prentice-Hall, Inc., 1977.

This book introduces a structured approach to programming and how to manage it. Topics include HIPO charts, structured walk-throughs, and testing .

IBM Data Processing Techniques: Coding Methods (F20-8093). White Plains: IBM Technical Publications Department.

This manual lists and describes the requirements for constructing adequate codes. It contains many examples of the common types of codes.

IBM System/3: Card System Introduction (GC21-7505-0). Rochester: IBM Corporation, Programming Publications, Department 425, 1969.

This manual includes a detailed description of the 96 column card and of the 96 column card multiple layout form, with planning guidelines for card layout.

Improved Programming Technologies: Management Overview (GE19-5086). Zoetermeer: IBM World Trade Systems Center, CPTO Support Group, 1976.

This manual introduces several techniques of top-down design including HIPO and structured walk-throughs.

Jackson, Clyde W. "Documentation is Spelled C-o-m-m-u-n-i-c-a-t-i-n-g," *Journal of Systems Management,* June 1973 (pp. 34-35).

This is a short, pithy article that stresses the importance of documentation to communication and to effective system operation. Several solutions to communications problems are discussed.

Kraus, Leonard I. *Administering and Controlling the Company Data Processing Function.* Englewood Cliffs: Prentice-Hall, 1969.

This book covers many topics related to systems analysis in a computer environment. Chapter 4, Using Project Management in EDP, is particularly pertinent. In this chapter, the phases in the life cycle of a computer-based business system are described in convenient outline form, and project management control techniques are presented.

Chapter 8 discusses the management of data processing operations. An appendix provides many detailed job descriptions.

Likert, Rensis. *New Patterns of Management.* New York: McGraw-Hill, 1961.

The author discusses different approaches to management, ranging from an authoritarian approach to a participative approach. His findings show that participative management systems tend to be the most productive.

Management Planning Guide for a Manual of Data Processing Standards (C20-1670-0). White Plains: IBM Technical Publications Department.

This manual is designated to assist computer installations in the choice and implementation of standards. It contains suggestions for management, machine configuration, systems analysis, programming, and operation standards. The management section includes a detailed listing of job responsibilities, ranging from data processing manager to keypunch operator.

Mathews, Don O. *The Design of the Management Information System.* Princeton: Auerbach Publishers, 1971 (pp. 23-39).

Chapter 3 is a very readable presentation of the management system's life-cycle concept. The difficulties encountered in defining milestones when hardware products are not present is emphasized.

McKinsey and Company, Inc. *Getting the Most Out of Your Computer.* New York, 1963.

This report presents the results of a survey of 27 large companies, representing a cross-section of industry. It is a classic among the early investigations of the effectiveness of computers in business. It concluded that the companies that had made best use of their computers were those in which executive leadership was provided by active top management participation.

Nelson, Edward A. *Management Handbook for the Estimation of Computer Programming Costs.* Santa Monica: Systems Development Corporation, 1967 (pp. 60-75).

This handbook presents guidelines to help managers estimate the cost of computer programming projects. The guidelines are based upon the analysis of cost factors associated with 169 completed computer programming projects.

Ratynski, Milton V. *The Air Force Computer Program Acquisition Concept*. AFIPS Conference Proceedings, vol. 30, 1967 (Spring Joint Computer Conference) (pp. 33-44).

This paper distinguishes between hardware and software end-items. It identifies the four phases in the development of a computer program and provides an overview of the principal activities associated with each phase.

Sanders, Donald H. *Computers in Business: Introduction*. New York: McGraw-Hill Book Company, 1972 (pp. 111-115).

The author describes the interaction between horizontal management levels and vertical business specialties; he discusses some of the problems of data-base-oriented management information systems.

Shaw, John C. and William Atkins. *Managing Computer System Projects*. New York: McGraw-Hill Book Company, 1970 (Chapters 1 and 2).

Chapter 1 reviews past failures of computerized management systems and describes a transition to a project management environment. Chapter 2 outlines a system development process from initial investigation to ongoing maintenance, of which a key element is cumulative documentation.

Weiss, Harold. "Computer Security, An Overview," *Datamation*, January 1974 (pp. 42-47).

This informative article is a concise discussion of security considerations in the data processing center. A distinction is made between protection against fraud and against natural disaster.

Wiederhold, Gio. *Database Design*. New York: McGraw-Hill Book Company, 1977.

This book covers file and data base techniques. It includes a chapter on data base operation and management, and defines DBMS terminology

INDEX